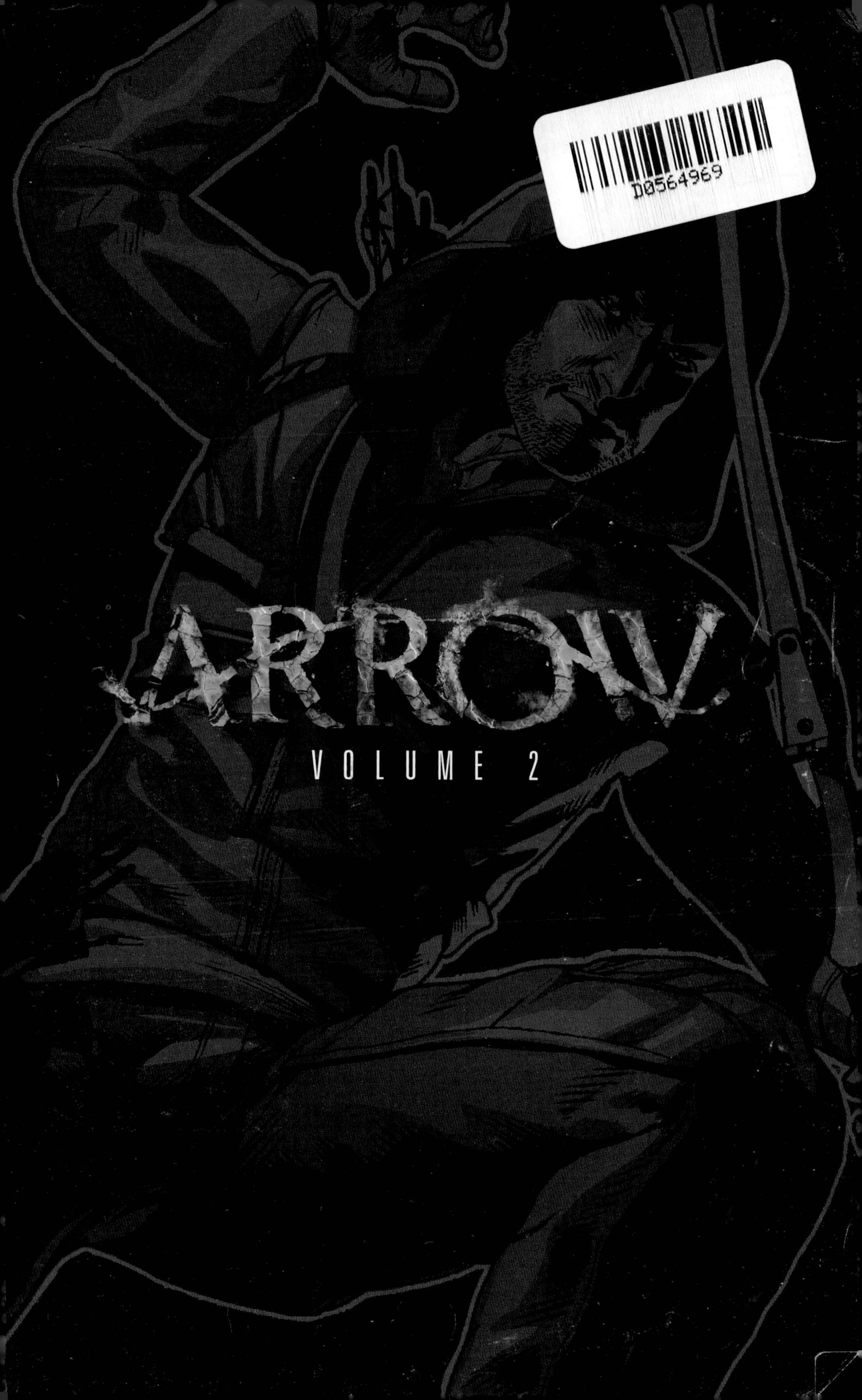
ARROW
VOLUME 2

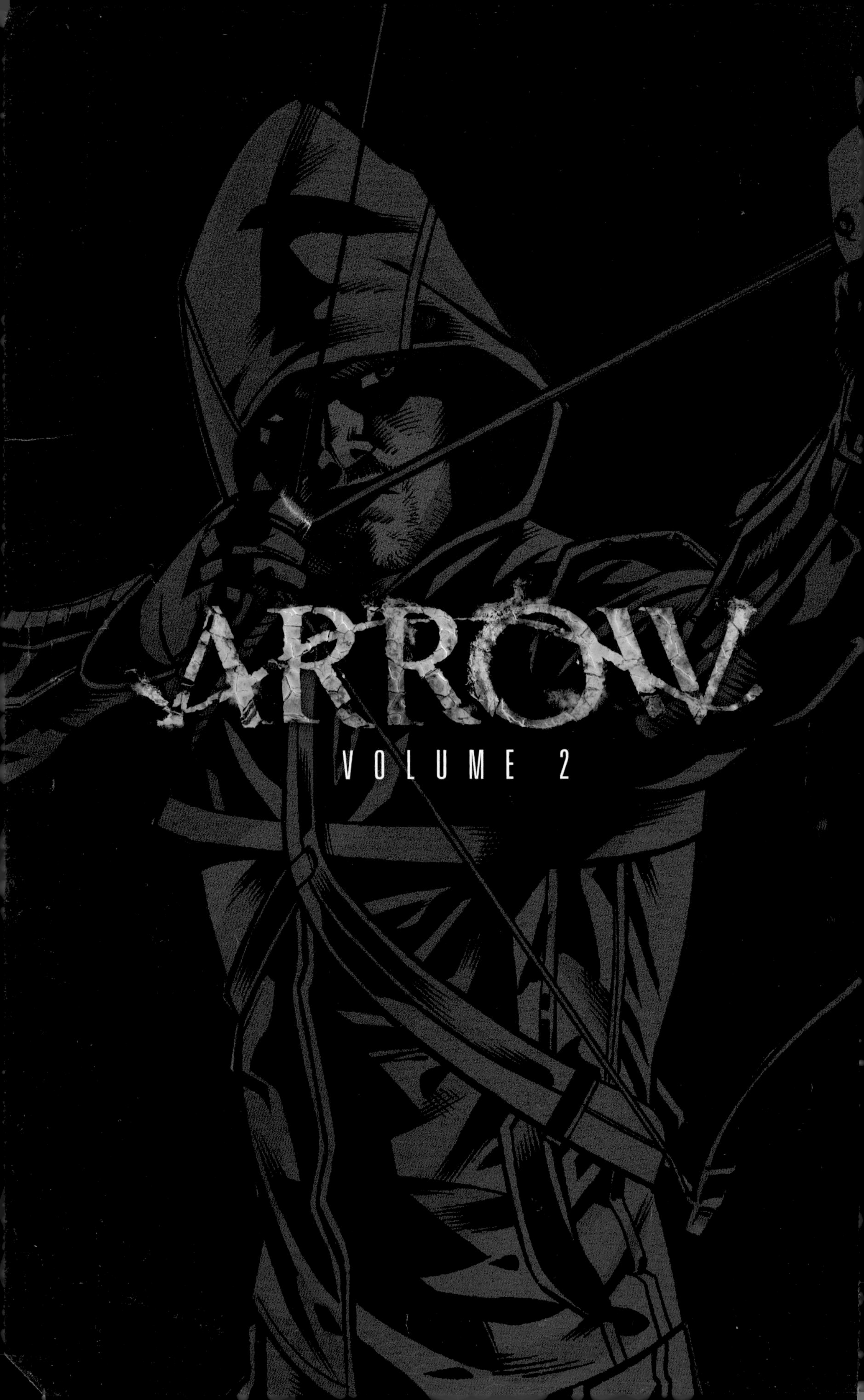
ARROW
VOLUME 2

CHAPTER 19: WINTERGREEN
Story: Marc Guggenheim & Andrew Kreisberg
Script: Lana Cho & Ben Sokolowski
Pencils: Allan Jefferson
Inks: Le Beau Underwood

CHAPTER 20: MAKE IT RAIN
Story: Marc Guggenheim & Andrew Kreisberg
Script: Katherine Walczak
Pencils: Victor Drujiniu
Inks: Juan Castro

CHAPTER 21: DETOUR
Story: Marc Guggenheim & Andrew Kreisberg
Script: Mary Iacono
Art: Xermanico

CHAPTER 22: BACK FROM THE DEADSHOT
Story: Marc Guggenheim & Andrew Kreisberg
Script: Wendy Mericle & Ben Sokolowski
Pencils: Sergio Sandoval
Inks: Pol Gas

CHAPTER 23: HUNTERS
Story: Marc Guggenheim & Andrew Kreisberg
Script: Emilio Aldrich
Art: Omar Francia

CHAPTER 24: DIAMOND IN THE ROUGH
Story: Marc Guggenheim & Andrew Kreisberg
Script: Tiffany Williams
Art: Victor Drujiniu

CHAPTER 25: THE PIECES MISSING
Story: Marc Guggenheim
Script: Marc Guggenheim
Art: Mike Grell

CHAPTER 26: LAPSE
Story: Marc Guggenheim
Script: Mary Iacono & Tiffany Williams
Pencils: Allan Jefferson
Inks: Le Beau Underwood

CHAPTER 27: LONE HUNTER
Story: Marc Guggenheim
Script: Emilio Aldrich
Art: Eric Nguyen

CHAPTER 28: AFTERMATH
Story: Marc Guggenheim
Script: Katherine Walczak
Art: Xermanico

CHAPTER 29: SHADO OF THE PAST
Story: Marc Guggenheim
Script: Marc Guggenheim
Art: Mike Grell

CHAPTER 30: PATIENT ZERO
Story: Marc Guggenheim
Script: Mary Iacono
Art: Sergio Sandoval

CHAPTER 31: NO WAY OUT
Story: Marc Guggenheim
Script: Emilio Aldrich
Art: Omar Francia

CHAPTER 32: FROM THE DARKNESS
Story: Marc Guggenheim
Script: Wendy Mericle & Ben Sokolowski
Pencils: Allan Jefferson
Inks: Jonas Trindade

CHAPTER 33: POTENTIAL
Story: Marc Guggenheim
Script: Drew Z. Greenberg
Art: Xermanico

CHAPTER 34: YOU OWE ME
Story: Marc Guggenheim
Script: Ben Sokolowski
Pencils: Victor Drujiniu
Inks: Juan Castro

CHAPTERS 35 & 36: SACRIFICES
Story: Marc Guggenheim
Script: Marc Guggenheim
Pencils: Allan Jefferson
Inks: Jonas Trindade

Colors by David Lopez, Santi Casas, Mado Peña & Sergi Erra of Ikari Studio
Randy Mayor
Letters by Wes Abbott

ALEX ANTONE Editor—Original Series
ROBIN WILDMAN Editor
ROBBIN BROSTERMAN Design Director—Books
DAMIAN RYLAND Publication Design

HANK KANALZ Senior VP—Vertigo and Integrated Publishing

DIANE NELSON President
DAN DIDIO and JIM LEE Co-Publishers
GEOFF JOHNS Chief Creative Officer
JOHN ROOD Executive VP—Sales, Marketing and Business Development
AMY GENKINS Senior VP—Business and Legal Affairs
NAIRI GARDINER Senior VP—Finance
JEFF BOISON VP — Publishing Planning
MARK CHIARELLO VP—Art Direction and Design
JOHN CUNNINGHAM VP—Marketing
TERRI CUNNINGHAM Editorial Administration
ALISON GILL Senior VP—Manufacturing and Operations
JAY KOGAN VP—Business and Legal Affairs, Publishing
JACK MAHAN VP—Business Affairs, Talent
NICK NAPOLITANO VP—Manufacturing Administration
SUE POHJA VP—Book Sales
COURTNEY SIMMONS Senior VP—Publicity
BOB WAYNE Senior VP—Sales

ARROW VOLUME 2

Published by DC Comics. Copyright © 2014 DC Comics. All Rights Reserved.

Originally published in single magazine form as ARROW 7-12 © 2013 DC Comics. All Rights Reserved. All characters, their distinctive likenesses and related
elements featured in this publication are trademarks of DC Comics. The stories, characters and incidents featured in this publication are entirely fictional.
DC Comics does not read or accept unsolicited ideas, stories or artwork.

DC Comics, 1700 Broadway, New York, NY 10019. A Warner Bros. Entertainment Company.
Printed by RR Donnelley, Salem, VA, USA. 3/28/14. First Printing.

ISBN: 978-1-4012-4603-7

Library of Congress Cataloging-in-Publication Data

Guggenheim, Marc.
  Arrow. Volume 2 / Marc Guggenheim.
      pages cm
  Summary: "Spinning out of the hit CW television show, these digital-first chapters, written by show creators Marc Guggenheim and Andrew Kreisberg,
fill in the gaps between the television show and the comics." —Provided by publisher.
  ISBN 978-1-4012-4603-7 (paperback)
  1. Graphic novels. I. Title.
  PN6728.G725G85 2014
  741.5'973—dc23
                    2014000324

SUSTAINABLE
FORESTRY
INITIATIVE
Certified Chain of Custody
At Least 20% Certified Forest Content
www.sfiprogram.org
SFI-01042
APPLIES TO TEXT STOCK ONLY

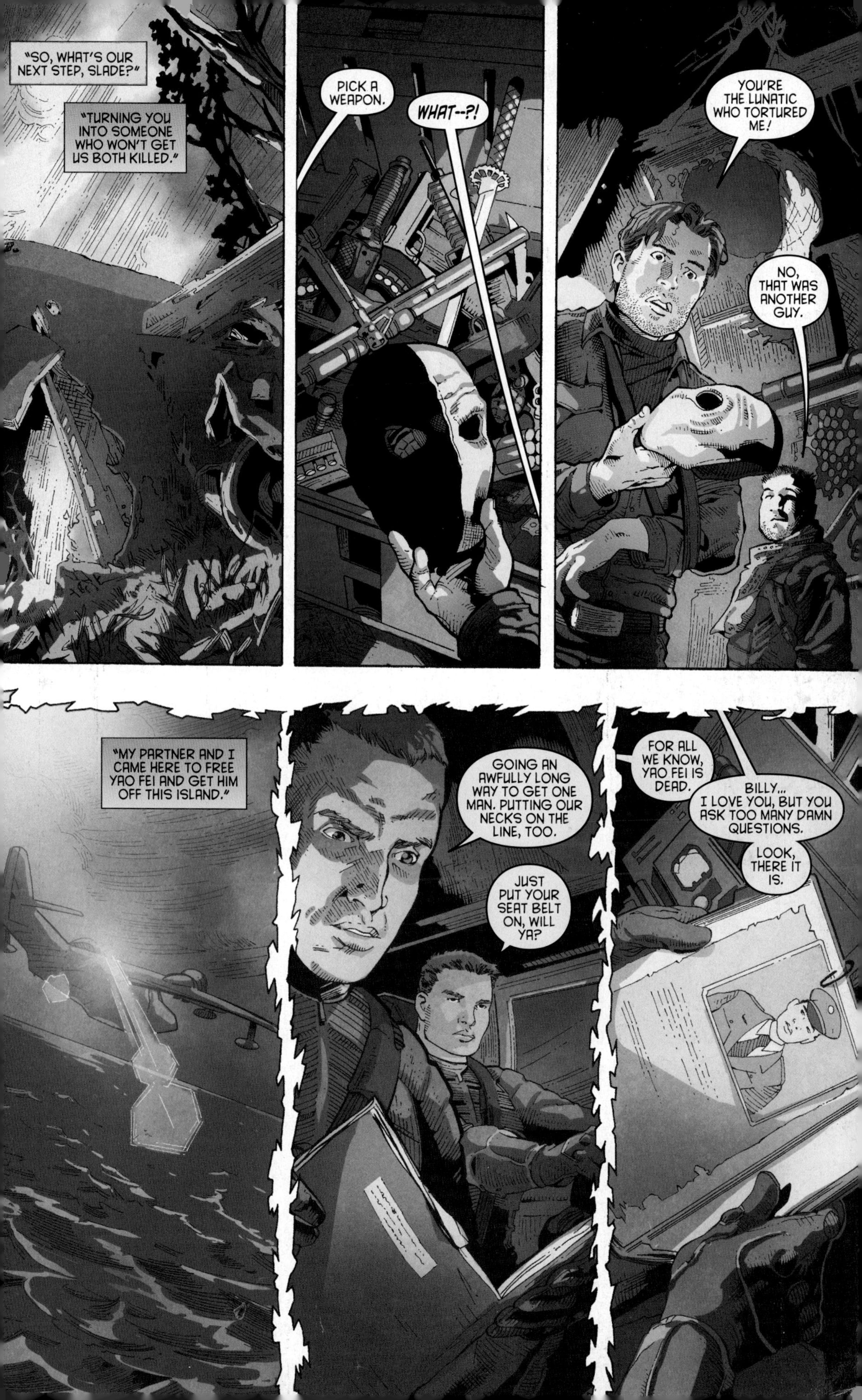
"SO, WHAT'S OUR NEXT STEP, SLADE?"
"TURNING YOU INTO SOMEONE WHO WON'T GET US BOTH KILLED."
PICK A WEAPON.
WHAT--?!
YOU'RE THE LUNATIC WHO TORTURED ME!
NO, THAT WAS ANOTHER GUY.
"MY PARTNER AND I CAME HERE TO FREE YAO FEI AND GET HIM OFF THIS ISLAND."
GOING AN AWFULLY LONG WAY TO GET ONE MAN. PUTTING OUR NECKS ON THE LINE, TOO.
JUST PUT YOUR SEAT BELT ON, WILL YA?
FOR ALL WE KNOW, YAO FEI IS DEAD.
BILLY... I LOVE YOU, BUT YOU ASK TOO MANY DAMN QUESTIONS.
LOOK, THERE IT IS.

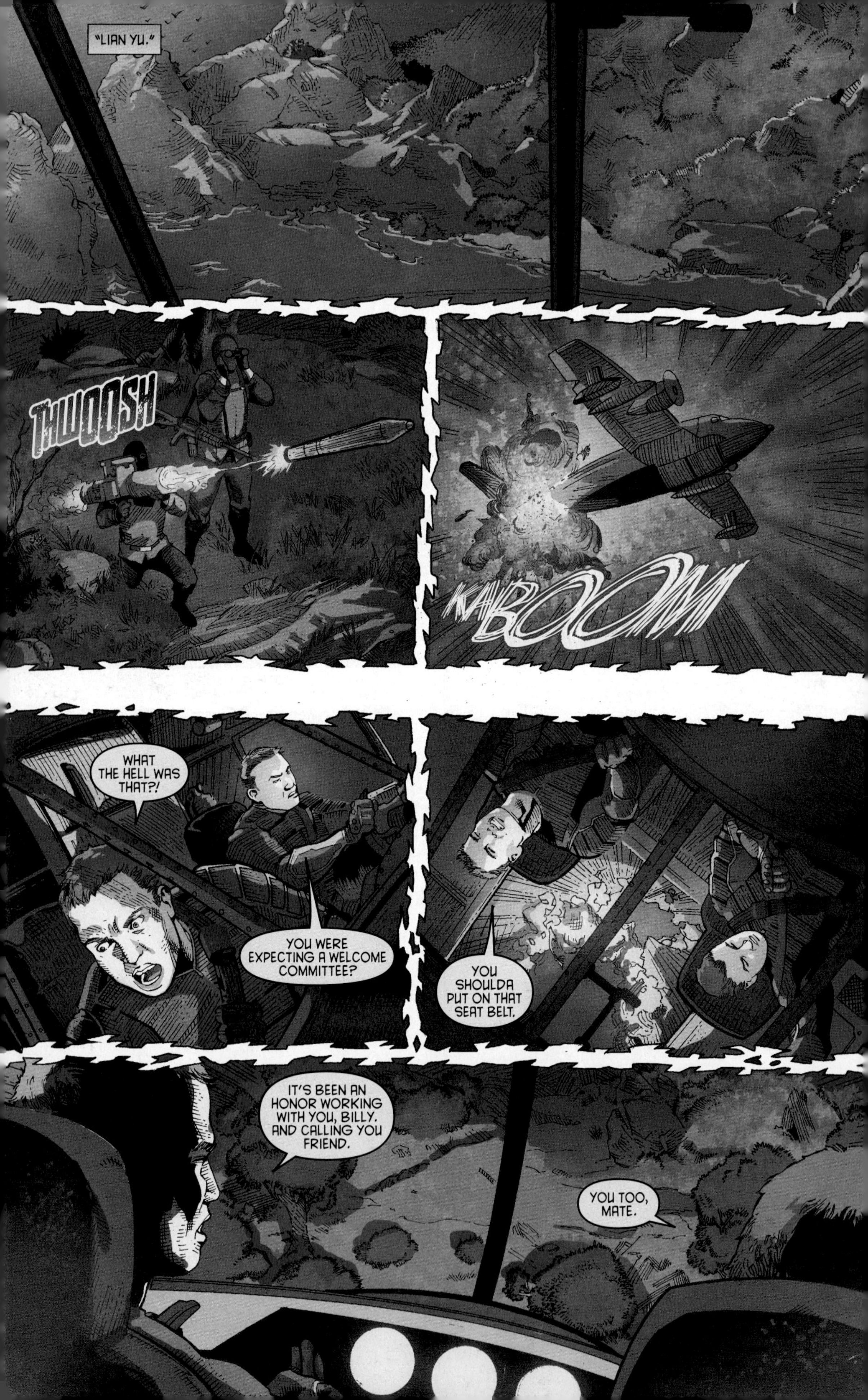
"LIAN YU."
THWOOSH
KABOOM
WHAT THE HELL WAS THAT?!
YOU WERE EXPECTING A WELCOME COMMITTEE?
YOU SHOULDA PUT ON THAT SEAT BELT.
IT'S BEEN AN HONOR WORKING WITH YOU, BILLY. AND CALLING YOU FRIEND.
YOU TOO, MATE.

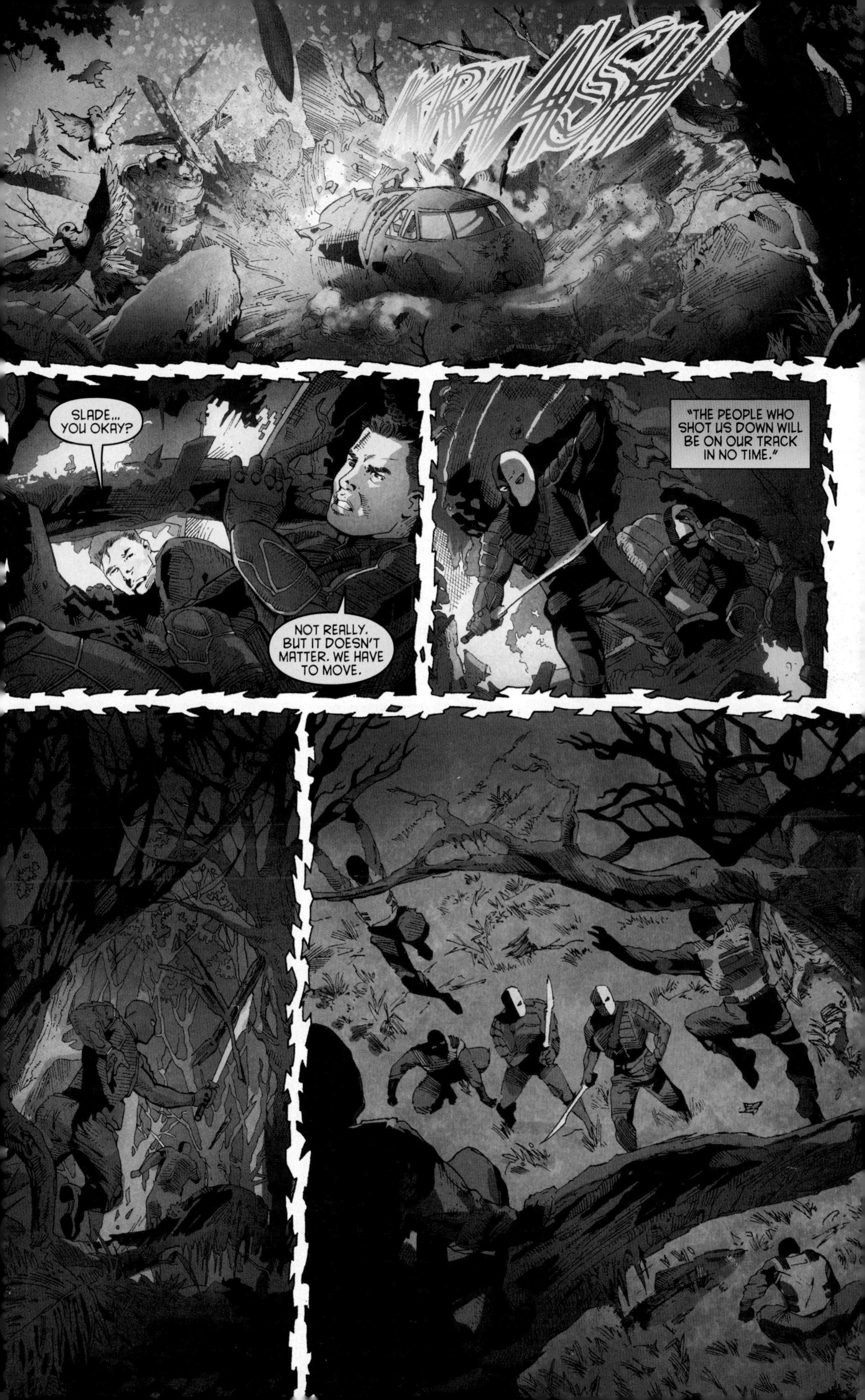
KRAASH
SLADE... YOU OKAY?
NOT REALLY. BUT IT DOESN'T MATTER. WE HAVE TO MOVE.
"THE PEOPLE WHO SHOT US DOWN WILL BE ON OUR TRACK IN NO TIME."

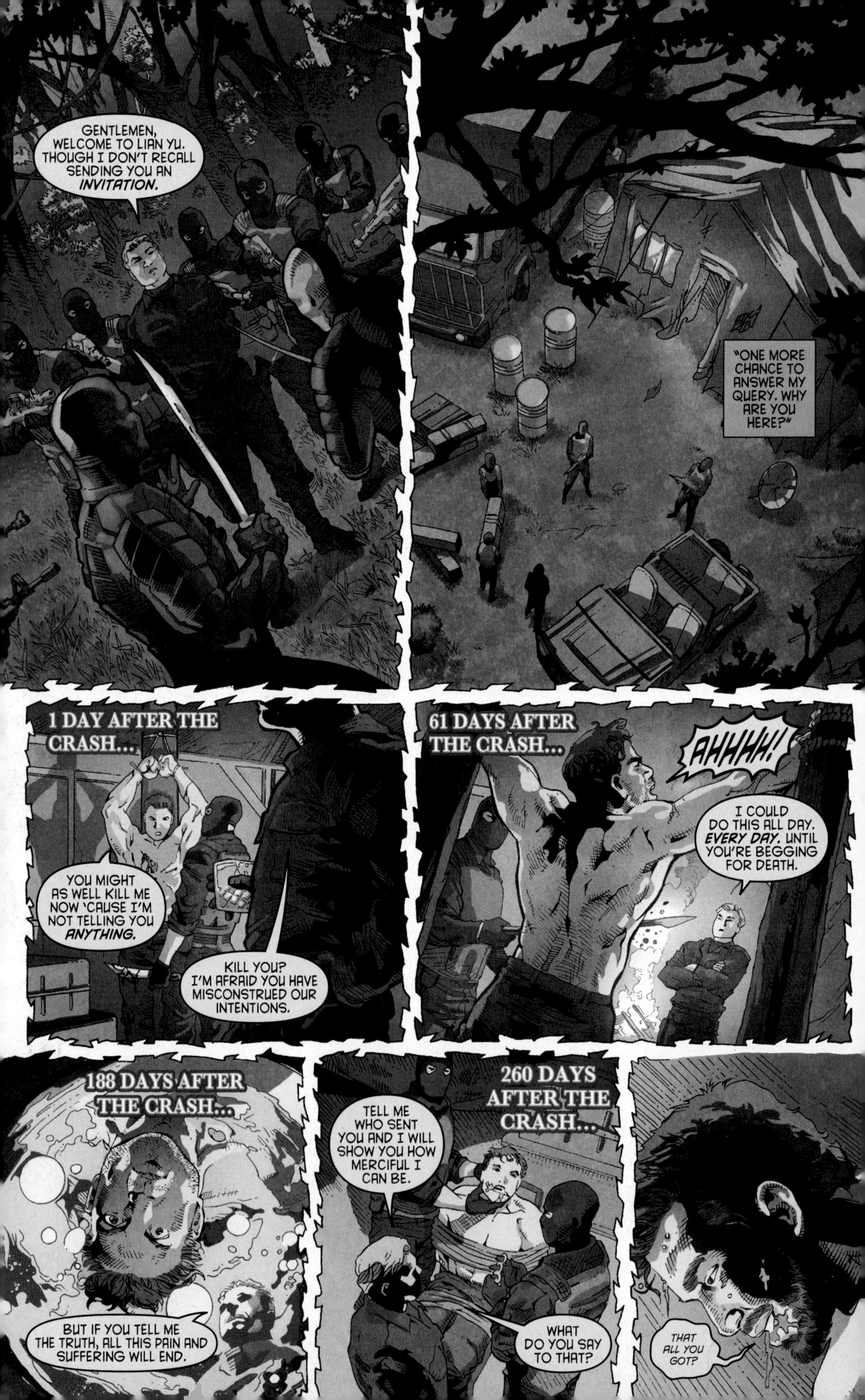
GENTLEMEN, WELCOME TO LIAN YU. THOUGH I DON'T RECALL SENDING YOU AN *INVITATION.*
"ONE MORE CHANCE TO ANSWER MY QUERY. WHY ARE YOU HERE?"
1 DAY AFTER THE CRASH...
YOU MIGHT AS WELL KILL ME NOW 'CAUSE I'M NOT TELLING YOU *ANYTHING.*
KILL YOU? I'M AFRAID YOU HAVE MISCONSTRUED OUR INTENTIONS.
61 DAYS AFTER THE CRASH...
AHHHH!
I COULD DO THIS ALL DAY. *EVERY DAY.* UNTIL YOU'RE BEGGING FOR DEATH.
188 DAYS AFTER THE CRASH...
BUT IF YOU TELL ME THE TRUTH, ALL THIS PAIN AND SUFFERING WILL END.
260 DAYS AFTER THE CRASH...
TELL ME WHO SENT YOU AND I WILL SHOW YOU HOW MERCIFUL I CAN BE.
WHAT DO YOU SAY TO THAT?
THAT ALL YOU GOT?

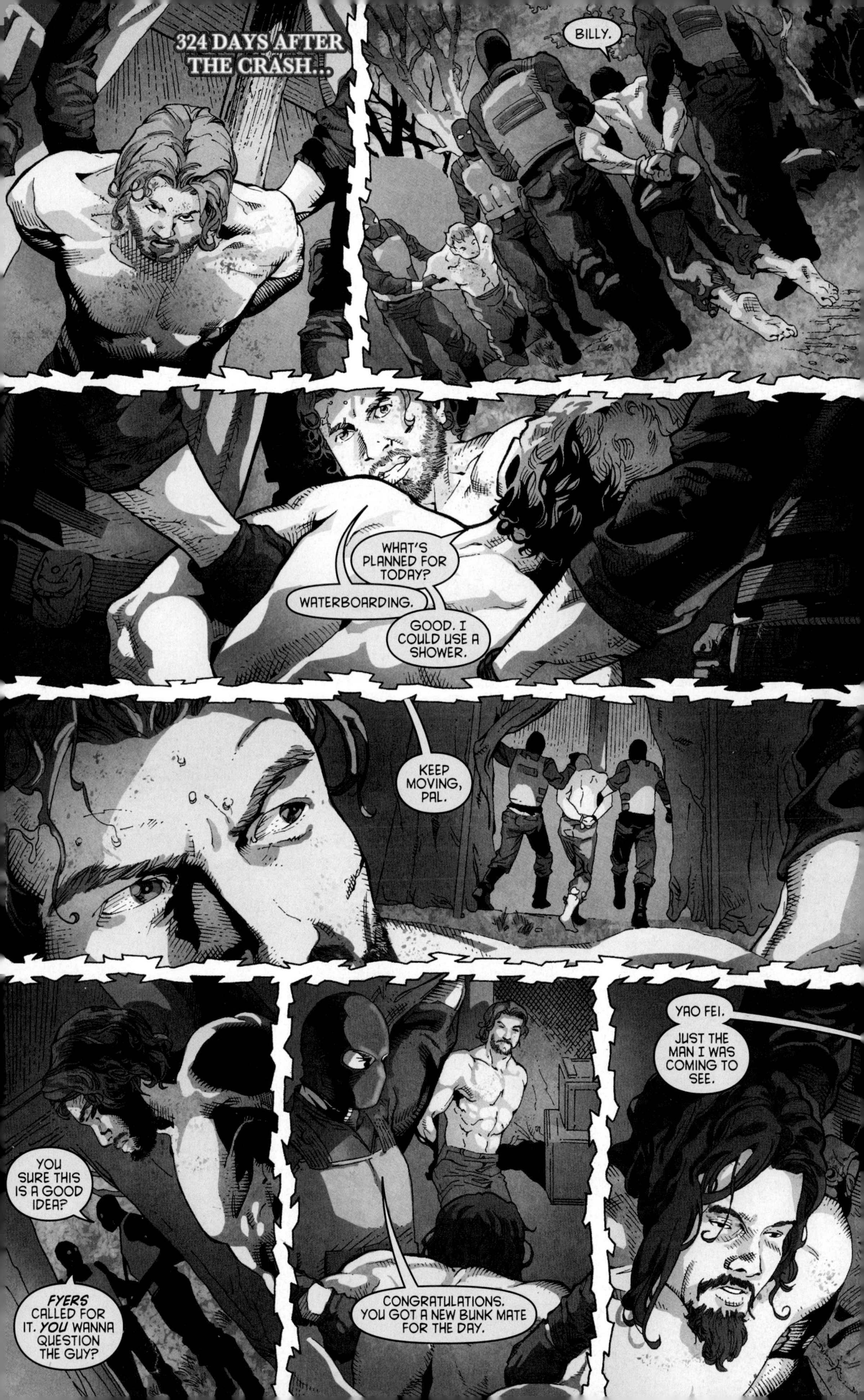
324 DAYS AFTER THE CRASH...
BILLY.
WHAT'S PLANNED FOR TODAY?
WATERBOARDING.
GOOD. I COULD USE A SHOWER.
KEEP MOVING, PAL.
YOU SURE THIS IS A GOOD IDEA?
FYERS CALLED FOR IT. YOU WANNA QUESTION THE GUY?
CONGRATULATIONS. YOU GOT A NEW BUNK MATE FOR THE DAY.
YAO FEI.
JUST THE MAN I WAS COMING TO SEE.

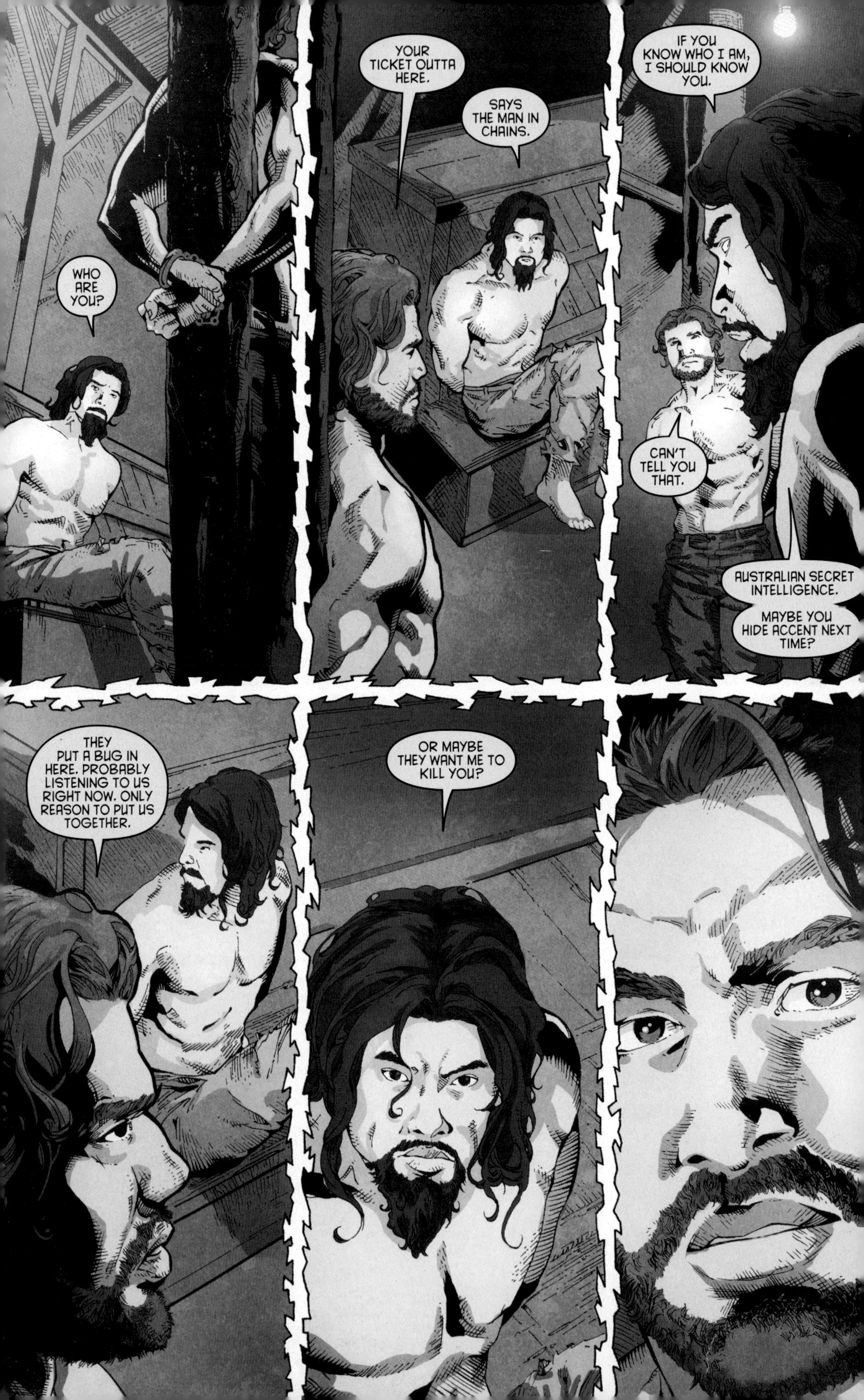
WHO ARE YOU?
YOUR TICKET OUTTA HERE.
SAYS THE MAN IN CHAINS.
IF YOU KNOW WHO I AM, I SHOULD KNOW YOU.
CAN'T TELL YOU THAT.
AUSTRALIAN SECRET INTELLIGENCE.
MAYBE YOU HIDE ACCENT NEXT TIME?
THEY PUT A BUG IN HERE. PROBABLY LISTENING TO US RIGHT NOW. ONLY REASON TO PUT US TOGETHER.
OR MAYBE THEY WANT ME TO KILL YOU?

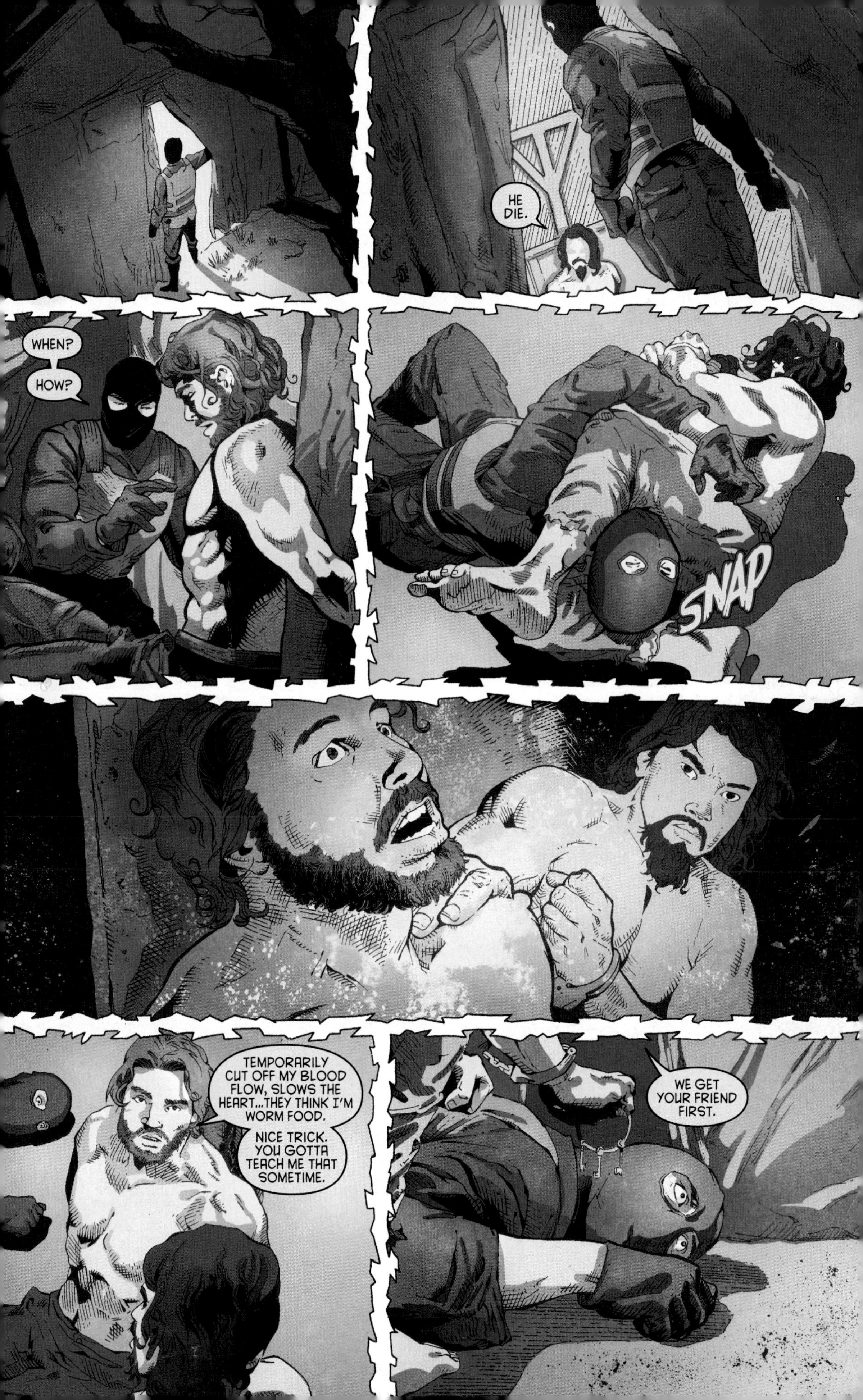
HE DIE.
WHEN?
HOW?
SNAP
TEMPORARILY CUT OFF MY BLOOD FLOW, SLOWS THE HEART...THEY THINK I'M WORM FOOD.
NICE TRICK. YOU GOTTA TEACH ME THAT SOMETIME.
WE GET YOUR FRIEND FIRST.

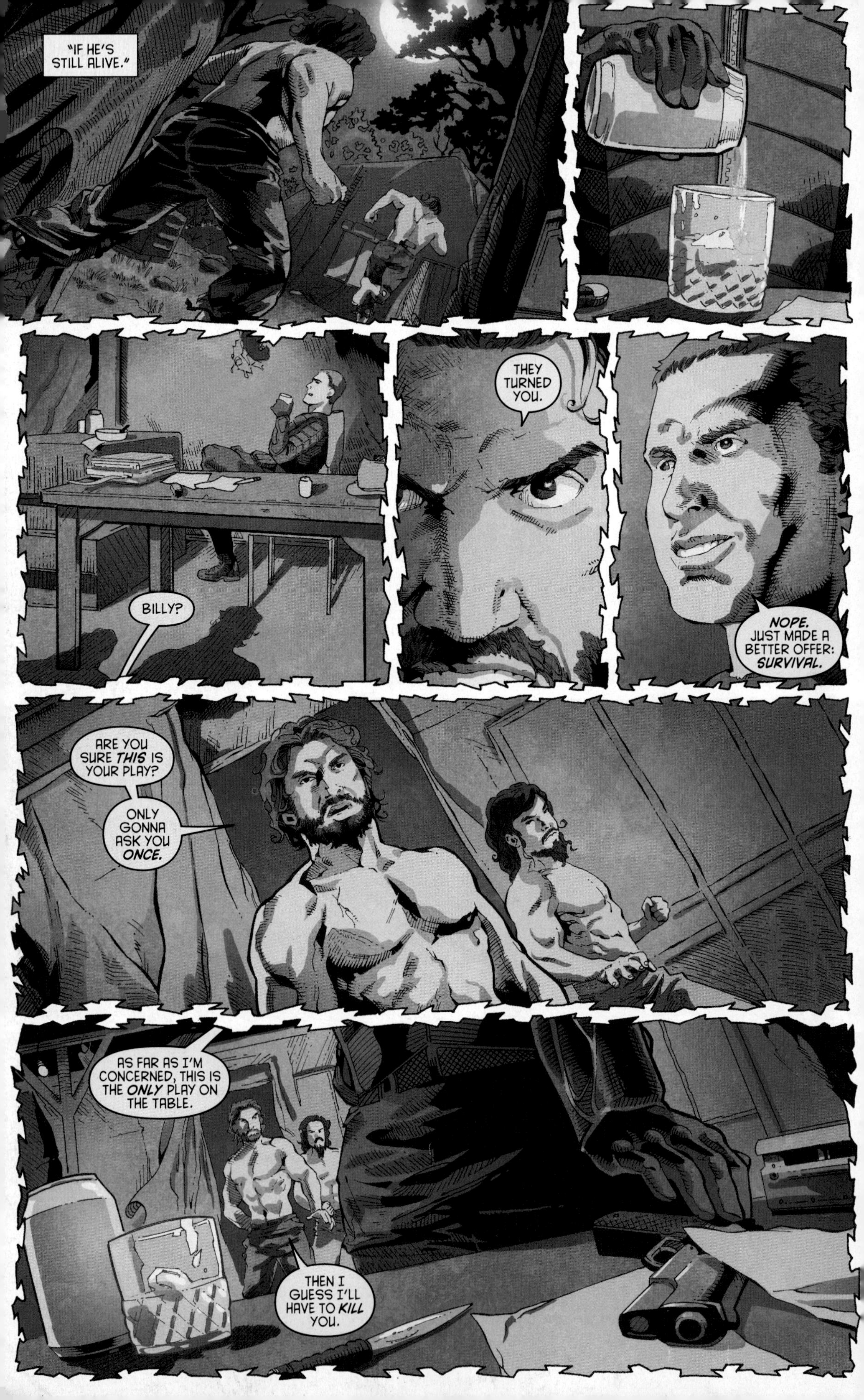
"IF HE'S STILL ALIVE."
BILLY?
THEY TURNED YOU.
NOPE. JUST MADE A BETTER OFFER: SURVIVAL.
ARE YOU SURE THIS IS YOUR PLAY?
ONLY GONNA ASK YOU ONCE.
AS FAR AS I'M CONCERNED, THIS IS THE ONLY PLAY ON THE TABLE.
THEN I GUESS I'LL HAVE TO KILL YOU.

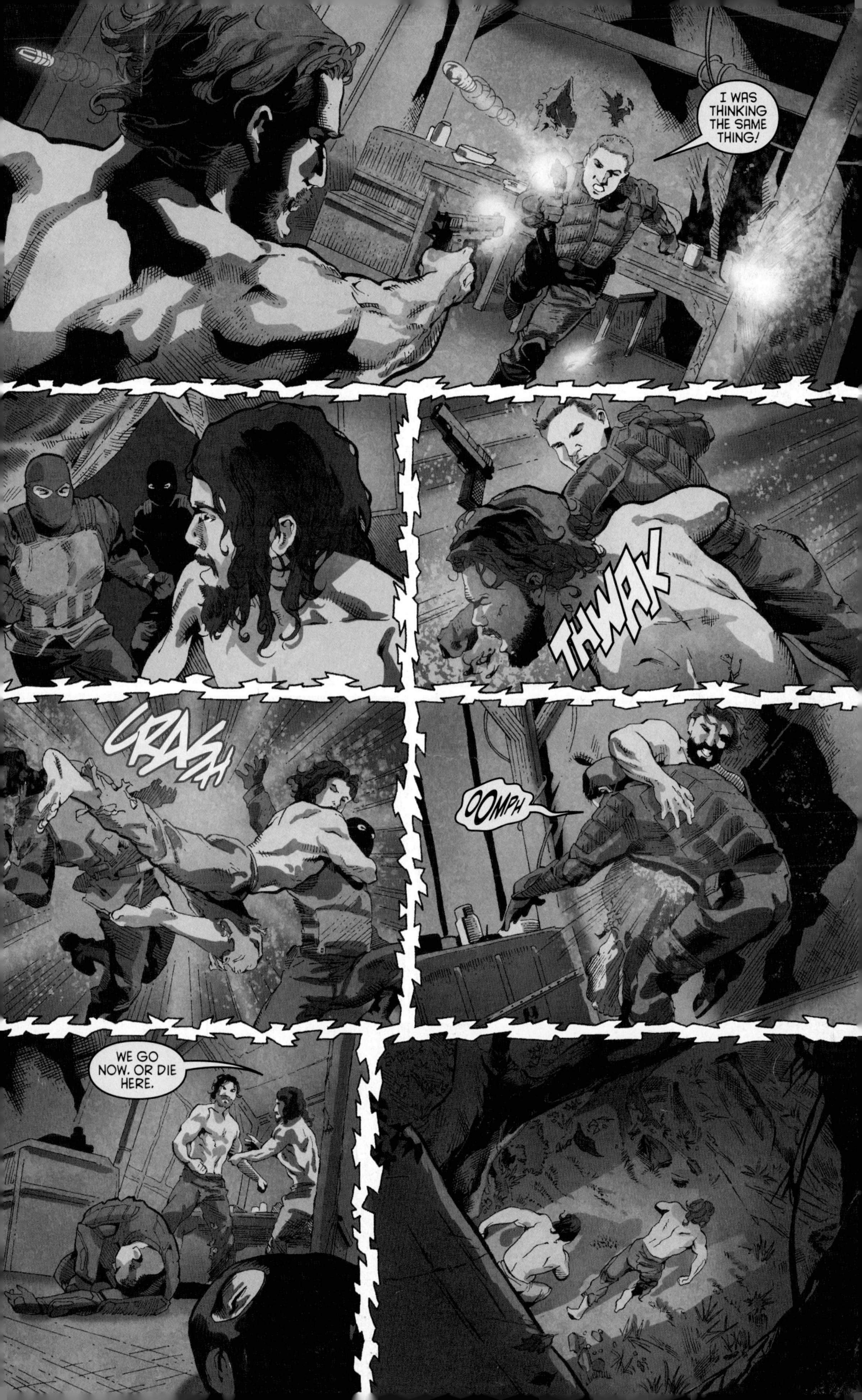
I WAS THINKING THE SAME THING!
THWAK
CRASH
OOMPH
WE GO NOW. OR DIE HERE.

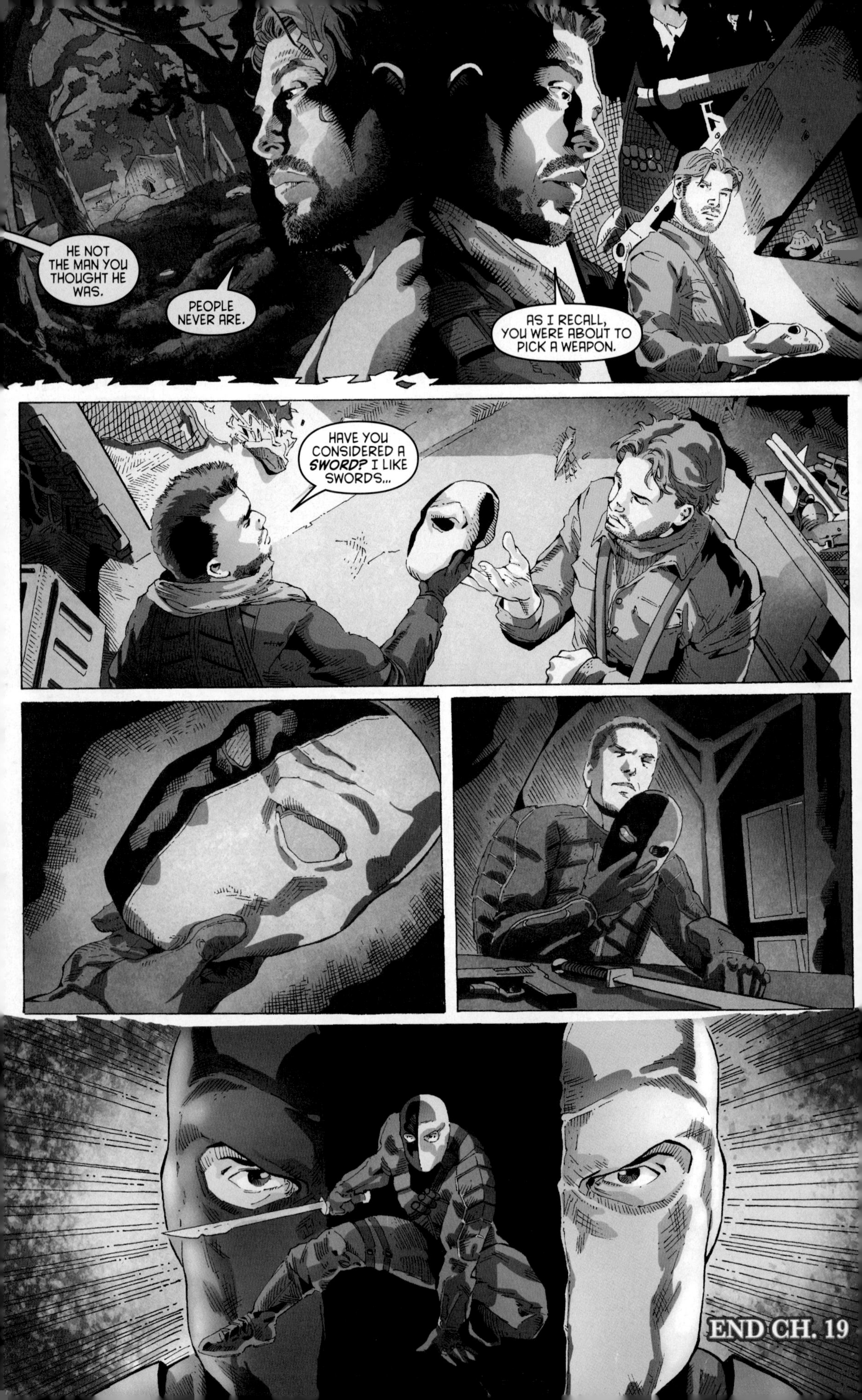
HE NOT THE MAN YOU THOUGHT HE WAS.
PEOPLE NEVER ARE.
AS I RECALL, YOU WERE ABOUT TO PICK A WEAPON.
HAVE YOU CONSIDERED A SWORD? I LIKE SWORDS...
END CH. 19

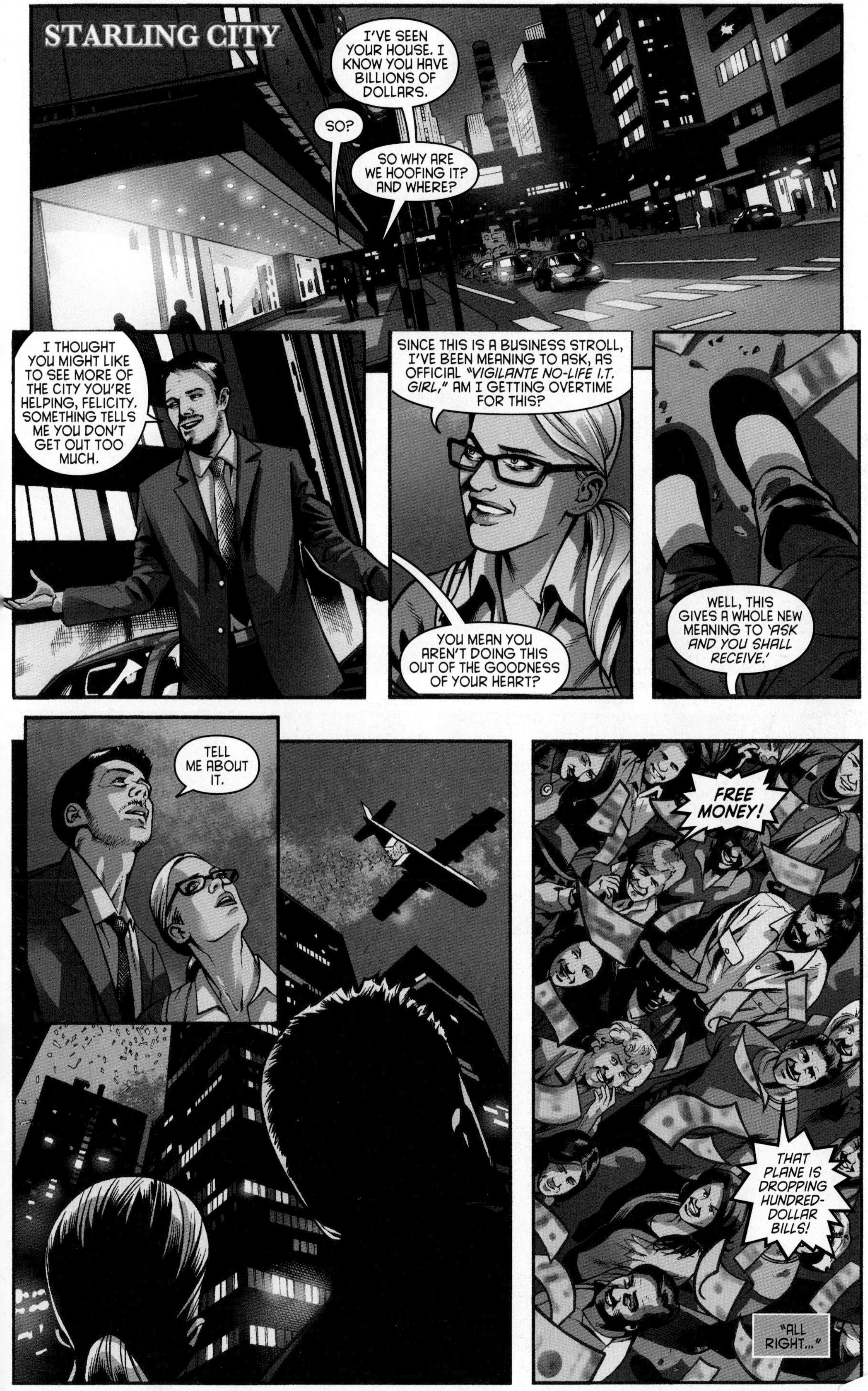
STARLING CITY
I'VE SEEN YOUR HOUSE. I KNOW YOU HAVE BILLIONS OF DOLLARS.
SO?
SO WHY ARE WE HOOFING IT? AND WHERE?
I THOUGHT YOU MIGHT LIKE TO SEE MORE OF THE CITY YOU'RE HELPING, FELICITY. SOMETHING TELLS ME YOU DON'T GET OUT TOO MUCH.
SINCE THIS IS A BUSINESS STROLL, I'VE BEEN MEANING TO ASK, AS OFFICIAL "VIGILANTE NO-LIFE I.T. GIRL," AM I GETTING OVERTIME FOR THIS?
YOU MEAN YOU AREN'T DOING THIS OUT OF THE GOODNESS OF YOUR HEART?
WELL, THIS GIVES A WHOLE NEW MEANING TO 'ASK AND YOU SHALL RECEIVE.'
TELL ME ABOUT IT.
FREE MONEY!
THAT PLANE IS DROPPING HUNDRED-DOLLAR BILLS!
"ALL RIGHT..."

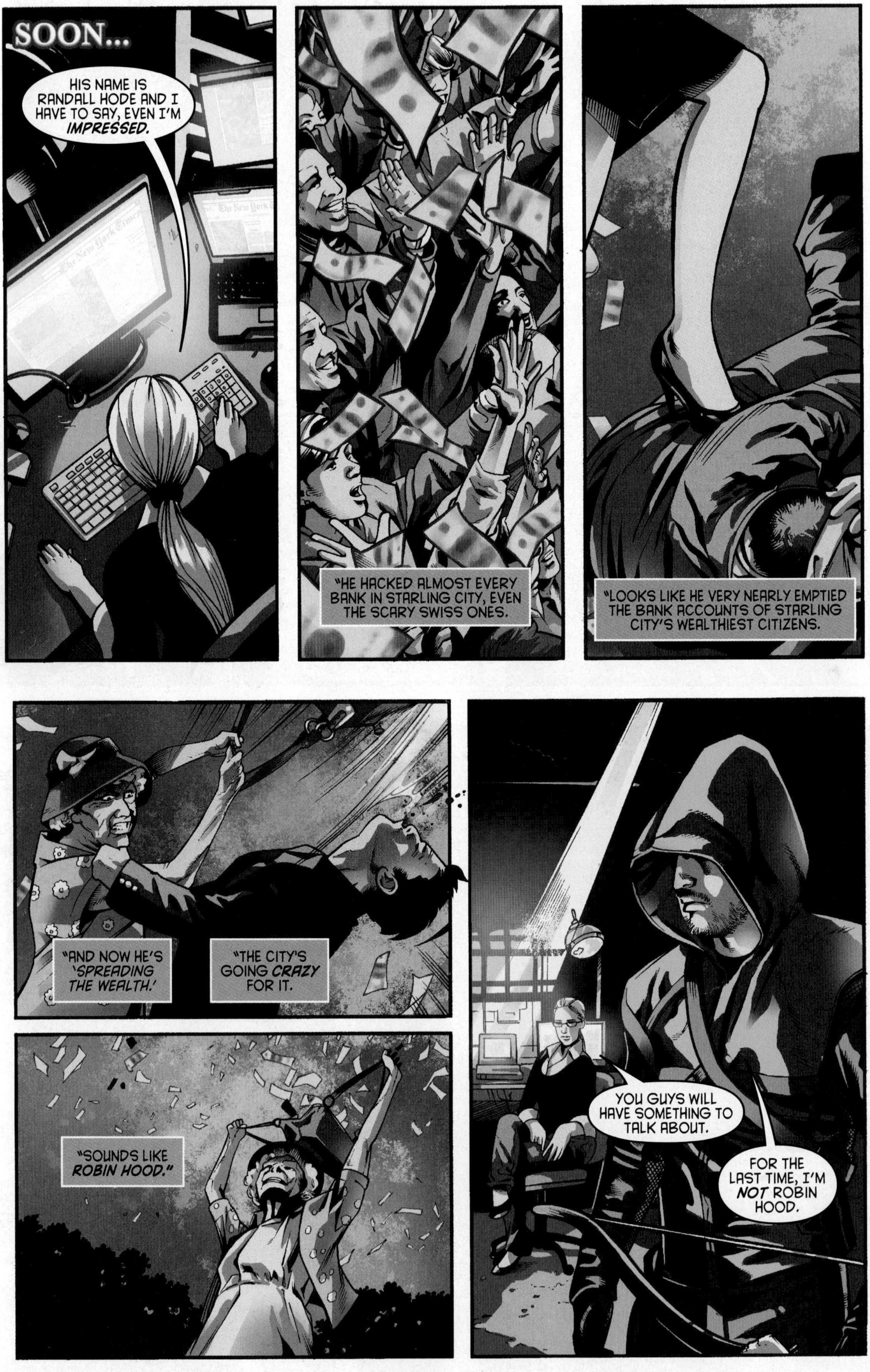
SOON...
HIS NAME IS RANDALL HODE AND I HAVE TO SAY, EVEN I'M *IMPRESSED.*
"HE HACKED ALMOST EVERY BANK IN STARLING CITY, EVEN THE SCARY SWISS ONES.
"LOOKS LIKE HE VERY NEARLY EMPTIED THE BANK ACCOUNTS OF STARLING CITY'S WEALTHIEST CITIZENS.
"AND NOW HE'S '*SPREADING THE WEALTH.*'
"THE CITY'S GOING *CRAZY* FOR IT.
"SOUNDS LIKE *ROBIN HOOD.*"
YOU GUYS WILL HAVE SOMETHING TO TALK ABOUT.
FOR THE LAST TIME, I'M *NOT* ROBIN HOOD.

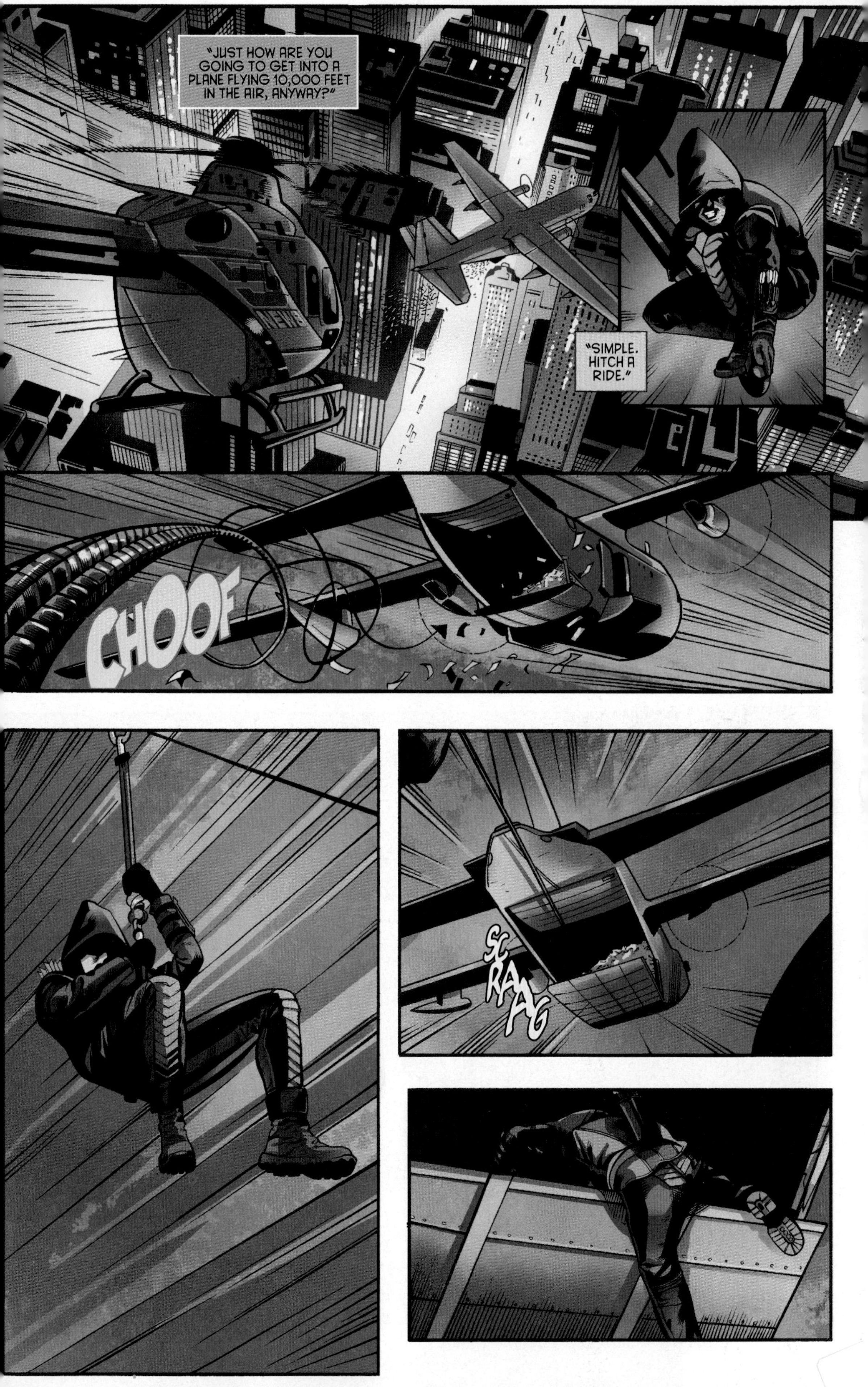
"JUST HOW ARE YOU GOING TO GET INTO A PLANE FLYING 10,000 FEET IN THE AIR, ANYWAY?"
"SIMPLE. HITCH A RIDE."
CHOOF
SCRAAAG

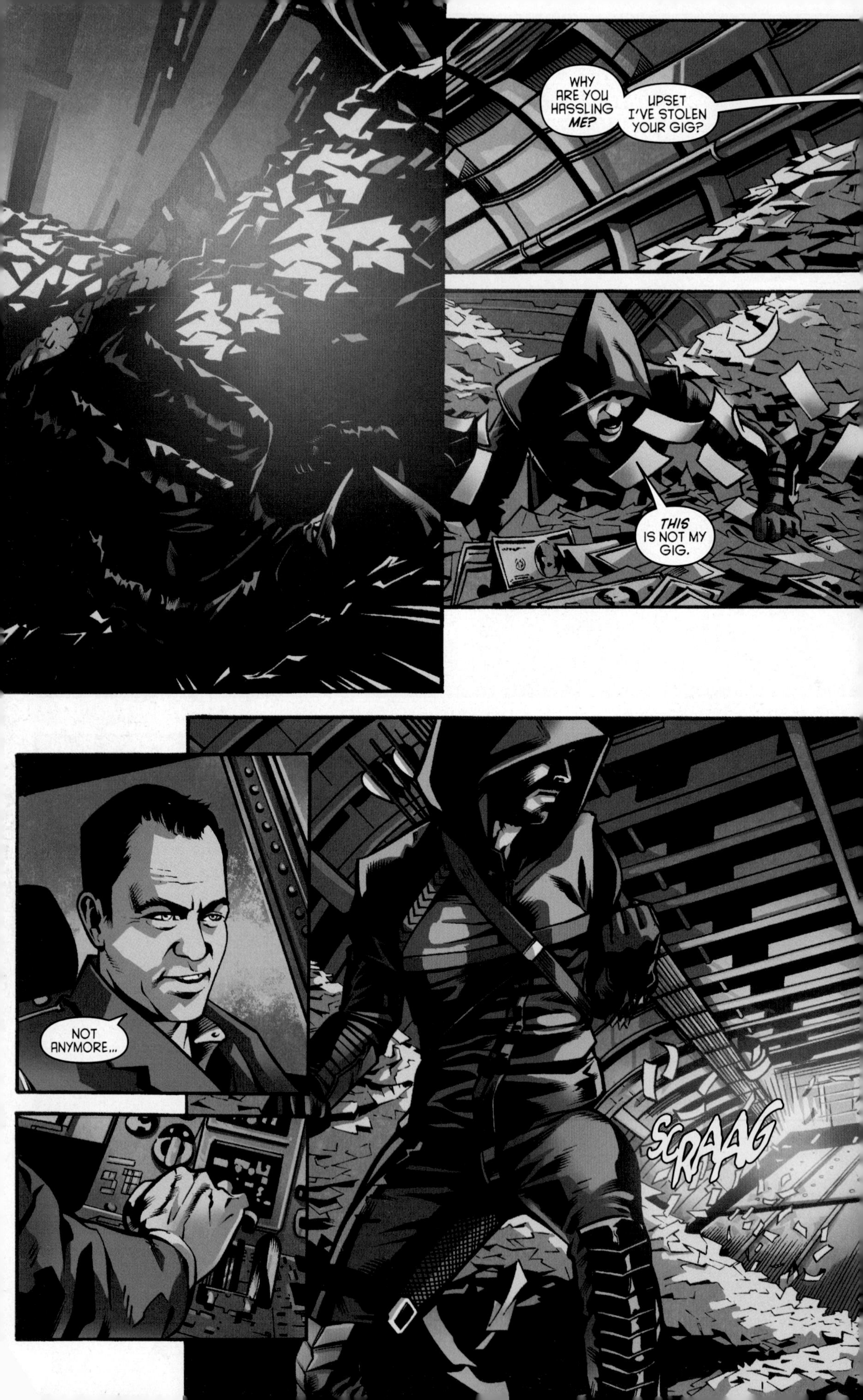
WHY ARE YOU HASSLING *ME?*
UPSET I'VE STOLEN YOUR GIG?
THIS IS NOT MY GIG.
NOT ANYMORE...
SCRAAAG

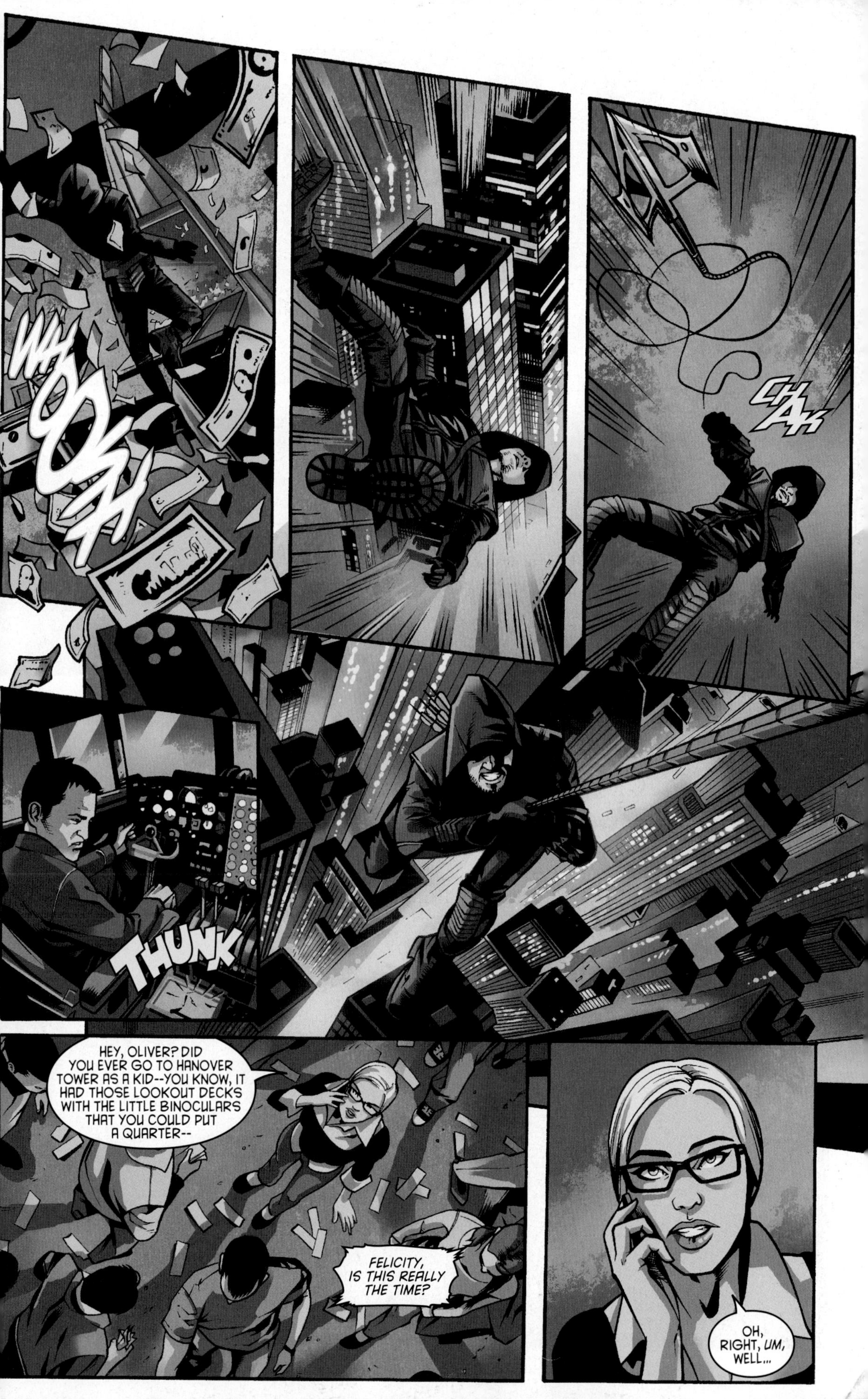
WHOOM
CHAK
THUNK
HEY, OLIVER? DID YOU EVER GO TO HANOVER TOWER AS A KID--YOU KNOW, IT HAD THOSE LOOKOUT DECKS WITH THE LITTLE BINOCULARS THAT YOU COULD PUT A QUARTER--
FELICITY, IS THIS REALLY THE TIME?
OH, RIGHT, UM, WELL...

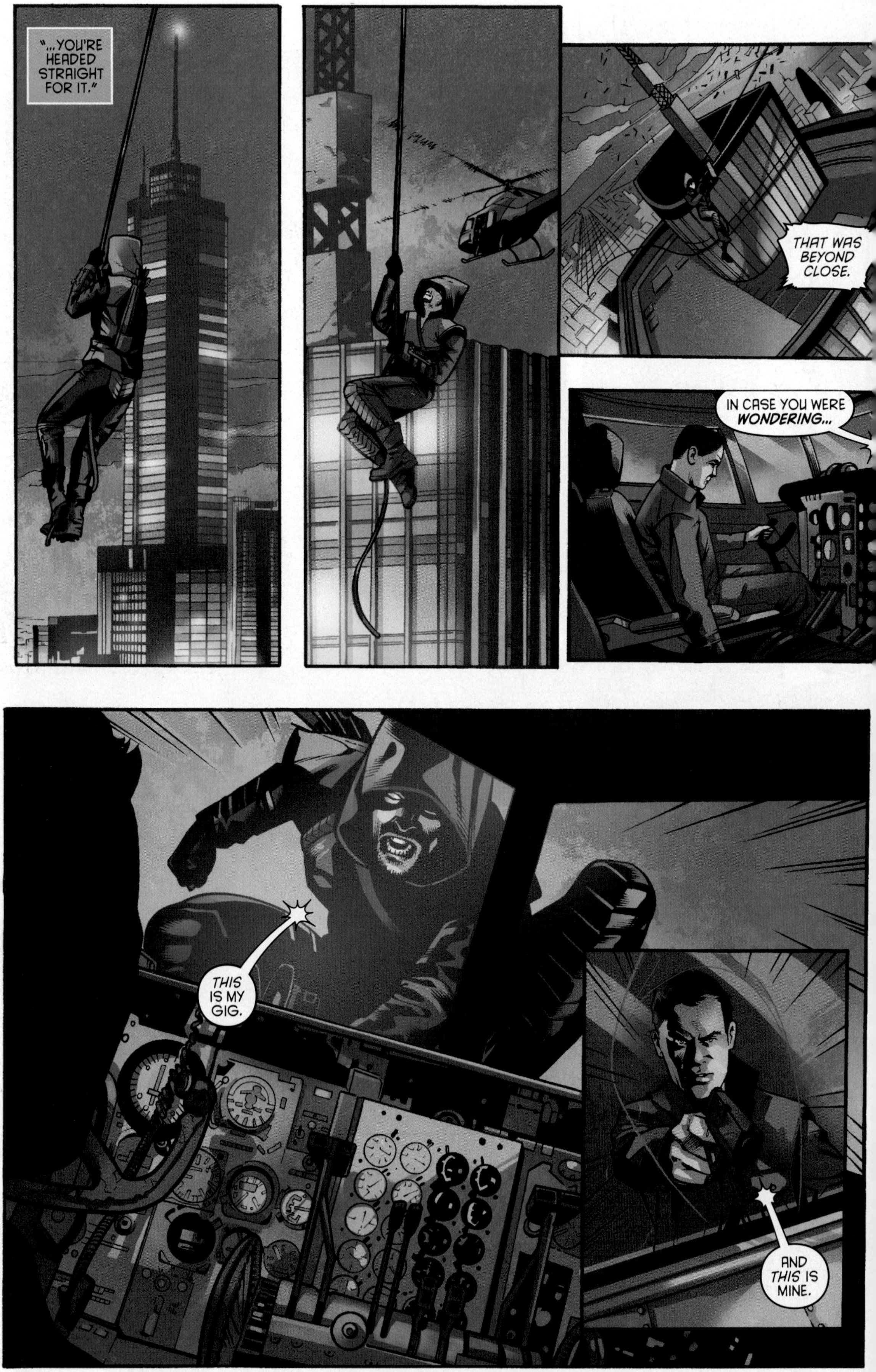
"...YOU'RE HEADED STRAIGHT FOR IT."
THAT WAS BEYOND CLOSE.
IN CASE YOU WERE WONDERING...
THIS IS MY GIG.
AND THIS IS MINE.

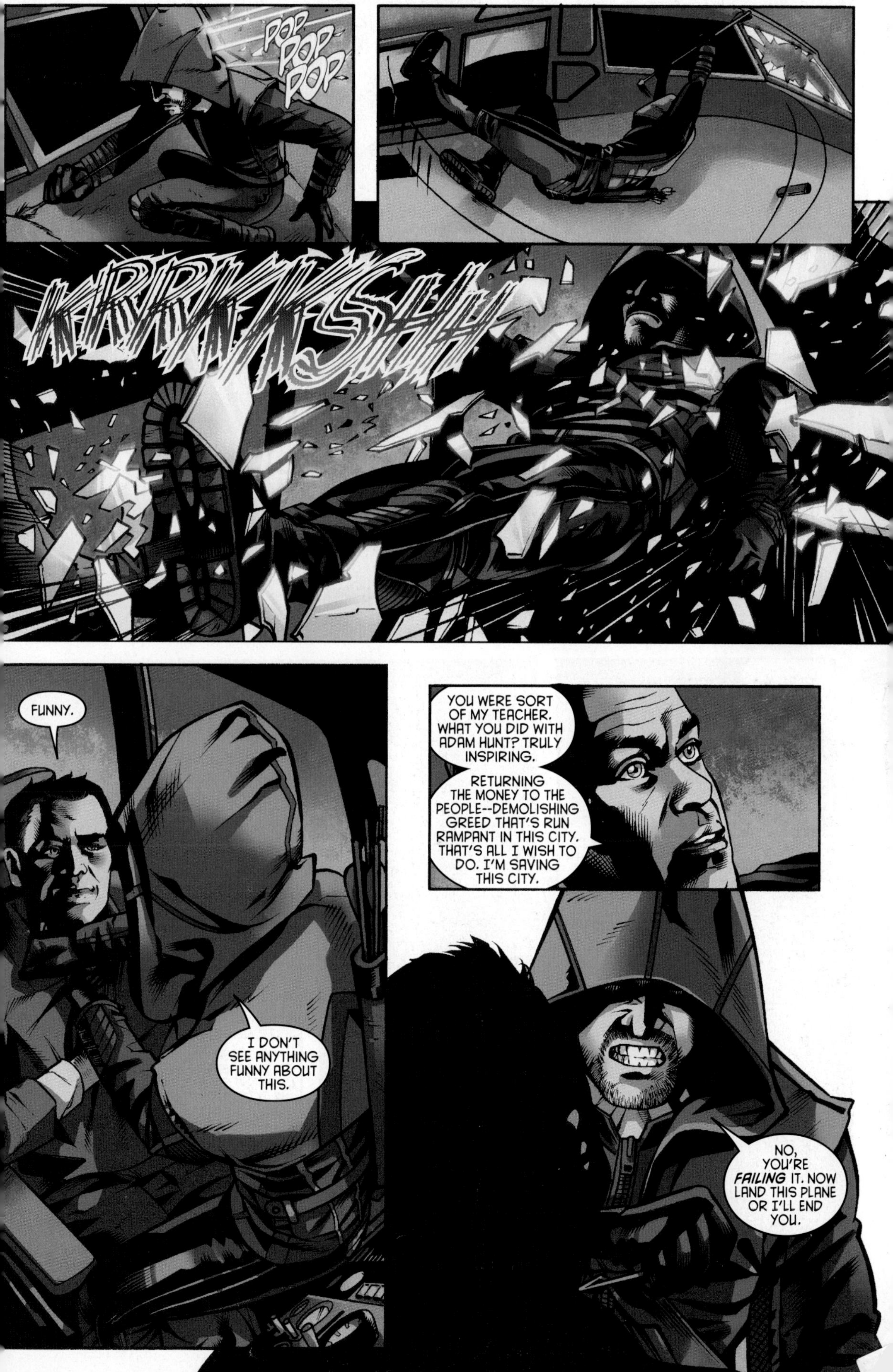
POP POP POP
KRRKKSHH
FUNNY.
I DON'T SEE ANYTHING FUNNY ABOUT THIS.
YOU WERE SORT OF MY TEACHER. WHAT YOU DID WITH ADAM HUNT? TRULY INSPIRING.
RETURNING THE MONEY TO THE PEOPLE--DEMOLISHING GREED THAT'S RUN RAMPANT IN THIS CITY. THAT'S ALL I WISH TO DO. I'M SAVING THIS CITY.
NO, YOU'RE FAILING IT. NOW LAND THIS PLANE OR I'LL END YOU.

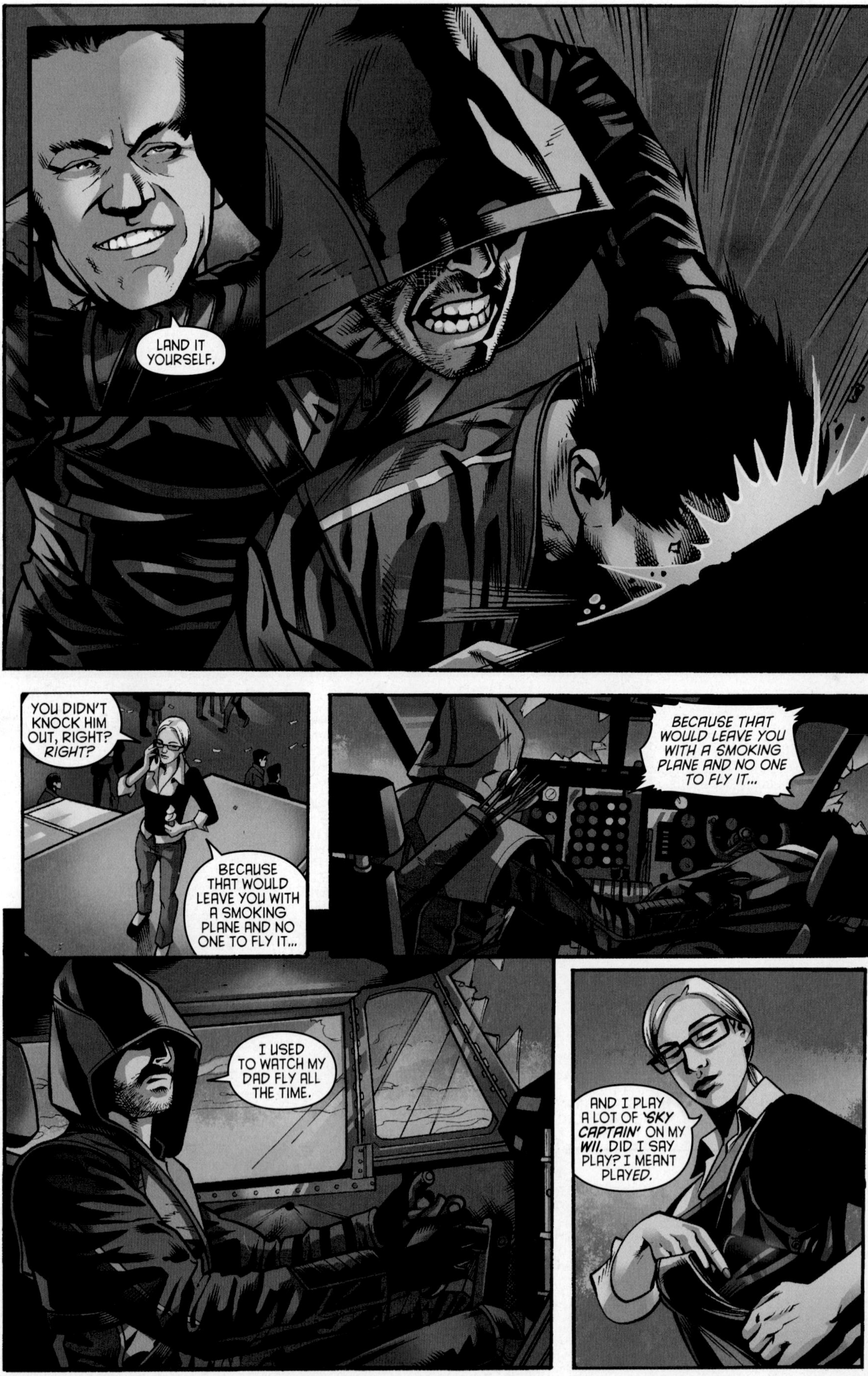
LAND IT YOURSELF.
YOU DIDN'T KNOCK HIM OUT, RIGHT? RIGHT?
BECAUSE THAT WOULD LEAVE YOU WITH A SMOKING PLANE AND NO ONE TO FLY IT...
BECAUSE THAT WOULD LEAVE YOU WITH A SMOKING PLANE AND NO ONE TO FLY IT...
I USED TO WATCH MY DAD FLY ALL THE TIME.
AND I PLAY A LOT OF 'SKY CAPTAIN' ON MY WII. DID I SAY PLAY? I MEANT PLAYED.

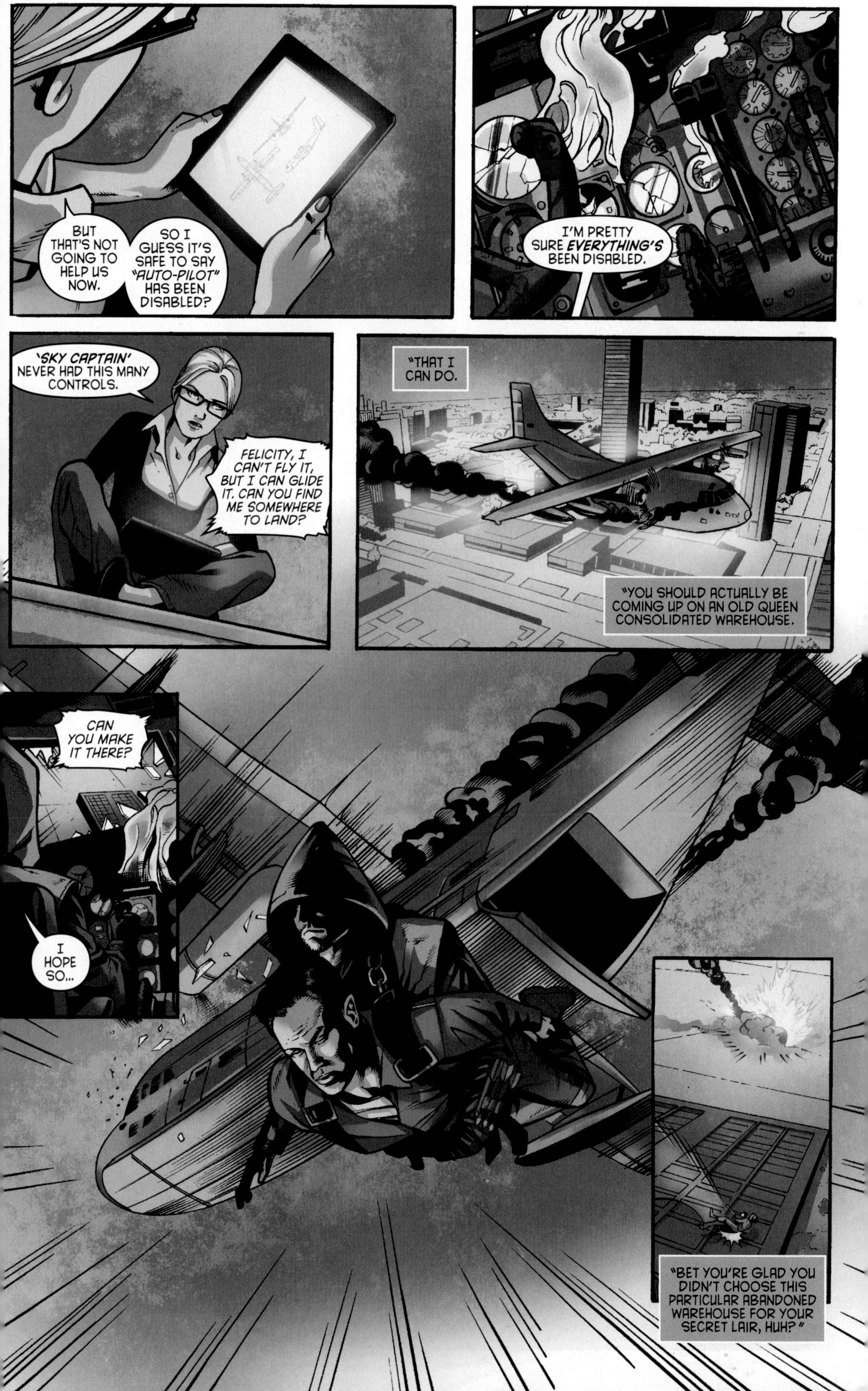

BUT THAT'S NOT GOING TO HELP US NOW.
SO I GUESS IT'S SAFE TO SAY "AUTO-PILOT" HAS BEEN DISABLED?
I'M PRETTY SURE EVERYTHING'S BEEN DISABLED.
'SKY CAPTAIN' NEVER HAD THIS MANY CONTROLS.
FELICITY, I CAN'T FLY IT, BUT I CAN GLIDE IT. CAN YOU FIND ME SOMEWHERE TO LAND?
"THAT I CAN DO.
"YOU SHOULD ACTUALLY BE COMING UP ON AN OLD QUEEN CONSOLIDATED WAREHOUSE.
CAN YOU MAKE IT THERE?
I HOPE SO...
"BET YOU'RE GLAD YOU DIDN'T CHOOSE THIS PARTICULAR ABANDONED WAREHOUSE FOR YOUR SECRET LAIR, HUH?"

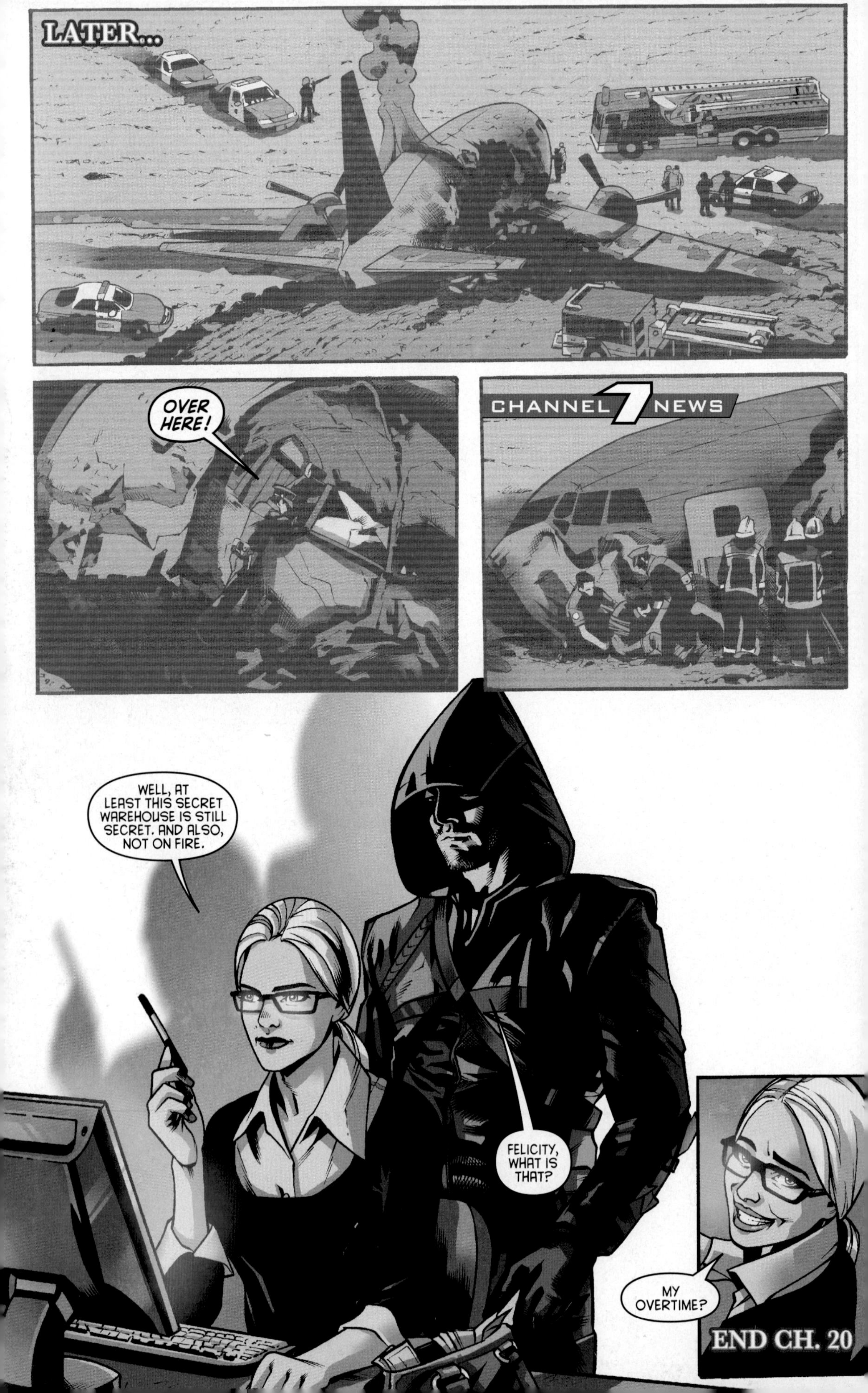
LATER...
OVER HERE!
CHANNEL 7 NEWS
WELL, AT LEAST THIS SECRET WAREHOUSE IS STILL SECRET. AND ALSO, NOT ON FIRE.
FELICITY, WHAT IS THAT?
MY OVERTIME?
END CH. 20

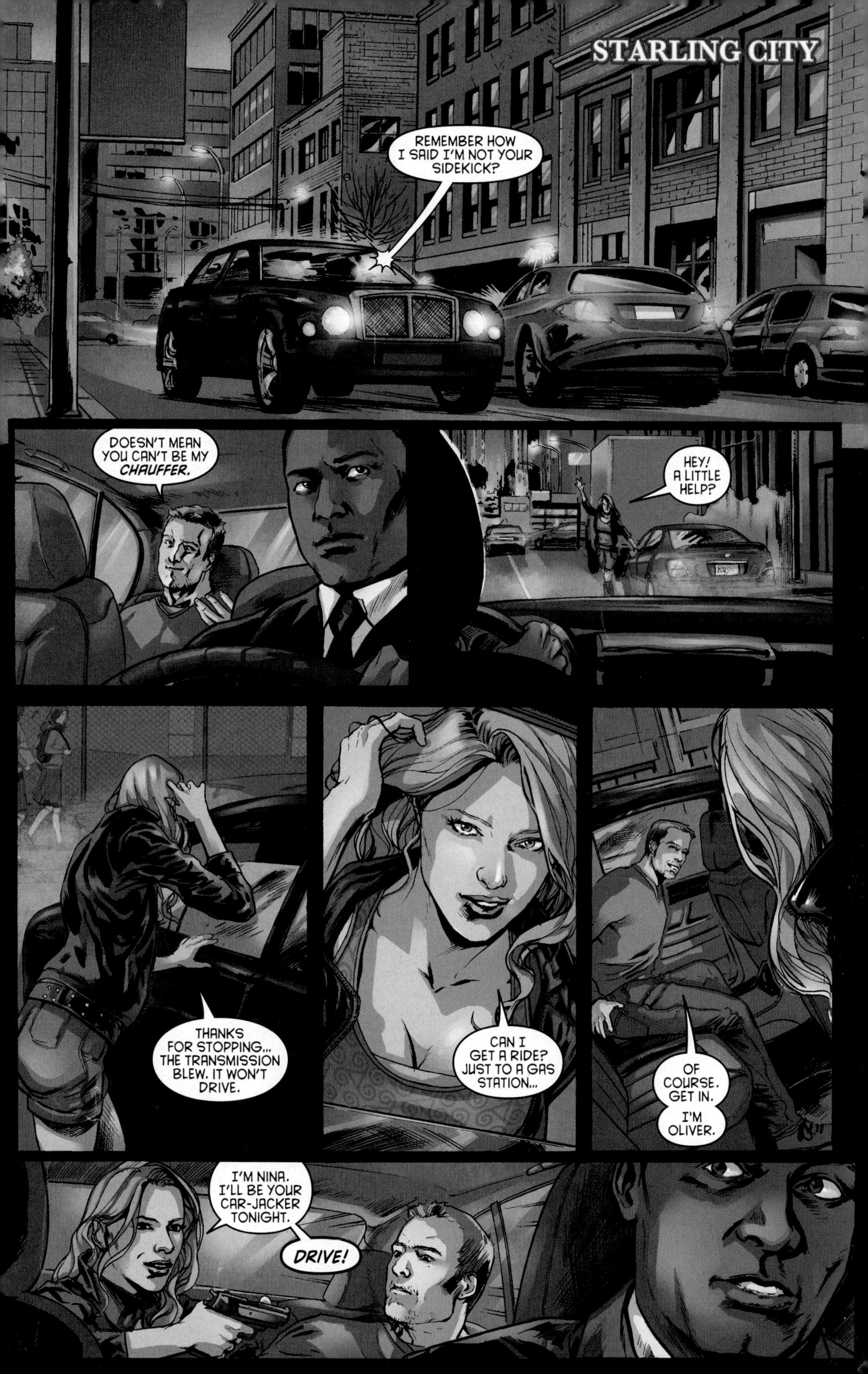
STARLING CITY
REMEMBER HOW I SAID I'M NOT YOUR SIDEKICK?
DOESN'T MEAN YOU CAN'T BE MY CHAUFFER.
HEY! A LITTLE HELP?
THANKS FOR STOPPING... THE TRANSMISSION BLEW. IT WON'T DRIVE.
CAN I GET A RIDE? JUST TO A GAS STATION...
OF COURSE. GET IN.
I'M OLIVER.
I'M NINA. I'LL BE YOUR CAR-JACKER TONIGHT.
DRIVE!

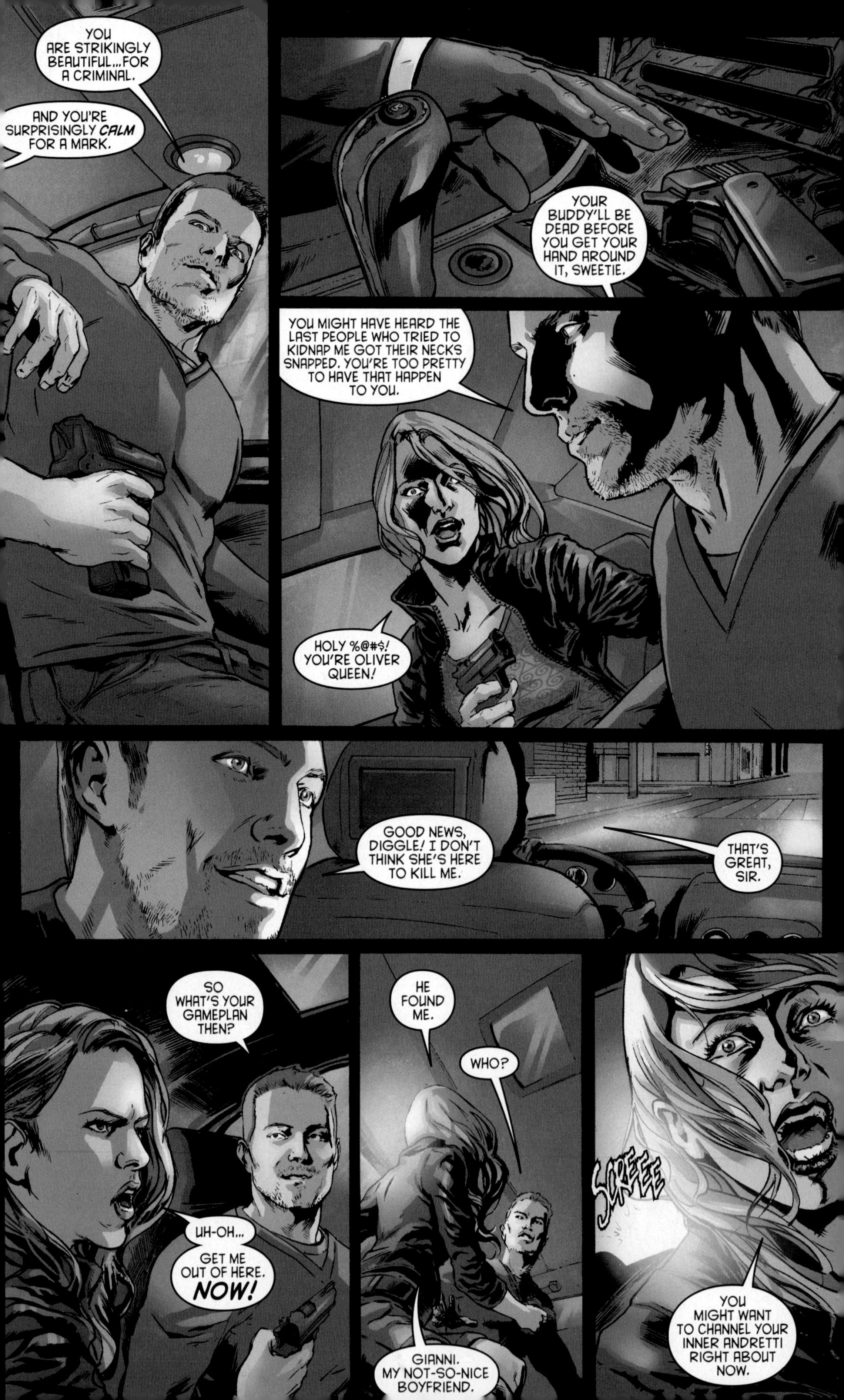
YOU ARE STRIKINGLY BEAUTIFUL...FOR A CRIMINAL.
AND YOU'RE SURPRISINGLY *CALM* FOR A MARK.
YOUR BUDDY'LL BE DEAD BEFORE YOU GET YOUR HAND AROUND IT, SWEETIE.
YOU MIGHT HAVE HEARD THE LAST PEOPLE WHO TRIED TO KIDNAP ME GOT THEIR NECKS SNAPPED. YOU'RE TOO PRETTY TO HAVE THAT HAPPEN TO YOU.
HOLY %@#$! YOU'RE OLIVER QUEEN!
GOOD NEWS, DIGGLE! I DON'T THINK SHE'S HERE TO KILL ME.
THAT'S GREAT, SIR.
SO WHAT'S YOUR GAMEPLAN THEN?
UH-OH...
GET ME OUT OF HERE. **NOW!**
HE FOUND ME.
WHO?
GIANNI. MY NOT-SO-NICE BOYFRIEND.
SCREEE
YOU MIGHT WANT TO CHANNEL YOUR INNER ANDRETTI RIGHT ABOUT NOW.

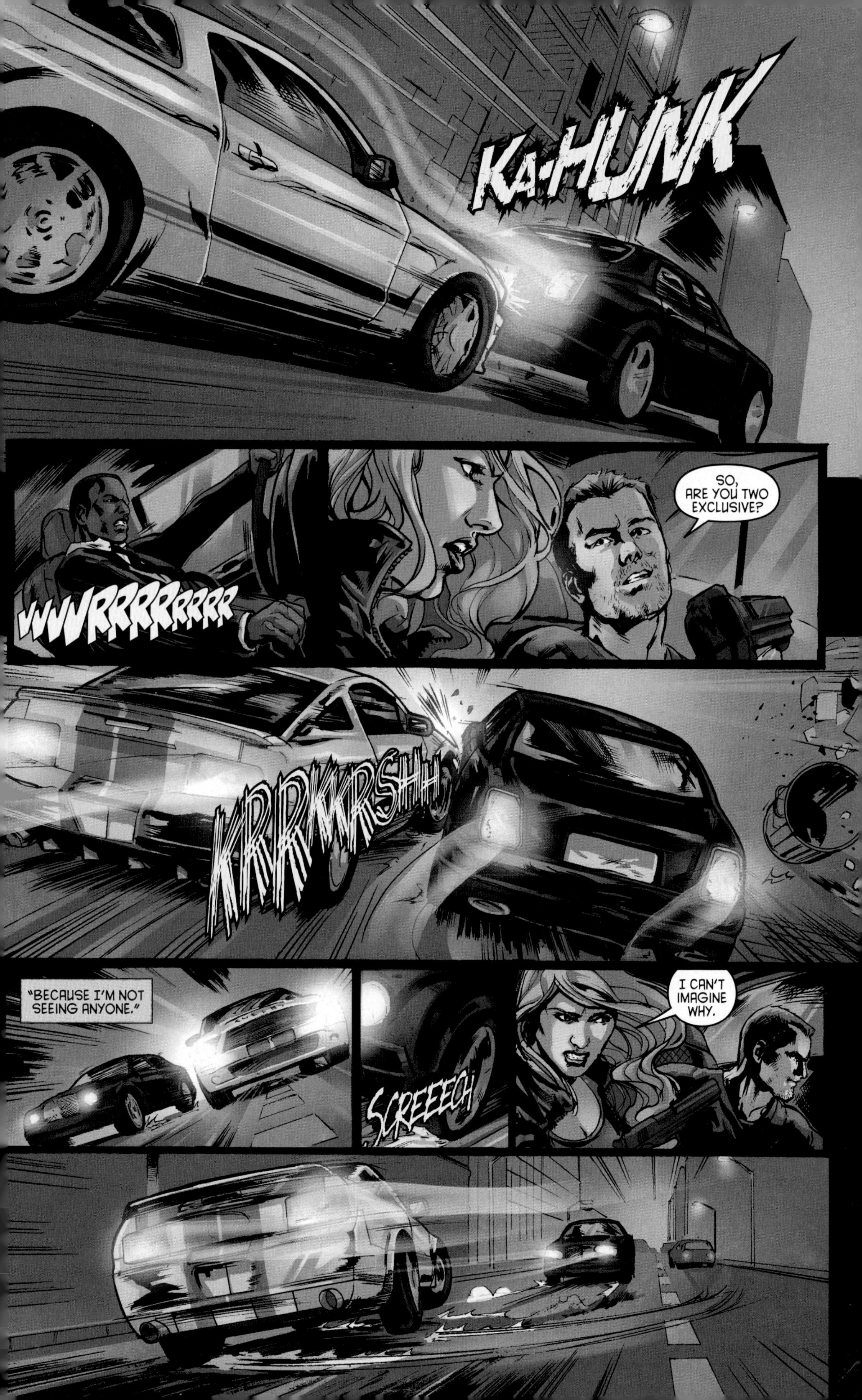
KA-HUNK
SO, ARE YOU TWO EXCLUSIVE?
VVVVRRRRRRRR
KRRKKRSHH
"BECAUSE I'M NOT SEEING ANYONE."
SCREEEECH
I CAN'T IMAGINE WHY.

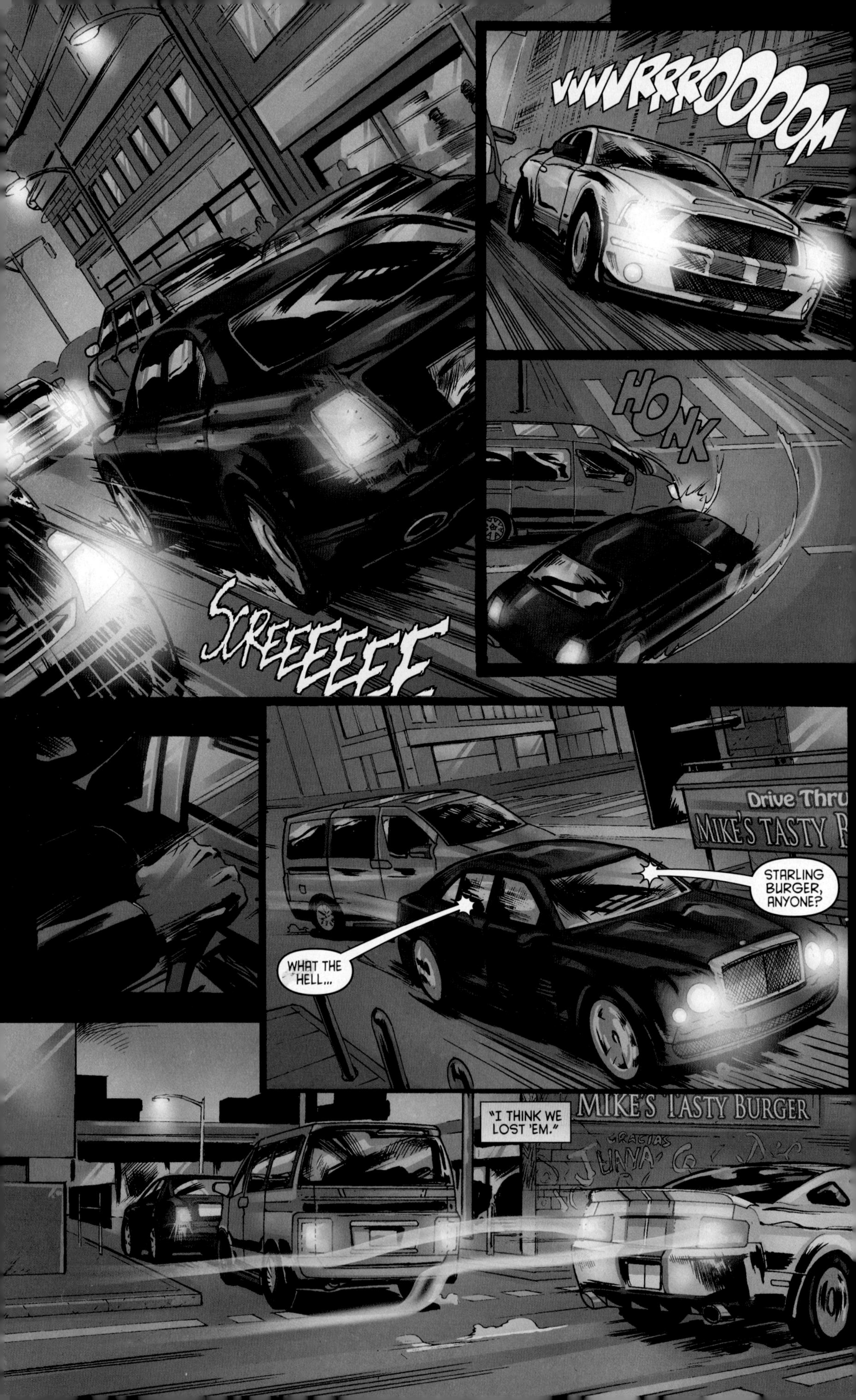
VVVVRRRROOOOM
HONK
SCREEEEEE
Drive Thru
MIKE'S TASTY B
STARLING BURGER, ANYONE?
WHAT THE HELL...
"I THINK WE LOST 'EM."
MIKE'S TASTY BURGER

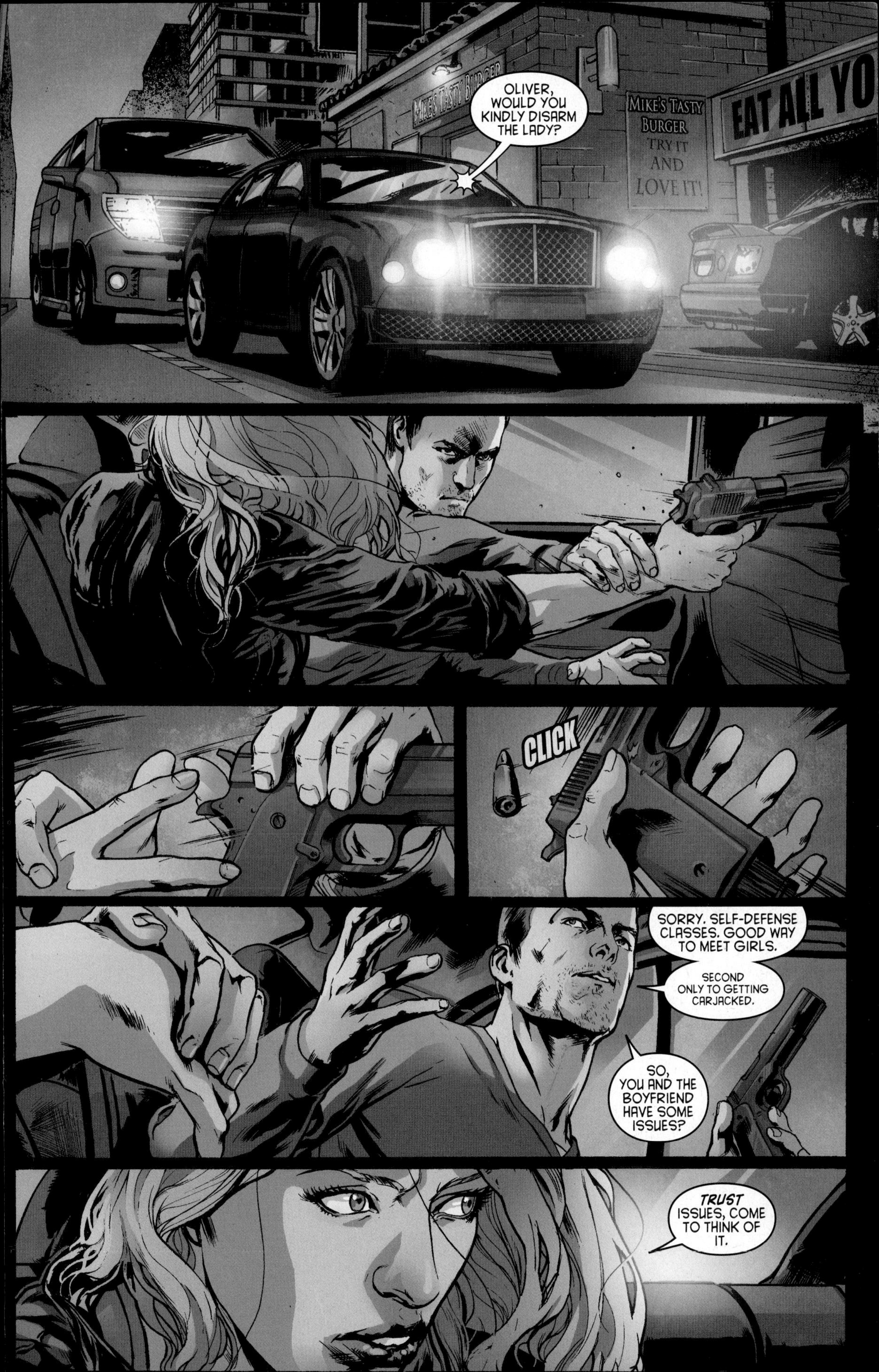
OLIVER, WOULD YOU KINDLY DISARM THE LADY?
MIKE'S TASTY BURGER
MIKE'S TASTY BURGER TRY IT AND LOVE IT!
EAT ALL YO
CLICK
SORRY. SELF-DEFENSE CLASSES. GOOD WAY TO MEET GIRLS.
SECOND ONLY TO GETTING CARJACKED.
SO, YOU AND THE BOYFRIEND HAVE SOME ISSUES?
TRUST ISSUES, COME TO THINK OF IT.

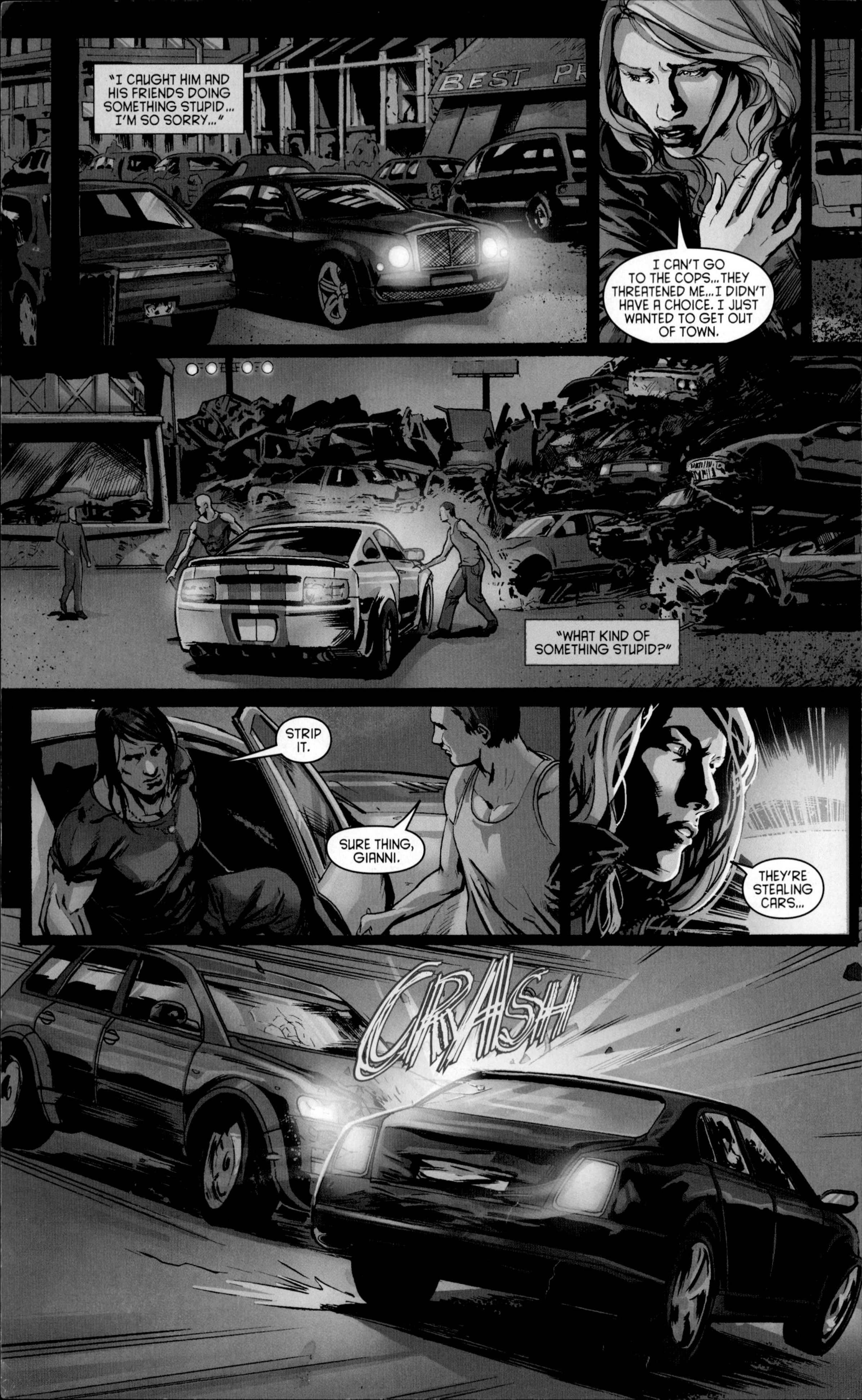
"I CAUGHT HIM AND HIS FRIENDS DOING SOMETHING STUPID... I'M SO SORRY..."
BEST PR
I CAN'T GO TO THE COPS... THEY THREATENED ME... I DIDN'T HAVE A CHOICE. I JUST WANTED TO GET OUT OF TOWN.
"WHAT KIND OF SOMETHING STUPID?"
STRIP IT.
SURE THING, GIANNI.
THEY'RE STEALING CARS...
CRASH

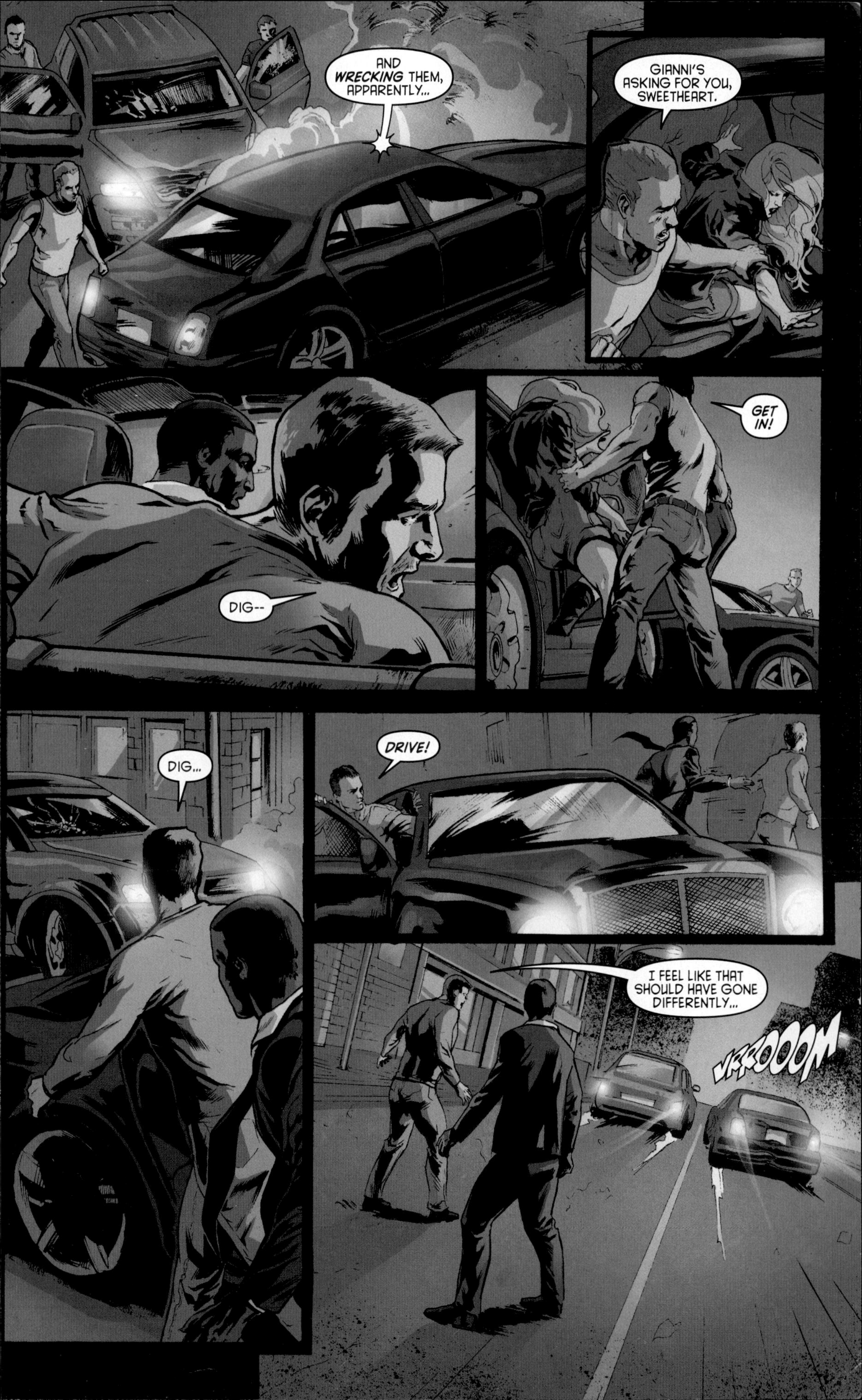
AND WRECKING THEM, APPARENTLY...
GIANNI'S ASKING FOR YOU, SWEETHEART.
DIG--
GET IN!
DIG...
DRIVE!
I FEEL LIKE THAT SHOULD HAVE GONE DIFFERENTLY...
VRROOOM

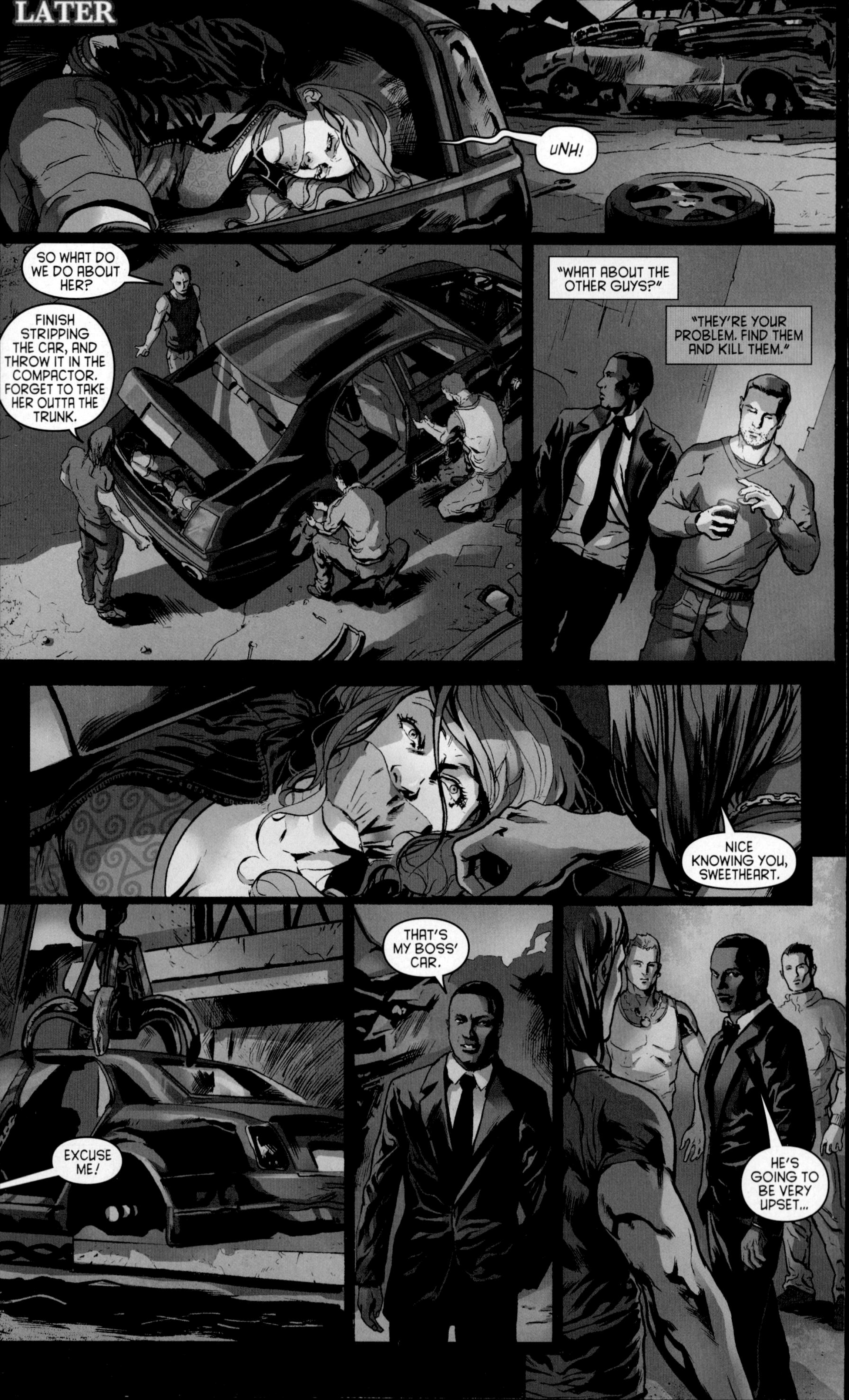
LATER
UNH!
SO WHAT DO WE DO ABOUT HER?
FINISH STRIPPING THE CAR, AND THROW IT IN THE COMPACTOR. FORGET TO TAKE HER OUTTA THE TRUNK.
"WHAT ABOUT THE OTHER GUYS?"
"THEY'RE YOUR PROBLEM. FIND THEM AND KILL THEM."
NICE KNOWING YOU, SWEETHEART.
EXCUSE ME!
THAT'S MY BOSS' CAR.
HE'S GOING TO BE VERY UPSET...

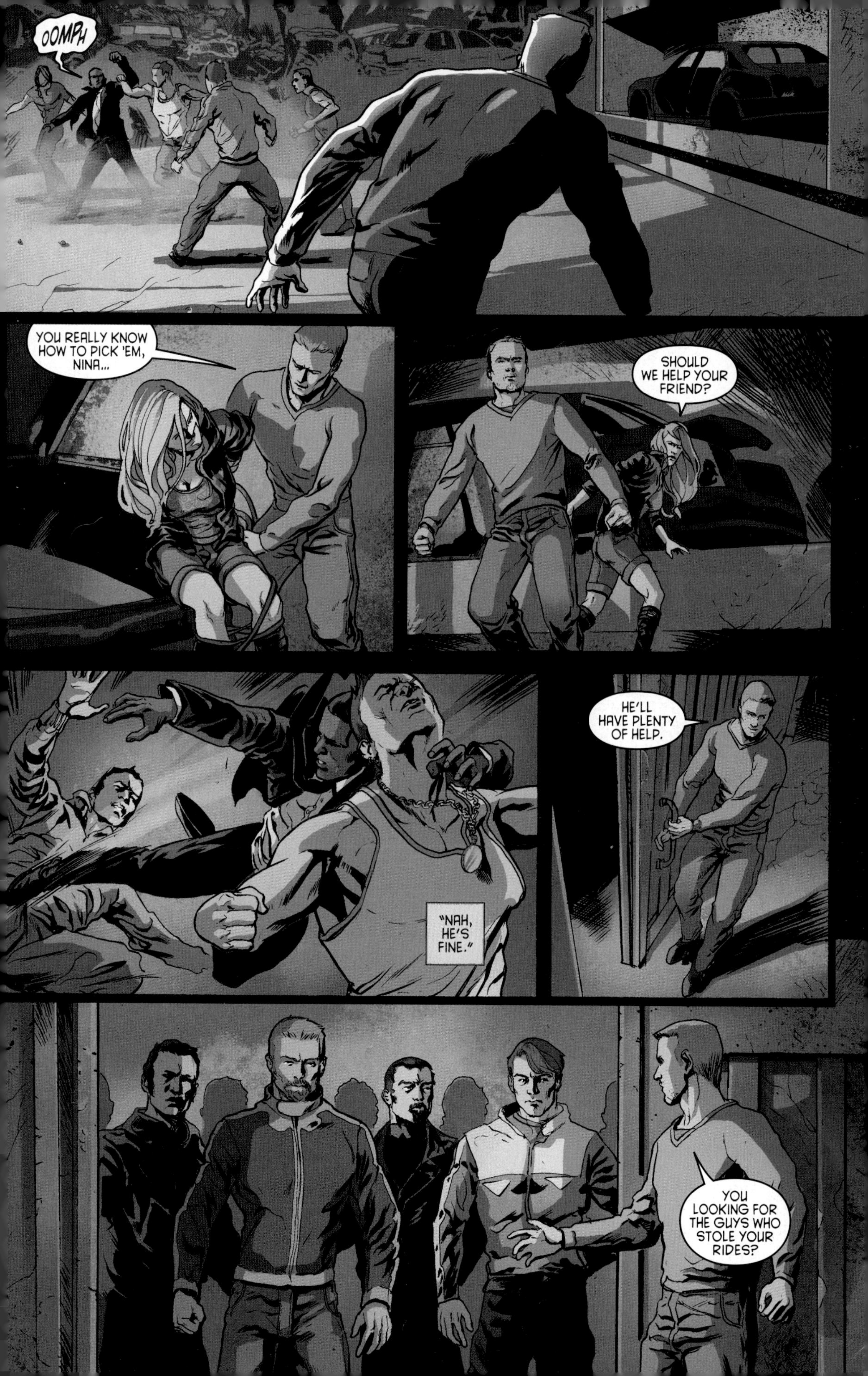
OOMPH
YOU REALLY KNOW HOW TO PICK 'EM, NINA...
SHOULD WE HELP YOUR FRIEND?
"NAH, HE'S FINE."
HE'LL HAVE PLENTY OF HELP.
YOU LOOKING FOR THE GUYS WHO STOLE YOUR RIDES?

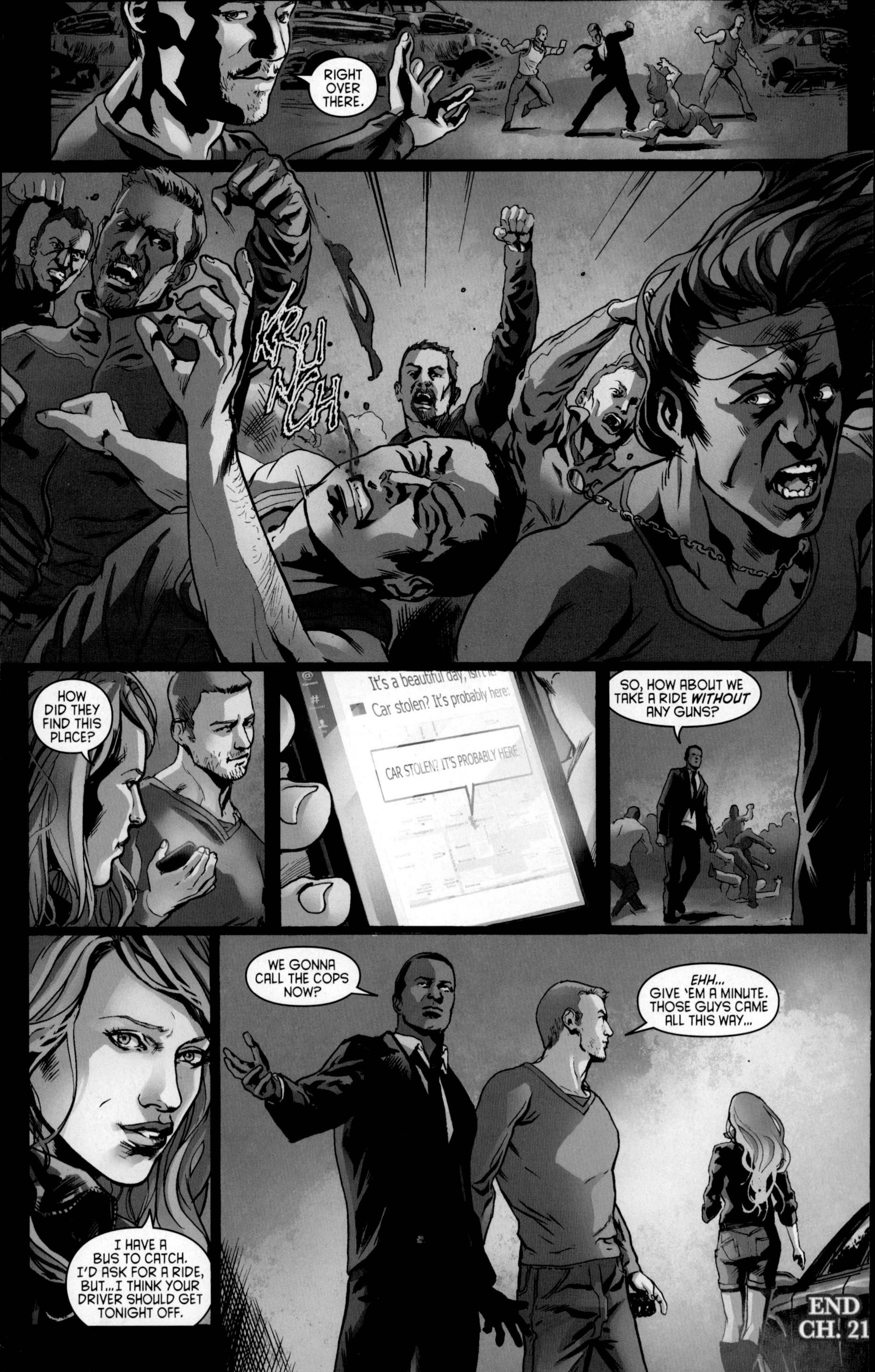
RIGHT OVER THERE.
KRUNCH
HOW DID THEY FIND THIS PLACE?
It's a beautiful day, isn't it?
Car stolen? It's probably here:
CAR STOLEN? IT'S PROBABLY HERE.
SO, HOW ABOUT WE TAKE A RIDE *WITHOUT* ANY GUNS?
I HAVE A BUS TO CATCH. I'D ASK FOR A RIDE, BUT... I THINK YOUR DRIVER SHOULD GET TONIGHT OFF.
WE GONNA CALL THE COPS NOW?
EHH... GIVE 'EM A MINUTE. THOSE GUYS CAME ALL THIS WAY...
END CH. 21

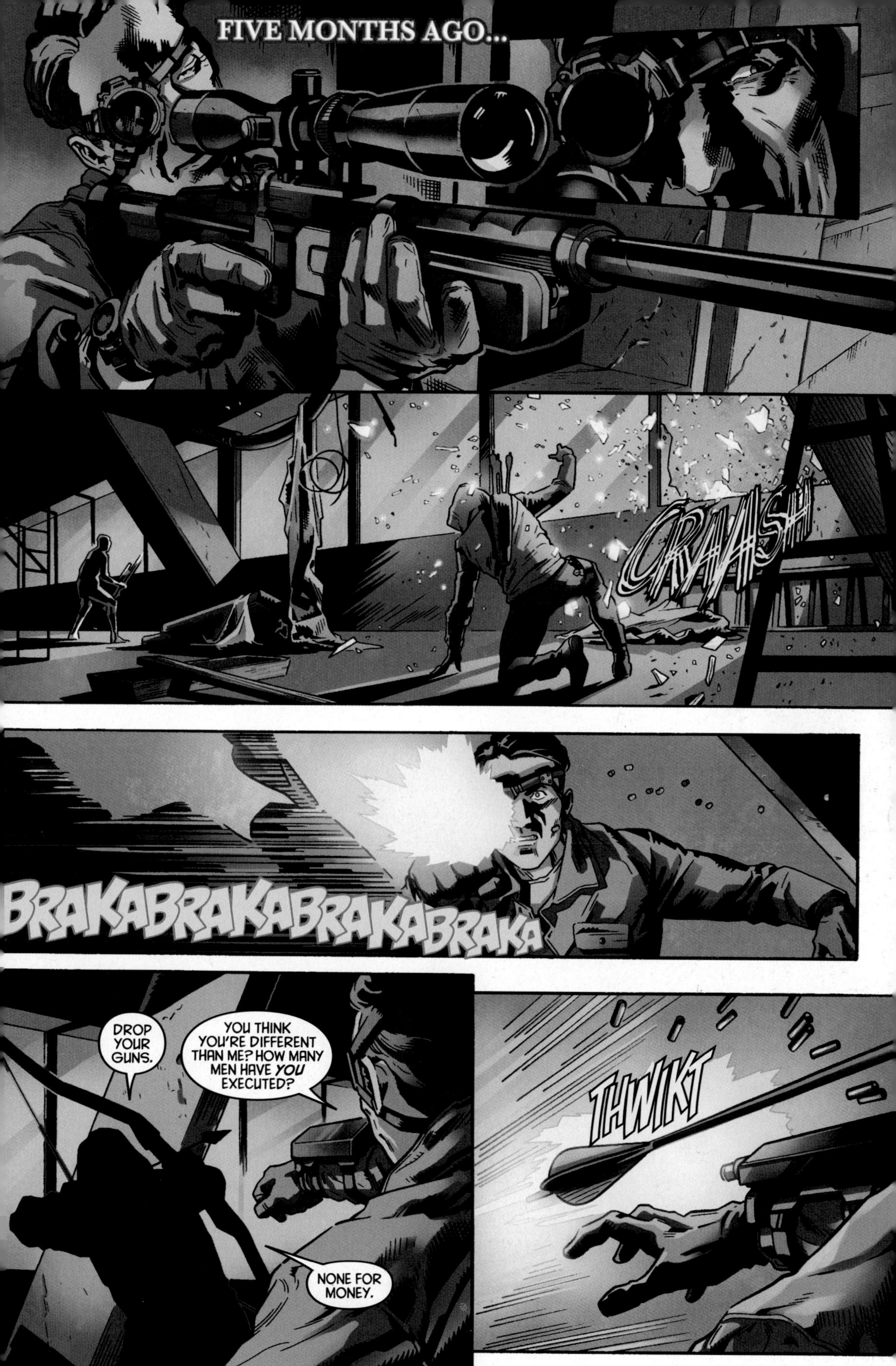
FIVE MONTHS AGO...
CRAAASH!
BRAKABRAKABRAKABRAKA
DROP YOUR GUNS.
YOU THINK YOU'RE DIFFERENT THAN ME? HOW MANY MEN HAVE *YOU* EXECUTED?
NONE FOR MONEY.
THWIKT

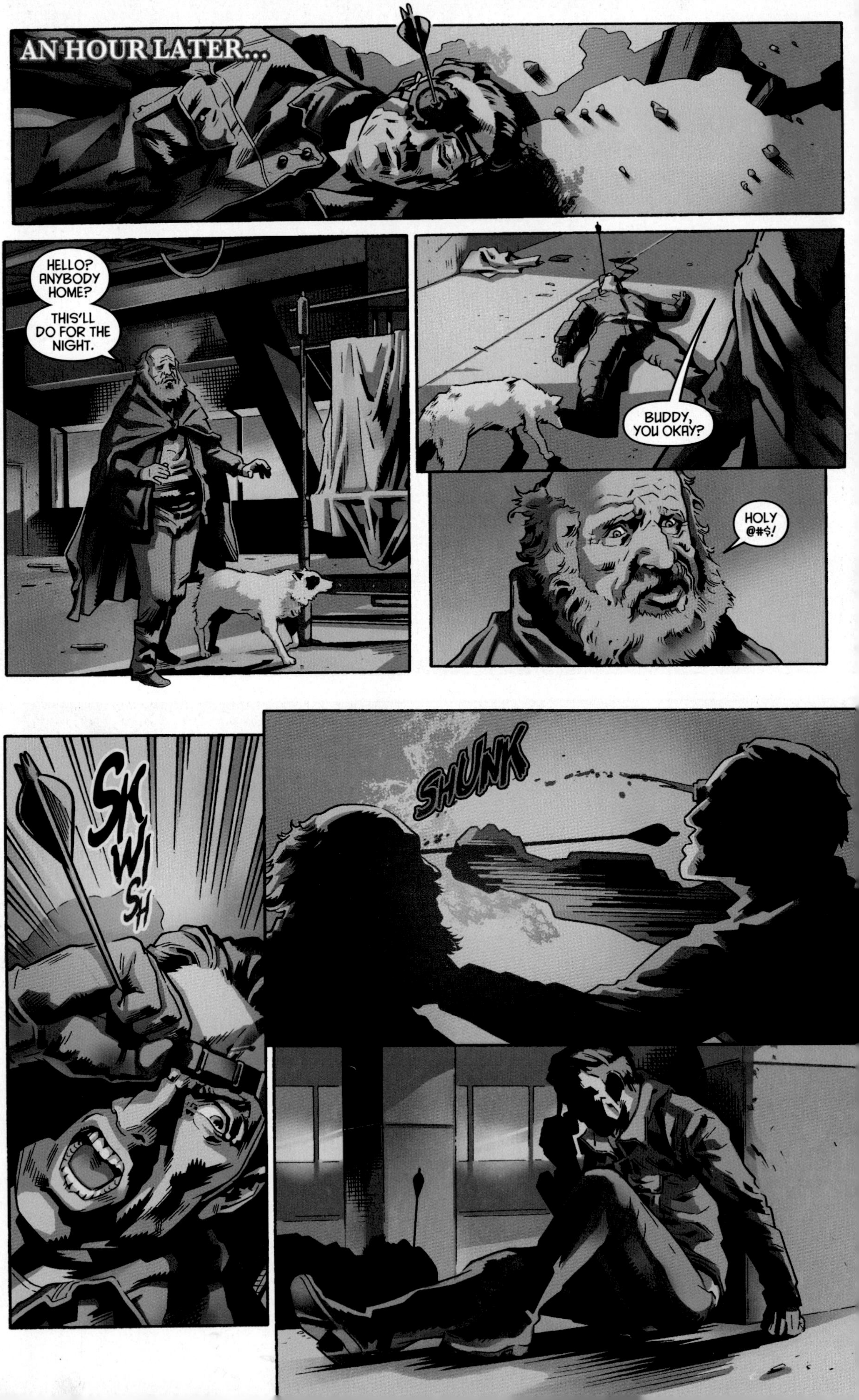
AN HOUR LATER...
HELLO? ANYBODY HOME?
THIS'LL DO FOR THE NIGHT.
BUDDY, YOU OKAY?
HOLY @#$!
SKWISH
SHUNK

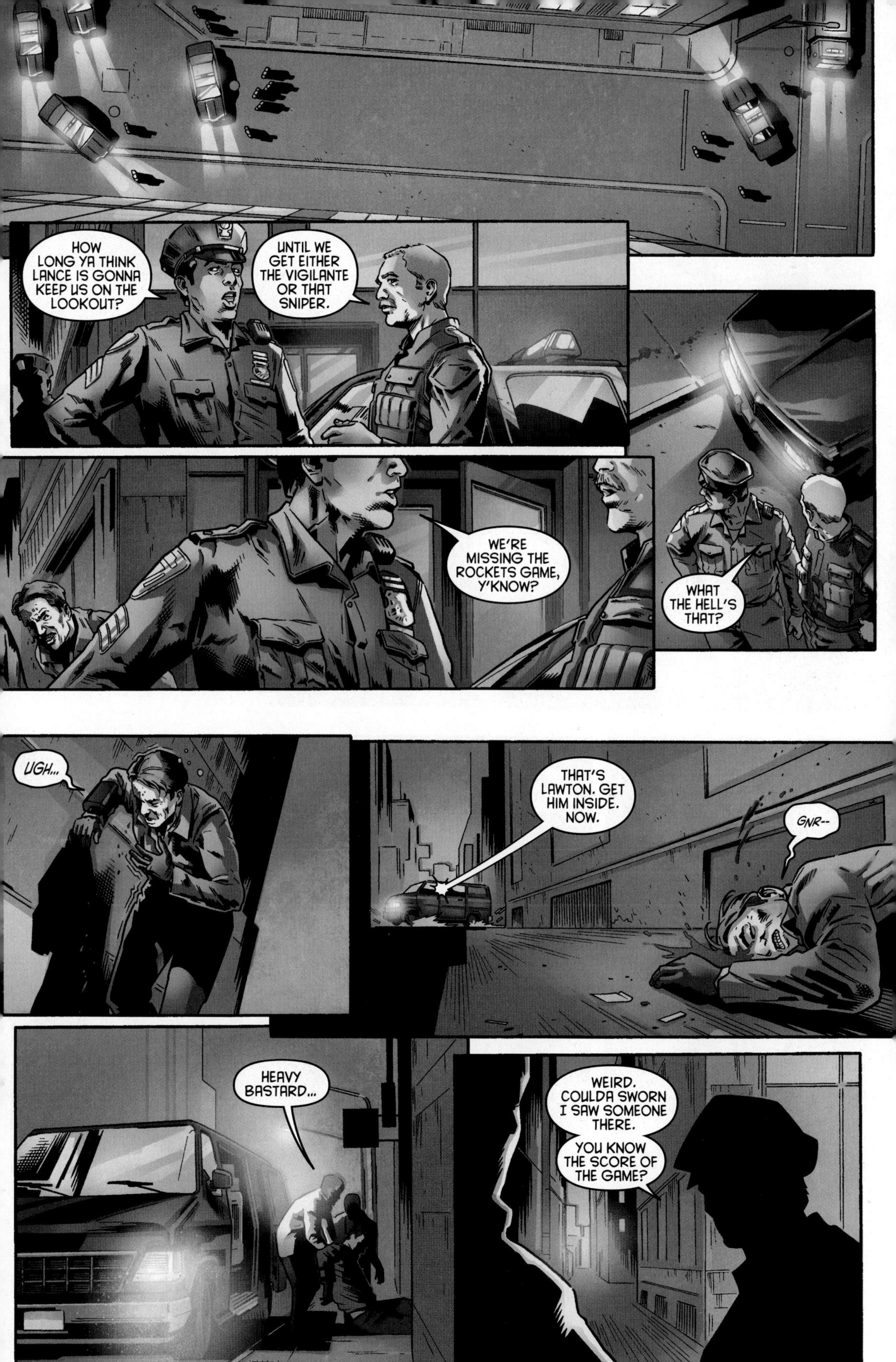
HOW LONG YA THINK LANCE IS GONNA KEEP US ON THE LOOKOUT?
UNTIL WE GET EITHER THE VIGILANTE OR THAT SNIPER.
WE'RE MISSING THE ROCKETS GAME, Y'KNOW?
WHAT THE HELL'S THAT?
UGH...
THAT'S LAWTON. GET HIM INSIDE. NOW.
GNR--
HEAVY BASTARD...
WEIRD. COULDA SWORN I SAW SOMEONE THERE.
YOU KNOW THE SCORE OF THE GAME?

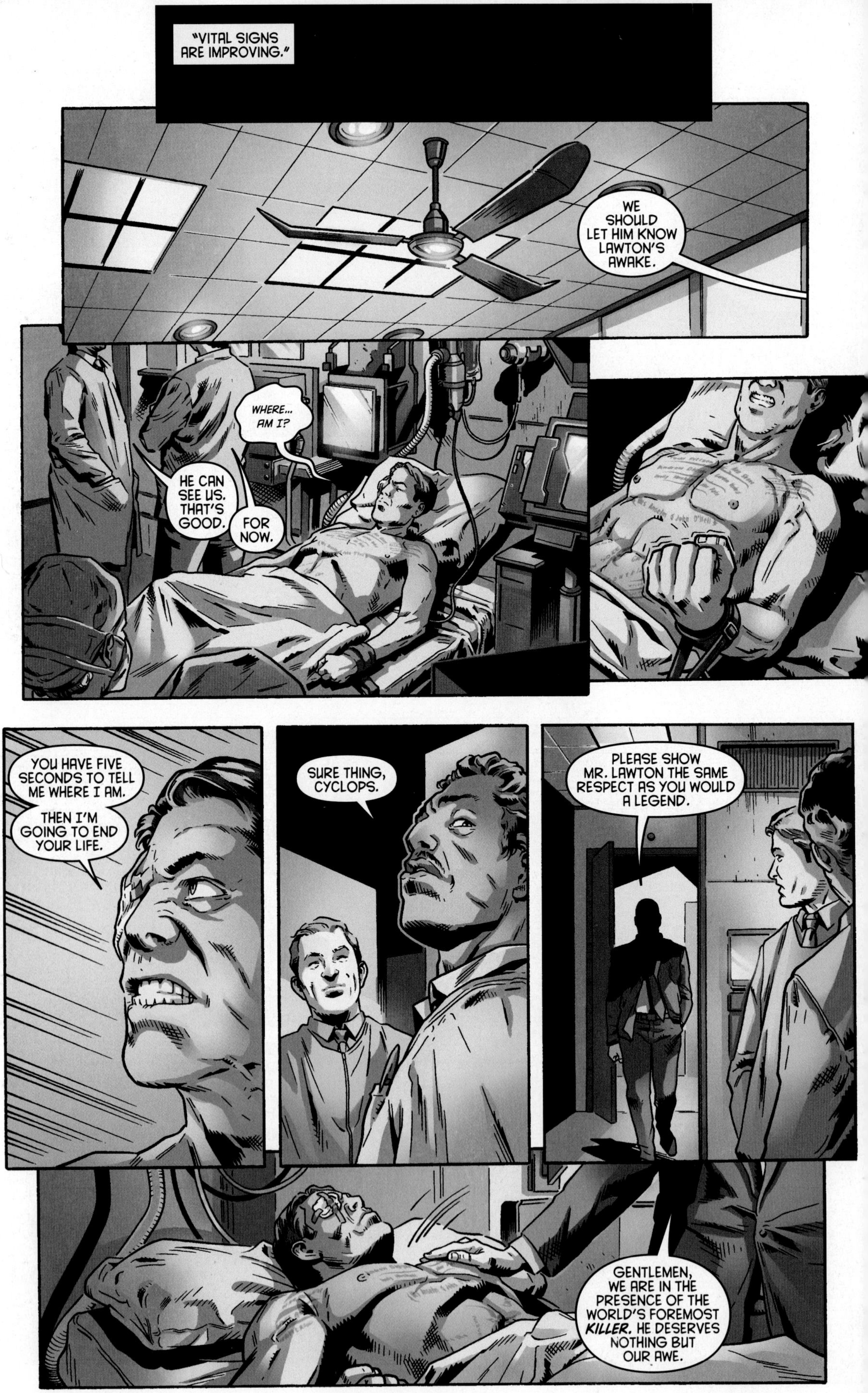
"VITAL SIGNS ARE IMPROVING."
WE SHOULD LET HIM KNOW LAWTON'S AWAKE.
WHERE... AM I?
HE CAN SEE US. THAT'S GOOD.
FOR NOW.
YOU HAVE FIVE SECONDS TO TELL ME WHERE I AM.
THEN I'M GOING TO END YOUR LIFE.
SURE THING, CYCLOPS.
PLEASE SHOW MR. LAWTON THE SAME RESPECT AS YOU WOULD A LEGEND.
GENTLEMEN, WE ARE IN THE PRESENCE OF THE WORLD'S FOREMOST KILLER. HE DESERVES NOTHING BUT OUR AWE.

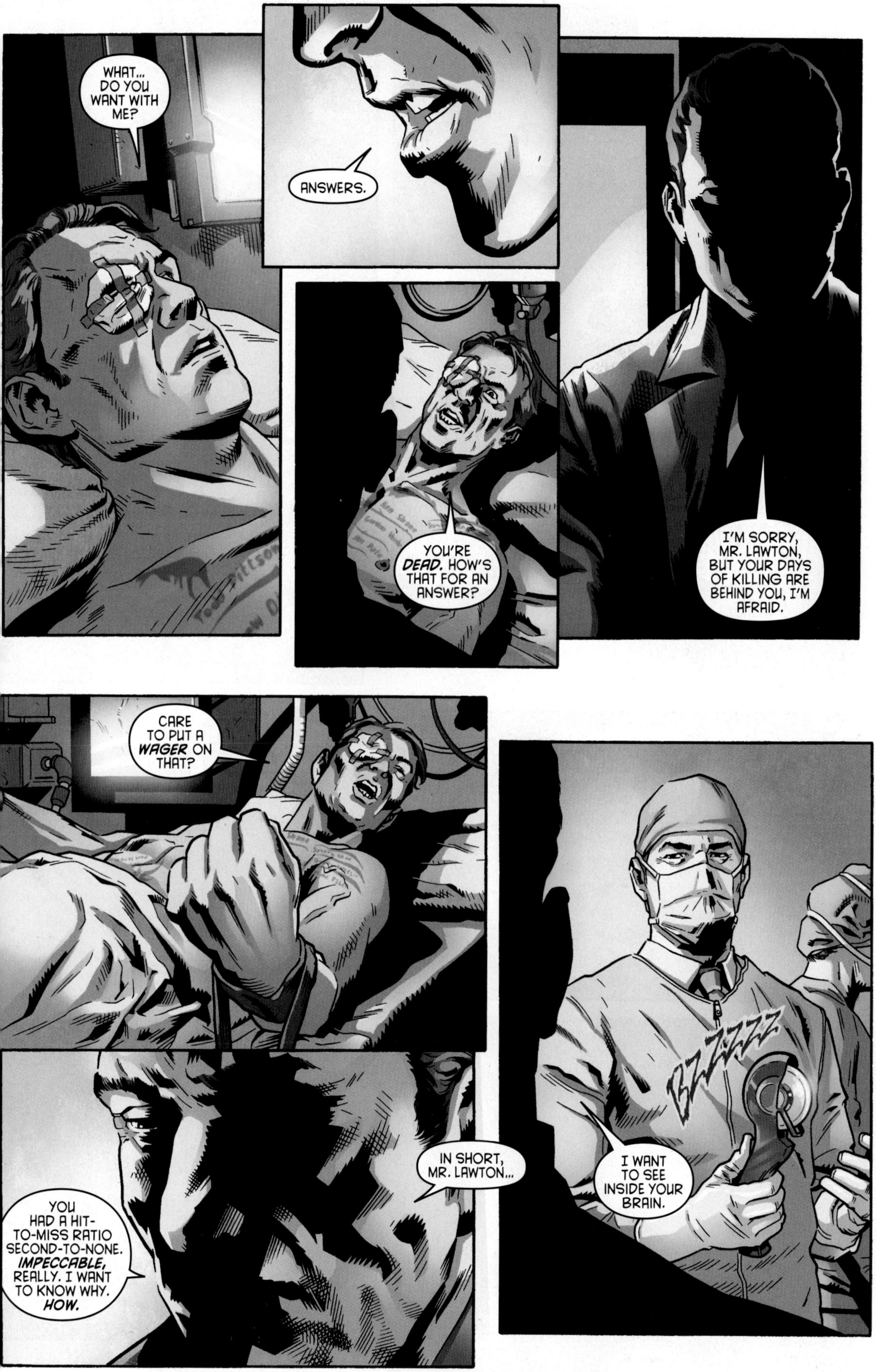

WHAT... DO YOU WANT WITH ME?
ANSWERS.
YOU'RE *DEAD.* HOW'S THAT FOR AN ANSWER?
I'M SORRY, MR. LAWTON, BUT YOUR DAYS OF KILLING ARE BEHIND YOU, I'M AFRAID.
CARE TO PUT A *WAGER* ON THAT?
YOU HAD A HIT-TO-MISS RATIO SECOND-TO-NONE. *IMPECCABLE,* REALLY. I WANT TO KNOW WHY. *HOW.*
IN SHORT, MR. LAWTON...
BZZZZZ
I WANT TO SEE INSIDE YOUR BRAIN.

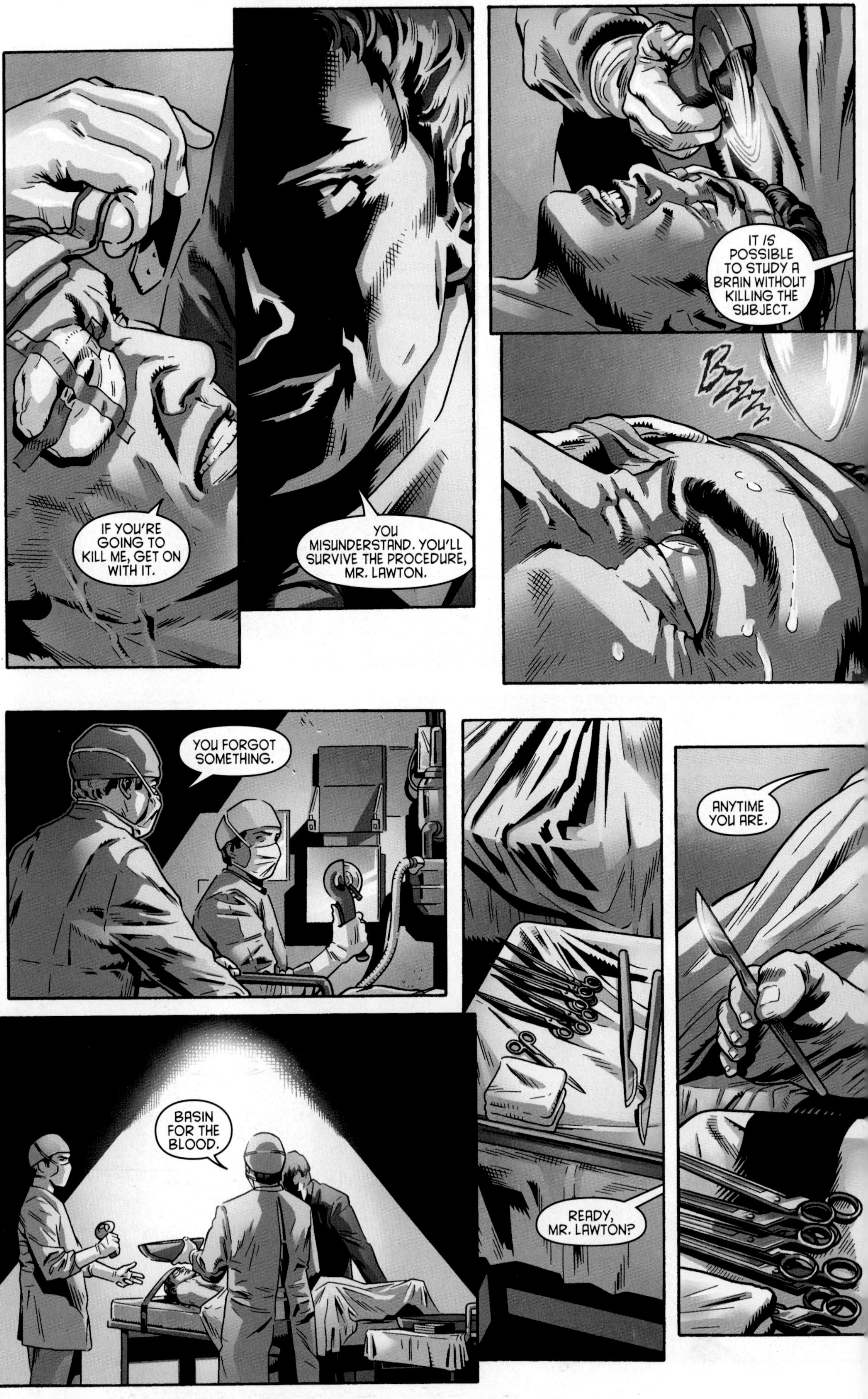
IF YOU'RE GOING TO KILL ME, GET ON WITH IT.
YOU MISUNDERSTAND. YOU'LL SURVIVE THE PROCEDURE, MR. LAWTON.
IT IS POSSIBLE TO STUDY A BRAIN WITHOUT KILLING THE SUBJECT.
BZZZZ
YOU FORGOT SOMETHING.
ANYTIME YOU ARE.
BASIN FOR THE BLOOD.
READY, MR. LAWTON?

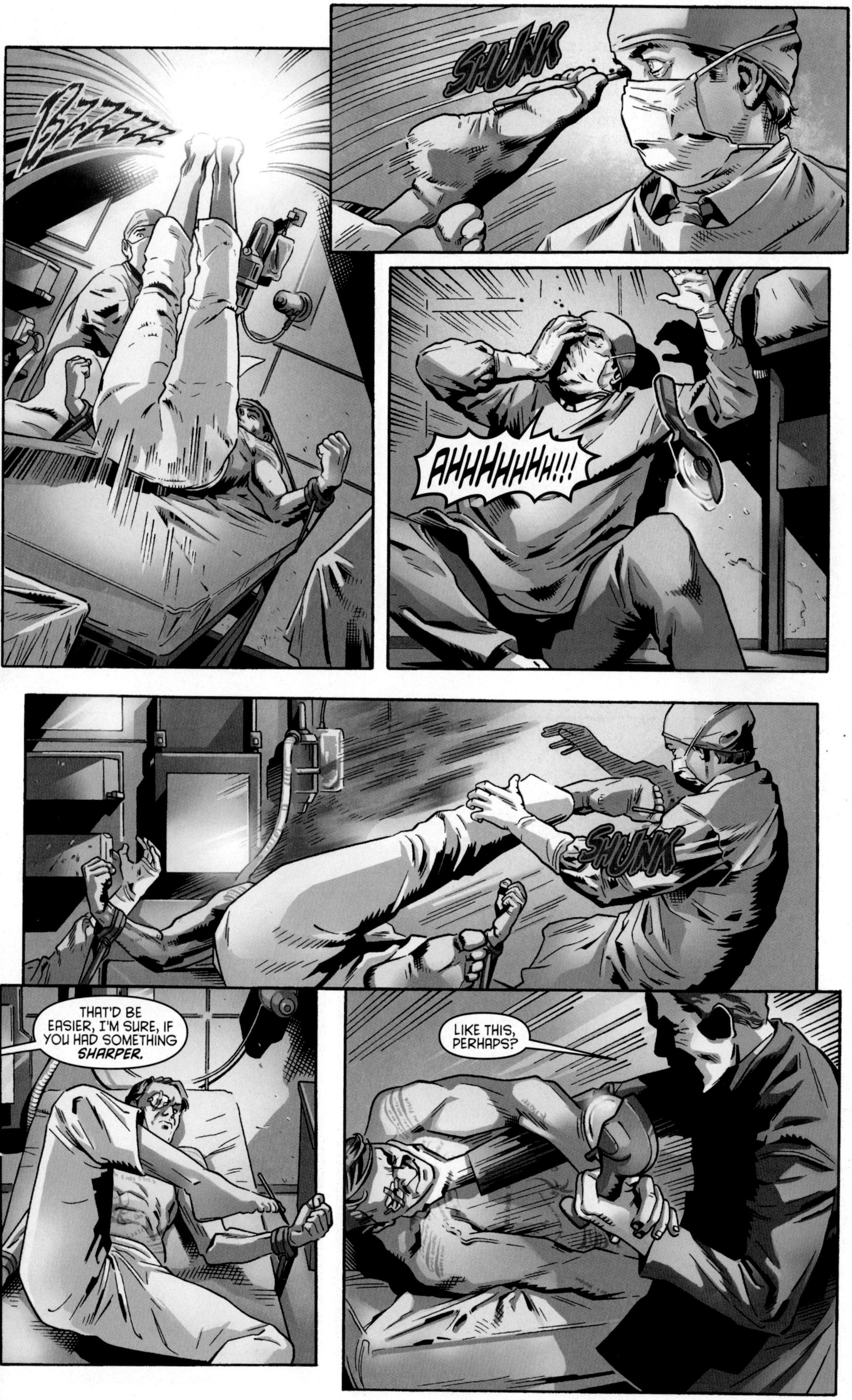
BZZZZZZ
SHUNK
AHHHHHHH!!!
SHUNK
THAT'D BE EASIER, I'M SURE, IF YOU HAD SOMETHING SHARPER.
LIKE THIS, PERHAPS?

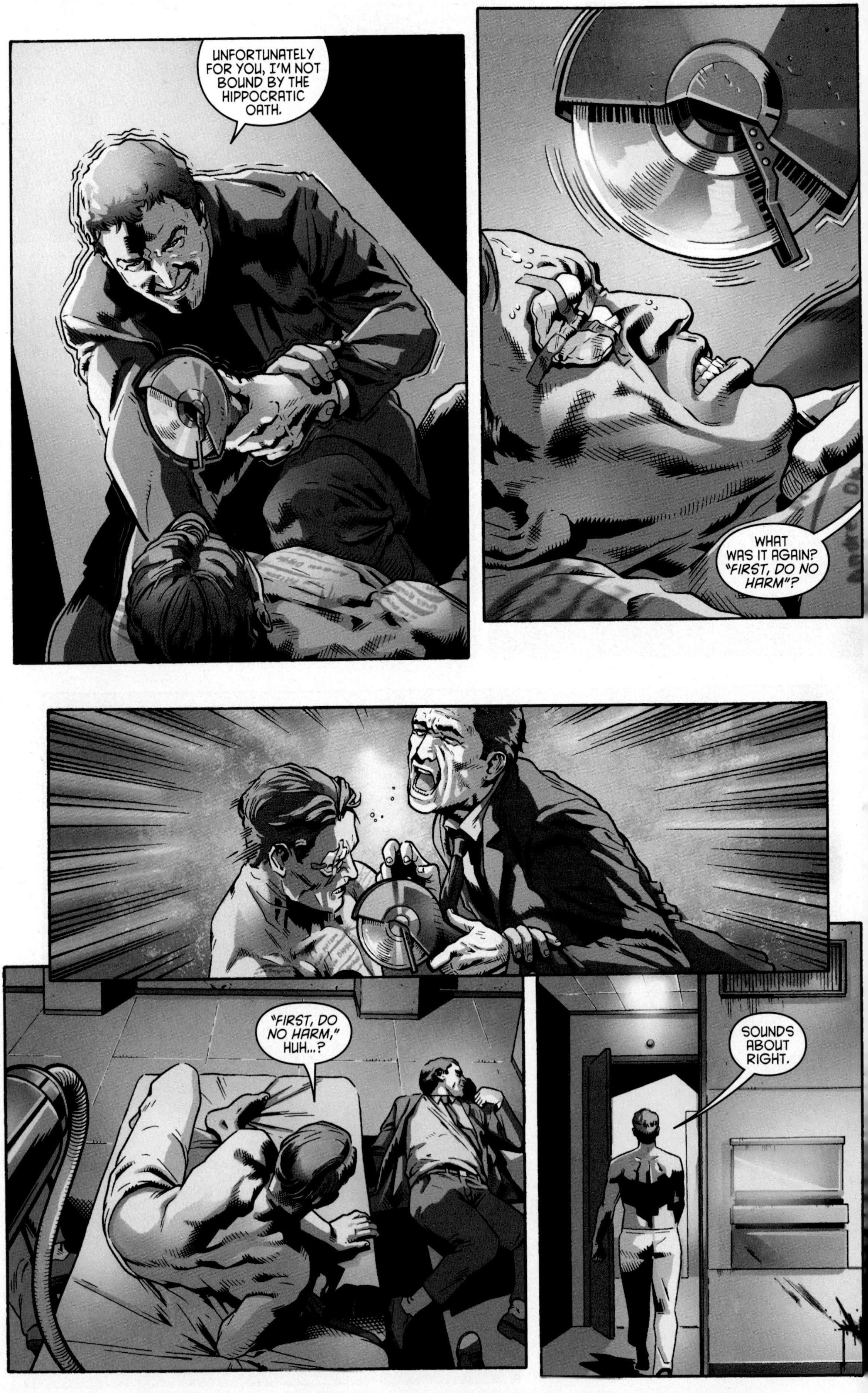
UNFORTUNATELY FOR YOU, I'M NOT BOUND BY THE HIPPOCRATIC OATH.
WHAT WAS IT AGAIN? "FIRST, DO NO HARM"?
"FIRST, DO NO HARM," HUH...?
SOUNDS ABOUT RIGHT.

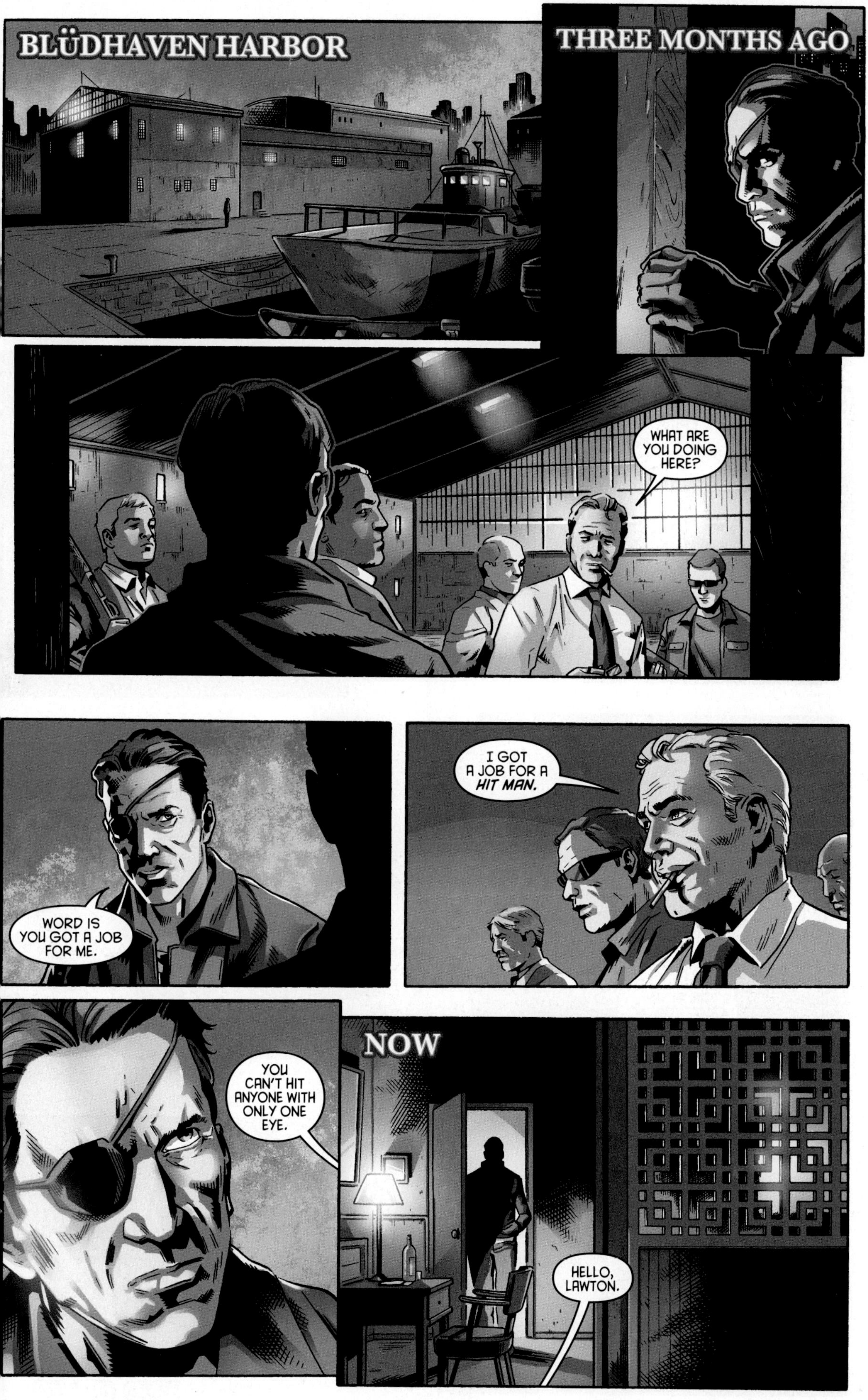
BLÜDHAVEN HARBOR
THREE MONTHS AGO
WHAT ARE YOU DOING HERE?
WORD IS YOU GOT A JOB FOR ME.
I GOT A JOB FOR A *HIT MAN.*
YOU CAN'T HIT ANYONE WITH ONLY ONE EYE.
NOW
HELLO, LAWTON.

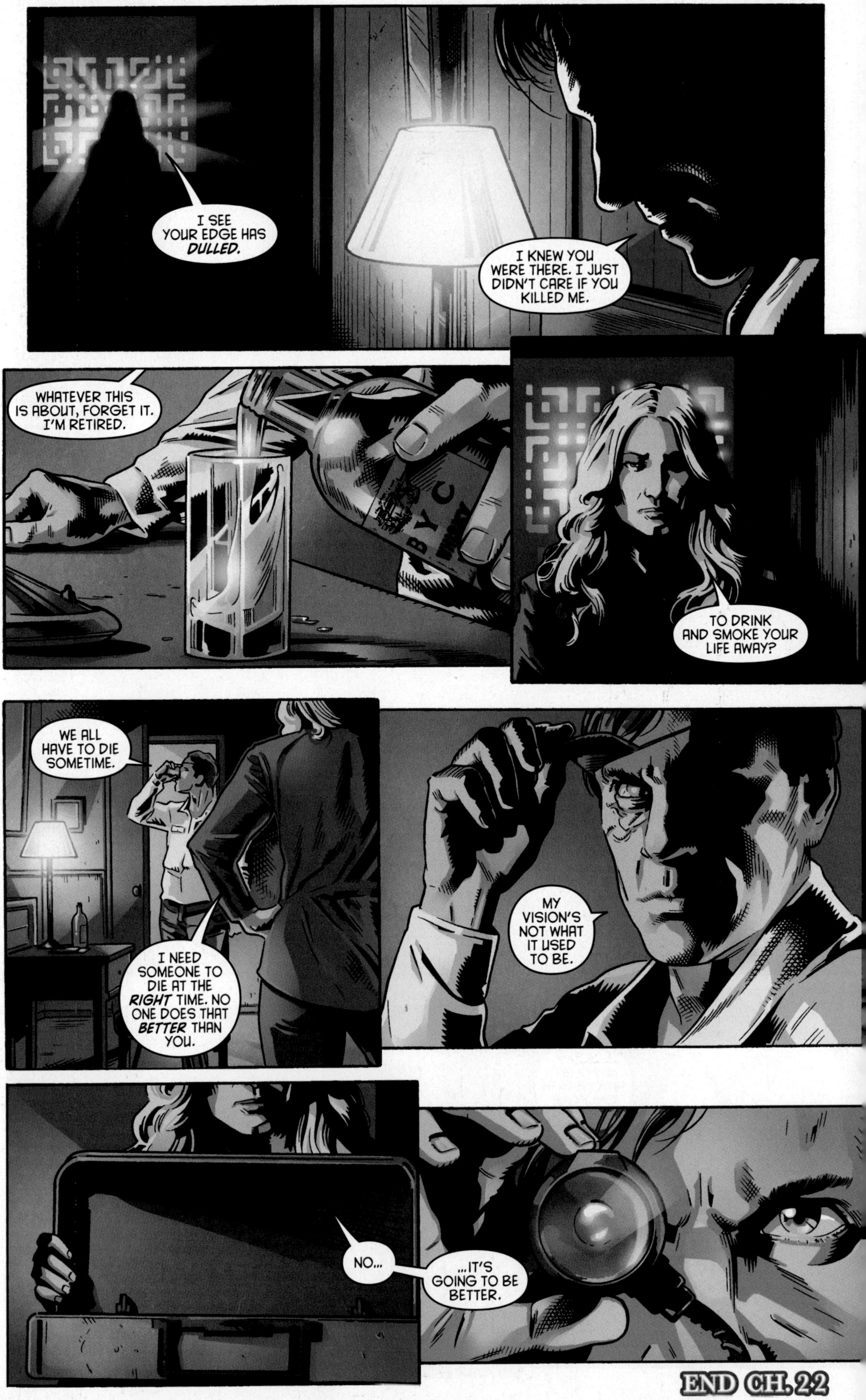
I SEE YOUR EDGE HAS *DULLED.*
I KNEW YOU WERE THERE. I JUST DIDN'T CARE IF YOU KILLED ME.
WHATEVER THIS IS ABOUT, FORGET IT. I'M RETIRED.
TO DRINK AND SMOKE YOUR LIFE AWAY?
WE ALL HAVE TO DIE SOMETIME.
I NEED SOMEONE TO DIE AT THE *RIGHT* TIME. NO ONE DOES THAT *BETTER* THAN YOU.
MY VISION'S NOT WHAT IT USED TO BE.
NO...
...IT'S GOING TO BE BETTER.
END CH. 22

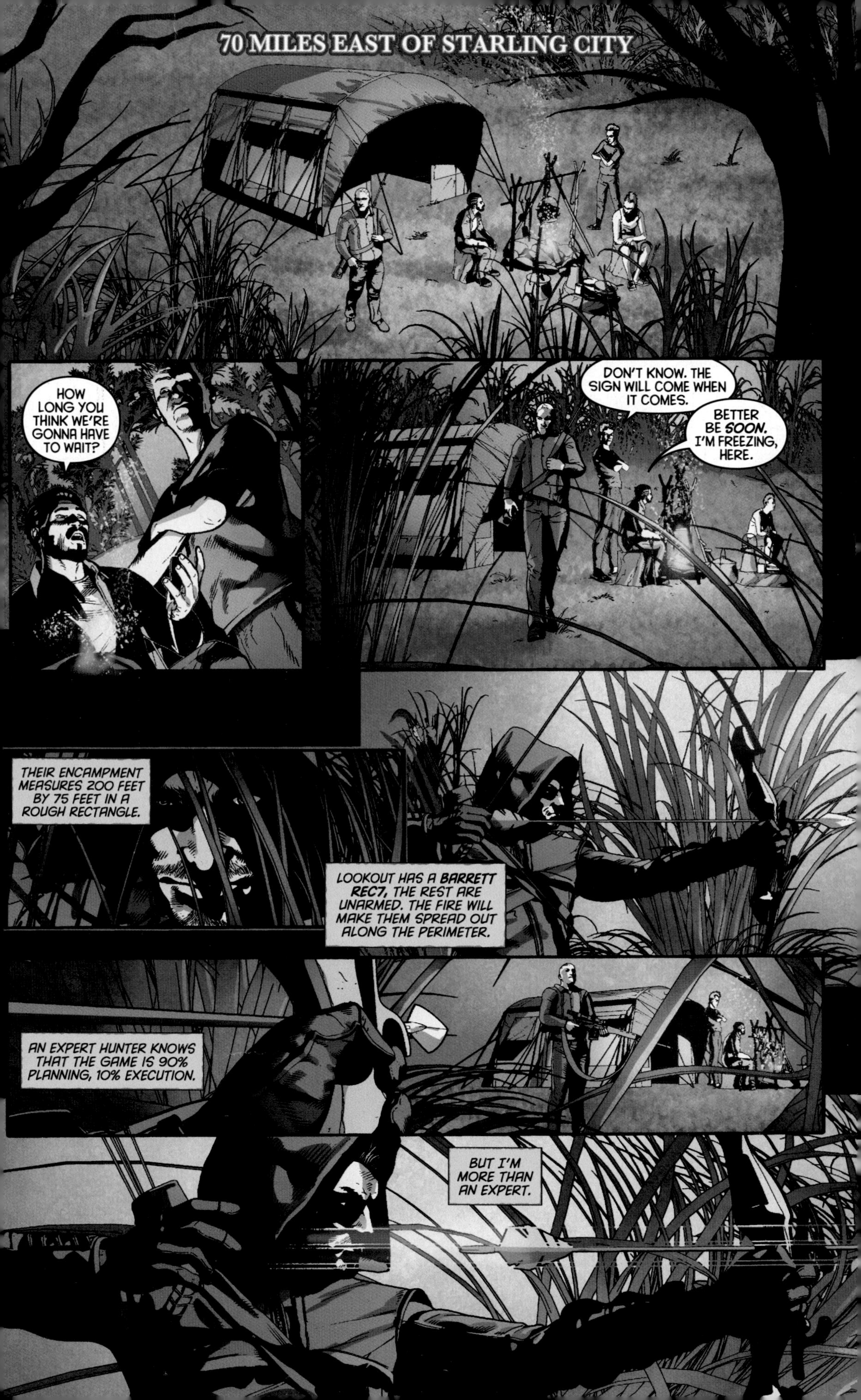
70 MILES EAST OF STARLING CITY
HOW LONG YOU THINK WE'RE GONNA HAVE TO WAIT?
DON'T KNOW. THE SIGN WILL COME WHEN IT COMES.
BETTER BE SOON. I'M FREEZING, HERE.
THEIR ENCAMPMENT MEASURES 200 FEET BY 75 FEET IN A ROUGH RECTANGLE.
LOOKOUT HAS A BARRETT REC7, THE REST ARE UNARMED. THE FIRE WILL MAKE THEM SPREAD OUT ALONG THE PERIMETER.
AN EXPERT HUNTER KNOWS THAT THE GAME IS 90% PLANNING, 10% EXECUTION.
BUT I'M MORE THAN AN EXPERT.

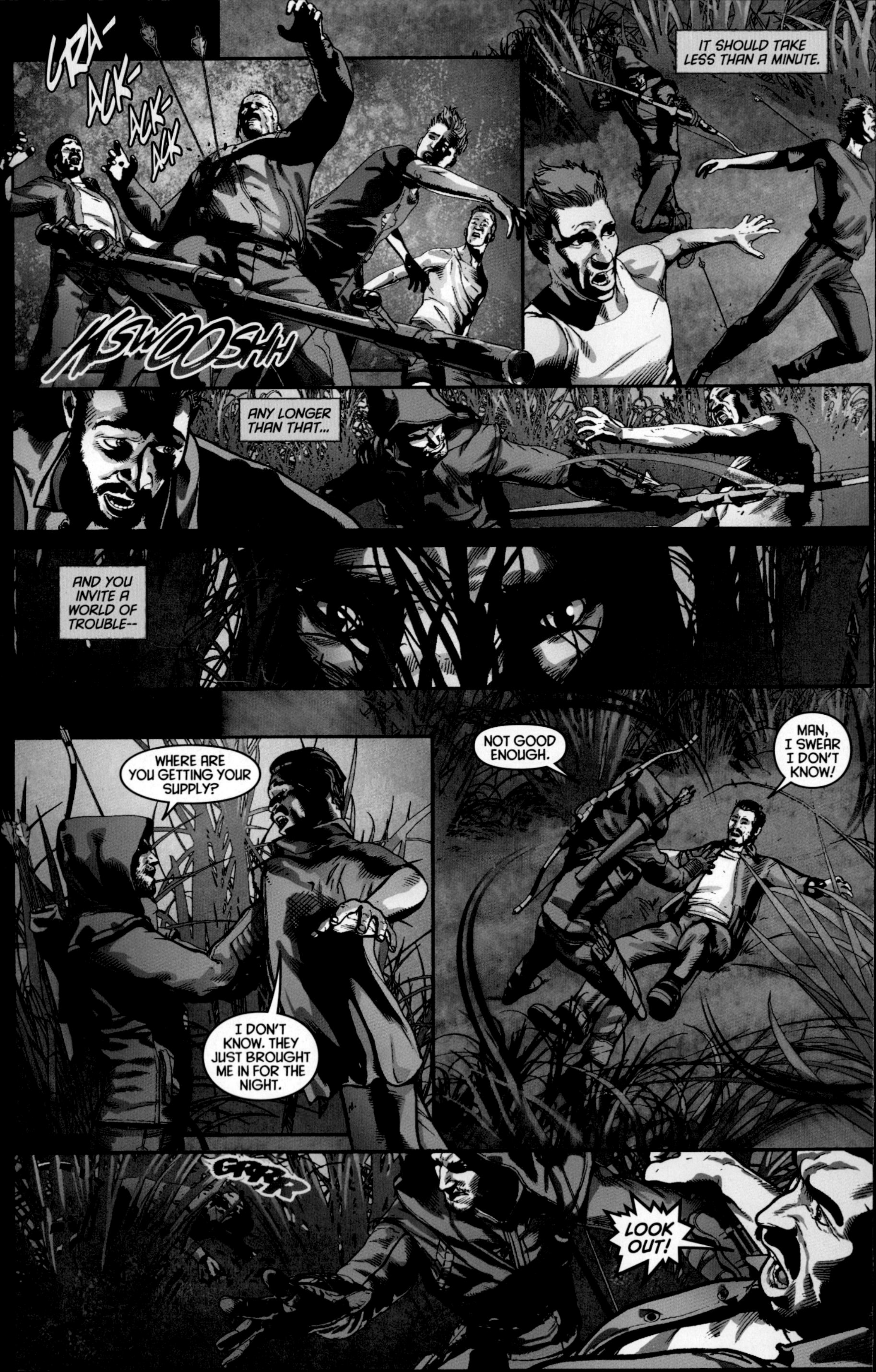
CRA-ACK-ACK-ACK
KSWOOSHH
IT SHOULD TAKE LESS THAN A MINUTE.
ANY LONGER THAN THAT...
AND YOU INVITE A WORLD OF TROUBLE--
WHERE ARE YOU GETTING YOUR SUPPLY?
I DON'T KNOW. THEY JUST BROUGHT ME IN FOR THE NIGHT.
NOT GOOD ENOUGH.
MAN, I SWEAR I DON'T KNOW!
GRRRR
LOOK OUT!

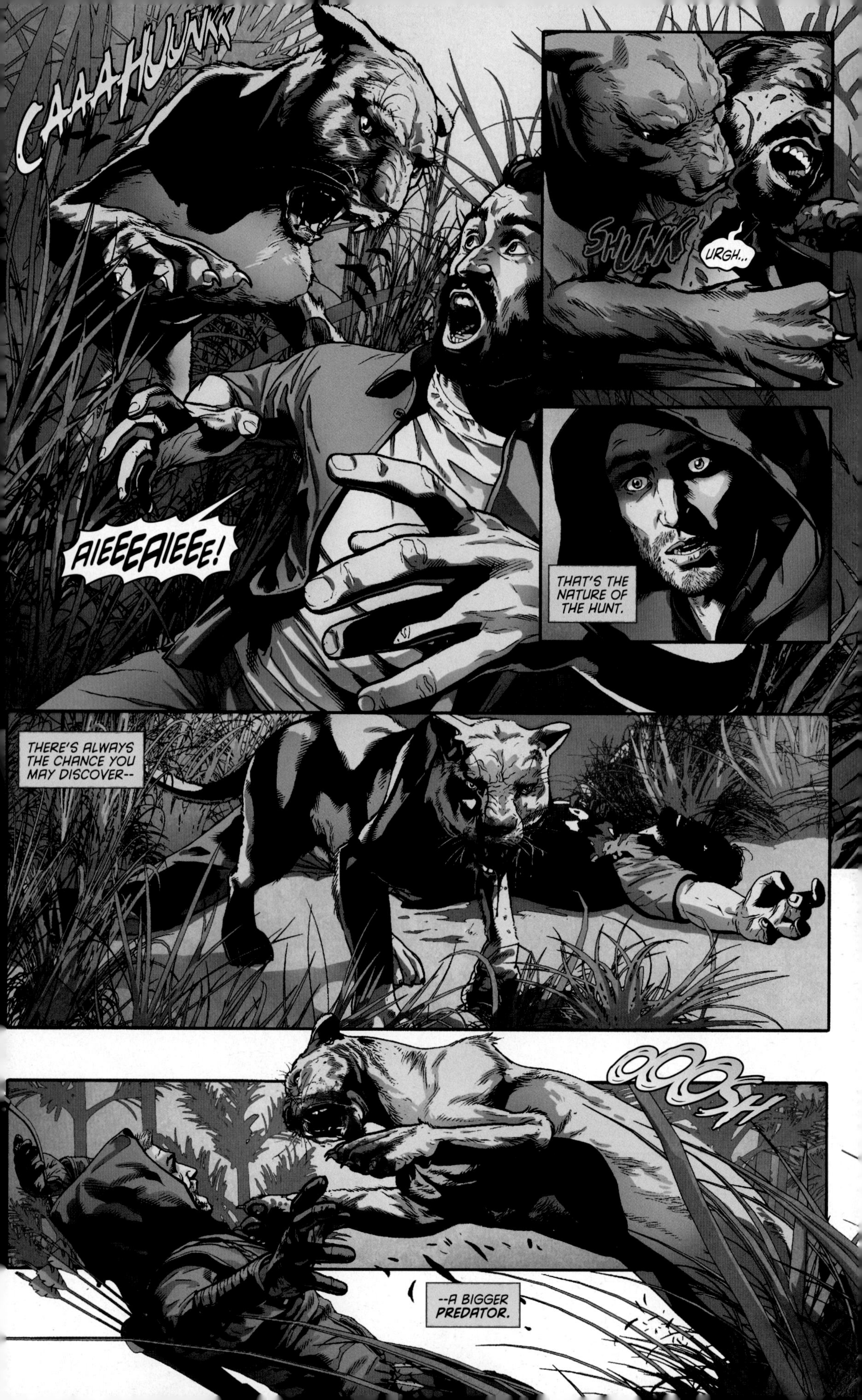
CAAAHUUNKK
AIEEEAIEEE!
SHUNKK
URGH...
THAT'S THE NATURE OF THE HUNT.
THERE'S ALWAYS THE CHANCE YOU MAY DISCOVER--
OOOOSH
--A BIGGER PREDATOR.

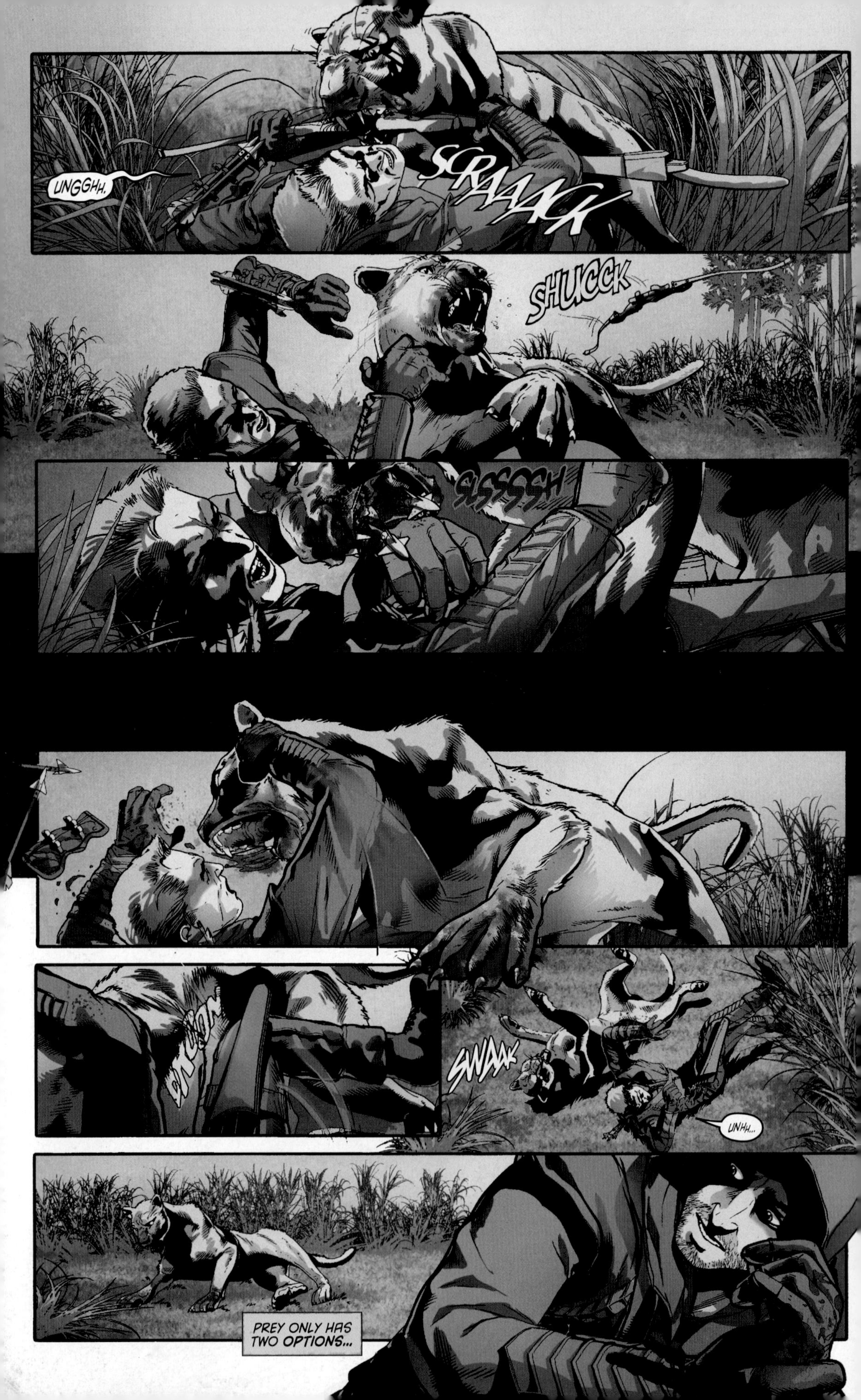
UNGGHH.
SCRAAAACK
SHUCCCK
SNAAK
UNHH...
PREY ONLY HAS TWO OPTIONS...

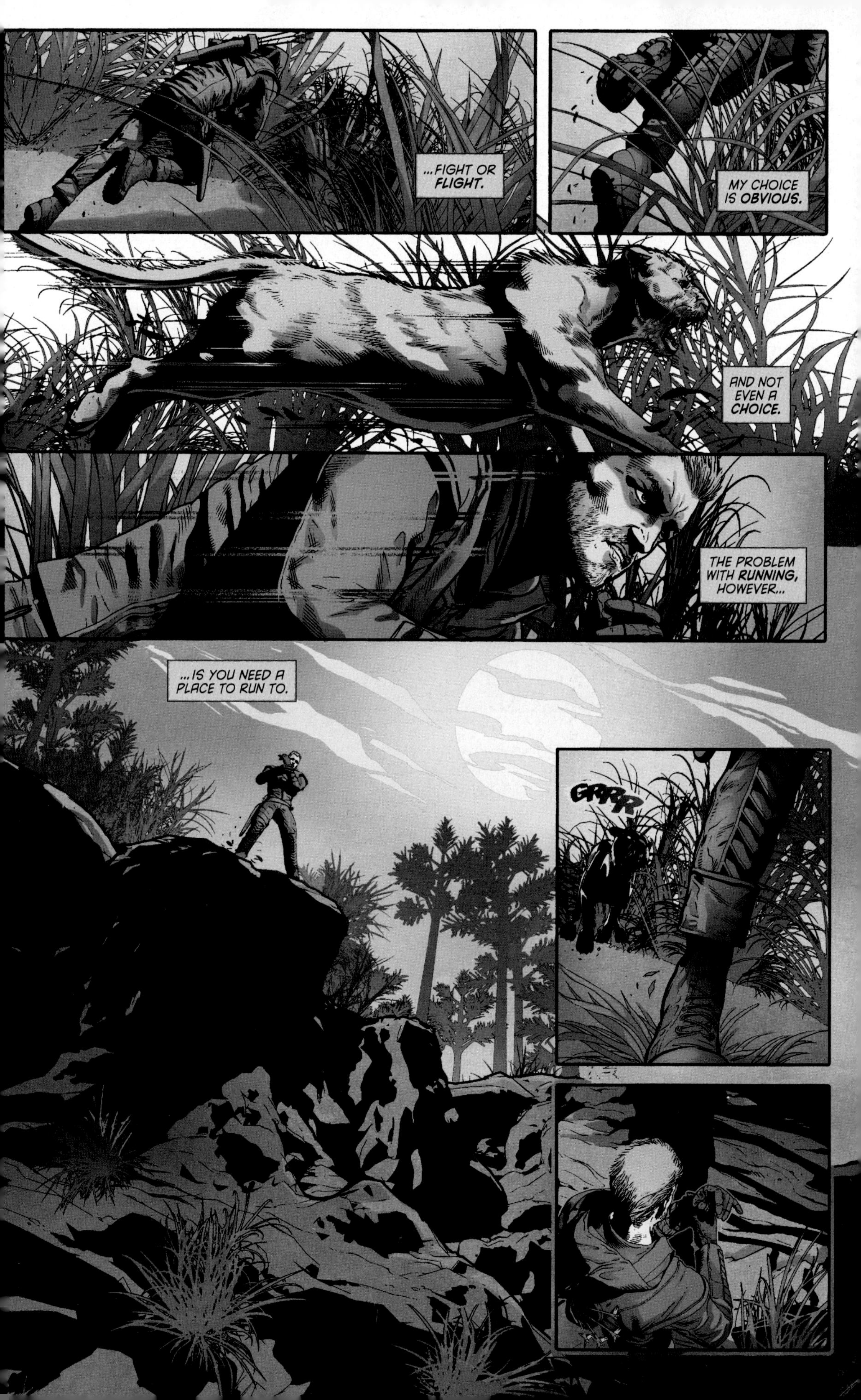
...FIGHT OR FLIGHT.
MY CHOICE IS OBVIOUS.
AND NOT EVEN A CHOICE.
THE PROBLEM WITH RUNNING, HOWEVER...
...IS YOU NEED A PLACE TO RUN TO.
GRRR

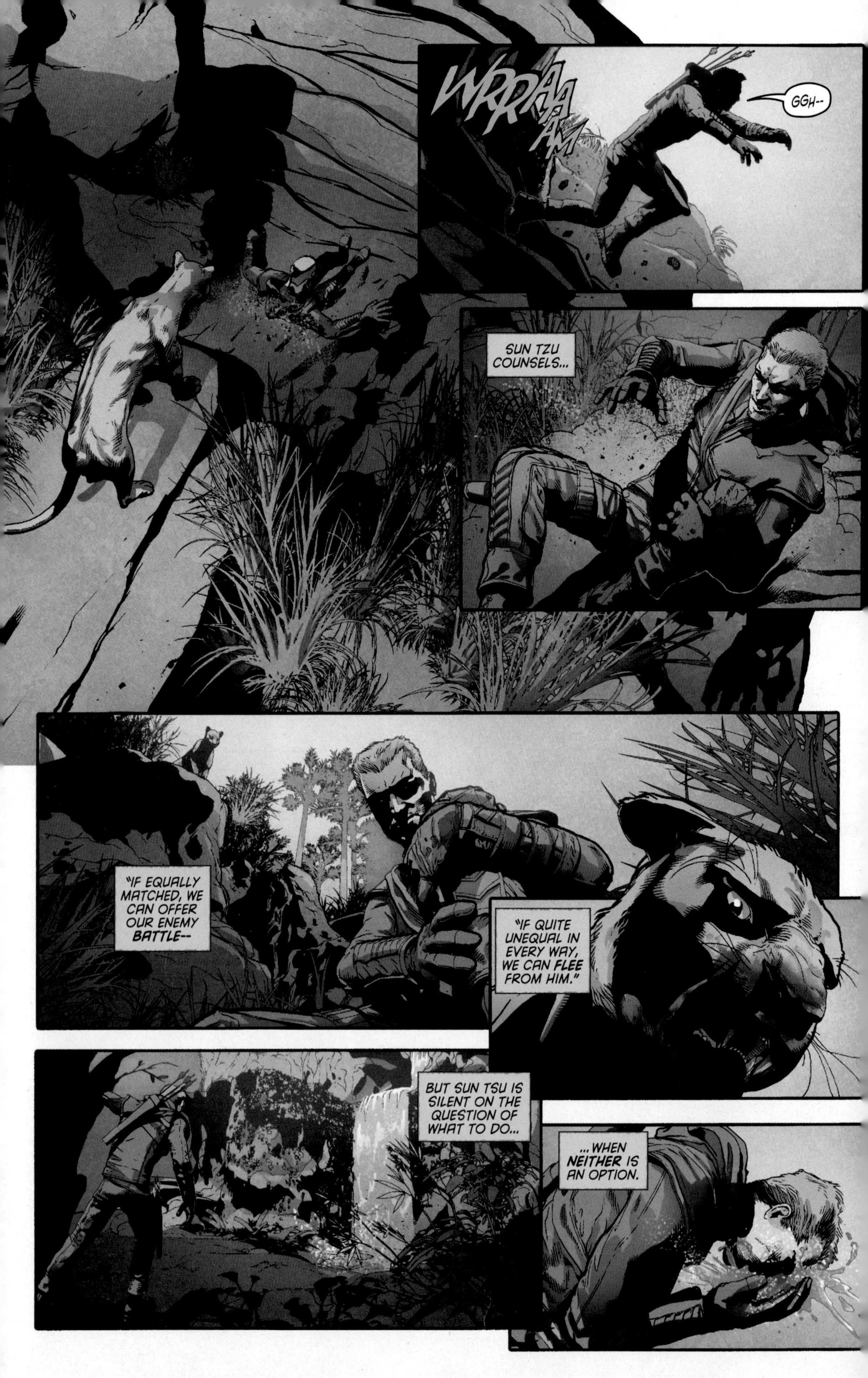
WRRAAAM
GGH--
SUN TZU COUNSELS...
"IF EQUALLY MATCHED, WE CAN OFFER OUR ENEMY BATTLE--
"IF QUITE UNEQUAL IN EVERY WAY, WE CAN FLEE FROM HIM."
BUT SUN TSU IS SILENT ON THE QUESTION OF WHAT TO DO...
...WHEN NEITHER IS AN OPTION.

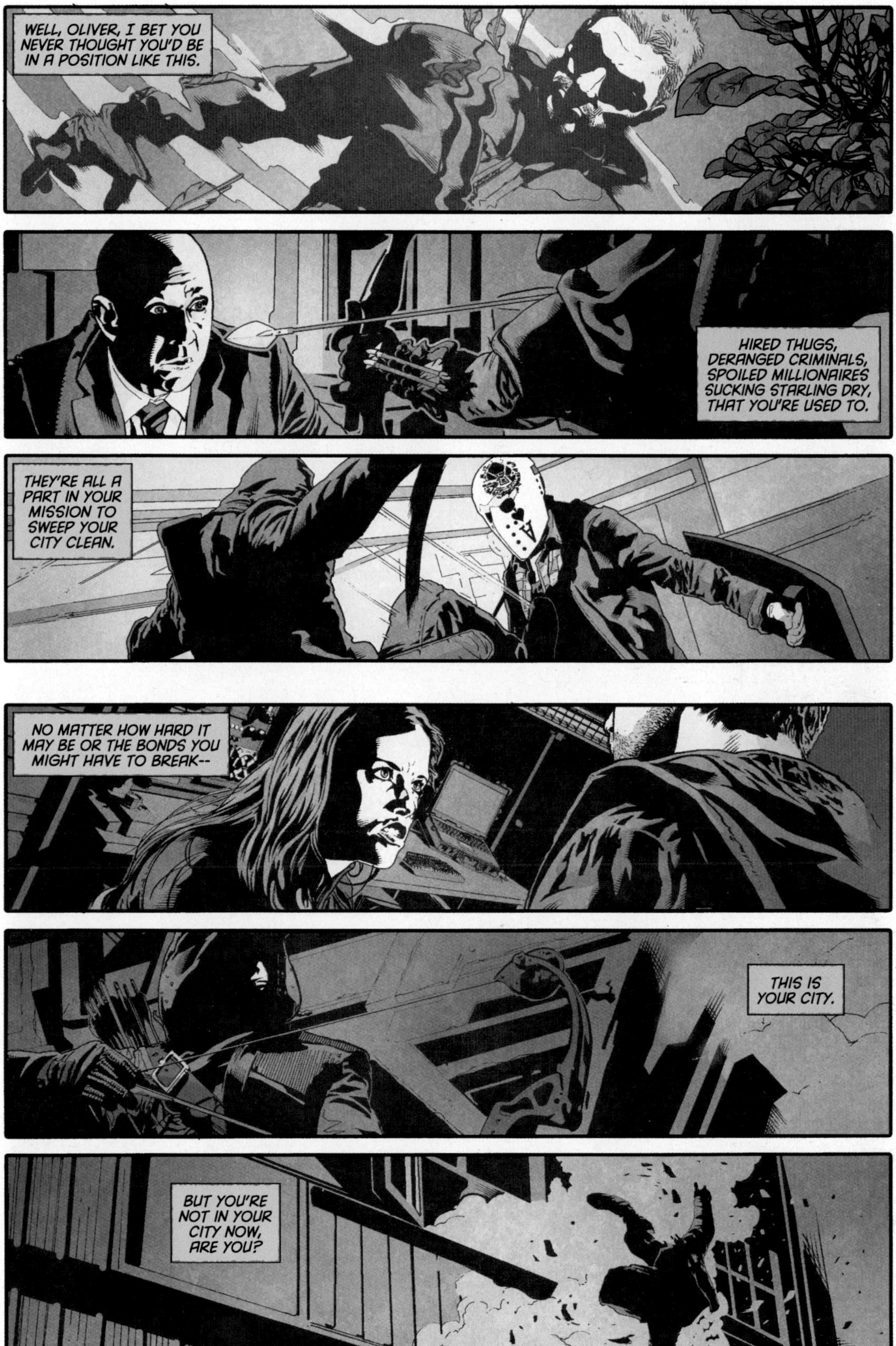
WELL, OLIVER, I BET YOU NEVER THOUGHT YOU'D BE IN A POSITION LIKE THIS.
HIRED THUGS, DERANGED CRIMINALS, SPOILED MILLIONAIRES SUCKING STARLING DRY, THAT YOU'RE USED TO.
THEY'RE ALL A PART IN YOUR MISSION TO SWEEP YOUR CITY CLEAN.
NO MATTER HOW HARD IT MAY BE OR THE BONDS YOU MIGHT HAVE TO BREAK--
THIS IS YOUR CITY.
BUT YOU'RE NOT IN YOUR CITY NOW, ARE YOU?

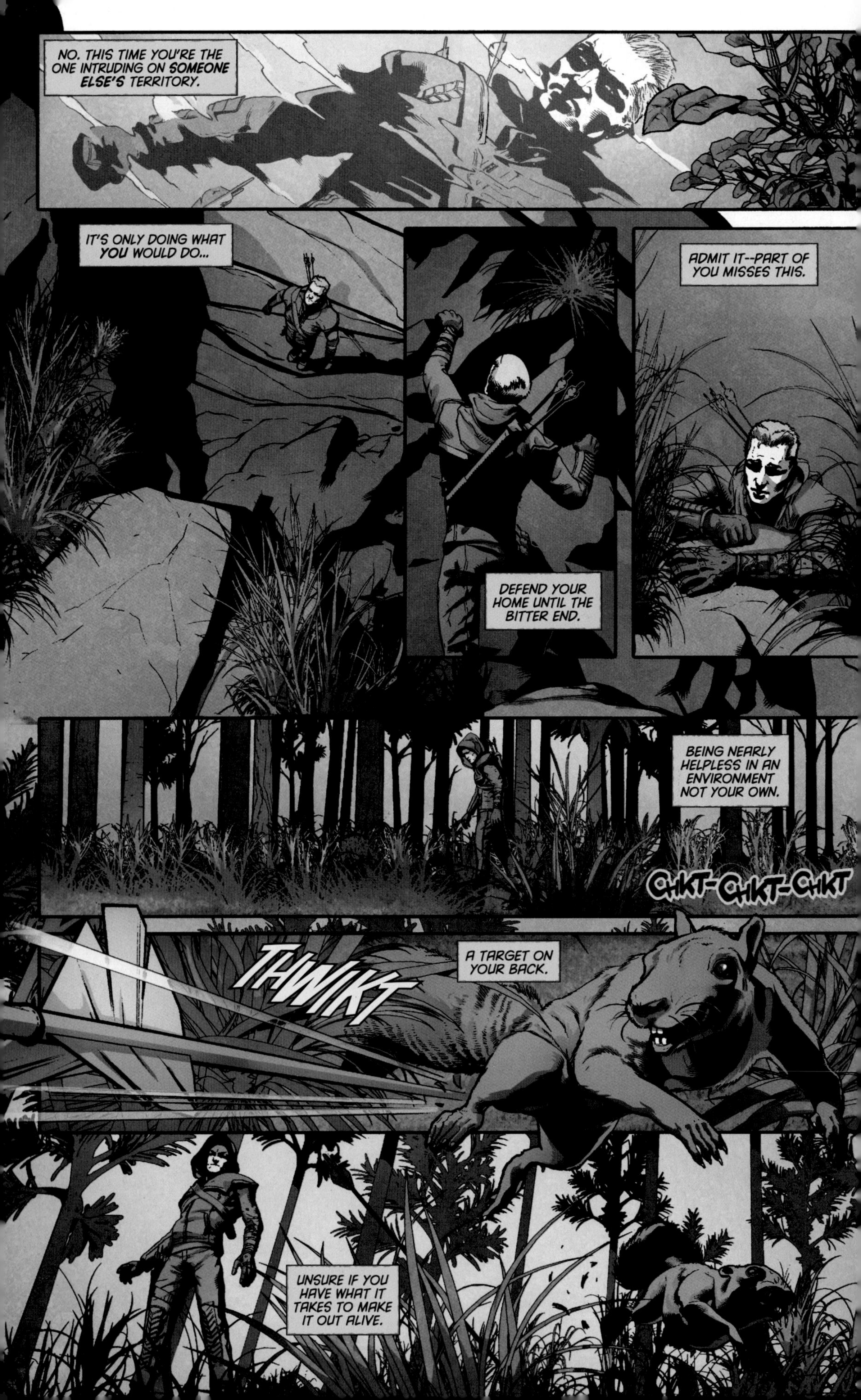

NO. THIS TIME YOU'RE THE ONE INTRUDING ON SOMEONE ELSE'S TERRITORY.
IT'S ONLY DOING WHAT YOU WOULD DO...
DEFEND YOUR HOME UNTIL THE BITTER END.
ADMIT IT--PART OF YOU MISSES THIS.
BEING NEARLY HELPLESS IN AN ENVIRONMENT NOT YOUR OWN.
CHKT-CHKT-CHKT
THWIKT
A TARGET ON YOUR BACK.
UNSURE IF YOU HAVE WHAT IT TAKES TO MAKE IT OUT ALIVE.

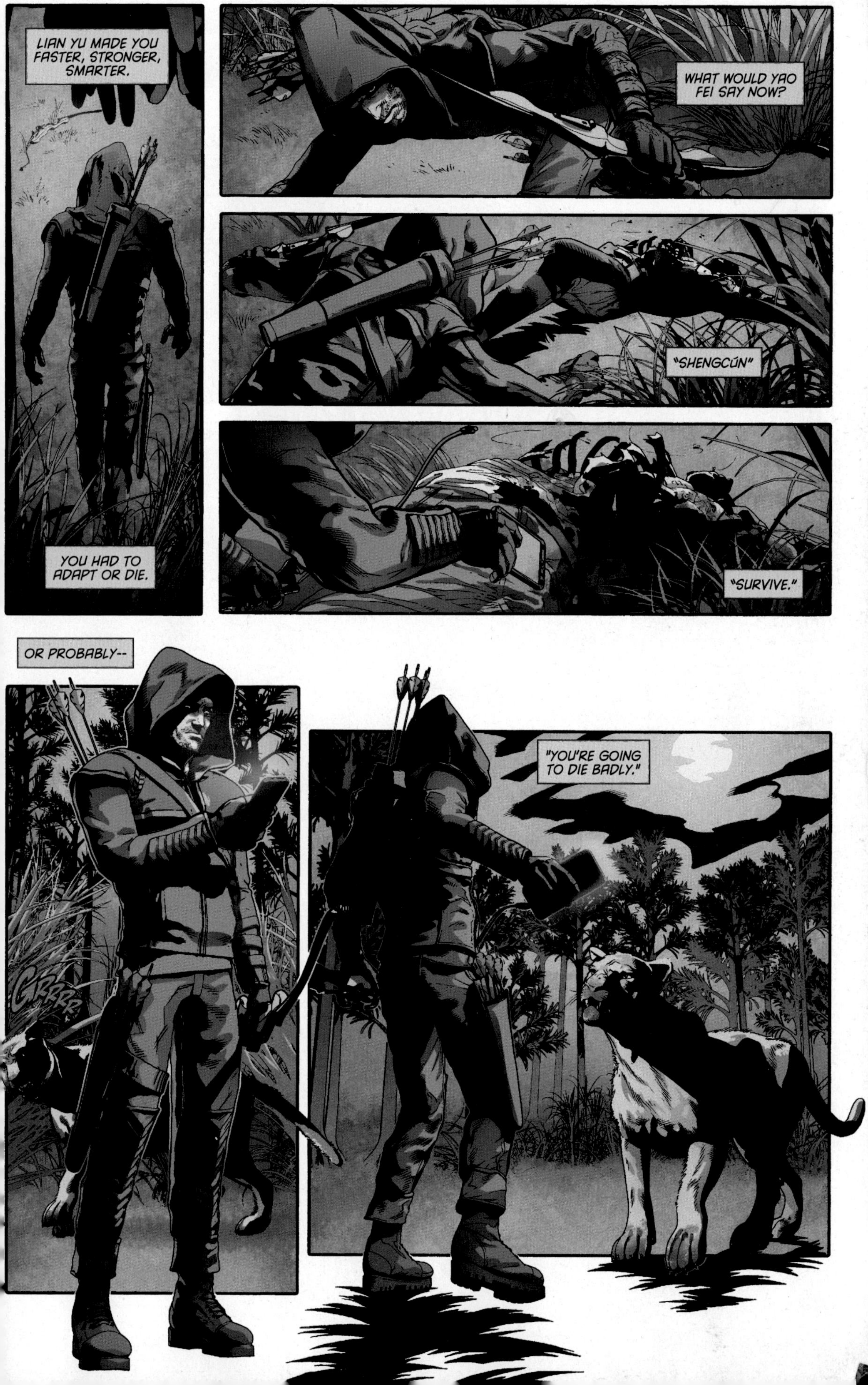

LIAN YU MADE YOU FASTER, STRONGER, SMARTER.
WHAT WOULD YAO FEI SAY NOW?
"SHENGCÚN"
"SURVIVE."
YOU HAD TO ADAPT OR DIE.
OR PROBABLY--
"YOU'RE GOING TO DIE BADLY."
GRRRR

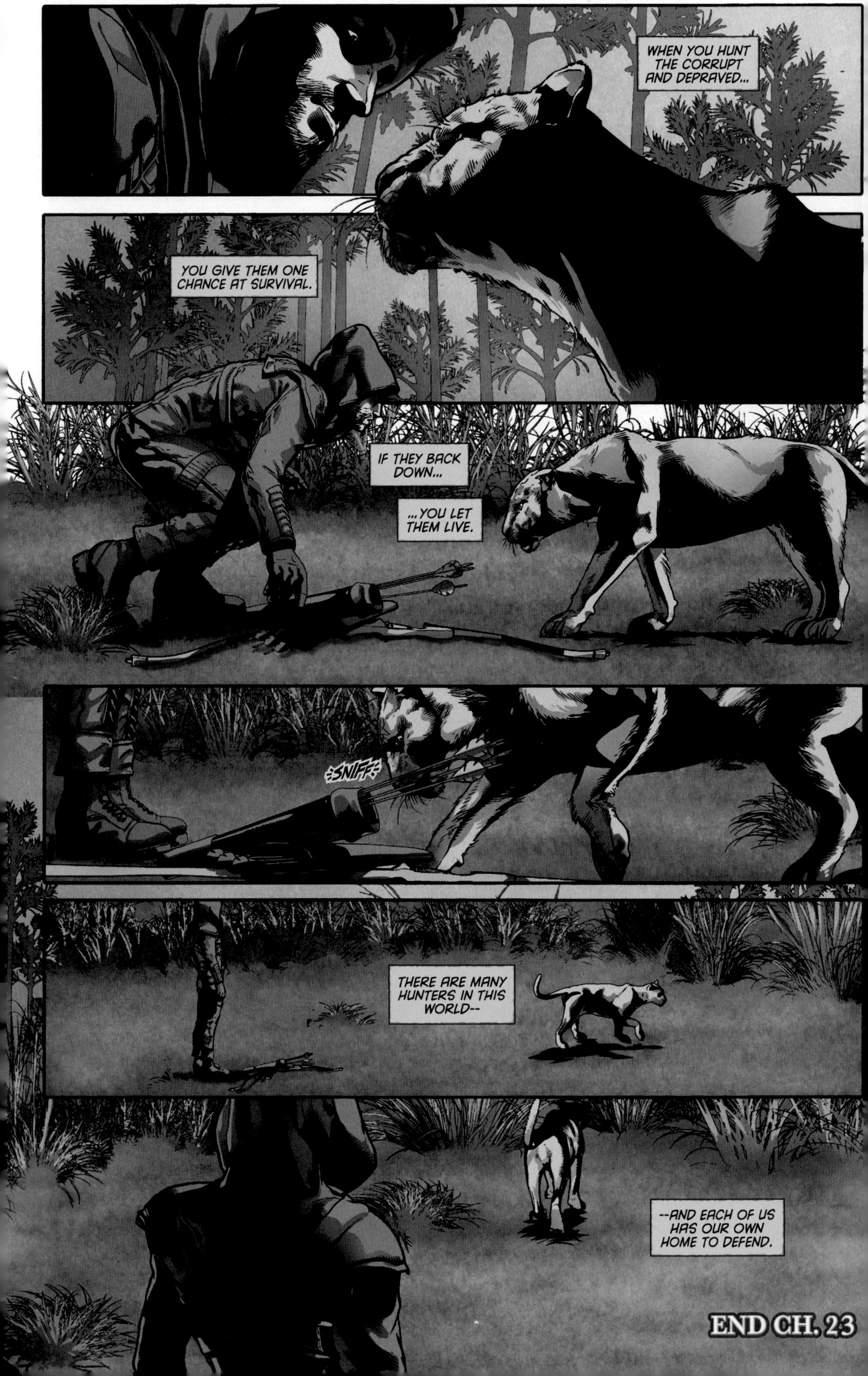
WHEN YOU HUNT THE CORRUPT AND DEPRAVED...
YOU GIVE THEM ONE CHANCE AT SURVIVAL.
IF THEY BACK DOWN...
...YOU LET THEM LIVE.
SNIFF
THERE ARE MANY HUNTERS IN THIS WORLD--
--AND EACH OF US HAS OUR OWN HOME TO DEFEND.
END CH. 23

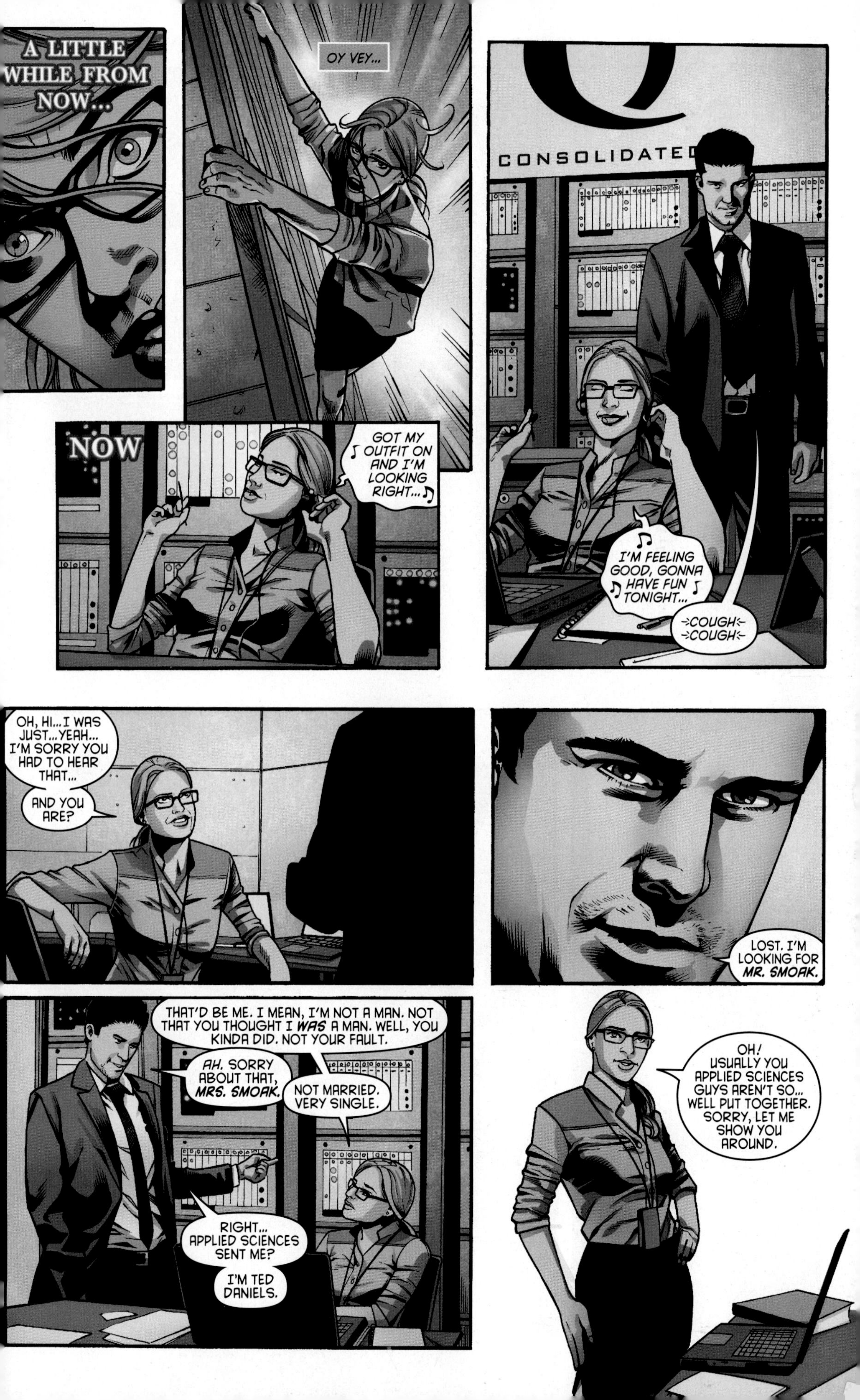
A LITTLE WHILE FROM NOW...
OY VEY...
NOW
GOT MY OUTFIT ON AND I'M LOOKING RIGHT...
CONSOLIDATED
I'M FEELING GOOD, GONNA HAVE FUN TONIGHT...
COUGH COUGH
OH, HI...I WAS JUST...YEAH... I'M SORRY YOU HAD TO HEAR THAT...
AND YOU ARE?
LOST. I'M LOOKING FOR MR. SMOAK.
THAT'D BE ME. I MEAN, I'M NOT A MAN. NOT THAT YOU THOUGHT I WAS A MAN. WELL, YOU KINDA DID. NOT YOUR FAULT.
AH. SORRY ABOUT THAT, MRS. SMOAK.
NOT MARRIED. VERY SINGLE.
RIGHT... APPLIED SCIENCES SENT ME?
I'M TED DANIELS.
OH! USUALLY YOU APPLIED SCIENCES GUYS AREN'T SO... WELL PUT TOGETHER. SORRY, LET ME SHOW YOU AROUND.

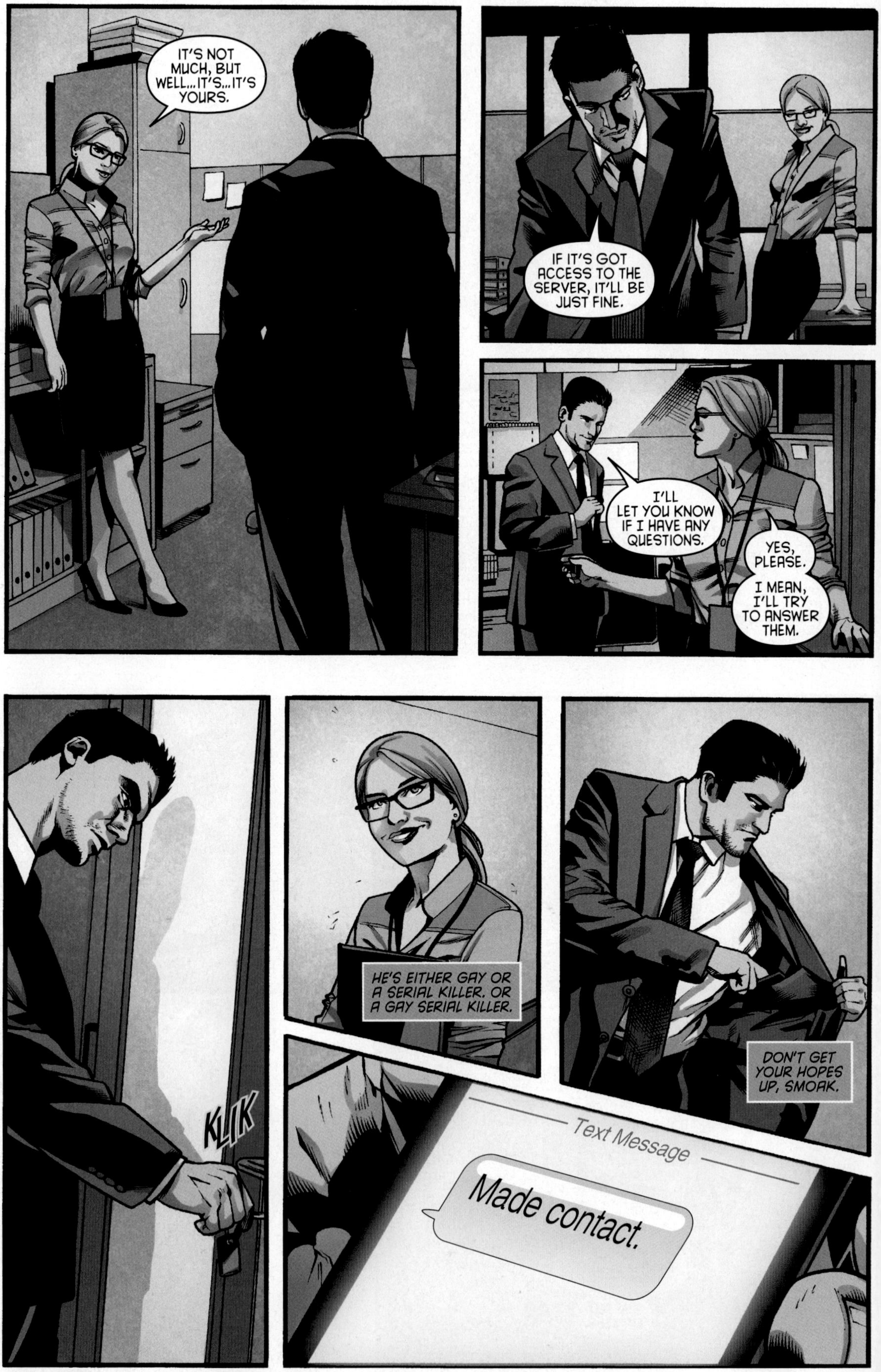
IT'S NOT MUCH, BUT WELL... IT'S... IT'S YOURS.
IF IT'S GOT ACCESS TO THE SERVER, IT'LL BE JUST FINE.
I'LL LET YOU KNOW IF I HAVE ANY QUESTIONS.
YES, PLEASE.
I MEAN, I'LL TRY TO ANSWER THEM.
KLIK
HE'S EITHER GAY OR A SERIAL KILLER. OR A GAY SERIAL KILLER.
DON'T GET YOUR HOPES UP, SMOAK.
Text Message
Made contact.

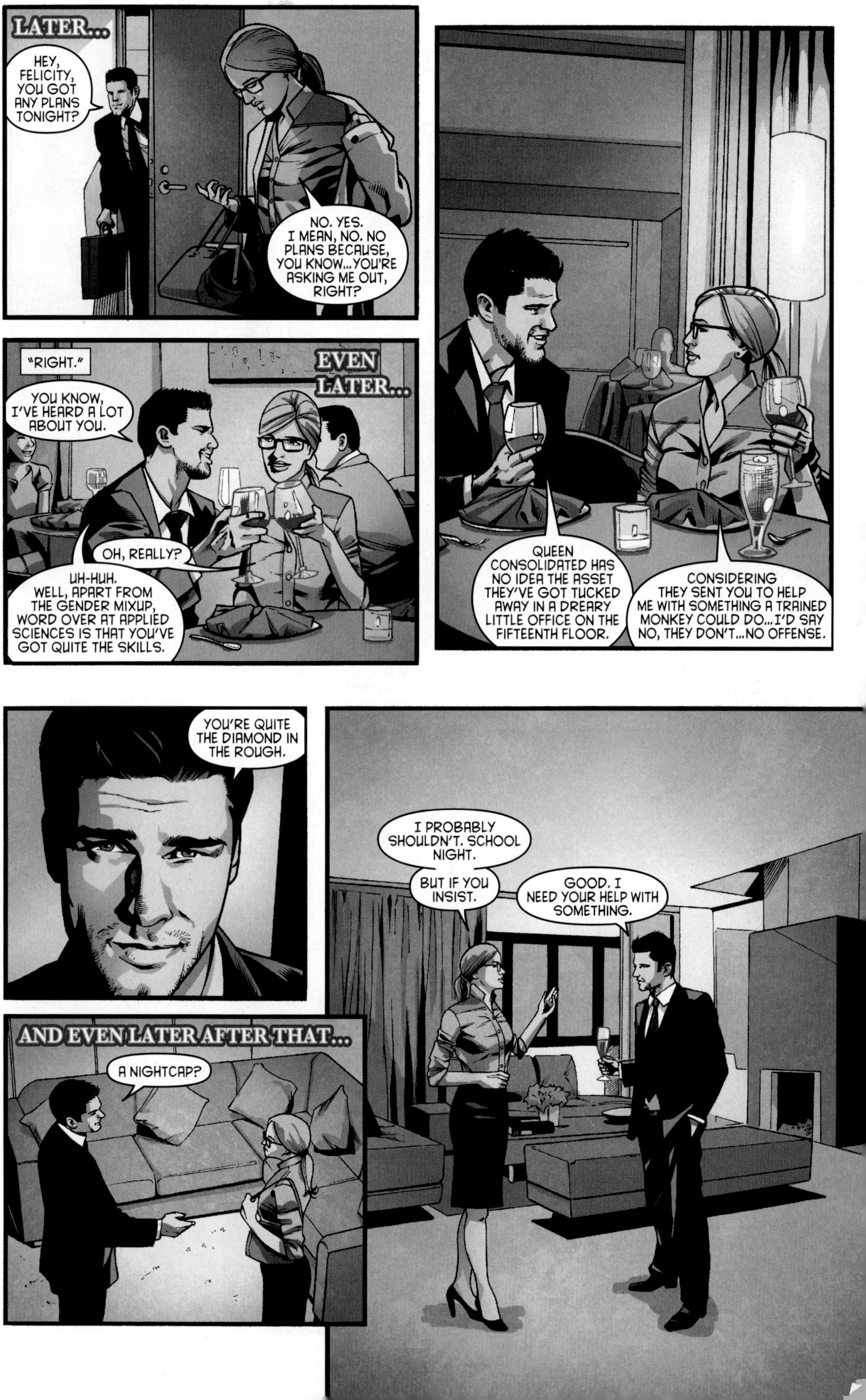
LATER...
HEY, FELICITY, YOU GOT ANY PLANS TONIGHT?
NO. YES. I MEAN, NO. NO PLANS BECAUSE, YOU KNOW...YOU'RE ASKING ME OUT, RIGHT?
"RIGHT."
EVEN LATER...
YOU KNOW, I'VE HEARD A LOT ABOUT YOU.
OH, REALLY?
UH-HUH. WELL, APART FROM THE GENDER MIXUP, WORD OVER AT APPLIED SCIENCES IS THAT YOU'VE GOT QUITE THE SKILLS.
QUEEN CONSOLIDATED HAS NO IDEA THE ASSET THEY'VE GOT TUCKED AWAY IN A DREARY LITTLE OFFICE ON THE FIFTEENTH FLOOR.
CONSIDERING THEY SENT YOU TO HELP ME WITH SOMETHING A TRAINED MONKEY COULD DO...I'D SAY NO, THEY DON'T...NO OFFENSE.
YOU'RE QUITE THE DIAMOND IN THE ROUGH.
AND EVEN LATER AFTER THAT...
A NIGHTCAP?
I PROBABLY SHOULDN'T. SCHOOL NIGHT.
BUT IF YOU INSIST.
GOOD. I NEED YOUR HELP WITH SOMETHING.

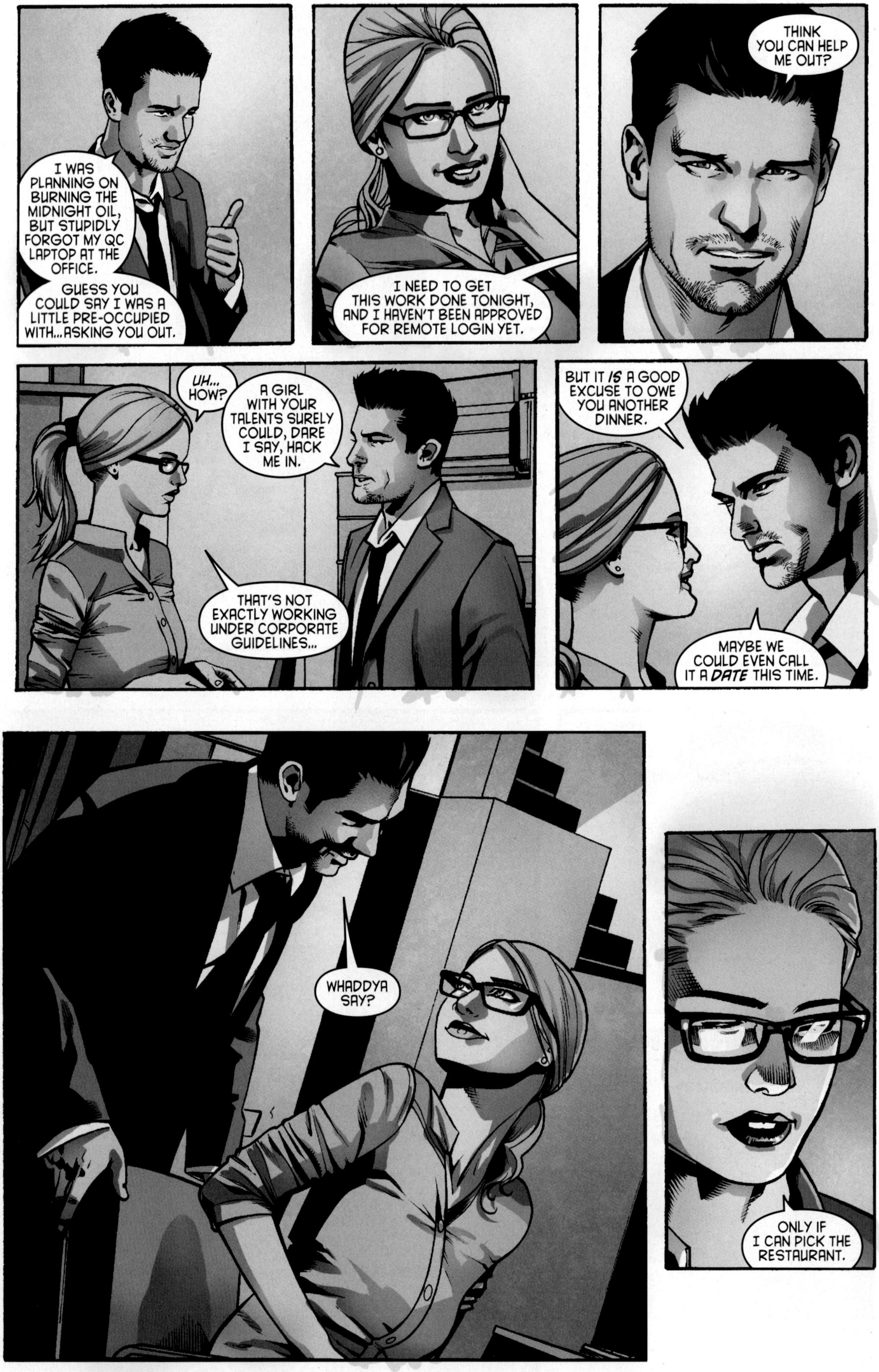

I WAS PLANNING ON BURNING THE MIDNIGHT OIL, BUT STUPIDLY FORGOT MY QC LAPTOP AT THE OFFICE.
GUESS YOU COULD SAY I WAS A LITTLE PRE-OCCUPIED WITH...ASKING YOU OUT.
I NEED TO GET THIS WORK DONE TONIGHT, AND I HAVEN'T BEEN APPROVED FOR REMOTE LOGIN YET.
THINK YOU CAN HELP ME OUT?
UH... HOW?
A GIRL WITH YOUR TALENTS SURELY COULD, DARE I SAY, HACK ME IN.
THAT'S NOT EXACTLY WORKING UNDER CORPORATE GUIDELINES...
BUT IT *IS* A GOOD EXCUSE TO OWE YOU ANOTHER DINNER.
MAYBE WE COULD EVEN CALL IT A ***DATE*** THIS TIME.
WHADDYA SAY?
ONLY IF I CAN PICK THE RESTAURANT.

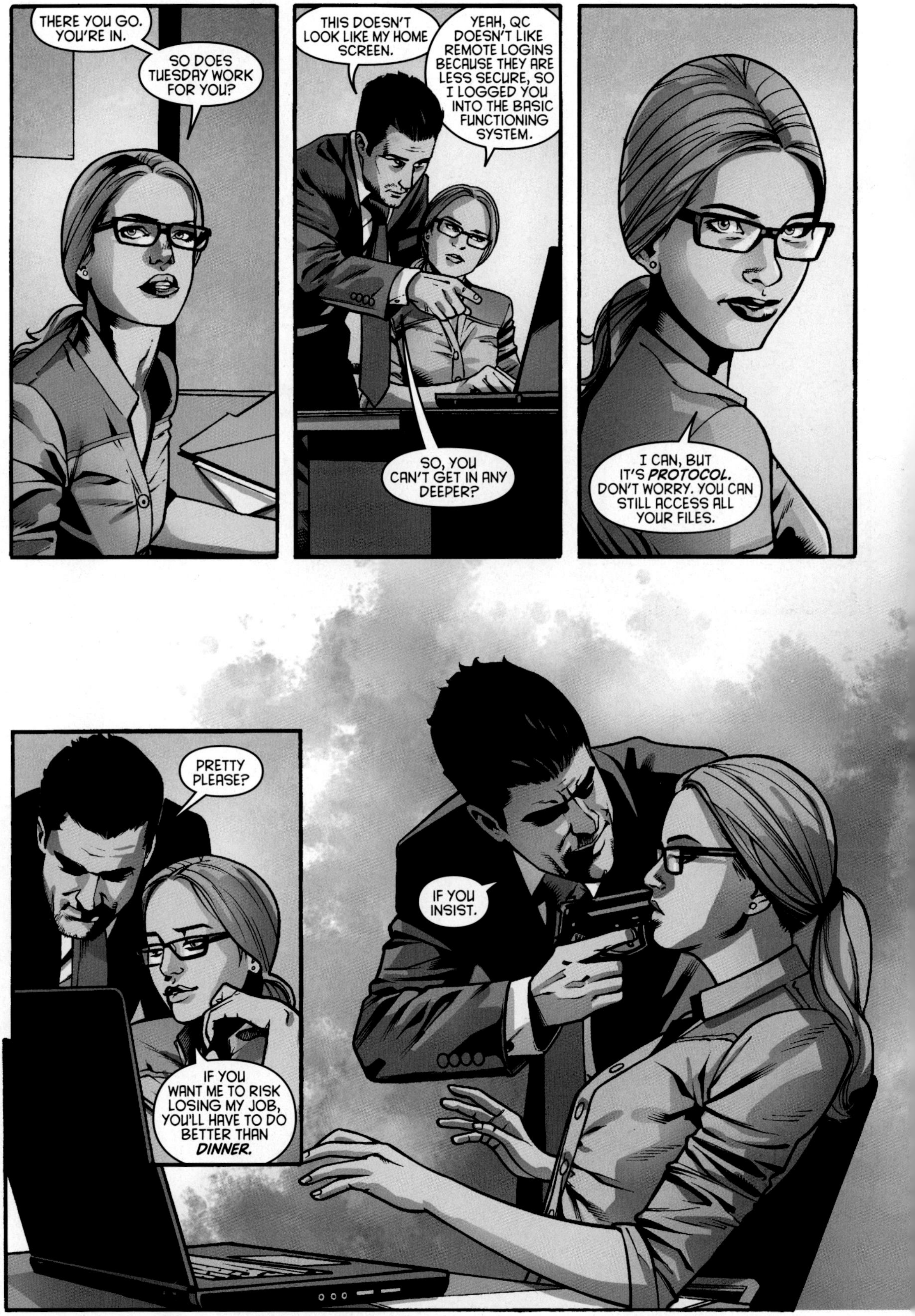
THERE YOU GO. YOU'RE IN.
SO DOES TUESDAY WORK FOR YOU?
THIS DOESN'T LOOK LIKE MY HOME SCREEN.
YEAH, QC DOESN'T LIKE REMOTE LOGINS BECAUSE THEY ARE LESS SECURE, SO I LOGGED YOU INTO THE BASIC FUNCTIONING SYSTEM.
SO, YOU CAN'T GET IN ANY DEEPER?
I CAN, BUT IT'S PROTOCOL. DON'T WORRY. YOU CAN STILL ACCESS ALL YOUR FILES.
PRETTY PLEASE?
IF YOU WANT ME TO RISK LOSING MY JOB, YOU'LL HAVE TO DO BETTER THAN DINNER.
IF YOU INSIST.

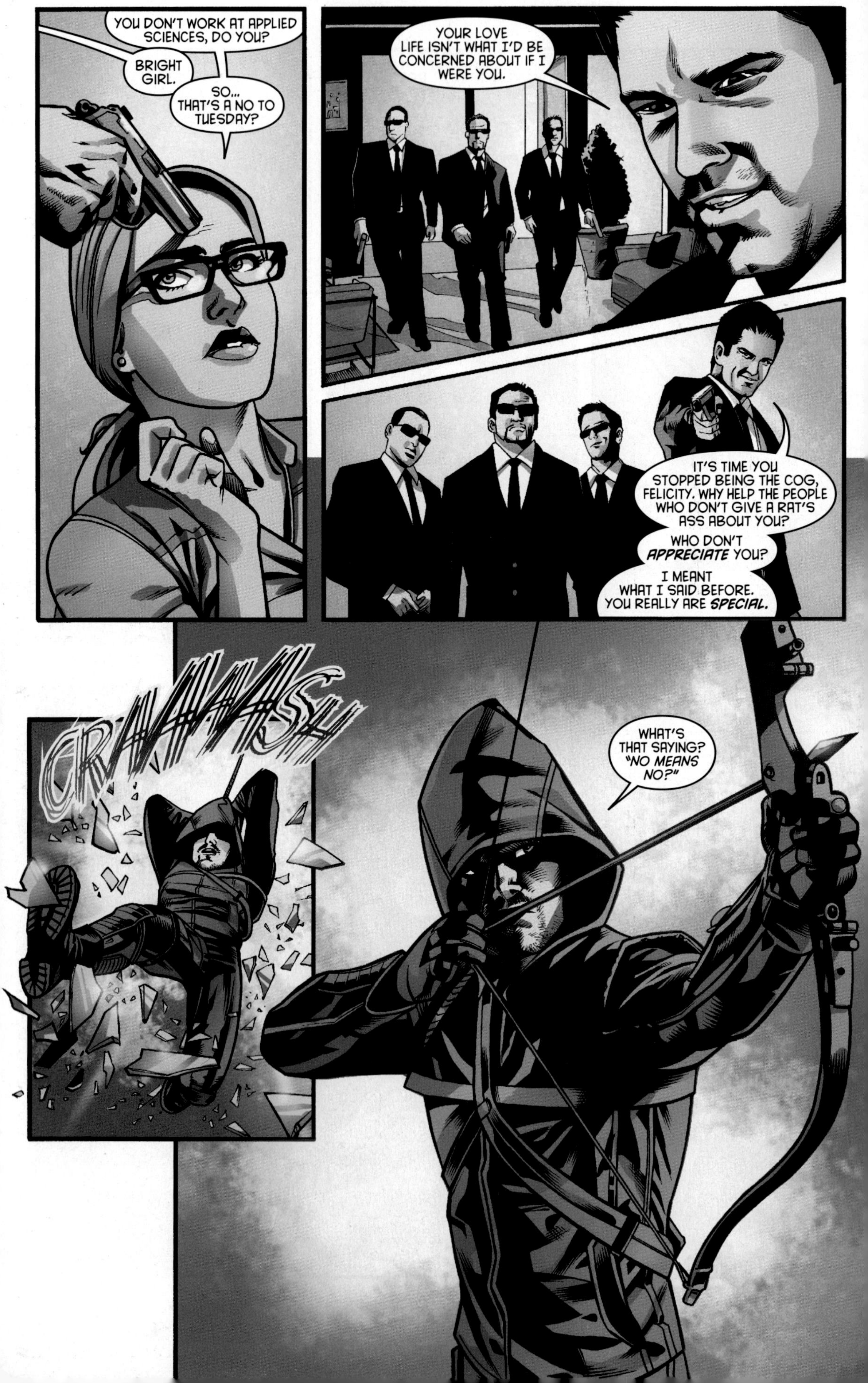
YOU DON'T WORK AT APPLIED SCIENCES, DO YOU?
BRIGHT GIRL.
SO... THAT'S A NO TO TUESDAY?
YOUR LOVE LIFE ISN'T WHAT I'D BE CONCERNED ABOUT IF I WERE YOU.
IT'S TIME YOU STOPPED BEING THE COG, FELICITY. WHY HELP THE PEOPLE WHO DON'T GIVE A RAT'S ASS ABOUT YOU?
WHO DON'T *APPRECIATE* YOU?
I MEANT WHAT I SAID BEFORE. YOU REALLY ARE *SPECIAL.*
CRAAASH
WHAT'S THAT SAYING? *"NO MEANS NO?"*

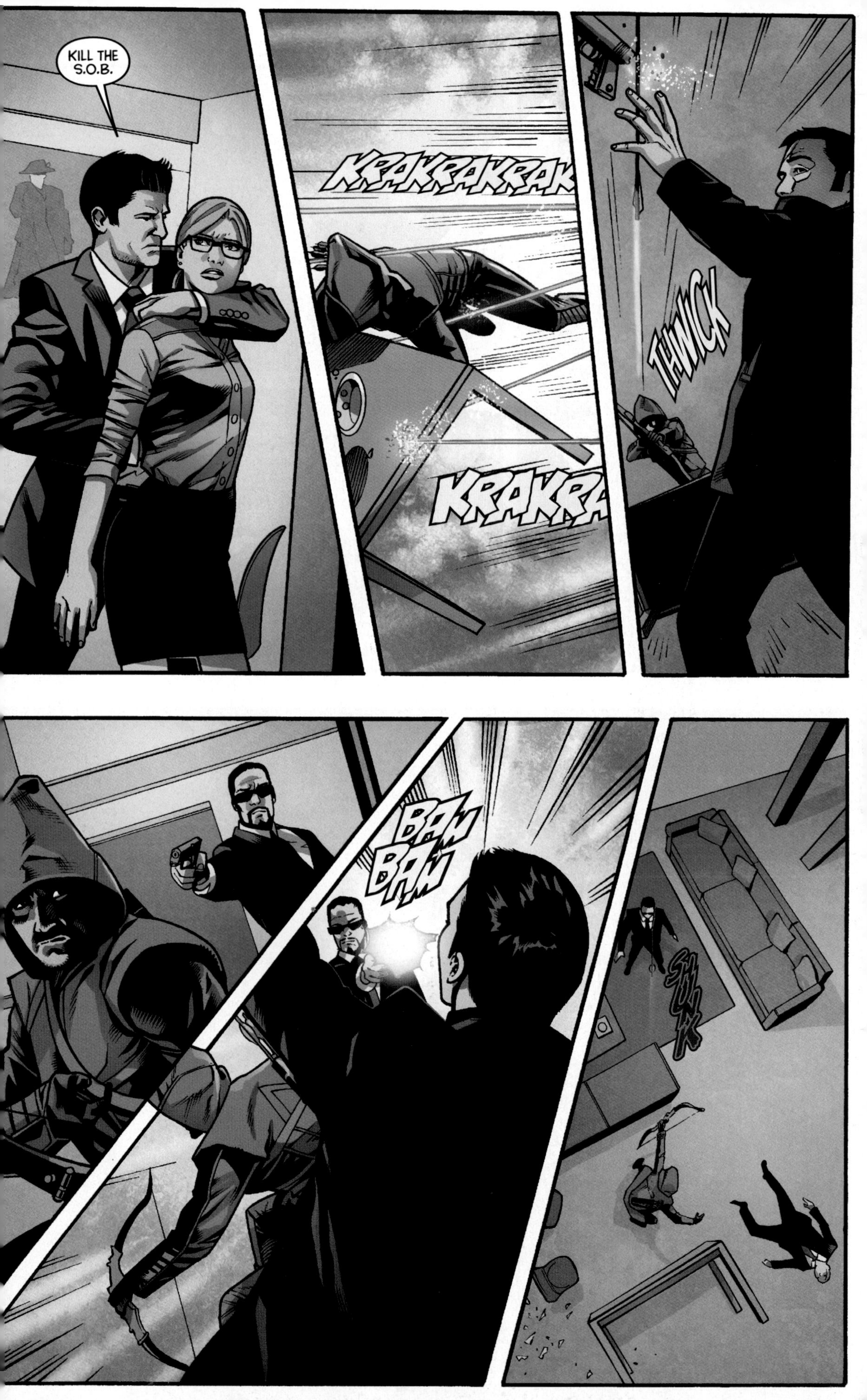
KILL THE S.O.B.
KRAKRAKRAKRAK
KRAKRA
THWICK
BAM
BAM
SHUNK

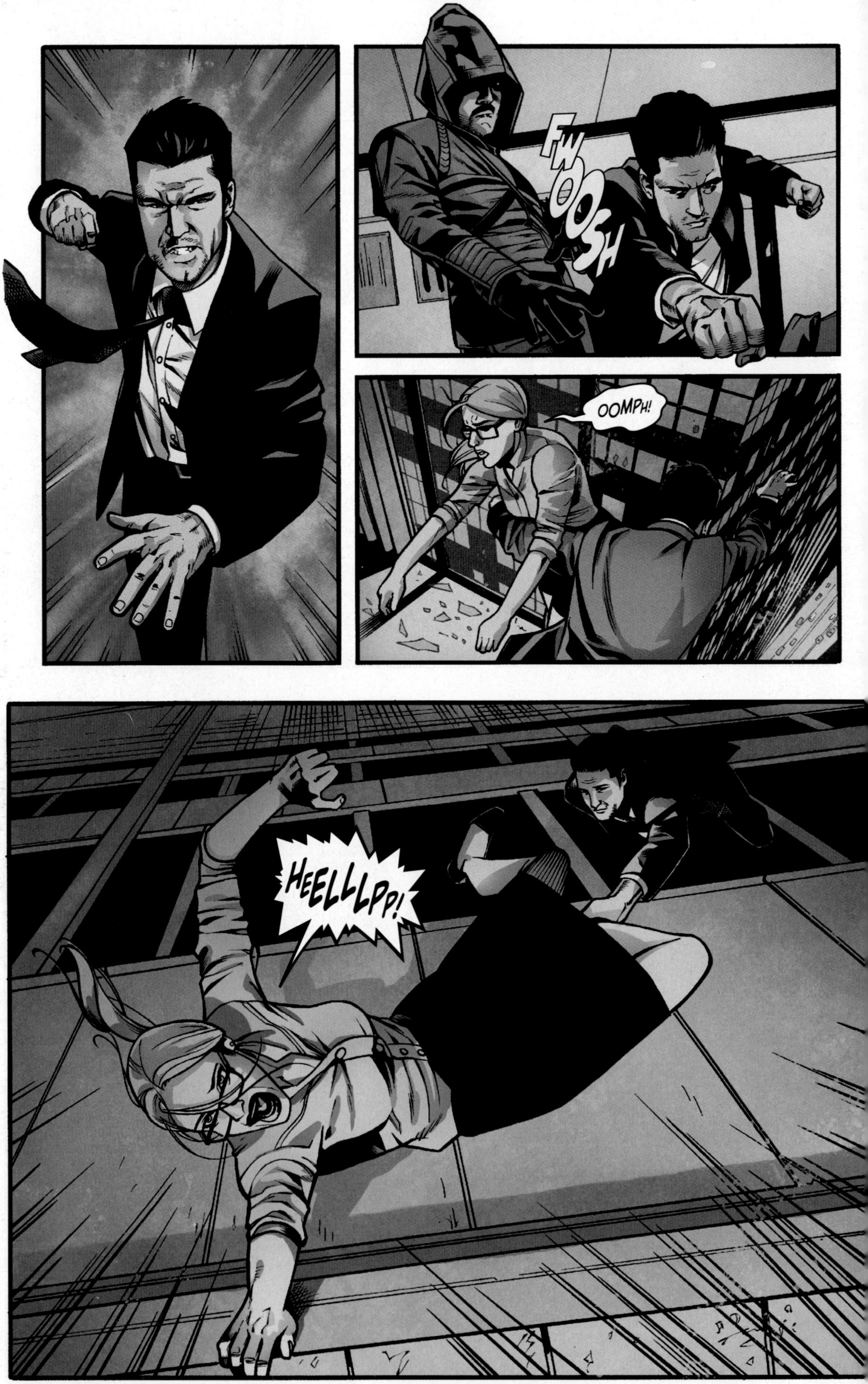
FWOOSH
OOMPH!
HEELLLPP!

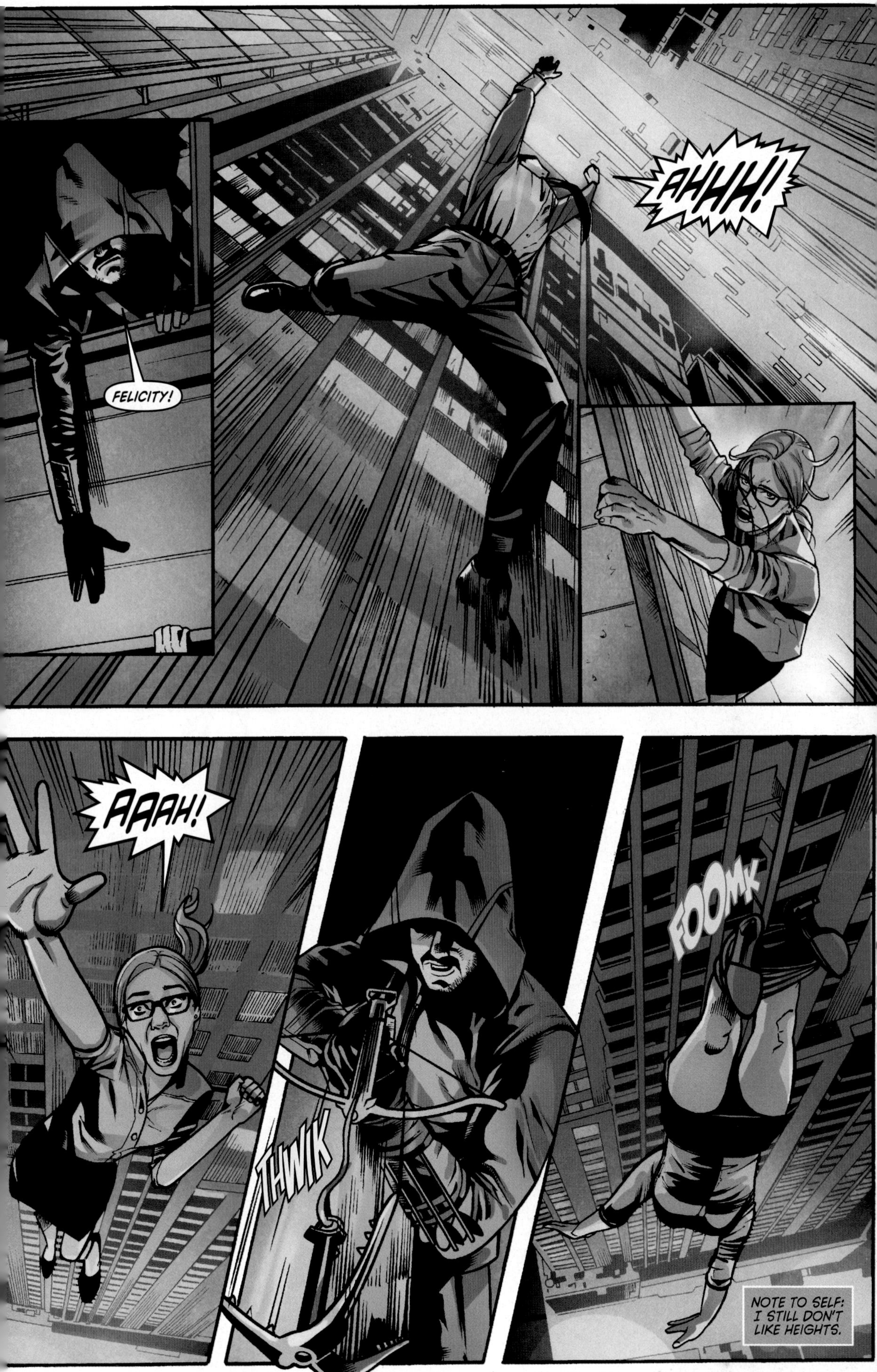
FELICITY!
AHHH!
AAAH!
THWIK
FOOMK
NOTE TO SELF:
I STILL DON'T
LIKE HEIGHTS.

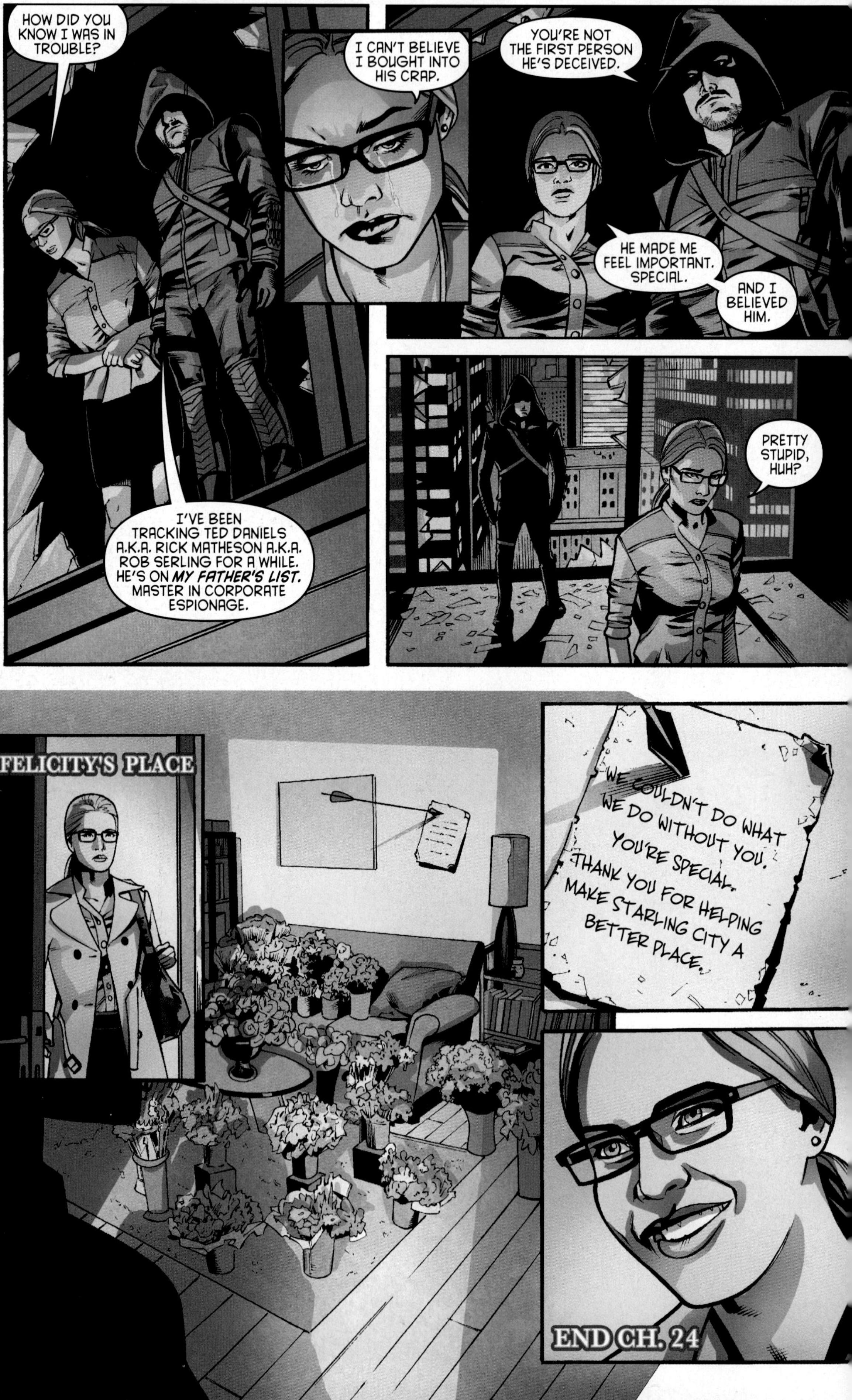
HOW DID YOU KNOW I WAS IN TROUBLE?
I'VE BEEN TRACKING TED DANIELS A.K.A. RICK MATHESON A.K.A. ROB SERLING FOR A WHILE. HE'S ON MY FATHER'S LIST. MASTER IN CORPORATE ESPIONAGE.
I CAN'T BELIEVE I BOUGHT INTO HIS CRAP.
YOU'RE NOT THE FIRST PERSON HE'S DECEIVED.
HE MADE ME FEEL IMPORTANT. SPECIAL.
AND I BELIEVED HIM.
PRETTY STUPID, HUH?
FELICITY'S PLACE
WE COULDN'T DO WHAT WE DO WITHOUT YOU. YOU'RE SPECIAL. THANK YOU FOR HELPING MAKE STARLING CITY A BETTER PLACE.
END CH. 24

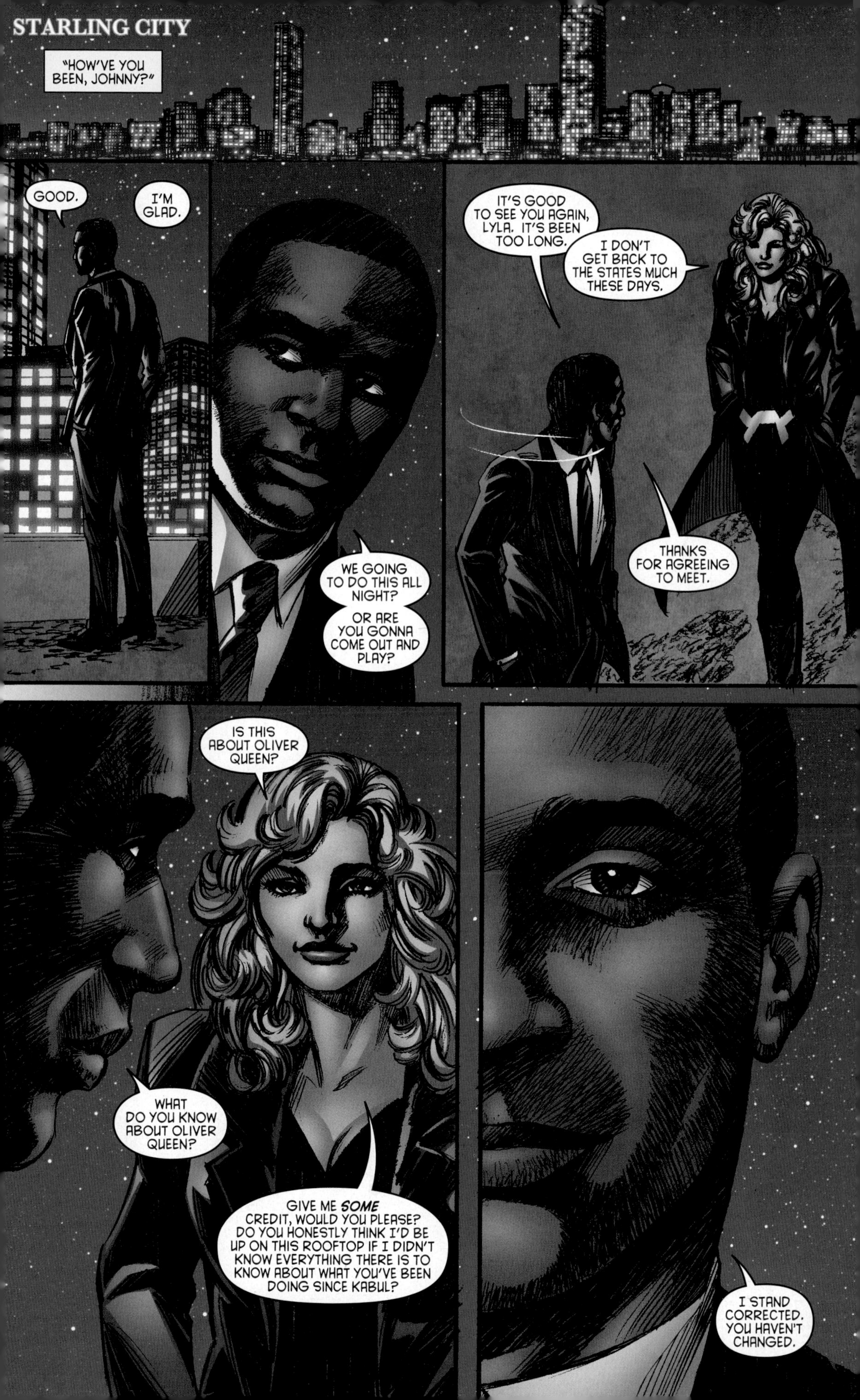
STARLING CITY
"HOW'VE YOU BEEN, JOHNNY?"
GOOD.
I'M GLAD.
WE GOING TO DO THIS ALL NIGHT?
OR ARE YOU GONNA COME OUT AND PLAY?
IT'S GOOD TO SEE YOU AGAIN, LYLA. IT'S BEEN TOO LONG.
I DON'T GET BACK TO THE STATES MUCH THESE DAYS.
THANKS FOR AGREEING TO MEET.
IS THIS ABOUT OLIVER QUEEN?
WHAT DO YOU KNOW ABOUT OLIVER QUEEN?
GIVE ME *SOME* CREDIT, WOULD YOU PLEASE? DO YOU HONESTLY THINK I'D BE UP ON THIS ROOFTOP IF I DIDN'T KNOW EVERYTHING THERE IS TO KNOW ABOUT WHAT YOU'VE BEEN DOING SINCE KABUL?
I STAND CORRECTED. YOU HAVEN'T CHANGED.

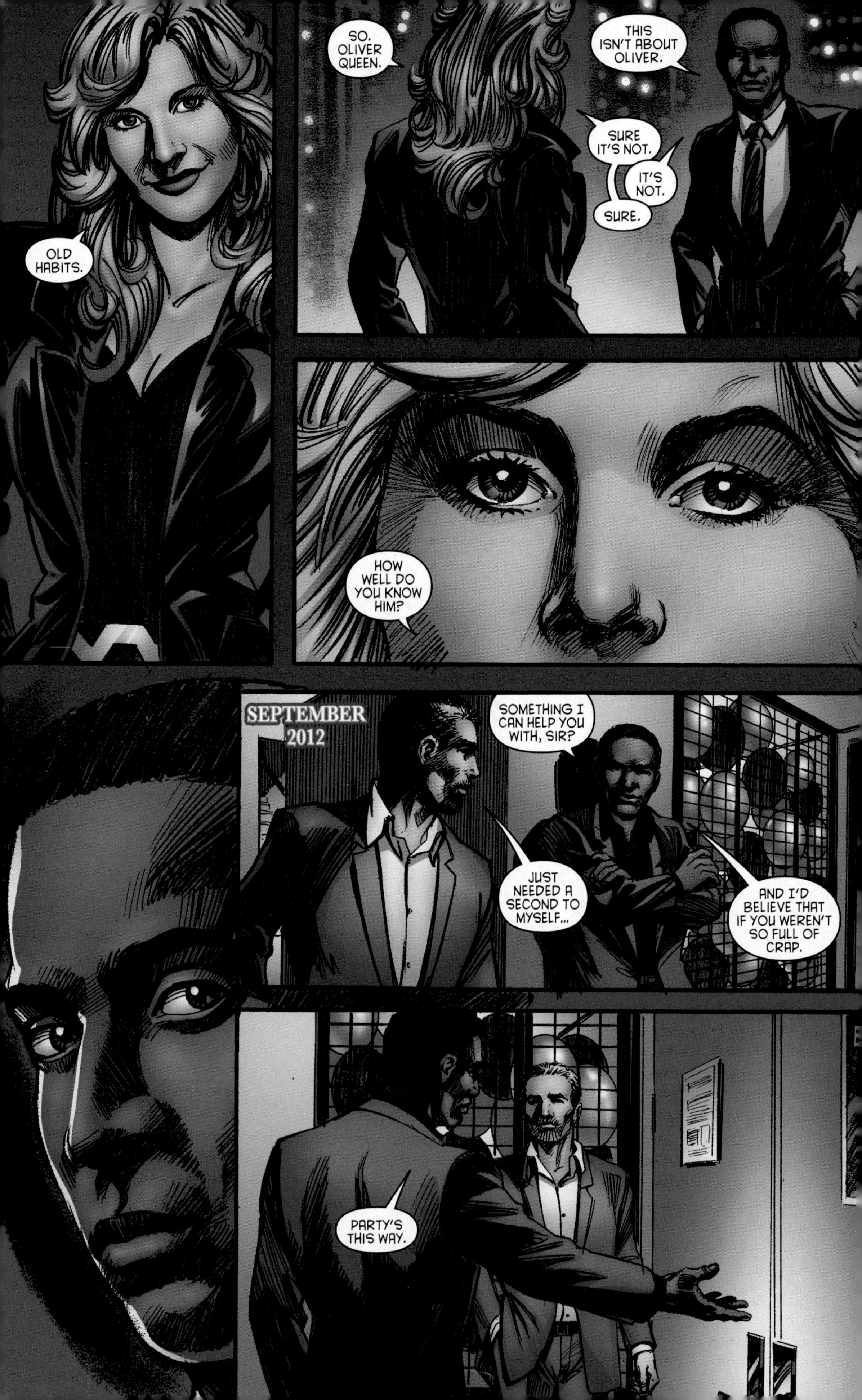
OLD HABITS.
SO. OLIVER QUEEN.
THIS ISN'T ABOUT OLIVER.
SURE IT'S NOT.
IT'S NOT.
SURE.
HOW WELL DO YOU KNOW HIM?
SEPTEMBER 2012
SOMETHING I CAN HELP YOU WITH, SIR?
JUST NEEDED A SECOND TO MYSELF...
AND I'D BELIEVE THAT IF YOU WEREN'T SO FULL OF CRAP.
PARTY'S THIS WAY.

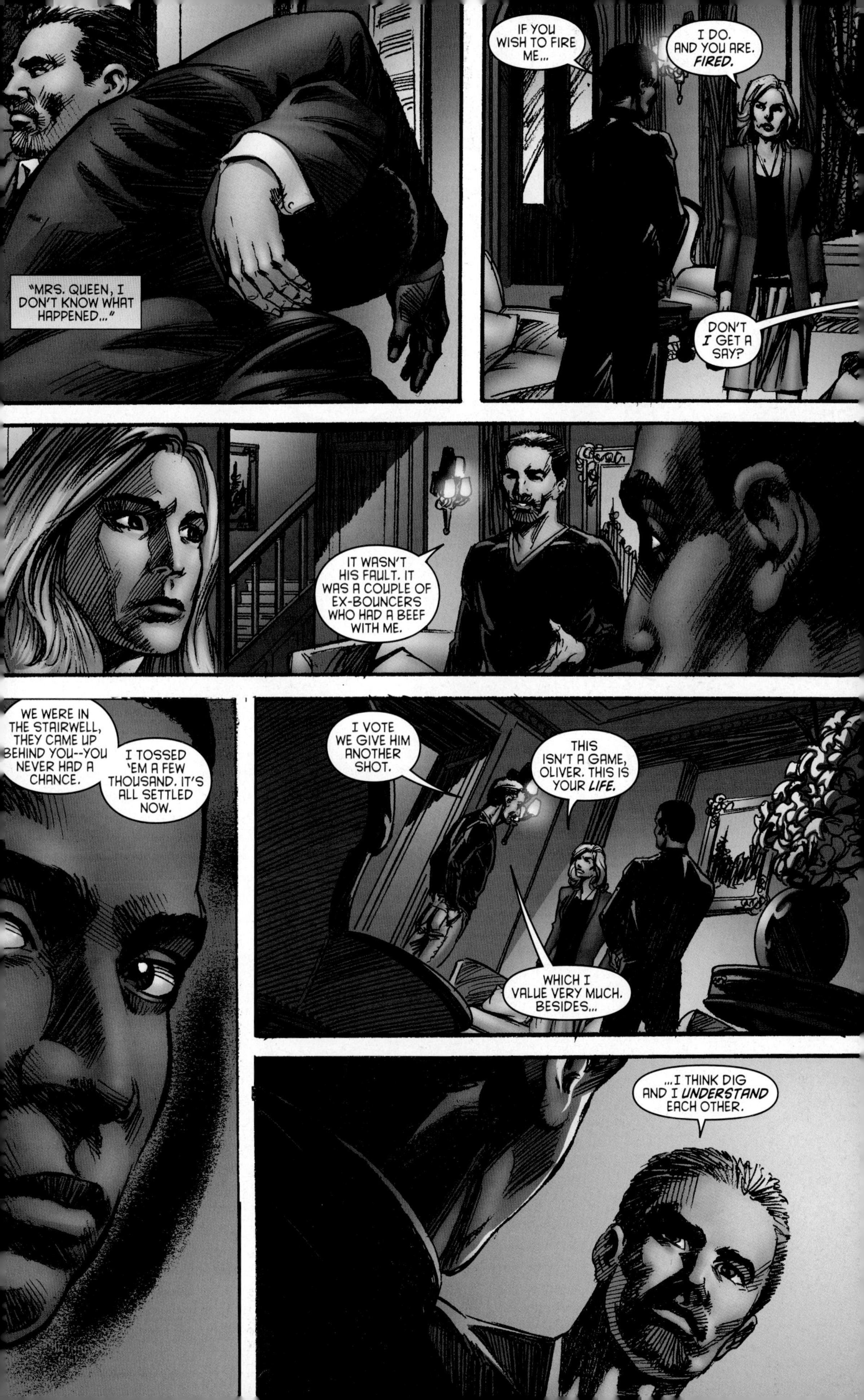
"MRS. QUEEN, I DON'T KNOW WHAT HAPPENED..."
IF YOU WISH TO FIRE ME...
I DO. AND YOU ARE. *FIRED.*
DON'T *I* GET A SAY?
IT WASN'T HIS FAULT. IT WAS A COUPLE OF EX-BOUNCERS WHO HAD A BEEF WITH ME.
WE WERE IN THE STAIRWELL, THEY CAME UP BEHIND YOU--YOU NEVER HAD A CHANCE.
I TOSSED 'EM A FEW THOUSAND. IT'S ALL SETTLED NOW.
I VOTE WE GIVE HIM ANOTHER SHOT.
THIS ISN'T A GAME, OLIVER. THIS IS YOUR *LIFE.*
WHICH I VALUE VERY MUCH. BESIDES...
...I THINK DIG AND I *UNDERSTAND* EACH OTHER.

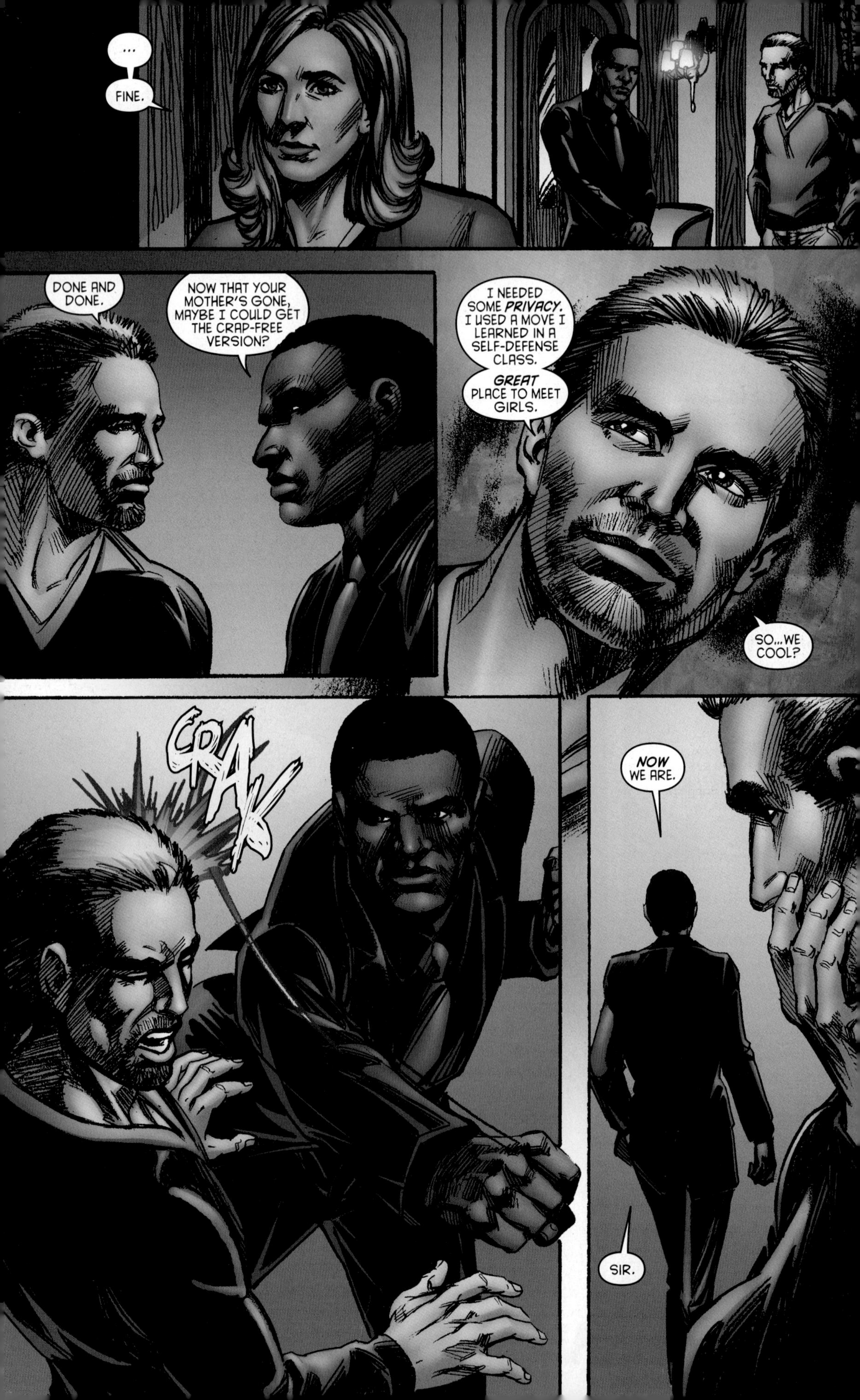
...
FINE.
DONE AND DONE.
NOW THAT YOUR MOTHER'S GONE, MAYBE I COULD GET THE CRAP-FREE VERSION?
I NEEDED SOME *PRIVACY*. I USED A MOVE I LEARNED IN A SELF-DEFENSE CLASS.
GREAT PLACE TO MEET GIRLS.
SO...WE COOL?
CRAK
NOW WE ARE.
SIR.

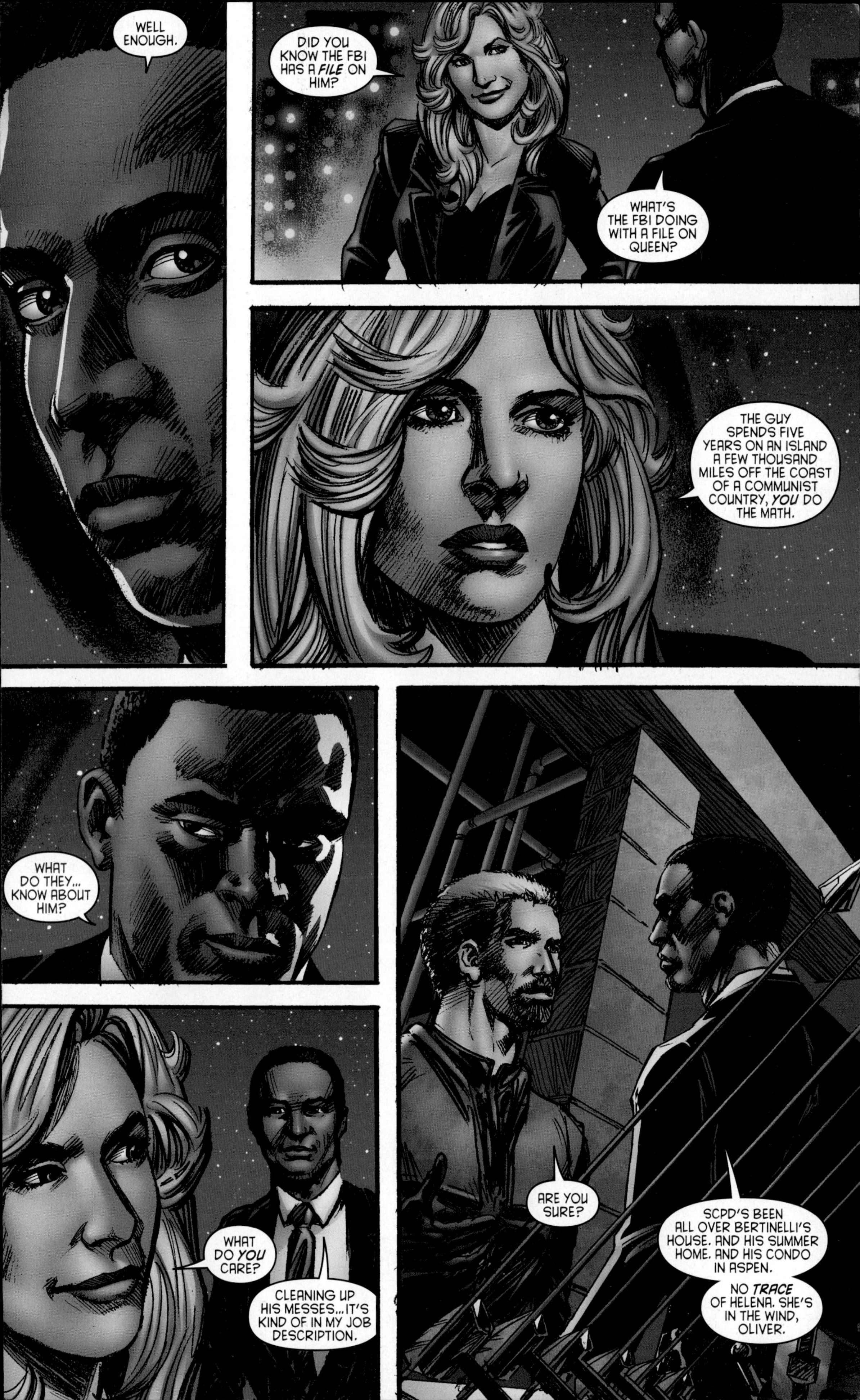
WELL ENOUGH.
DID YOU KNOW THE FBI HAS A *FILE* ON HIM?
WHAT'S THE FBI DOING WITH A FILE ON QUEEN?
THE GUY SPENDS FIVE YEARS ON AN ISLAND A FEW THOUSAND MILES OFF THE COAST OF A COMMUNIST COUNTRY, *YOU* DO THE MATH.
WHAT DO THEY... KNOW ABOUT HIM?
WHAT DO *YOU* CARE?
CLEANING UP HIS MESSES... IT'S KIND OF IN MY JOB DESCRIPTION.
SCPD'S BEEN ALL OVER BERTINELLI'S HOUSE. AND HIS SUMMER HOME. AND HIS CONDO IN ASPEN.
NO *TRACE* OF HELENA. SHE'S IN THE WIND, OLIVER.
ARE YOU SURE?

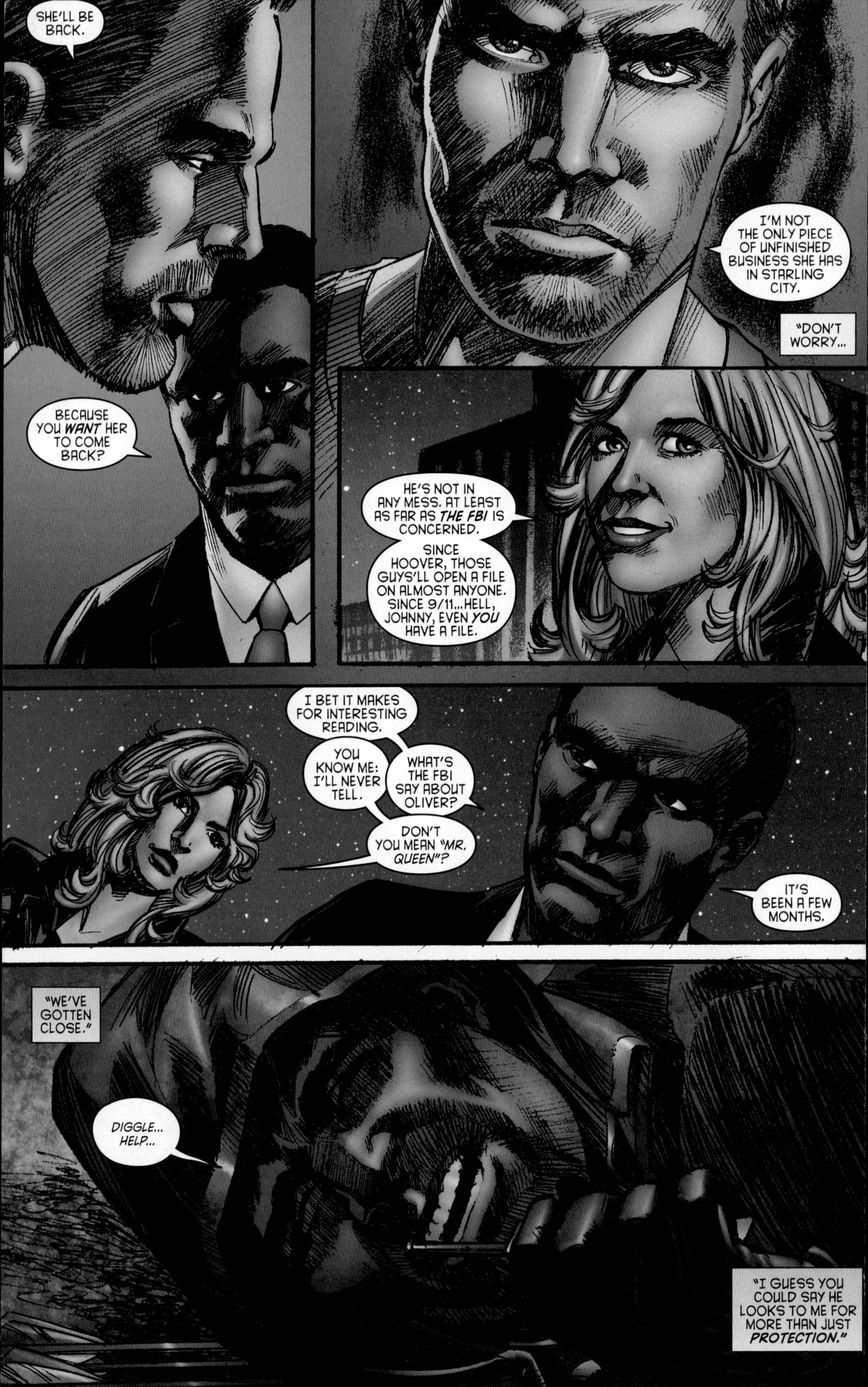
SHE'LL BE BACK.
I'M NOT THE ONLY PIECE OF UNFINISHED BUSINESS SHE HAS IN STARLING CITY.
"DON'T WORRY...
BECAUSE YOU *WANT* HER TO COME BACK?
HE'S NOT IN ANY MESS. AT LEAST AS FAR AS *THE FBI* IS CONCERNED.
SINCE HOOVER, THOSE GUYS'LL OPEN A FILE ON ALMOST ANYONE. SINCE 9/11...HELL, JOHNNY, EVEN *YOU* HAVE A FILE.
I BET IT MAKES FOR INTERESTING READING.
WHAT'S THE FBI SAY ABOUT OLIVER?
YOU KNOW ME: I'LL NEVER TELL.
DON'T YOU MEAN *"MR. QUEEN"*?
IT'S BEEN A FEW MONTHS.
"WE'VE GOTTEN CLOSE."
DIGGLE... HELP...
"I GUESS YOU COULD SAY HE LOOKS TO ME FOR MORE THAN JUST *PROTECTION*."

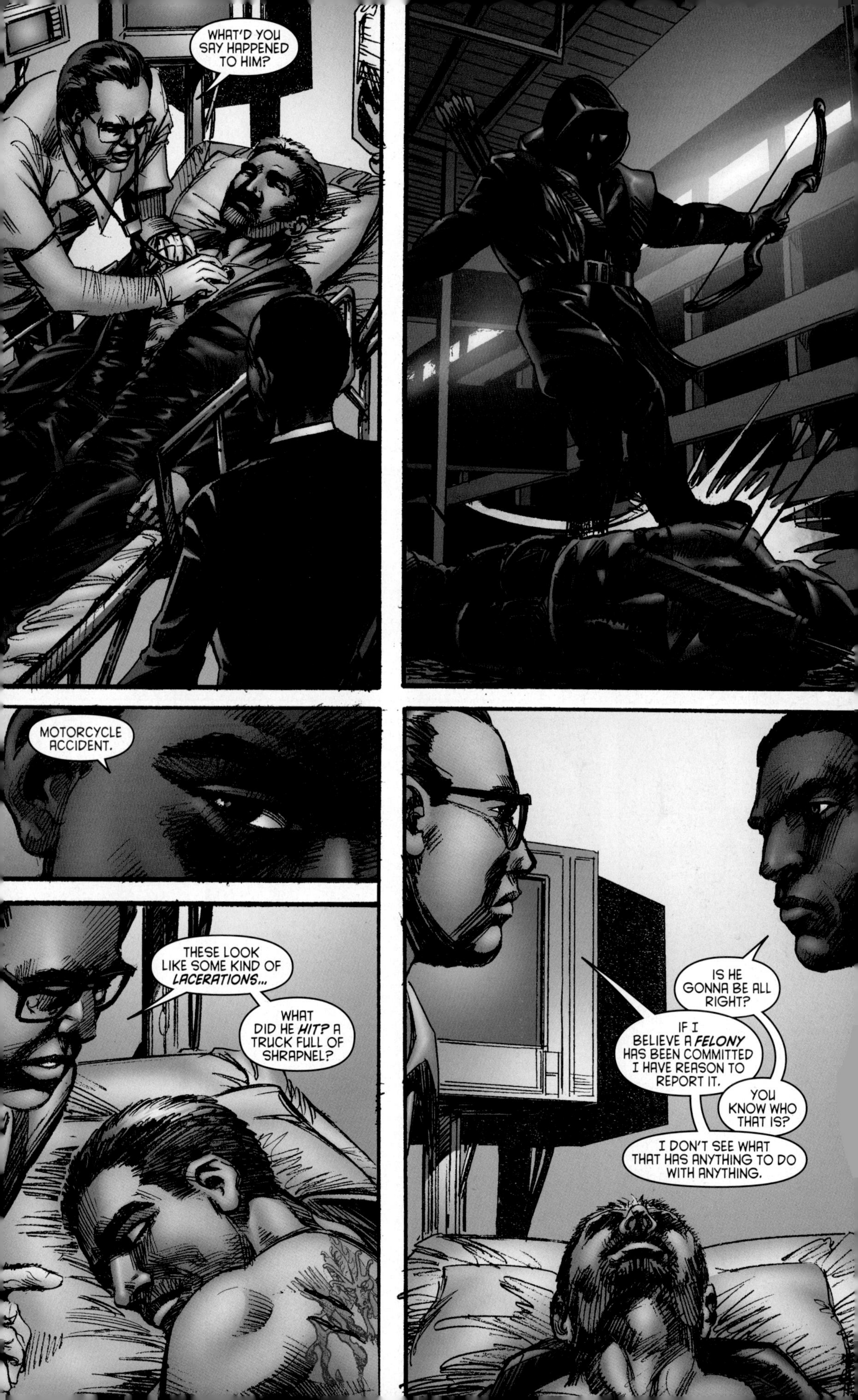
WHAT'D YOU SAY HAPPENED TO HIM?
MOTORCYCLE ACCIDENT.
THESE LOOK LIKE SOME KIND OF *LACERATIONS...*
WHAT DID HE *HIT?* A TRUCK FULL OF SHRAPNEL?
IS HE GONNA BE ALL RIGHT?
IF I BELIEVE A *FELONY* HAS BEEN COMMITTED I HAVE REASON TO REPORT IT.
YOU KNOW WHO THAT IS?
I DON'T SEE WHAT THAT HAS ANYTHING TO DO WITH ANYTHING.

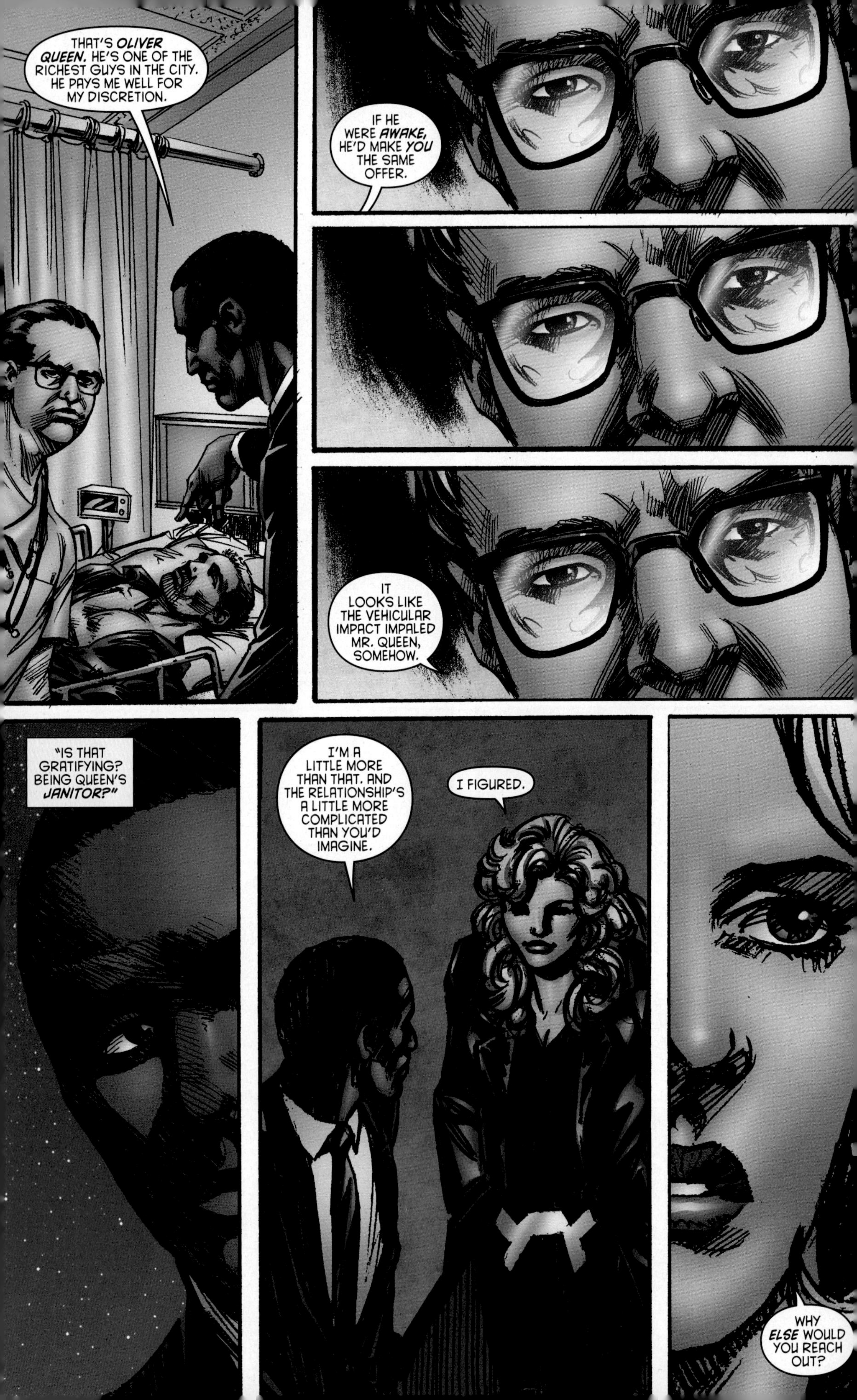
THAT'S OLIVER QUEEN. HE'S ONE OF THE RICHEST GUYS IN THE CITY. HE PAYS ME WELL FOR MY DISCRETION.
IF HE WERE AWAKE, HE'D MAKE YOU THE SAME OFFER.
IT LOOKS LIKE THE VEHICULAR IMPACT IMPALED MR. QUEEN, SOMEHOW.
"IS THAT GRATIFYING? BEING QUEEN'S JANITOR?"
I'M A LITTLE MORE THAN THAT. AND THE RELATIONSHIP'S A LITTLE MORE COMPLICATED THAN YOU'D IMAGINE.
I FIGURED.
WHY ELSE WOULD YOU REACH OUT?

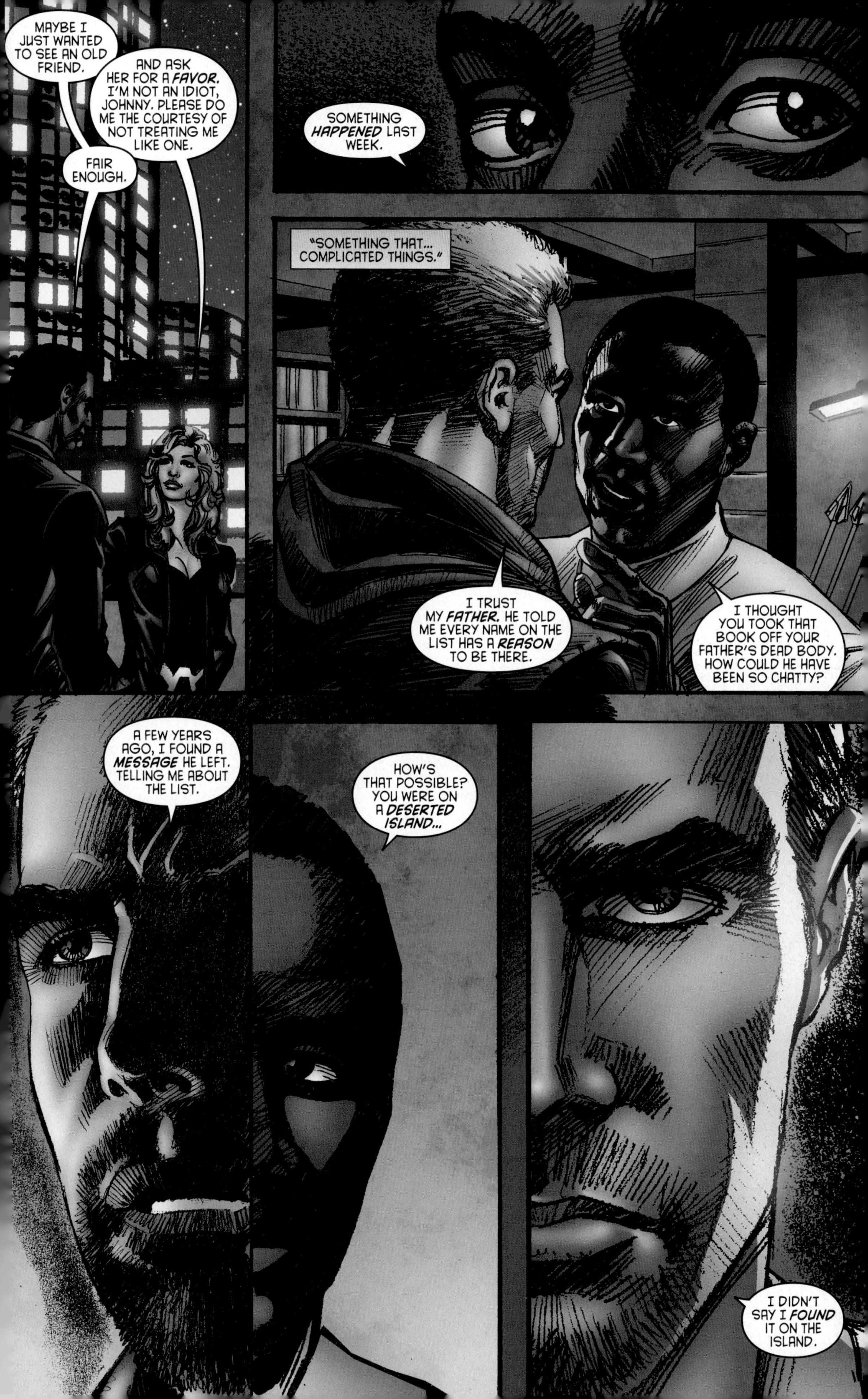
MAYBE I JUST WANTED TO SEE AN OLD FRIEND.
AND ASK HER FOR A FAVOR. I'M NOT AN IDIOT, JOHNNY. PLEASE DO ME THE COURTESY OF NOT TREATING ME LIKE ONE.
FAIR ENOUGH.
SOMETHING HAPPENED LAST WEEK.
"SOMETHING THAT... COMPLICATED THINGS."
I TRUST MY FATHER. HE TOLD ME EVERY NAME ON THE LIST HAS A REASON TO BE THERE.
I THOUGHT YOU TOOK THAT BOOK OFF YOUR FATHER'S DEAD BODY. HOW COULD HE HAVE BEEN SO CHATTY?
A FEW YEARS AGO, I FOUND A MESSAGE HE LEFT. TELLING ME ABOUT THE LIST.
HOW'S THAT POSSIBLE? YOU WERE ON A DESERTED ISLAND...
I DIDN'T SAY I FOUND IT ON THE ISLAND.

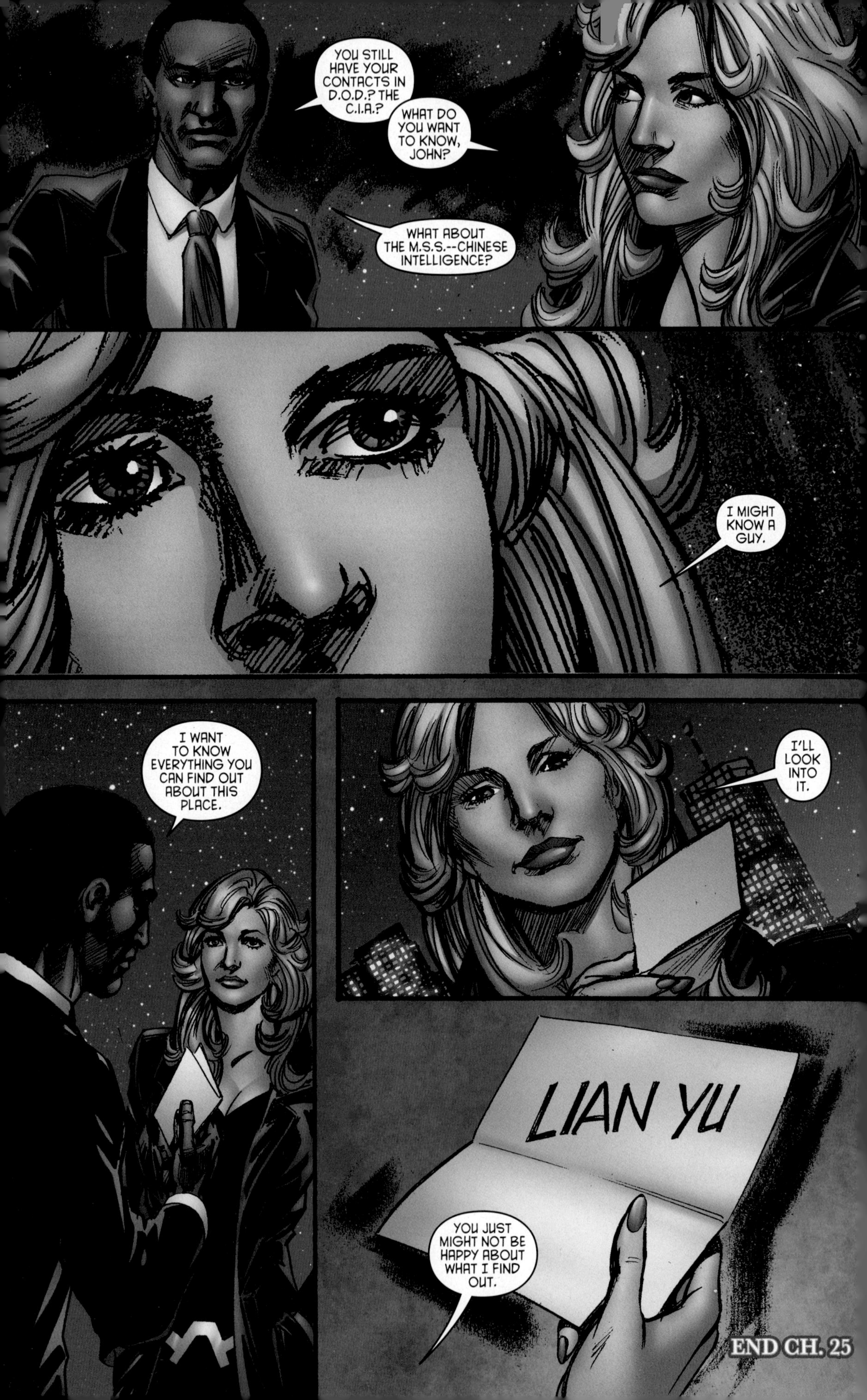
YOU STILL HAVE YOUR CONTACTS IN D.O.D.? THE C.I.A.?
WHAT DO YOU WANT TO KNOW, JOHN?
WHAT ABOUT THE M.S.S.--CHINESE INTELLIGENCE?
I MIGHT KNOW A GUY.
I WANT TO KNOW EVERYTHING YOU CAN FIND OUT ABOUT THIS PLACE.
I'LL LOOK INTO IT.
LIAN YU
YOU JUST MIGHT NOT BE HAPPY ABOUT WHAT I FIND OUT.
END CH. 25

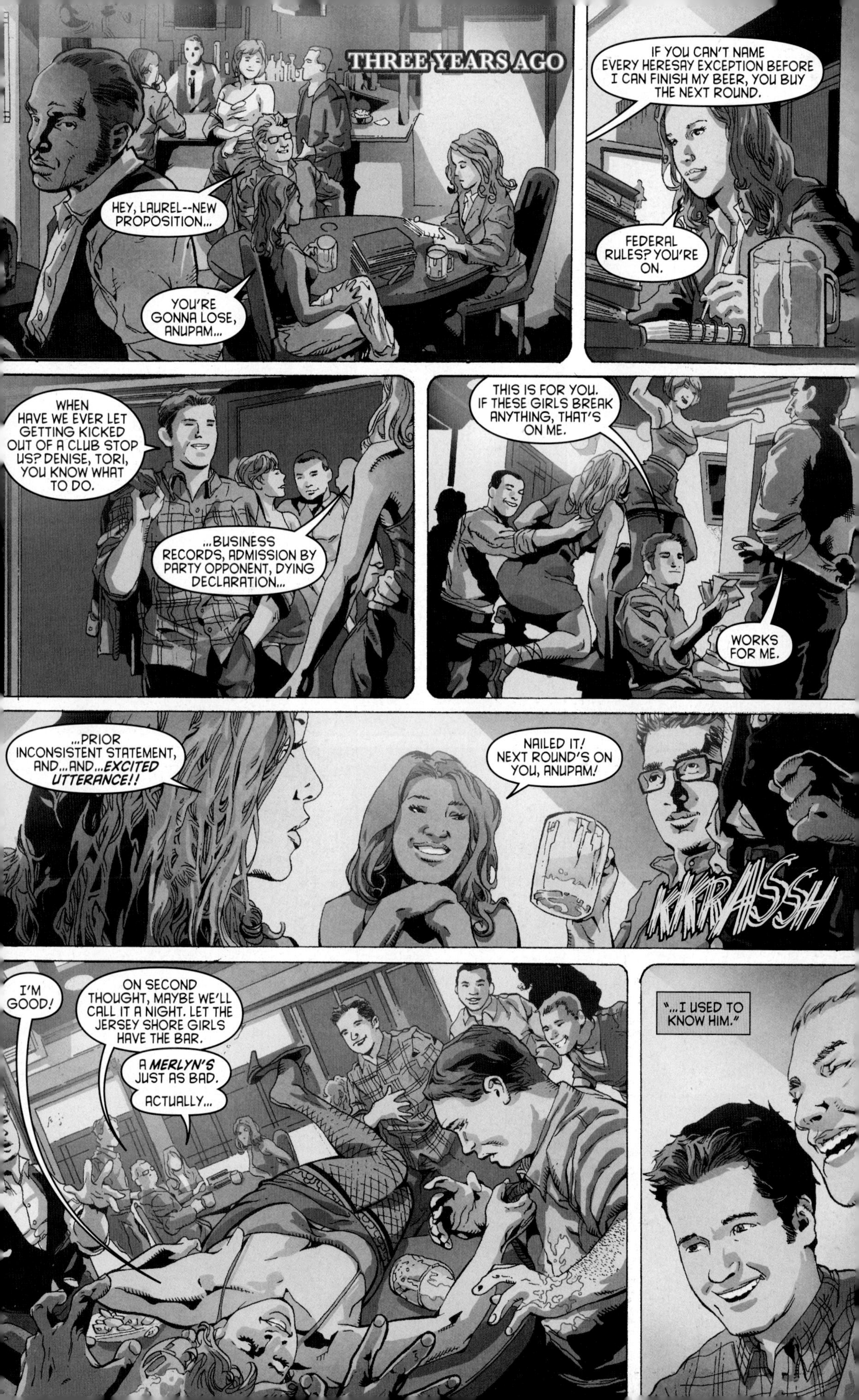
THREE YEARS AGO
HEY, LAUREL--NEW PROPOSITION...
YOU'RE GONNA LOSE, ANUPAM...
IF YOU CAN'T NAME EVERY HERESAY EXCEPTION BEFORE I CAN FINISH MY BEER, YOU BUY THE NEXT ROUND.
FEDERAL RULES? YOU'RE ON.
WHEN HAVE WE EVER LET GETTING KICKED OUT OF A CLUB STOP US? DENISE, TORI, YOU KNOW WHAT TO DO.
...BUSINESS RECORDS, ADMISSION BY PARTY OPPONENT, DYING DECLARATION...
THIS IS FOR YOU. IF THESE GIRLS BREAK ANYTHING, THAT'S ON ME.
WORKS FOR ME.
...PRIOR INCONSISTENT STATEMENT, AND...AND...EXCITED UTTERANCE!!
NAILED IT! NEXT ROUND'S ON YOU, ANUPAM!
KKRASSH
I'M GOOD!
ON SECOND THOUGHT, MAYBE WE'LL CALL IT A NIGHT. LET THE JERSEY SHORE GIRLS HAVE THE BAR.
A MERLYN'S JUST AS BAD.
ACTUALLY...
"...I USED TO KNOW HIM."

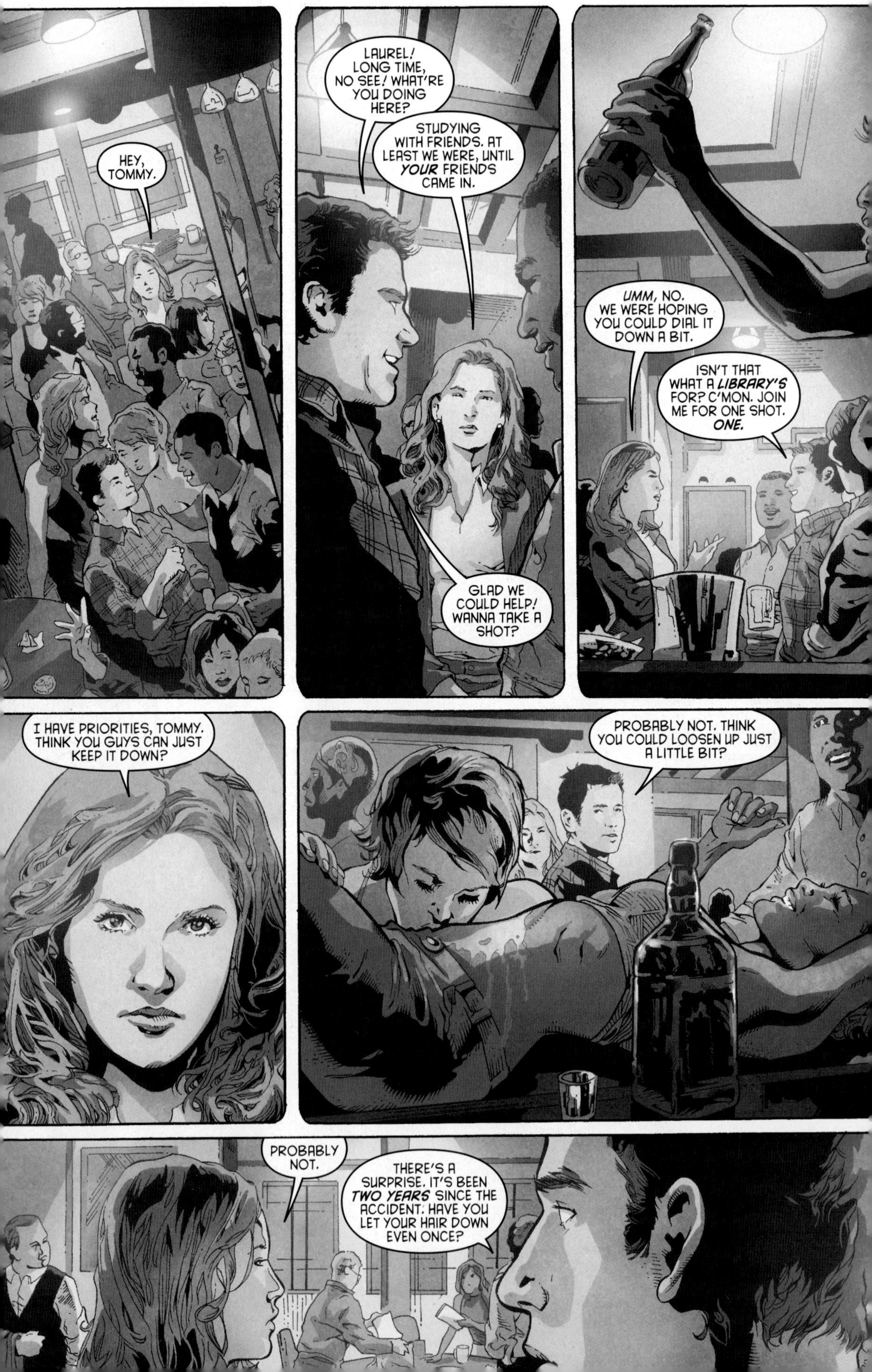
HEY, TOMMY.
LAUREL! LONG TIME, NO SEE! WHAT'RE YOU DOING HERE?
STUDYING WITH FRIENDS. AT LEAST WE WERE, UNTIL YOUR FRIENDS CAME IN.
GLAD WE COULD HELP! WANNA TAKE A SHOT?
UMM, NO. WE WERE HOPING YOU COULD DIAL IT DOWN A BIT.
ISN'T THAT WHAT A LIBRARY'S FOR? C'MON. JOIN ME FOR ONE SHOT. ONE.
I HAVE PRIORITIES, TOMMY. THINK YOU GUYS CAN JUST KEEP IT DOWN?
PROBABLY NOT. THINK YOU COULD LOOSEN UP JUST A LITTLE BIT?
PROBABLY NOT.
THERE'S A SURPRISE. IT'S BEEN TWO YEARS SINCE THE ACCIDENT. HAVE YOU LET YOUR HAIR DOWN EVEN ONCE?

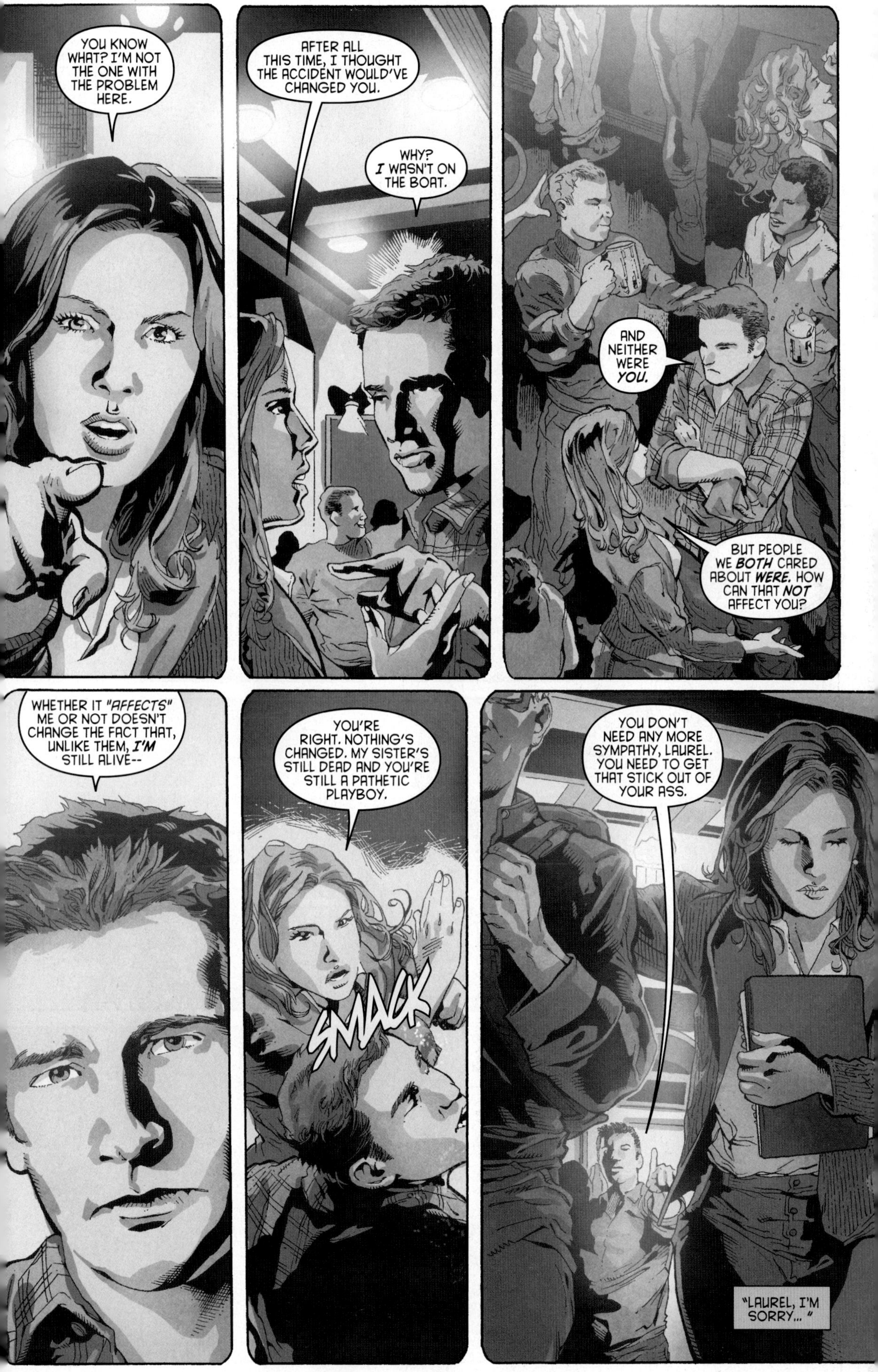
YOU KNOW WHAT? I'M NOT THE ONE WITH THE PROBLEM HERE.
AFTER ALL THIS TIME, I THOUGHT THE ACCIDENT WOULD'VE CHANGED YOU.
WHY? *I* WASN'T ON THE BOAT.
AND NEITHER WERE *YOU.*
BUT PEOPLE WE *BOTH* CARED ABOUT *WERE.* HOW CAN THAT *NOT* AFFECT YOU?
WHETHER IT *"AFFECTS"* ME OR NOT DOESN'T CHANGE THE FACT THAT, UNLIKE THEM, *I'M* STILL ALIVE--
YOU'RE RIGHT. NOTHING'S CHANGED. MY SISTER'S STILL DEAD AND YOU'RE STILL A PATHETIC PLAYBOY.
SMACK
YOU DON'T NEED ANY MORE SYMPATHY, LAUREL. YOU NEED TO GET THAT STICK OUT OF YOUR ASS.
"LAUREL, I'M SORRY..."

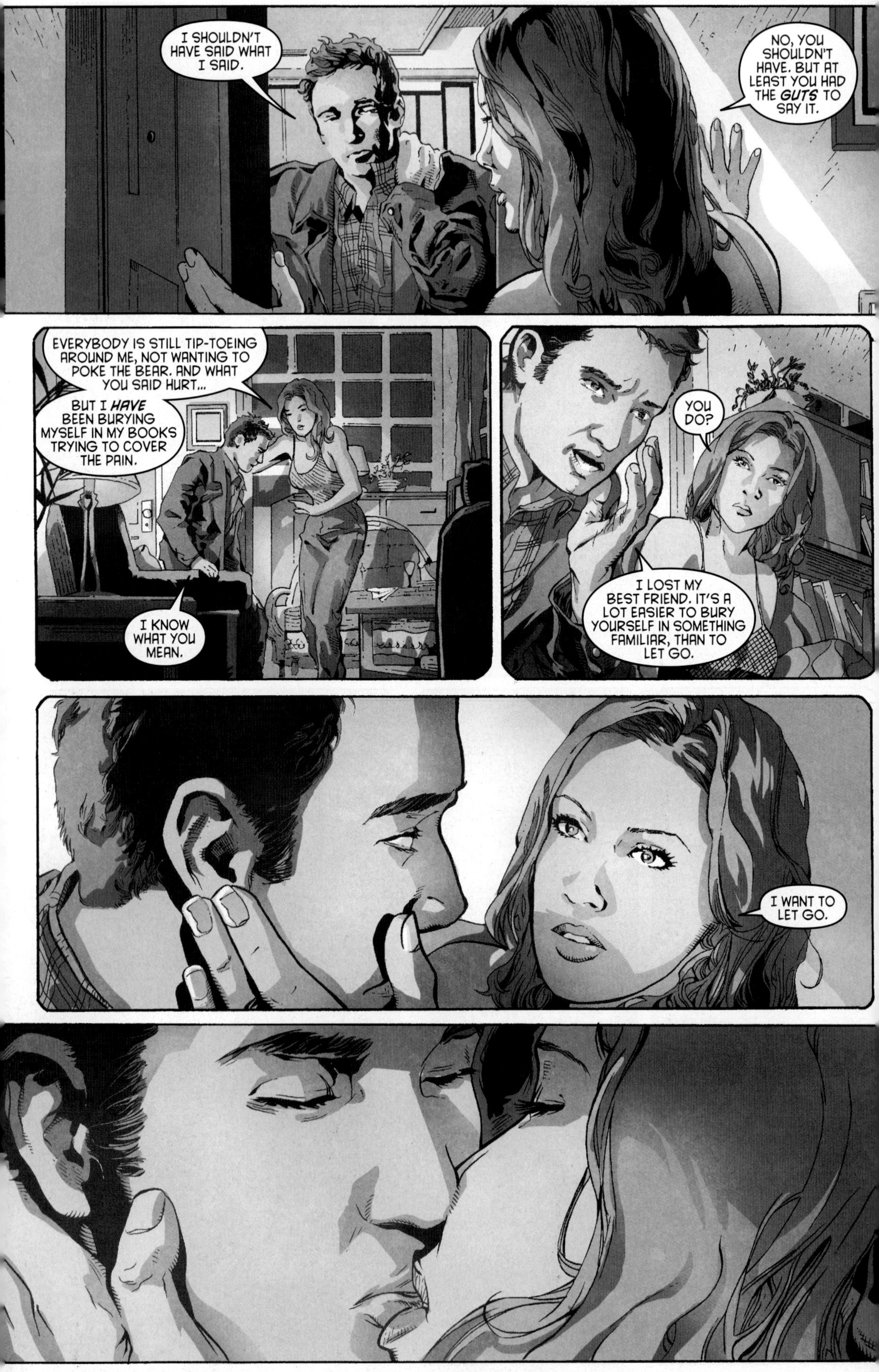
I SHOULDN'T HAVE SAID WHAT I SAID.
NO, YOU SHOULDN'T HAVE. BUT AT LEAST YOU HAD THE GUTS TO SAY IT.
EVERYBODY IS STILL TIP-TOEING AROUND ME, NOT WANTING TO POKE THE BEAR. AND WHAT YOU SAID HURT...
BUT I HAVE BEEN BURYING MYSELF IN MY BOOKS TRYING TO COVER THE PAIN.
I KNOW WHAT YOU MEAN.
YOU DO?
I LOST MY BEST FRIEND. IT'S A LOT EASIER TO BURY YOURSELF IN SOMETHING FAMILIAR, THAN TO LET GO.
I WANT TO LET GO.

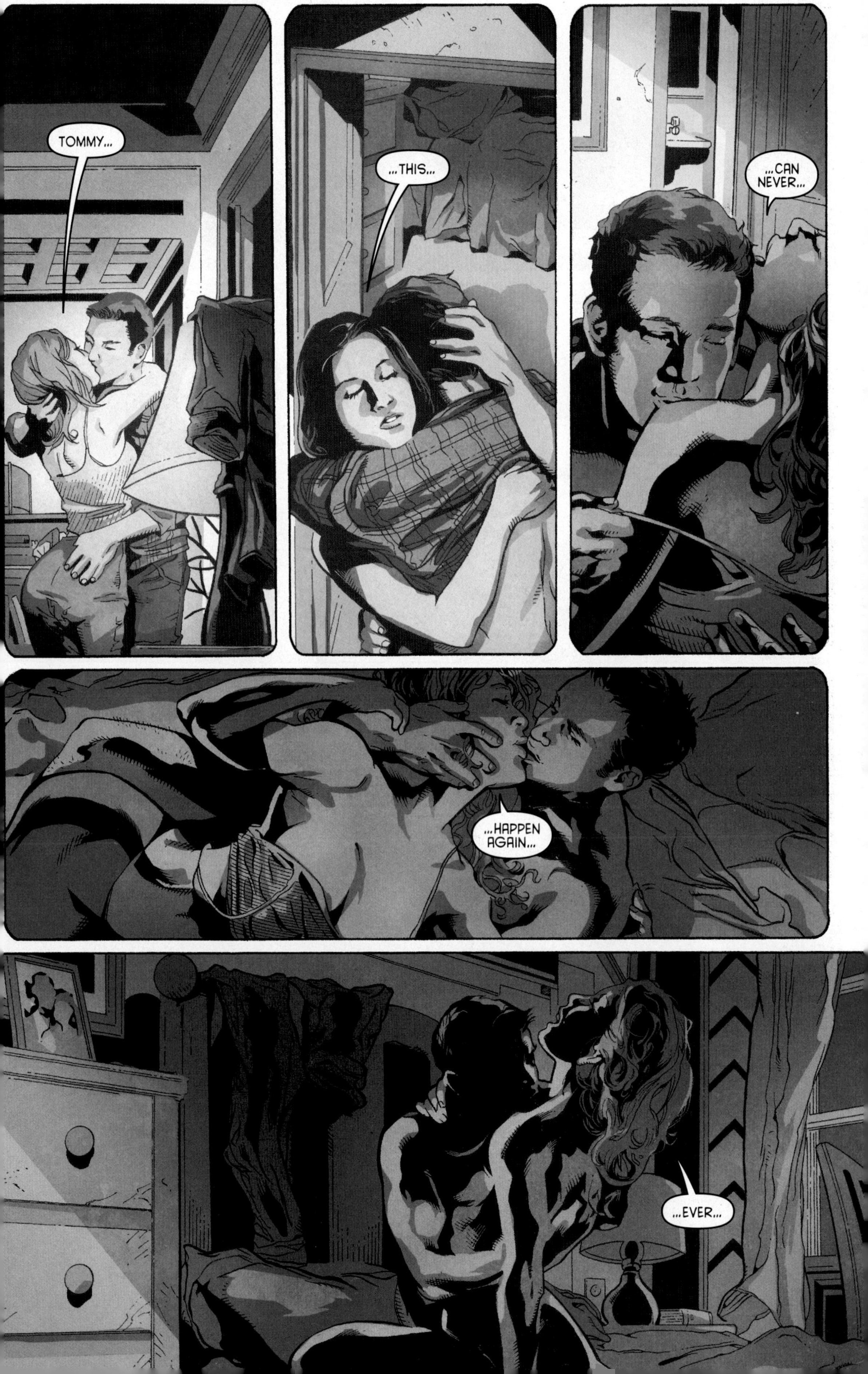
TOMMY...
...THIS...
...CAN NEVER...
...HAPPEN AGAIN...
...EVER...

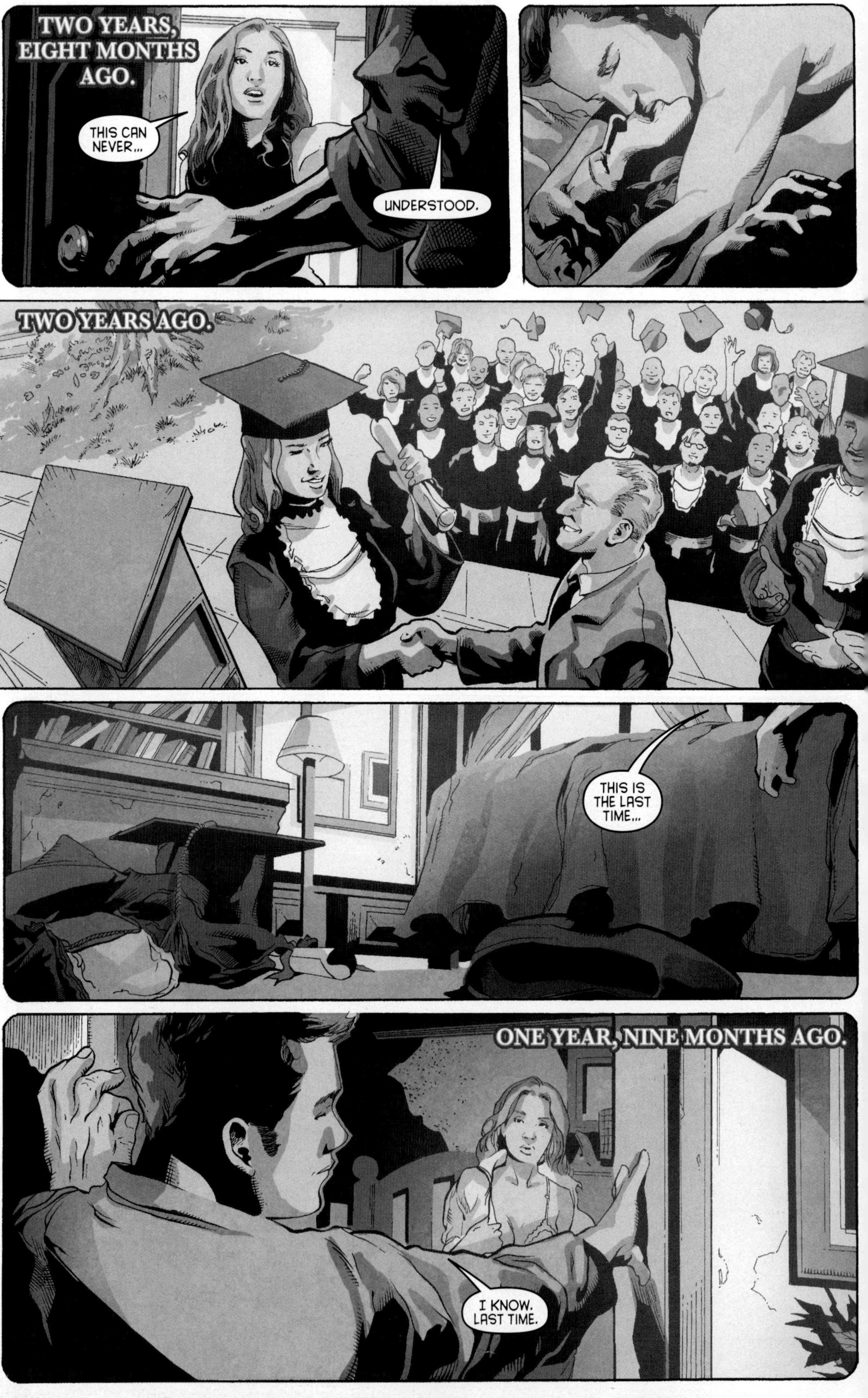

TWO YEARS, EIGHT MONTHS AGO.
THIS CAN NEVER...
UNDERSTOOD.
TWO YEARS AGO.
THIS IS THE LAST TIME...
ONE YEAR, NINE MONTHS AGO.
I KNOW. LAST TIME.

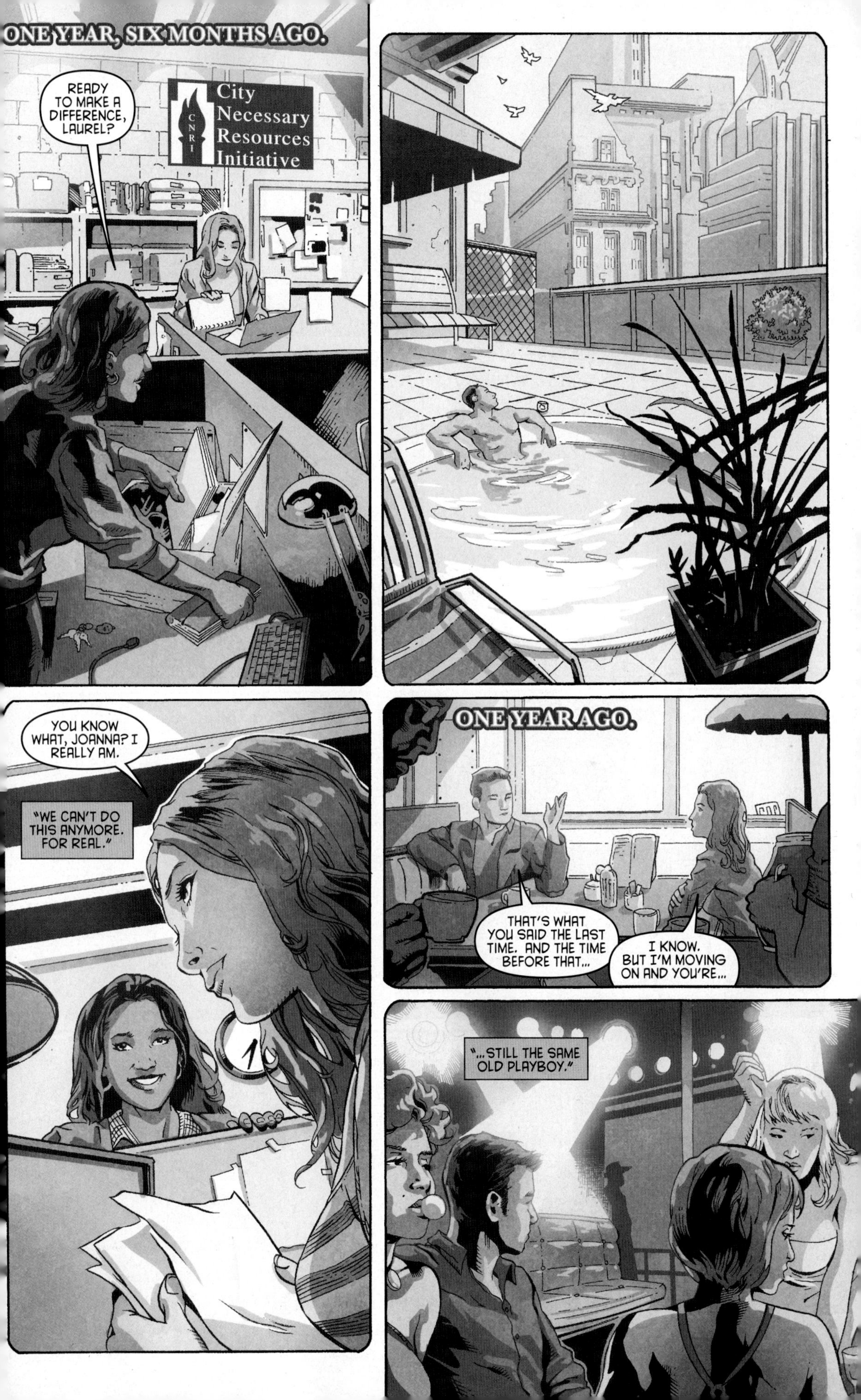
ONE YEAR, SIX MONTHS AGO.
READY TO MAKE A DIFFERENCE, LAUREL?
City Necessary Resources Initiative
CNRI
YOU KNOW WHAT, JOANNA? I REALLY AM.
"WE CAN'T DO THIS ANYMORE. FOR REAL."
ONE YEAR AGO.
THAT'S WHAT YOU SAID THE LAST TIME. AND THE TIME BEFORE THAT...
I KNOW. BUT I'M MOVING ON AND YOU'RE...
"...STILL THE SAME OLD PLAYBOY."

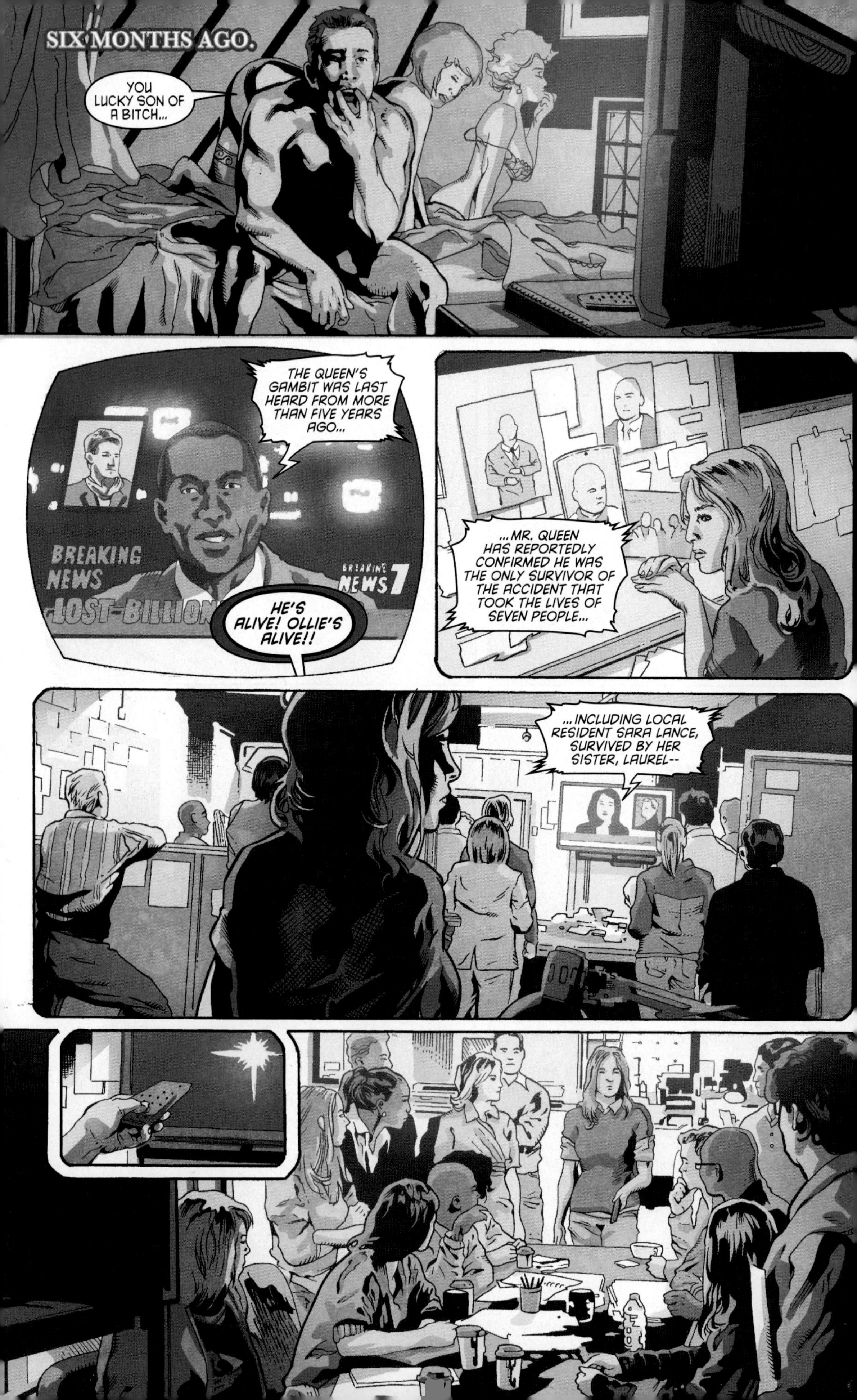
SIX MONTHS AGO.
YOU LUCKY SON OF A BITCH...
THE QUEEN'S GAMBIT WAS LAST HEARD FROM MORE THAN FIVE YEARS AGO...
BREAKING NEWS
BREAKING NEWS 7
LOST-BILLION
HE'S ALIVE! OLLIE'S ALIVE!!
...MR. QUEEN HAS REPORTEDLY CONFIRMED HE WAS THE ONLY SURVIVOR OF THE ACCIDENT THAT TOOK THE LIVES OF SEVEN PEOPLE...
...INCLUDING LOCAL RESIDENT SARA LANCE, SURVIVED BY HER SISTER, LAUREL--

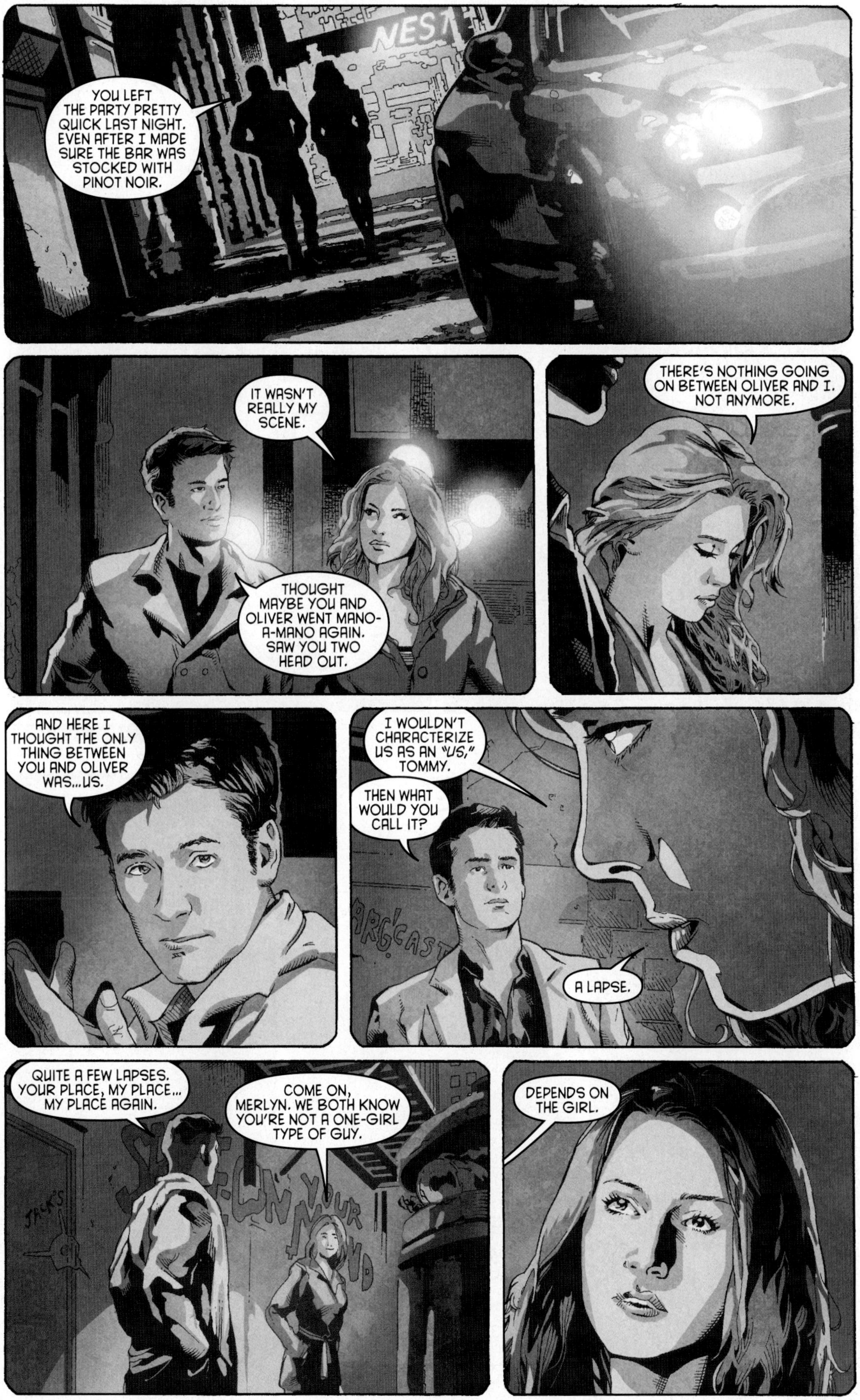
NEST
YOU LEFT THE PARTY PRETTY QUICK LAST NIGHT. EVEN AFTER I MADE SURE THE BAR WAS STOCKED WITH PINOT NOIR.
IT WASN'T REALLY MY SCENE.
THOUGHT MAYBE YOU AND OLIVER WENT MANO-A-MANO AGAIN. SAW YOU TWO HEAD OUT.
THERE'S NOTHING GOING ON BETWEEN OLIVER AND I. NOT ANYMORE.
AND HERE I THOUGHT THE ONLY THING BETWEEN YOU AND OLIVER WAS...US.
I WOULDN'T CHARACTERIZE US AS AN "US," TOMMY.
THEN WHAT WOULD YOU CALL IT?
A LAPSE.
QUITE A FEW LAPSES. YOUR PLACE, MY PLACE... MY PLACE AGAIN.
COME ON, MERLYN. WE BOTH KNOW YOU'RE NOT A ONE-GIRL TYPE OF GUY.
DEPENDS ON THE GIRL.

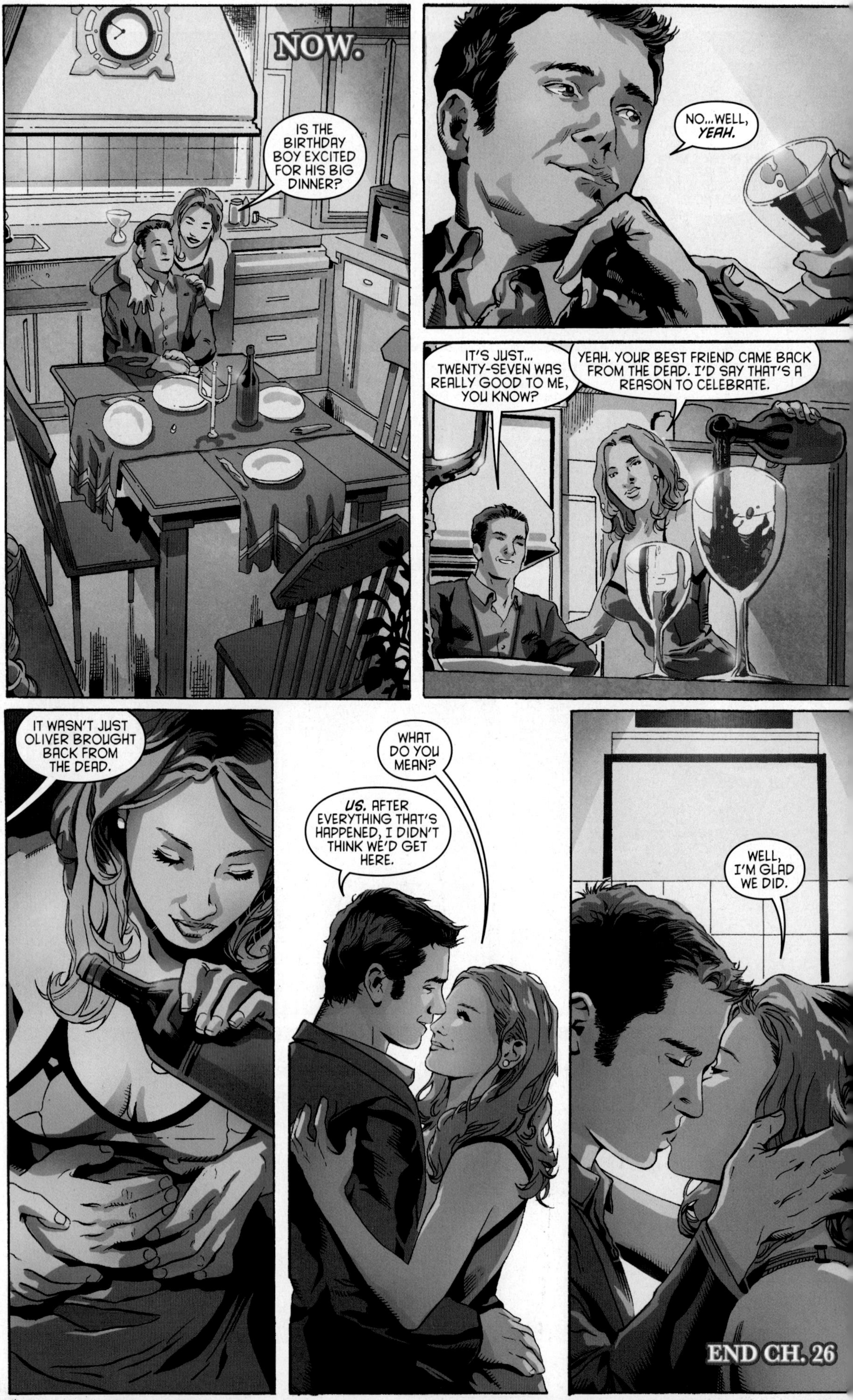
NOW.
IS THE BIRTHDAY BOY EXCITED FOR HIS BIG DINNER?
NO...WELL, *YEAH.*
IT'S JUST... TWENTY-SEVEN WAS REALLY GOOD TO ME, YOU KNOW?
YEAH. YOUR BEST FRIEND CAME BACK FROM THE DEAD. I'D SAY THAT'S A REASON TO CELEBRATE.
IT WASN'T JUST OLIVER BROUGHT BACK FROM THE DEAD.
WHAT DO YOU MEAN?
US. AFTER EVERYTHING THAT'S HAPPENED, I DIDN'T THINK WE'D GET HERE.
WELL, I'M GLAD WE DID.
END CH. 26

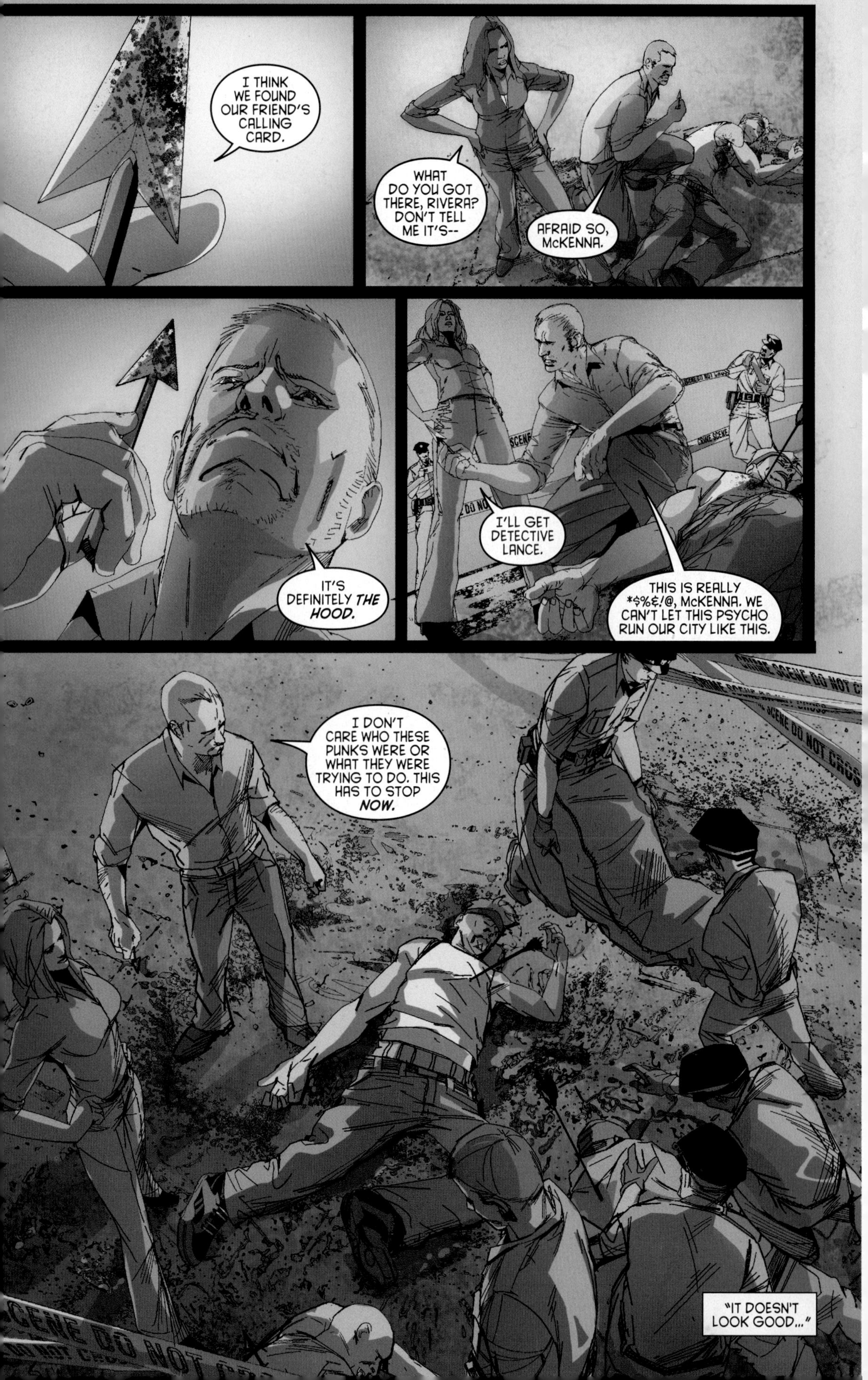
I THINK WE FOUND OUR FRIEND'S CALLING CARD.
WHAT DO YOU GOT THERE, RIVERA? DON'T TELL ME IT'S--
AFRAID SO, McKENNA.
IT'S DEFINITELY *THE HOOD.*
I'LL GET DETECTIVE LANCE.
THIS IS REALLY *$%&!@, McKENNA. WE CAN'T LET THIS PSYCHO RUN OUR CITY LIKE THIS.
I DON'T CARE WHO THESE PUNKS WERE OR WHAT THEY WERE TRYING TO DO. THIS HAS TO STOP *NOW.*
"IT DOESN'T LOOK GOOD..."

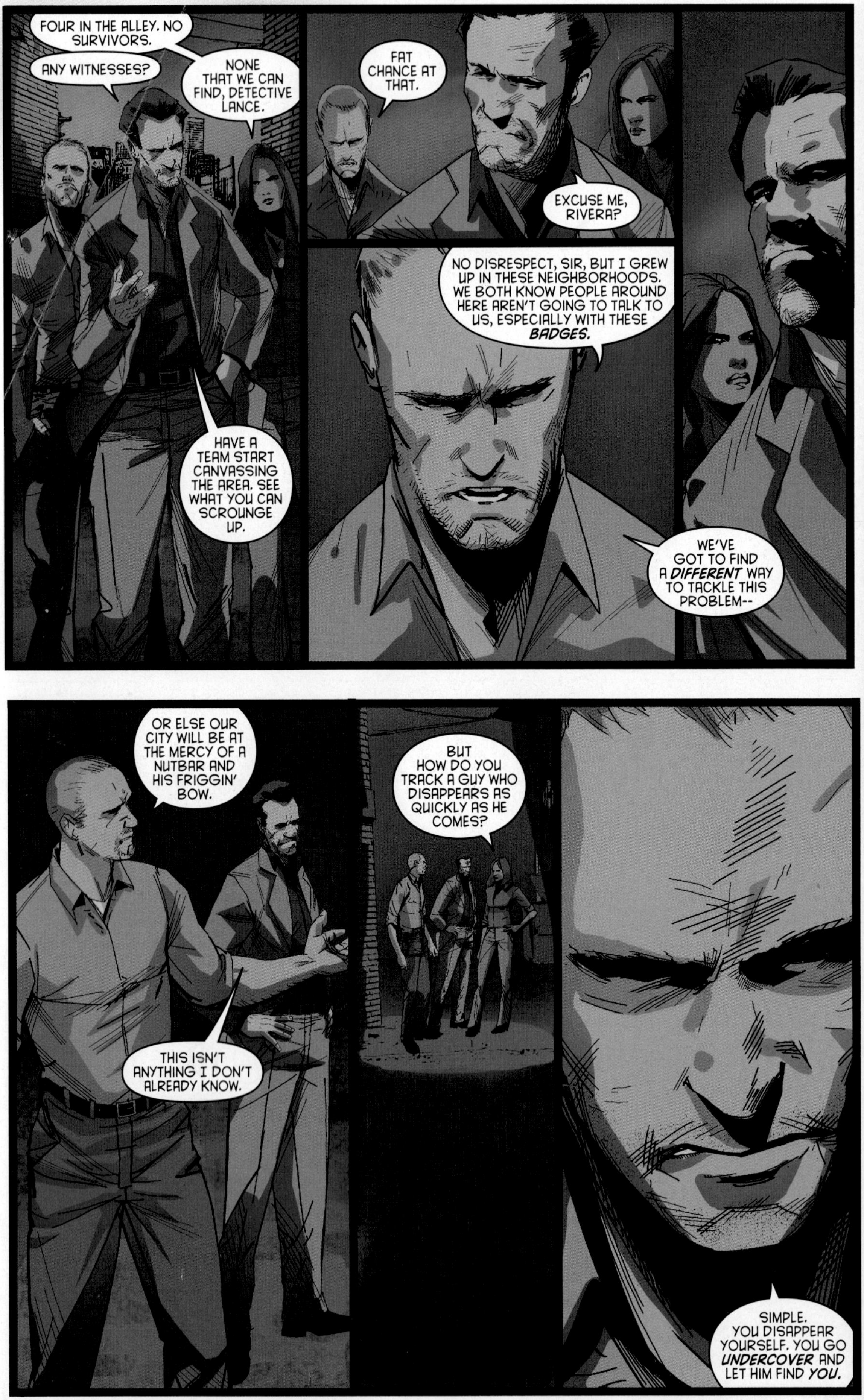
FOUR IN THE ALLEY. NO SURVIVORS.
ANY WITNESSES?
NONE THAT WE CAN FIND, DETECTIVE LANCE.
HAVE A TEAM START CANVASSING THE AREA. SEE WHAT YOU CAN SCROUNGE UP.
FAT CHANCE AT THAT.
EXCUSE ME, RIVERA?
NO DISRESPECT, SIR, BUT I GREW UP IN THESE NEIGHBORHOODS. WE BOTH KNOW PEOPLE AROUND HERE AREN'T GOING TO TALK TO US, ESPECIALLY WITH THESE BADGES.
WE'VE GOT TO FIND A DIFFERENT WAY TO TACKLE THIS PROBLEM--
OR ELSE OUR CITY WILL BE AT THE MERCY OF A NUTBAR AND HIS FRIGGIN' BOW.
THIS ISN'T ANYTHING I DON'T ALREADY KNOW.
BUT HOW DO YOU TRACK A GUY WHO DISAPPEARS AS QUICKLY AS HE COMES?
SIMPLE. YOU DISAPPEAR YOURSELF. YOU GO UNDERCOVER AND LET HIM FIND YOU.

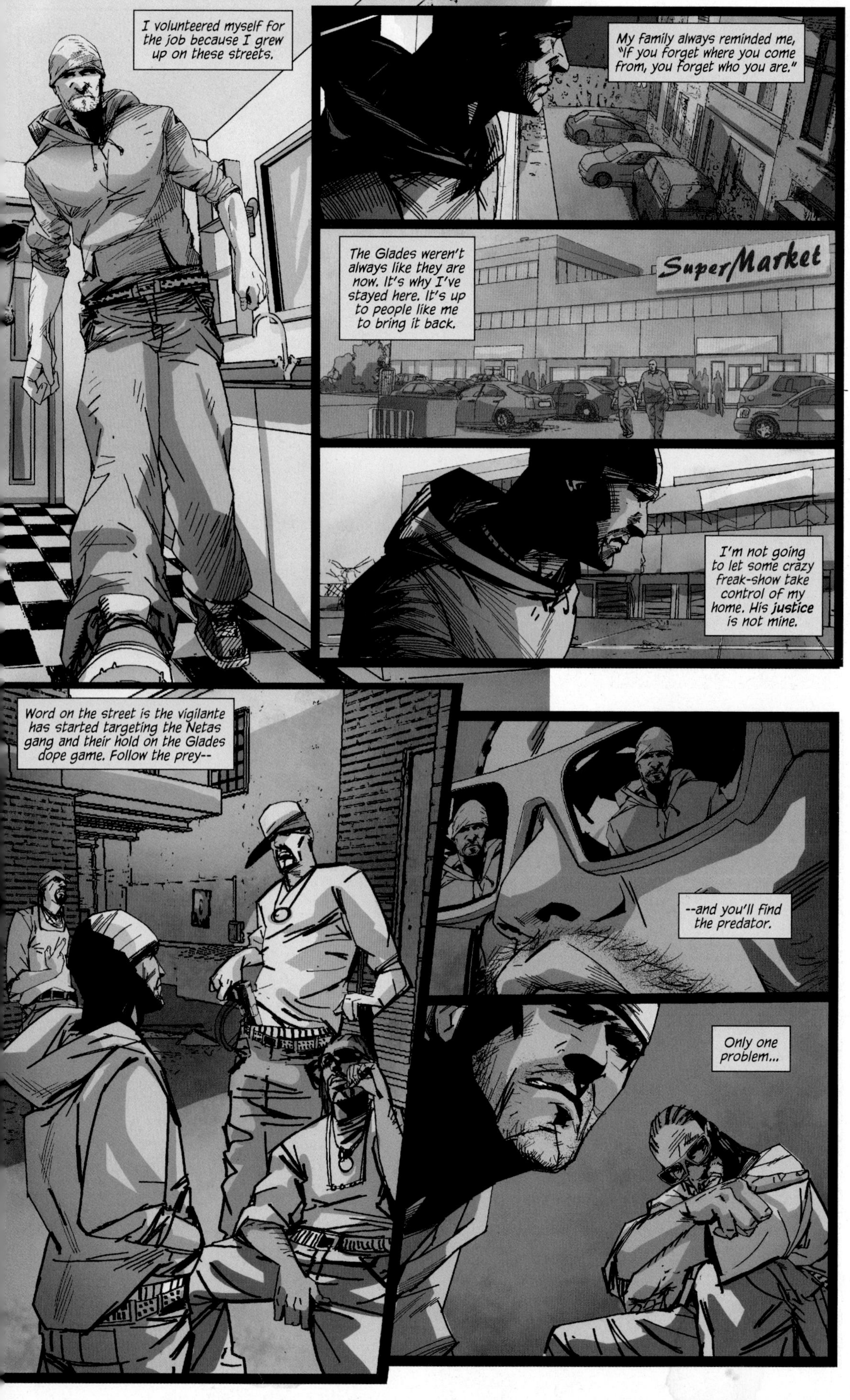
I volunteered myself for the job because I grew up on these streets.
My family always reminded me, "If you forget where you come from, you forget who you are."
The Glades weren't always like they are now. It's why I've stayed here. It's up to people like me to bring it back.
SuperMarket
I'm not going to let some crazy freak-show take control of my home. His justice is not mine.
Word on the street is the vigilante has started targeting the Netas gang and their hold on the Glades dope game. Follow the prey--
--and you'll find the predator.
Only one problem...

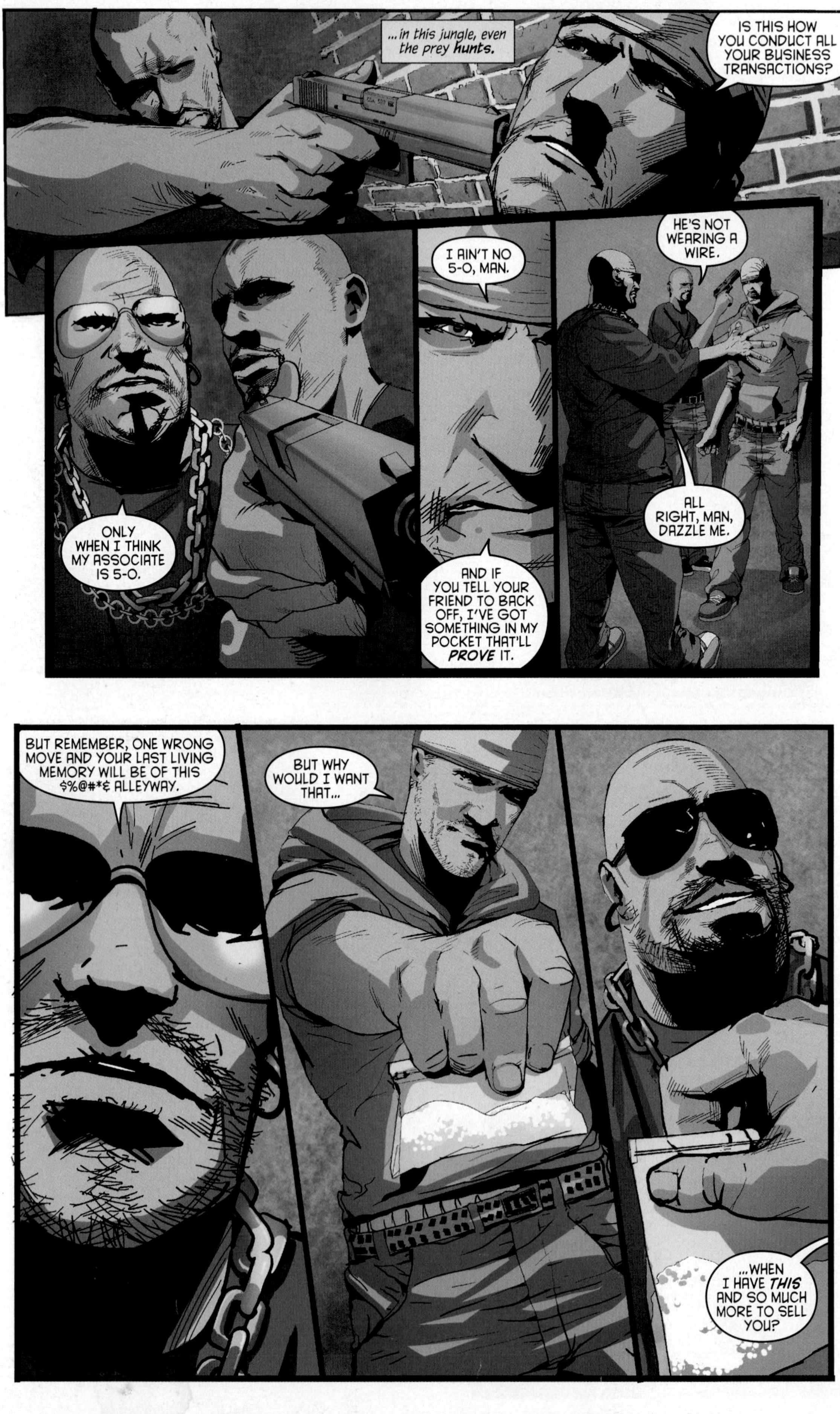
...in this jungle, even the prey hunts.
IS THIS HOW YOU CONDUCT ALL YOUR BUSINESS TRANSACTIONS?
ONLY WHEN I THINK MY ASSOCIATE IS 5-O.
I AIN'T NO 5-O, MAN.
AND IF YOU TELL YOUR FRIEND TO BACK OFF, I'VE GOT SOMETHING IN MY POCKET THAT'LL PROVE IT.
HE'S NOT WEARING A WIRE.
ALL RIGHT, MAN, DAZZLE ME.
BUT REMEMBER, ONE WRONG MOVE AND YOUR LAST LIVING MEMORY WILL BE OF THIS $%@#*& ALLEYWAY.
BUT WHY WOULD I WANT THAT...
...WHEN I HAVE THIS AND SO MUCH MORE TO SELL YOU?

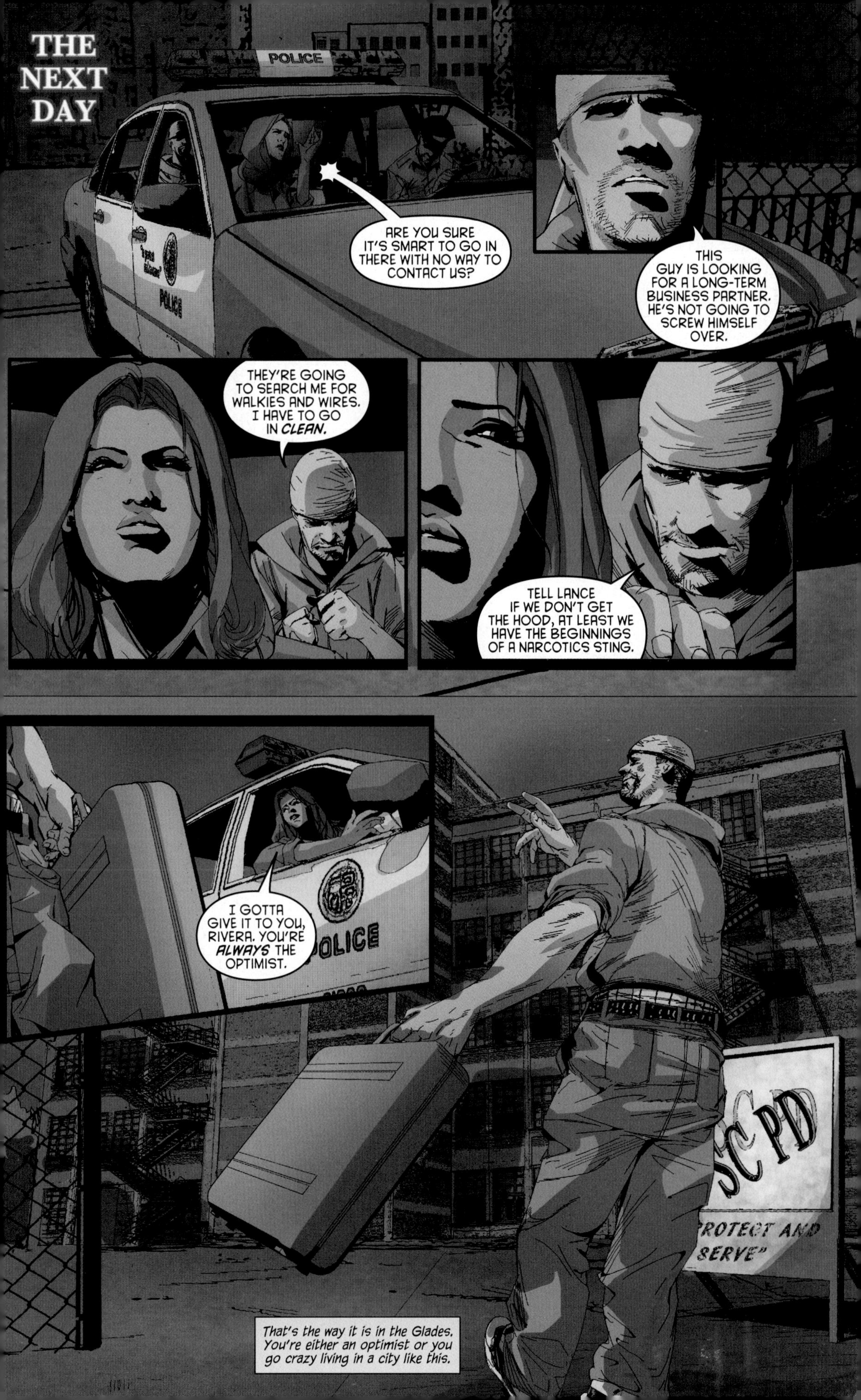
THE NEXT DAY
POLICE
ARE YOU SURE IT'S SMART TO GO IN THERE WITH NO WAY TO CONTACT US?
THIS GUY IS LOOKING FOR A LONG-TERM BUSINESS PARTNER. HE'S NOT GOING TO SCREW HIMSELF OVER.
THEY'RE GOING TO SEARCH ME FOR WALKIES AND WIRES. I HAVE TO GO IN *CLEAN.*
TELL LANCE IF WE DON'T GET THE HOOD, AT LEAST WE HAVE THE BEGINNINGS OF A NARCOTICS STING.
I GOTTA GIVE IT TO YOU, RIVERA. YOU'RE *ALWAYS* THE OPTIMIST.
POLICE
SCPD
"PROTECT AND SERVE"
That's the way it is in the Glades. You're either an optimist or you go crazy living in a city like this.

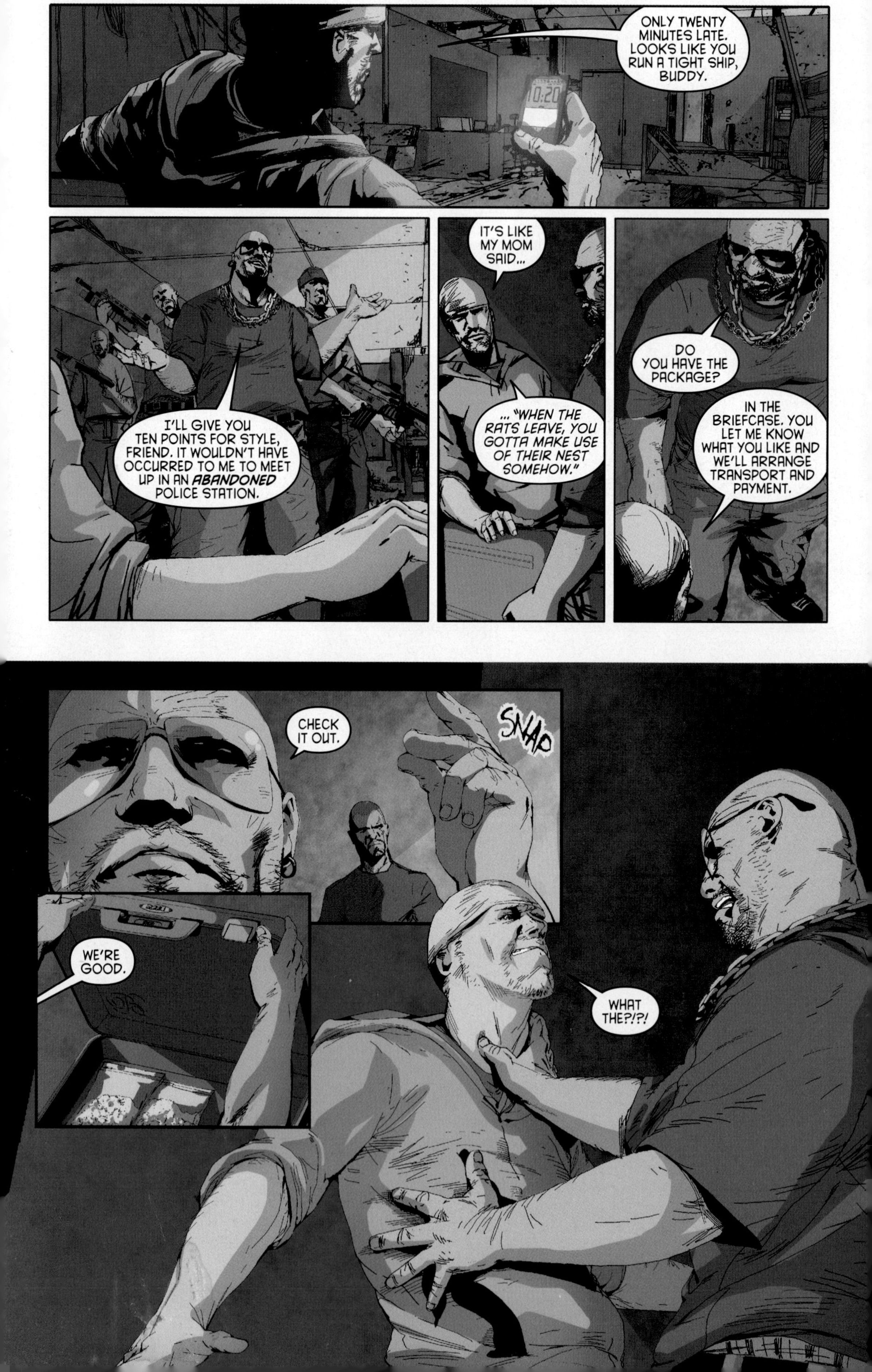
ONLY TWENTY MINUTES LATE. LOOKS LIKE YOU RUN A TIGHT SHIP, BUDDY.
10:20
I'LL GIVE YOU TEN POINTS FOR STYLE, FRIEND. IT WOULDN'T HAVE OCCURRED TO ME TO MEET UP IN AN ABANDONED POLICE STATION.
IT'S LIKE MY MOM SAID...
..."WHEN THE RATS LEAVE, YOU GOTTA MAKE USE OF THEIR NEST SOMEHOW."
DO YOU HAVE THE PACKAGE?
IN THE BRIEFCASE. YOU LET ME KNOW WHAT YOU LIKE AND WE'LL ARRANGE TRANSPORT AND PAYMENT.
CHECK IT OUT.
SNAP
WE'RE GOOD.
WHAT THE?!?!

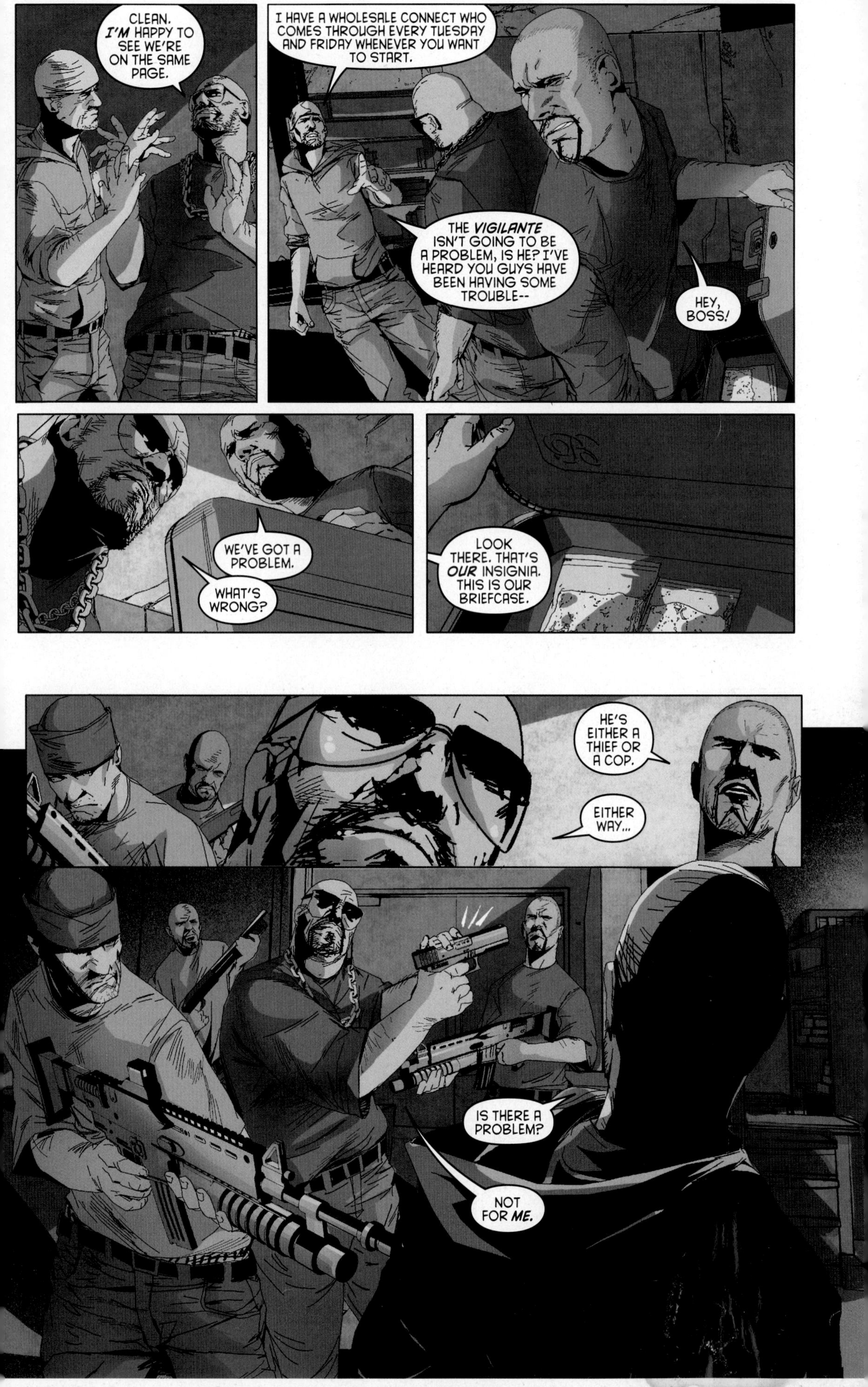
CLEAN. *I'M* HAPPY TO SEE WE'RE ON THE SAME PAGE.
I HAVE A WHOLESALE CONNECT WHO COMES THROUGH EVERY TUESDAY AND FRIDAY WHENEVER YOU WANT TO START.
THE *VIGILANTE* ISN'T GOING TO BE A PROBLEM, IS HE? I'VE HEARD YOU GUYS HAVE BEEN HAVING SOME TROUBLE--
HEY, BOSS!
WE'VE GOT A PROBLEM.
WHAT'S WRONG?
LOOK THERE. THAT'S *OUR* INSIGNIA. THIS IS OUR BRIEFCASE.
HE'S EITHER A THIEF OR A COP.
EITHER WAY...
IS THERE A PROBLEM?
NOT FOR *ME.*

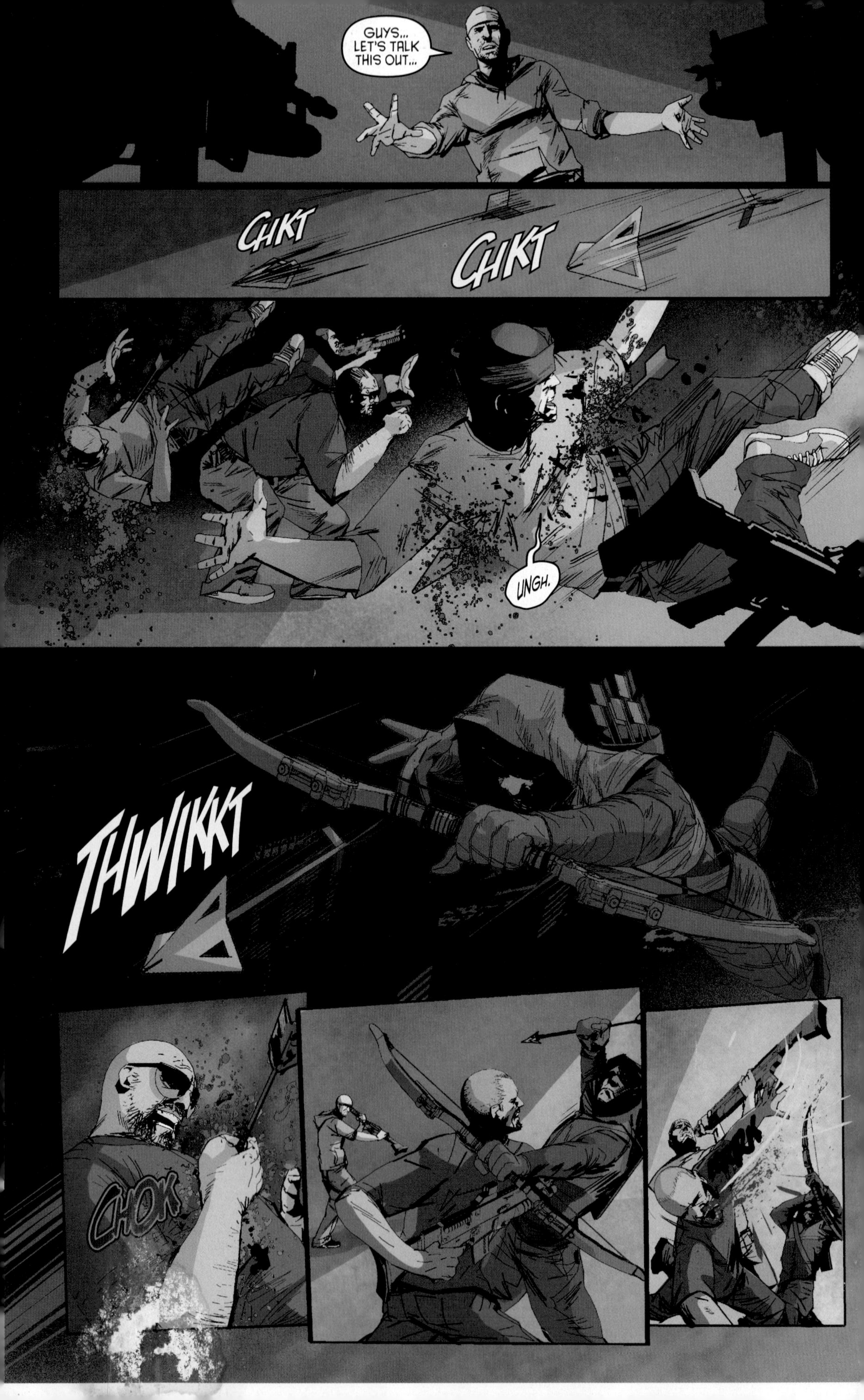
GUYS... LET'S TALK THIS OUT...
CHKT
CHKT
UNGH.
THWIKKT
CHOK

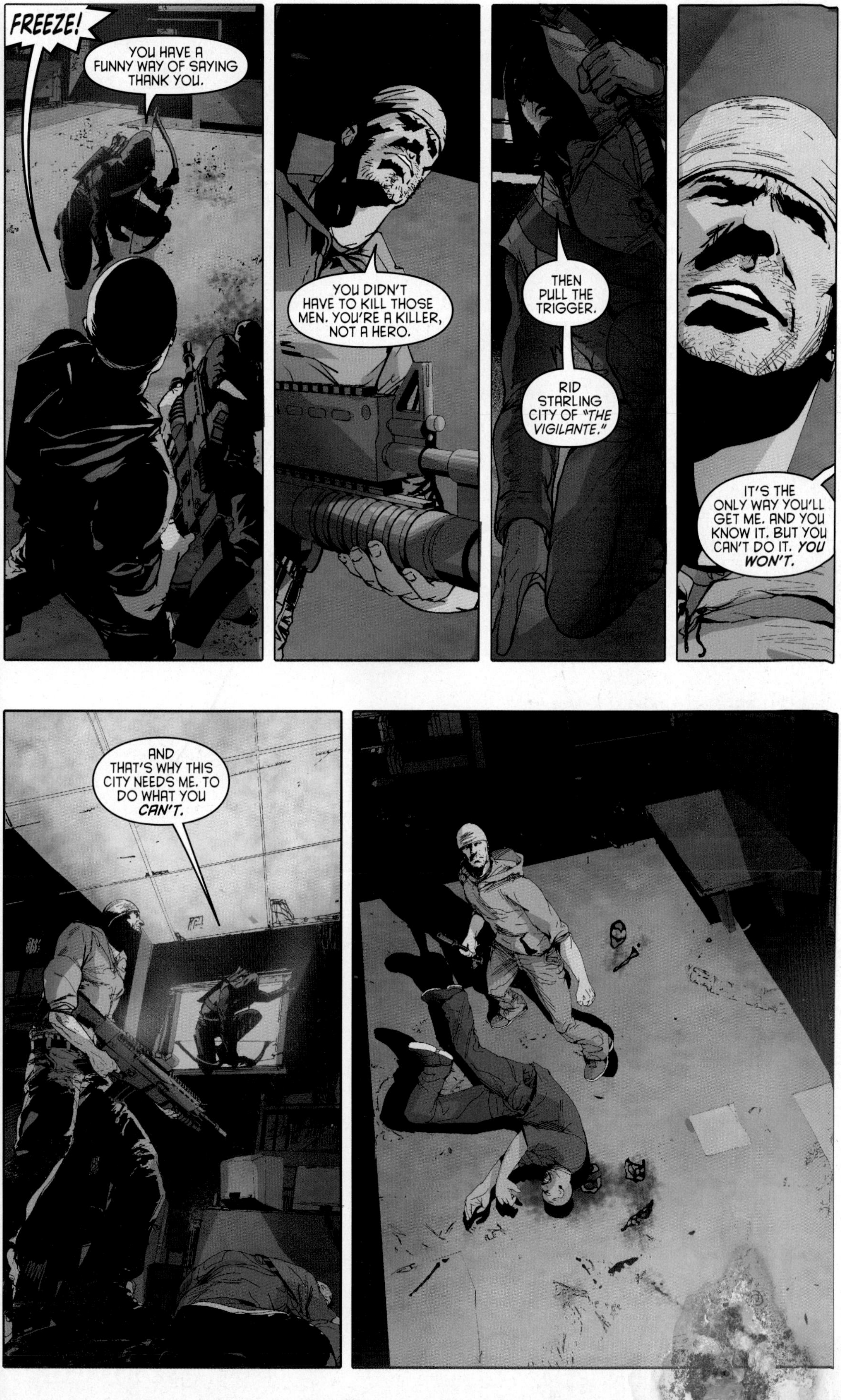
FREEZE!
YOU HAVE A FUNNY WAY OF SAYING THANK YOU.
YOU DIDN'T HAVE TO KILL THOSE MEN. YOU'RE A KILLER, NOT A HERO.
THEN PULL THE TRIGGER.
RID STARLING CITY OF "THE VIGILANTE."
IT'S THE ONLY WAY YOU'LL GET ME. AND YOU KNOW IT. BUT YOU CAN'T DO IT. YOU WON'T.
AND THAT'S WHY THIS CITY NEEDS ME. TO DO WHAT YOU CAN'T.

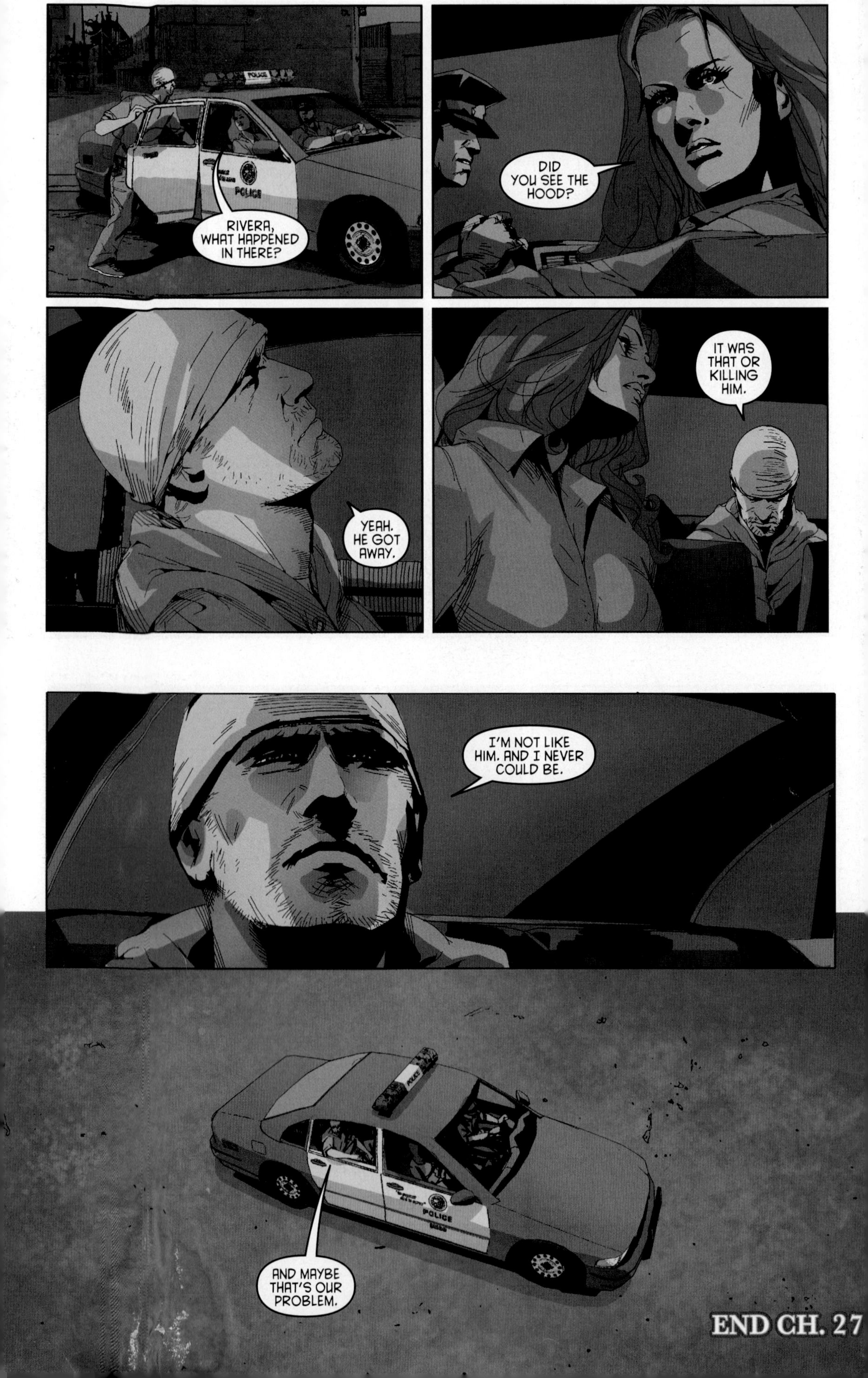
RIVERA, WHAT HAPPENED IN THERE?
DID YOU SEE THE HOOD?
YEAH. HE GOT AWAY.
IT WAS THAT OR KILLING HIM.
I'M NOT LIKE HIM. AND I NEVER COULD BE.
AND MAYBE THAT'S OUR PROBLEM.
END CH. 27

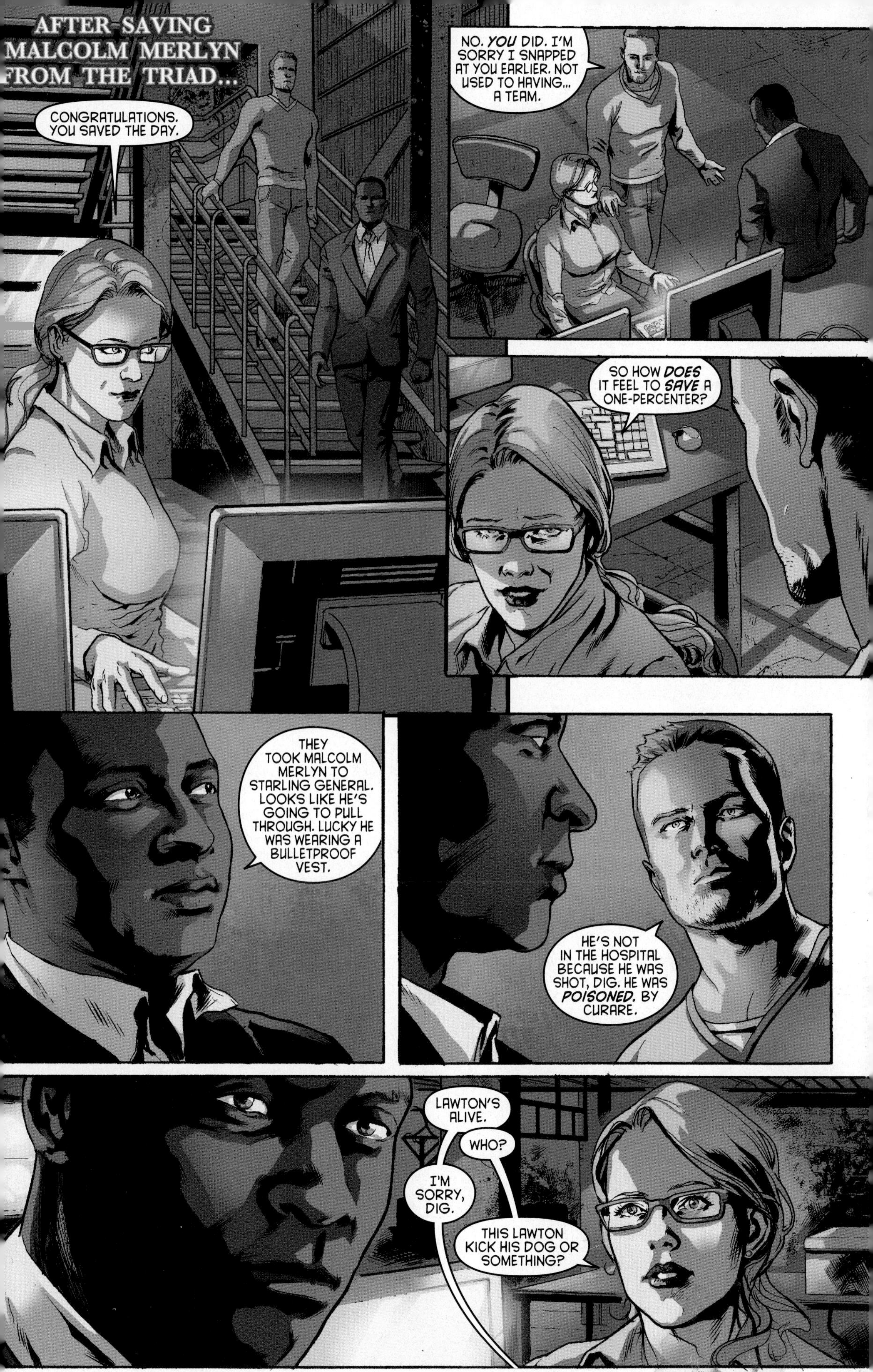
AFTER SAVING MALCOLM MERLYN FROM THE TRIAD...
CONGRATULATIONS. YOU SAVED THE DAY.
NO. YOU DID. I'M SORRY I SNAPPED AT YOU EARLIER. NOT USED TO HAVING... A TEAM.
SO HOW DOES IT FEEL TO SAVE A ONE-PERCENTER?
THEY TOOK MALCOLM MERLYN TO STARLING GENERAL. LOOKS LIKE HE'S GOING TO PULL THROUGH. LUCKY HE WAS WEARING A BULLETPROOF VEST.
HE'S NOT IN THE HOSPITAL BECAUSE HE WAS SHOT, DIG. HE WAS POISONED. BY CURARE.
LAWTON'S ALIVE.
WHO?
I'M SORRY, DIG.
THIS LAWTON KICK HIS DOG OR SOMETHING?

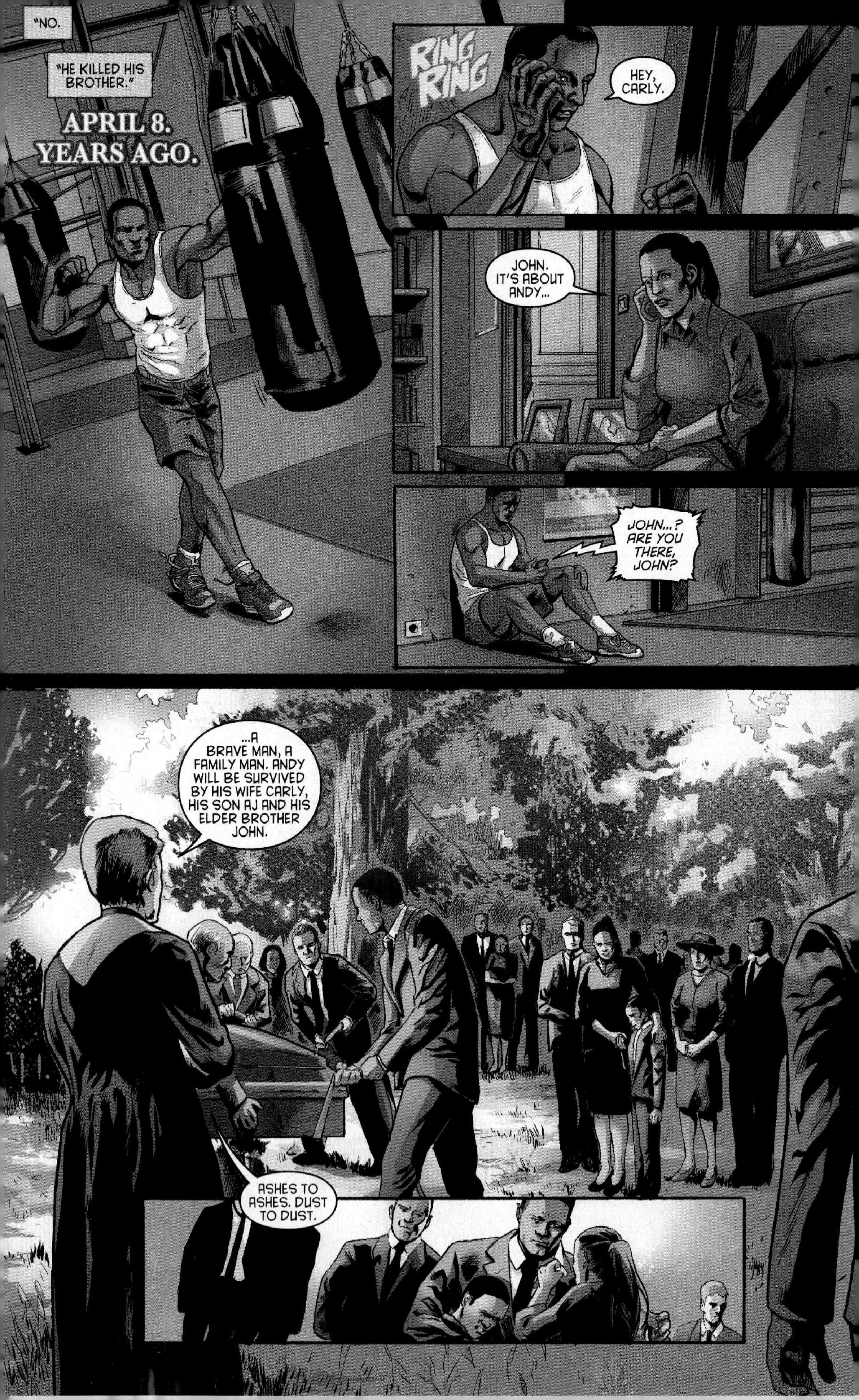
"NO.
"HE KILLED HIS BROTHER."
APRIL 8. YEARS AGO.
RING RING
HEY, CARLY.
JOHN. IT'S ABOUT ANDY...
JOHN...? ARE YOU THERE, JOHN?
...A BRAVE MAN, A FAMILY MAN. ANDY WILL BE SURVIVED BY HIS WIFE CARLY, HIS SON AJ AND HIS ELDER BROTHER JOHN.
ASHES TO ASHES. DUST TO DUST.

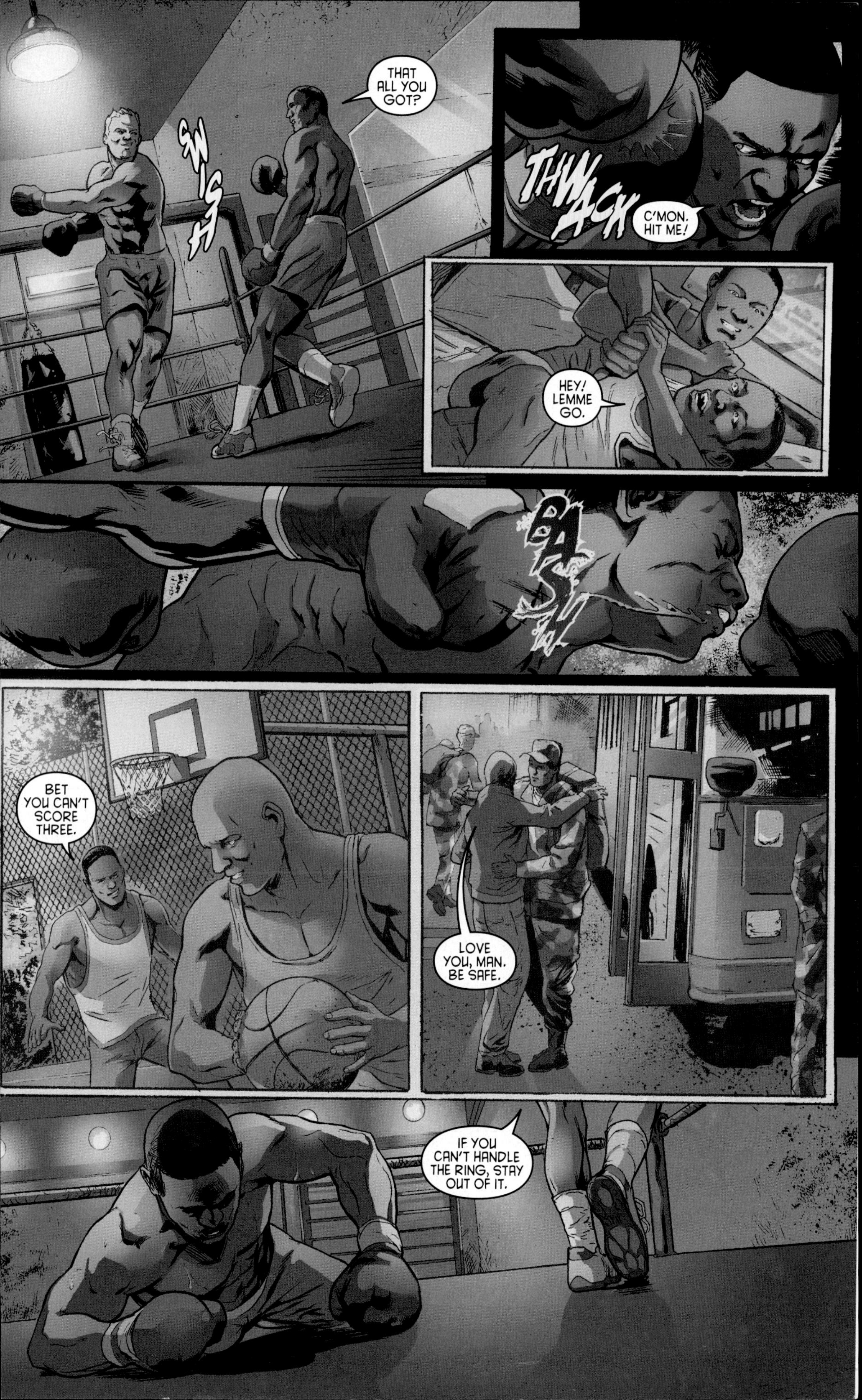
SWISH
THAT ALL YOU GOT?
THWACK
C'MON. HIT ME!
HEY! LEMME GO.
BASH
BET YOU CAN'T SCORE THREE.
LOVE YOU, MAN. BE SAFE.
IF YOU CAN'T HANDLE THE RING, STAY OUT OF IT.

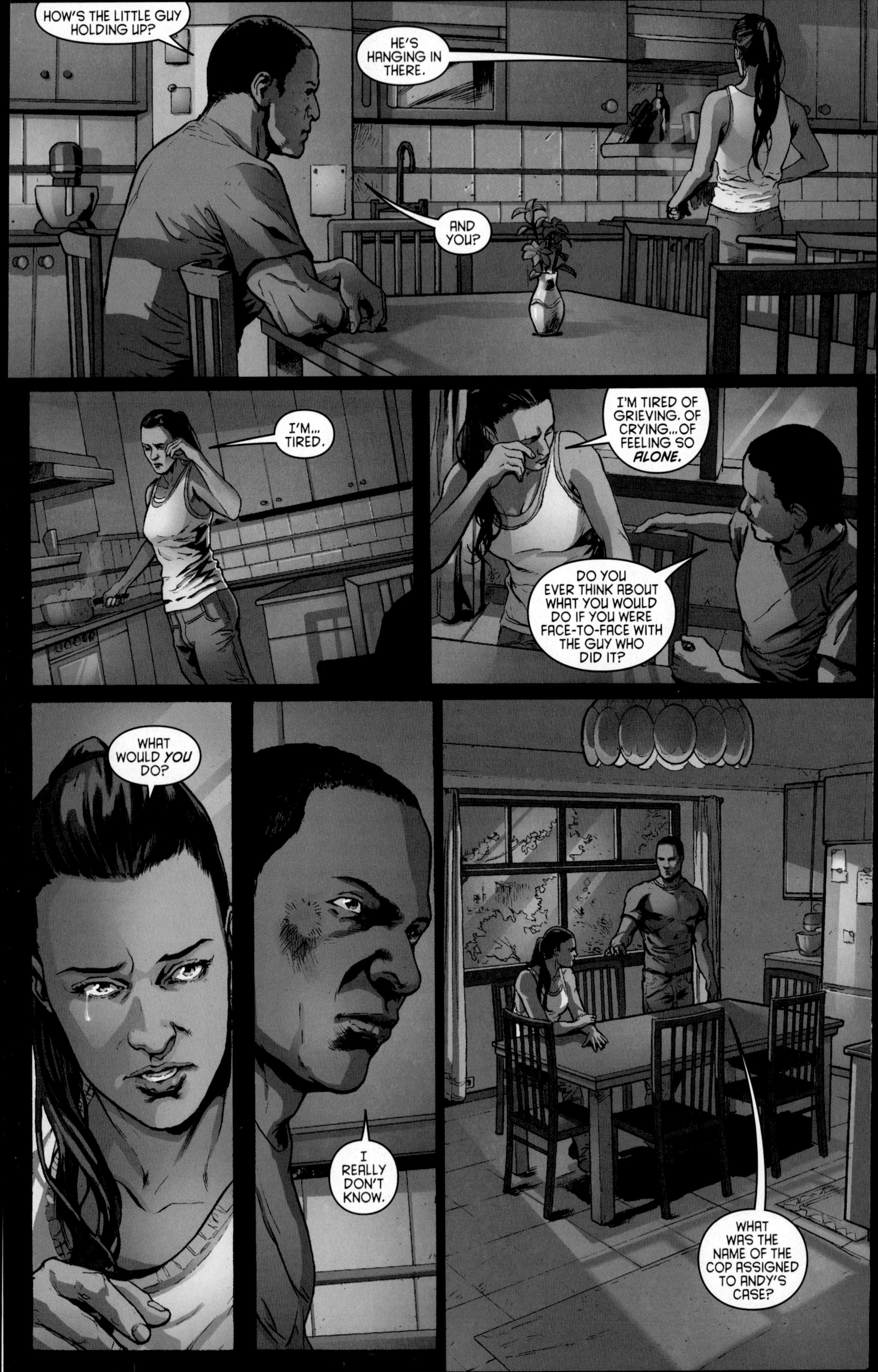
HOW'S THE LITTLE GUY HOLDING UP?
HE'S HANGING IN THERE.
AND YOU?
I'M... TIRED.
I'M TIRED OF GRIEVING. OF CRYING... OF FEELING SO *ALONE.*
DO YOU EVER THINK ABOUT WHAT YOU WOULD DO IF YOU WERE FACE-TO-FACE WITH THE GUY WHO DID IT?
WHAT WOULD *YOU* DO?
I REALLY DON'T KNOW.
WHAT WAS THE NAME OF THE COP ASSIGNED TO ANDY'S CASE?

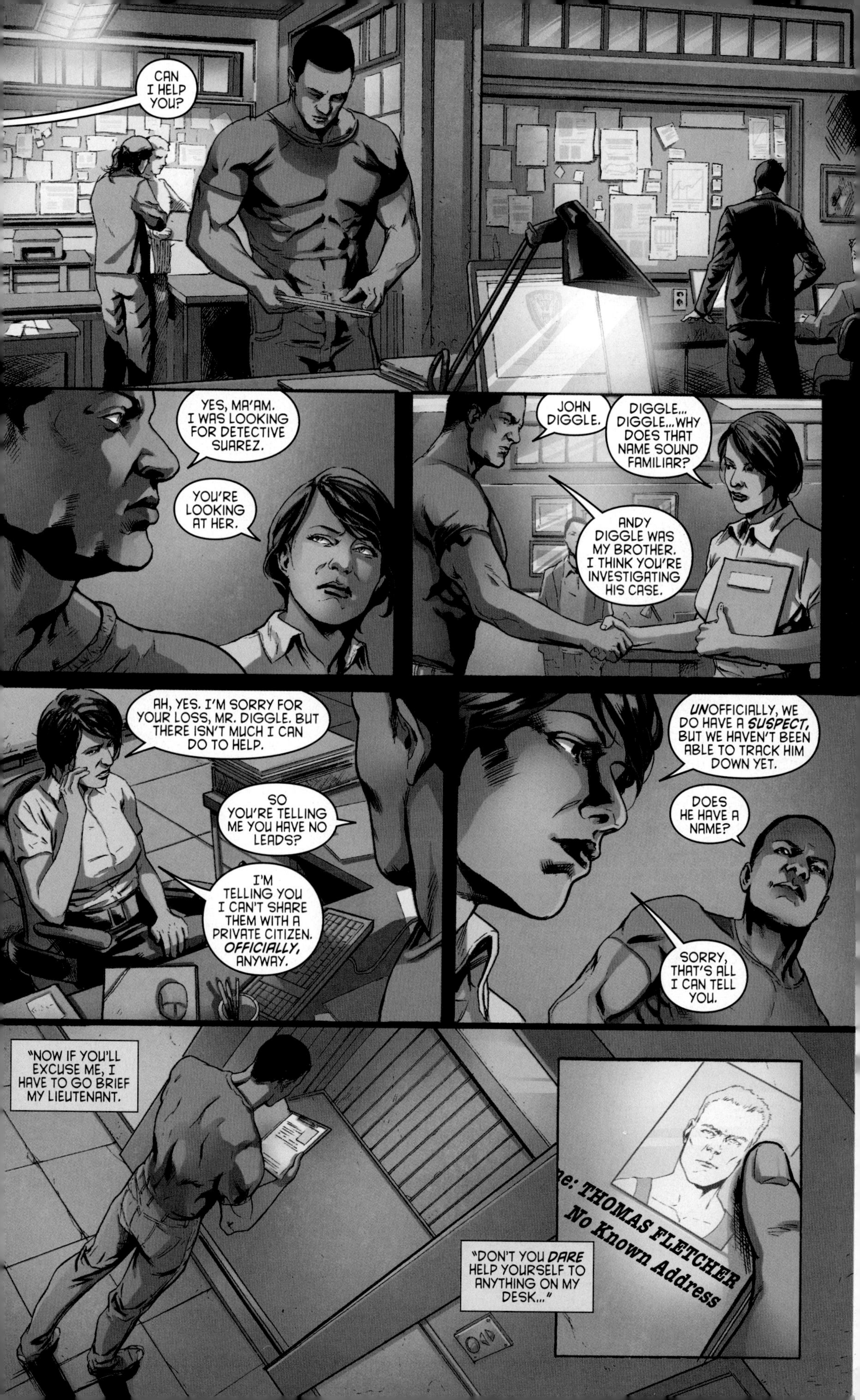
CAN I HELP YOU?
YES, MA'AM. I WAS LOOKING FOR DETECTIVE SUAREZ.
YOU'RE LOOKING AT HER.
JOHN DIGGLE.
DIGGLE... DIGGLE...WHY DOES THAT NAME SOUND FAMILIAR?
ANDY DIGGLE WAS MY BROTHER. I THINK YOU'RE INVESTIGATING HIS CASE.
AH, YES. I'M SORRY FOR YOUR LOSS, MR. DIGGLE. BUT THERE ISN'T MUCH I CAN DO TO HELP.
SO YOU'RE TELLING ME YOU HAVE NO LEADS?
I'M TELLING YOU I CAN'T SHARE THEM WITH A PRIVATE CITIZEN. OFFICIALLY, ANYWAY.
UNOFFICIALLY, WE DO HAVE A SUSPECT, BUT WE HAVEN'T BEEN ABLE TO TRACK HIM DOWN YET.
DOES HE HAVE A NAME?
SORRY, THAT'S ALL I CAN TELL YOU.
"NOW IF YOU'LL EXCUSE ME, I HAVE TO GO BRIEF MY LIEUTENANT.
"DON'T YOU DARE HELP YOURSELF TO ANYTHING ON MY DESK..."
e: THOMAS FLETCHER
No Known Address

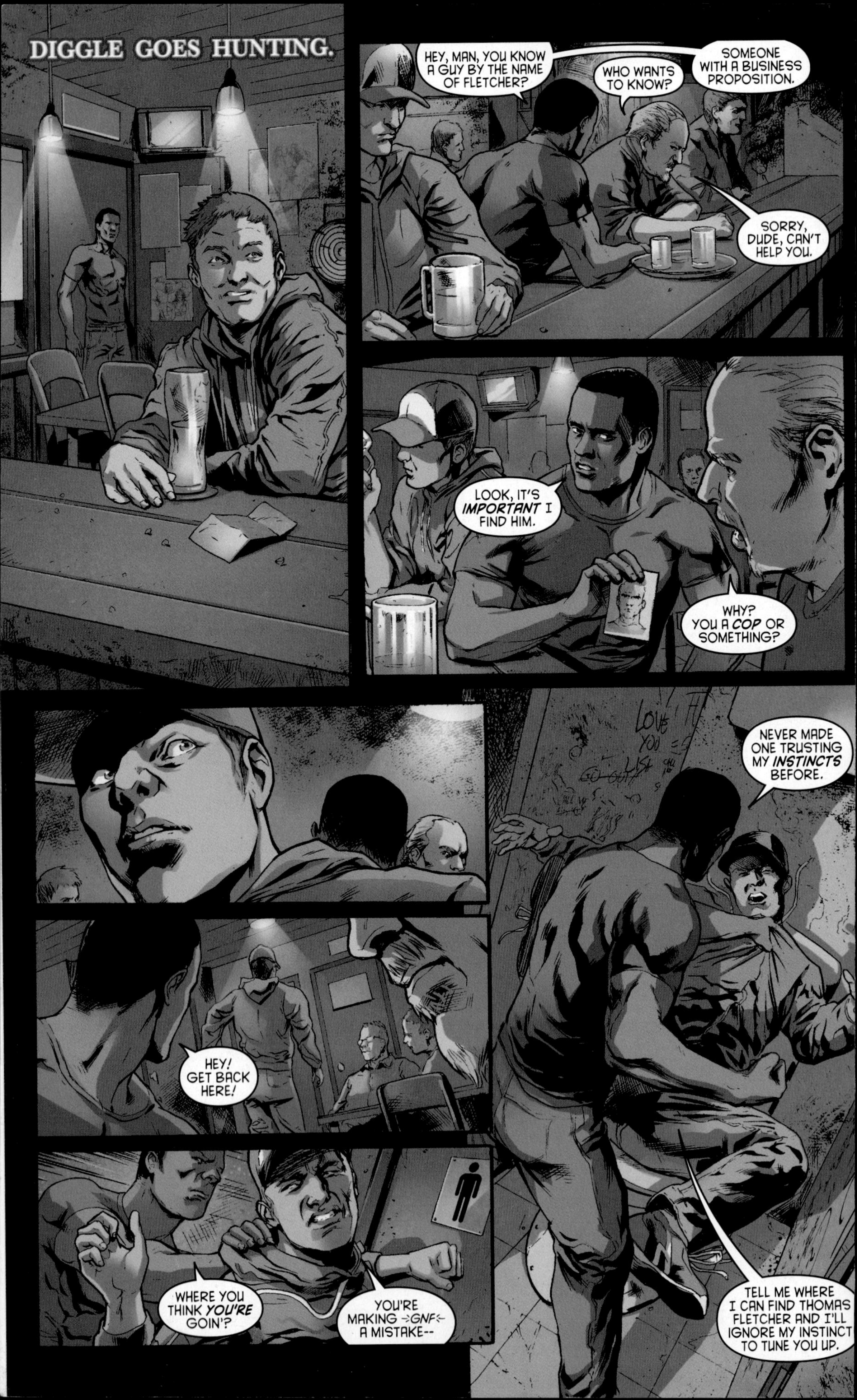
DIGGLE GOES HUNTING.
HEY, MAN, YOU KNOW A GUY BY THE NAME OF FLETCHER?
WHO WANTS TO KNOW?
SOMEONE WITH A BUSINESS PROPOSITION.
SORRY, DUDE, CAN'T HELP YOU.
LOOK, IT'S IMPORTANT I FIND HIM.
WHY? YOU A COP OR SOMETHING?
LOVE YOU
GO OUT
NEVER MADE ONE TRUSTING MY INSTINCTS BEFORE.
HEY! GET BACK HERE!
WHERE YOU THINK YOU'RE GOIN'?
YOU'RE MAKING -GNF- A MISTAKE--
TELL ME WHERE I CAN FIND THOMAS FLETCHER AND I'LL IGNORE MY INSTINCT TO TUNE YOU UP.

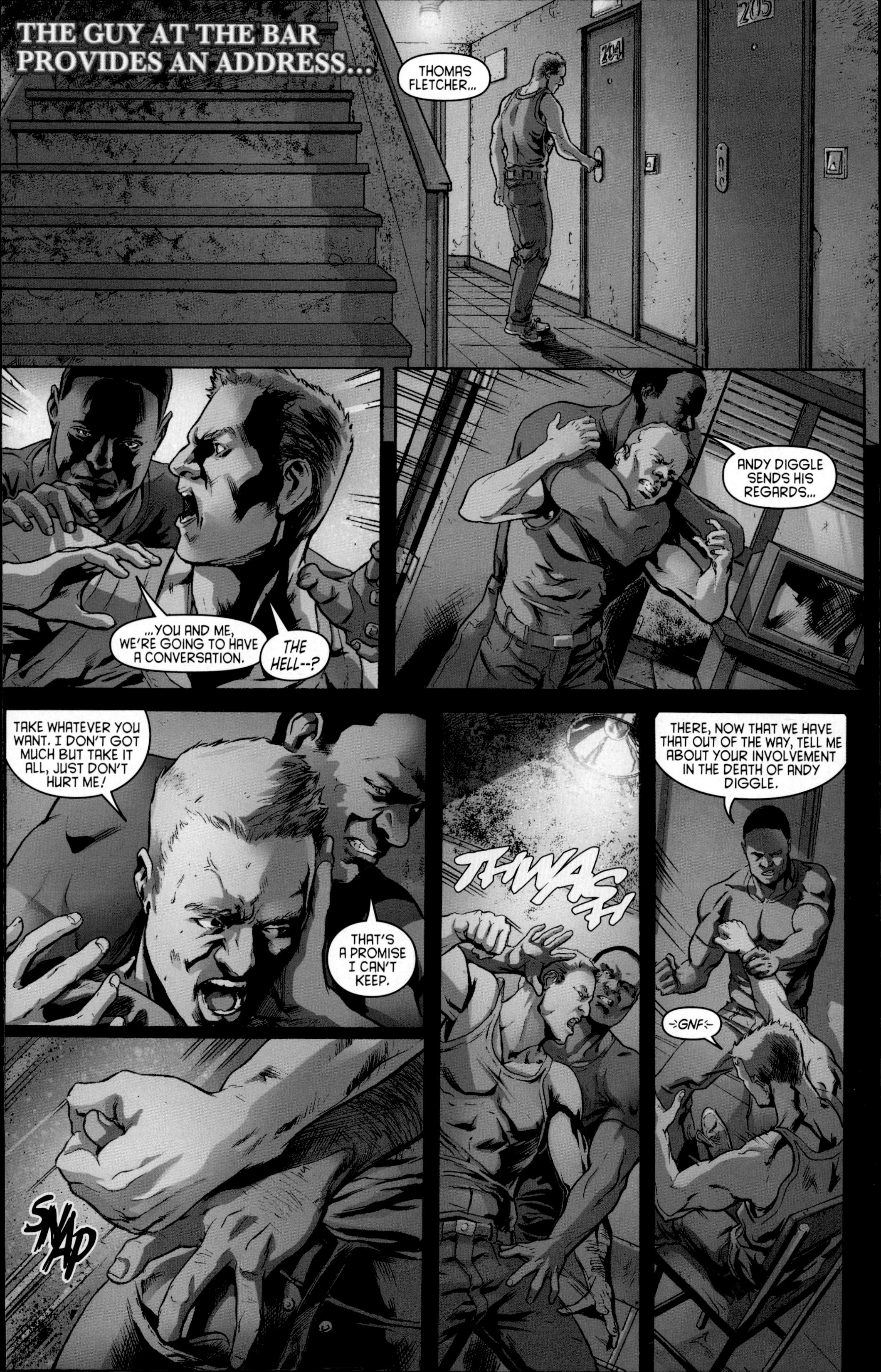
THE GUY AT THE BAR PROVIDES AN ADDRESS...
THOMAS FLETCHER...
...YOU AND ME, WE'RE GOING TO HAVE A CONVERSATION.
THE HELL--?
ANDY DIGGLE SENDS HIS REGARDS...
TAKE WHATEVER YOU WANT. I DON'T GOT MUCH BUT TAKE IT ALL, JUST DON'T HURT ME!
THAT'S A PROMISE I CAN'T KEEP.
SNAP
THWACK
THERE, NOW THAT WE HAVE THAT OUT OF THE WAY, TELL ME ABOUT YOUR INVOLVEMENT IN THE DEATH OF ANDY DIGGLE.
GNF

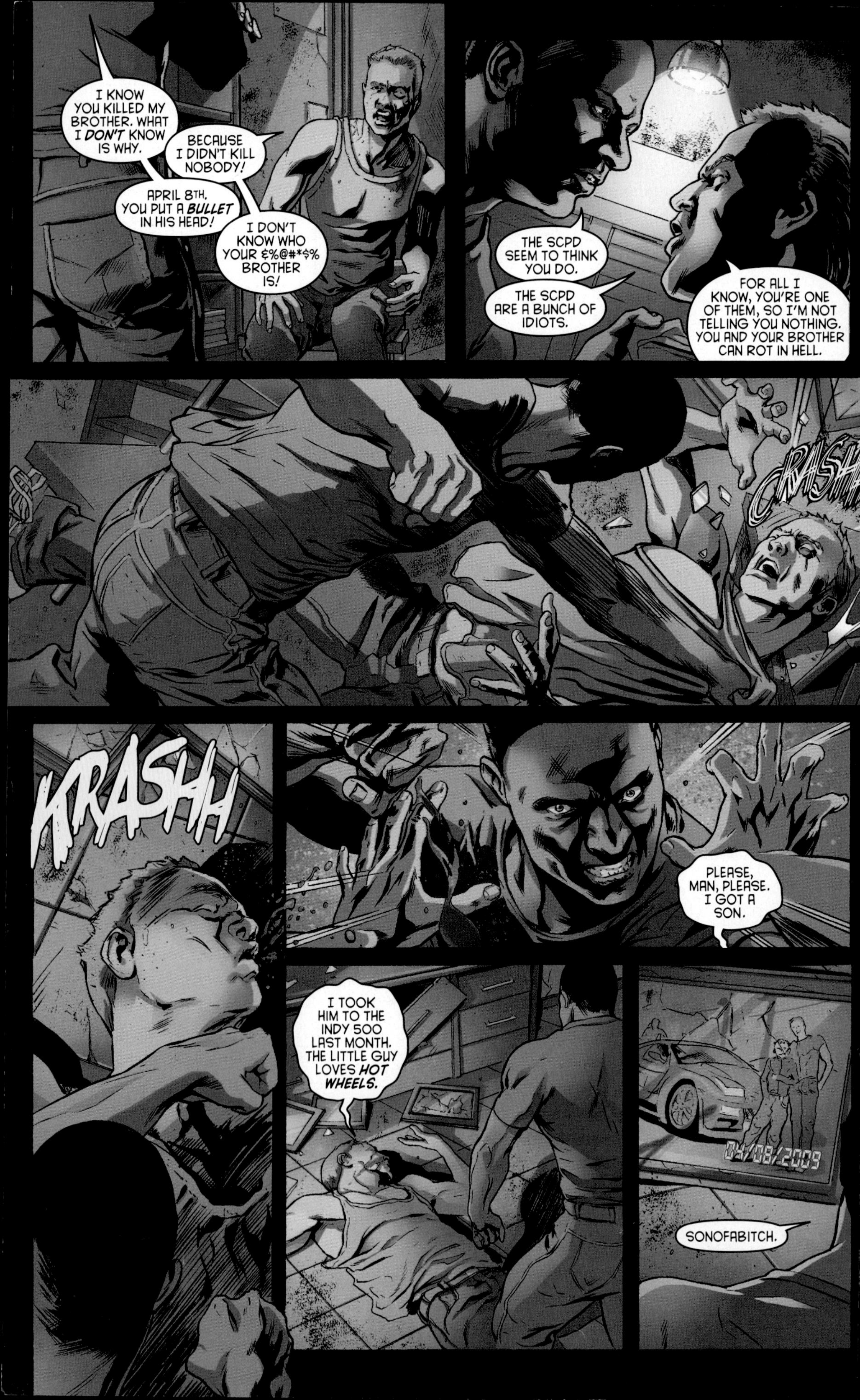
I KNOW YOU KILLED MY BROTHER. WHAT I *DON'T* KNOW IS WHY.
BECAUSE I DIDN'T KILL NOBODY!
APRIL 8TH. YOU PUT A *BULLET* IN HIS HEAD!
I DON'T KNOW WHO YOUR &%@#*$% BROTHER IS!
THE SCPD SEEM TO THINK YOU DO.
THE SCPD ARE A BUNCH OF IDIOTS.
FOR ALL I KNOW, YOU'RE ONE OF THEM, SO I'M NOT TELLING YOU NOTHING. YOU AND YOUR BROTHER CAN ROT IN HELL.
KRASHH
PLEASE, MAN, PLEASE. I GOT A SON.
I TOOK HIM TO THE INDY 500 LAST MONTH. THE LITTLE GUY LOVES *HOT WHEELS.*
04/08/2009
SONOFABITCH.

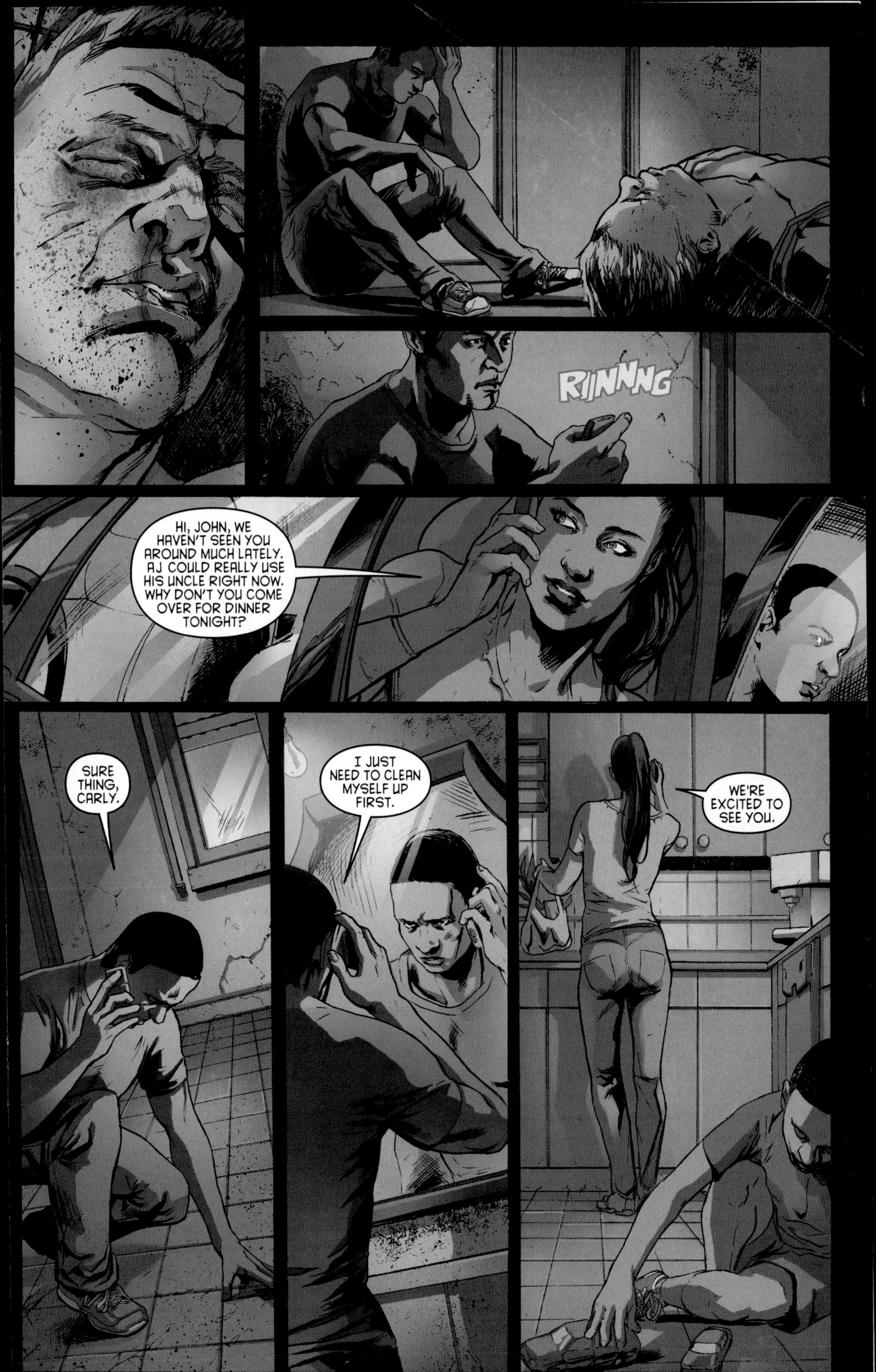
RIINNNG
HI, JOHN, WE HAVEN'T SEEN YOU AROUND MUCH LATELY. AJ COULD REALLY USE HIS UNCLE RIGHT NOW. WHY DON'T YOU COME OVER FOR DINNER TONIGHT?
SURE THING, CARLY.
I JUST NEED TO CLEAN MYSELF UP FIRST.
WE'RE EXCITED TO SEE YOU.

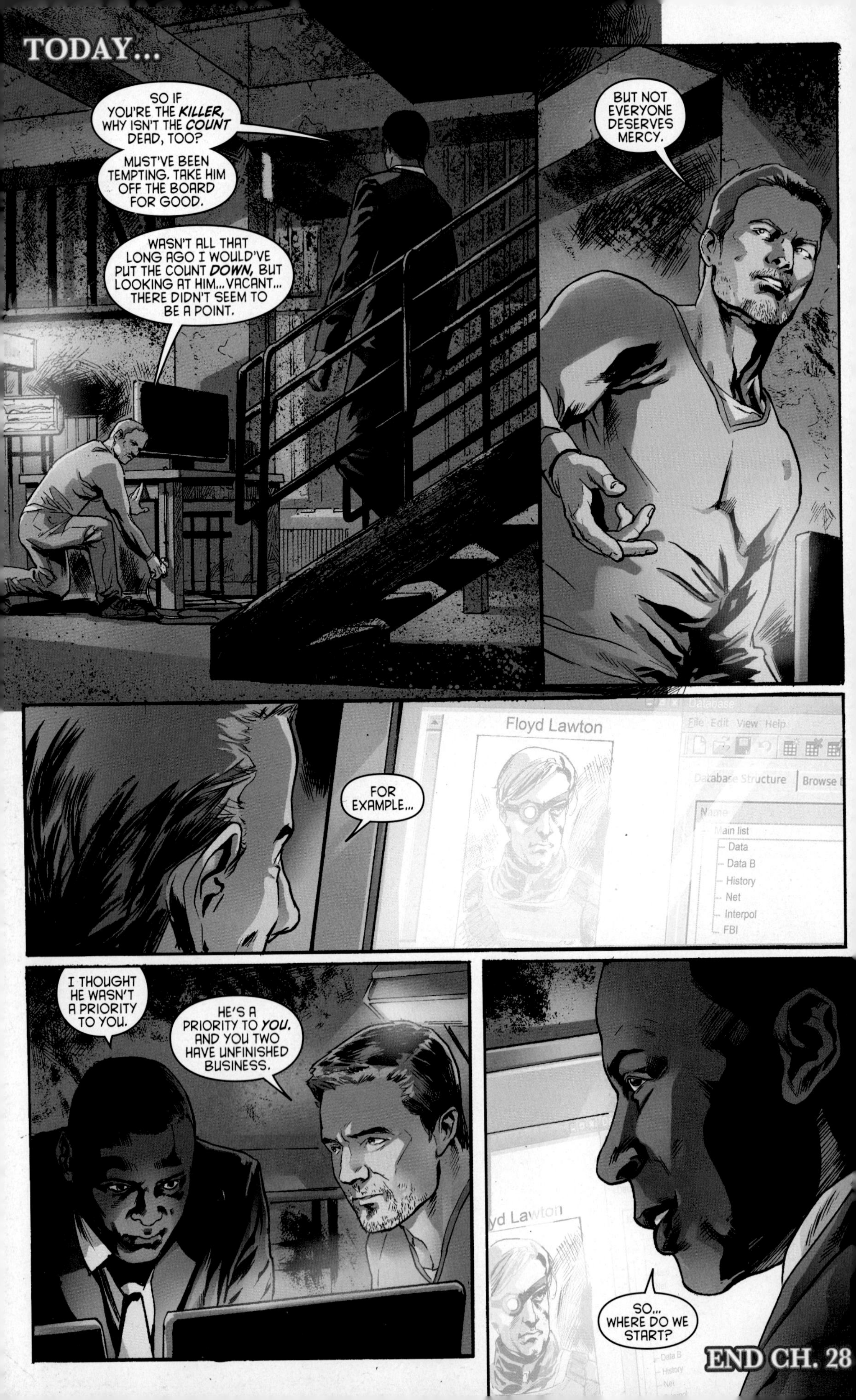
TODAY...
SO IF YOU'RE THE KILLER, WHY ISN'T THE COUNT DEAD, TOO?
MUST'VE BEEN TEMPTING. TAKE HIM OFF THE BOARD FOR GOOD.
WASN'T ALL THAT LONG AGO I WOULD'VE PUT THE COUNT DOWN, BUT LOOKING AT HIM... VACANT... THERE DIDN'T SEEM TO BE A POINT.
BUT NOT EVERYONE DESERVES MERCY.
Floyd Lawton
File Edit View Help
Database Structure
Browse
Name
Main list
Data
Data B
History
Net
Interpol
FBI
FOR EXAMPLE...
I THOUGHT HE WASN'T A PRIORITY TO YOU.
HE'S A PRIORITY TO YOU. AND YOU TWO HAVE UNFINISHED BUSINESS.
SO... WHERE DO WE START?
END CH. 28

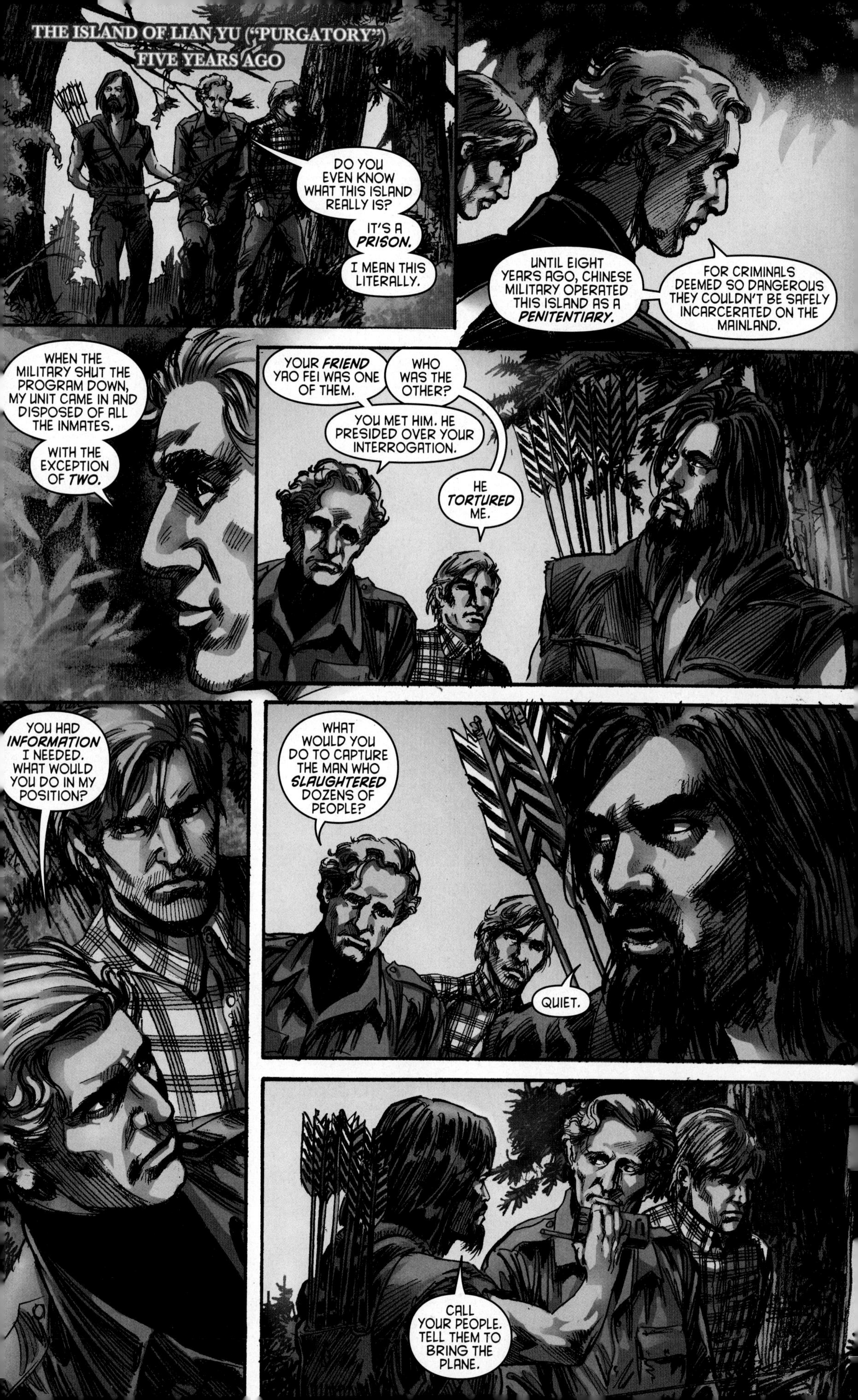
THE ISLAND OF LIAN YU ("PURGATORY")
FIVE YEARS AGO
DO YOU EVEN KNOW WHAT THIS ISLAND REALLY IS?
IT'S A PRISON.
I MEAN THIS LITERALLY.
UNTIL EIGHT YEARS AGO, CHINESE MILITARY OPERATED THIS ISLAND AS A PENITENTIARY.
FOR CRIMINALS DEEMED SO DANGEROUS THEY COULDN'T BE SAFELY INCARCERATED ON THE MAINLAND.
WHEN THE MILITARY SHUT THE PROGRAM DOWN, MY UNIT CAME IN AND DISPOSED OF ALL THE INMATES.
WITH THE EXCEPTION OF TWO.
YOUR FRIEND YAO FEI WAS ONE OF THEM.
WHO WAS THE OTHER?
YOU MET HIM. HE PRESIDED OVER YOUR INTERROGATION.
HE TORTURED ME.
YOU HAD INFORMATION I NEEDED. WHAT WOULD YOU DO IN MY POSITION?
WHAT WOULD YOU DO TO CAPTURE THE MAN WHO SLAUGHTERED DOZENS OF PEOPLE?
QUIET.
CALL YOUR PEOPLE. TELL THEM TO BRING THE PLANE.

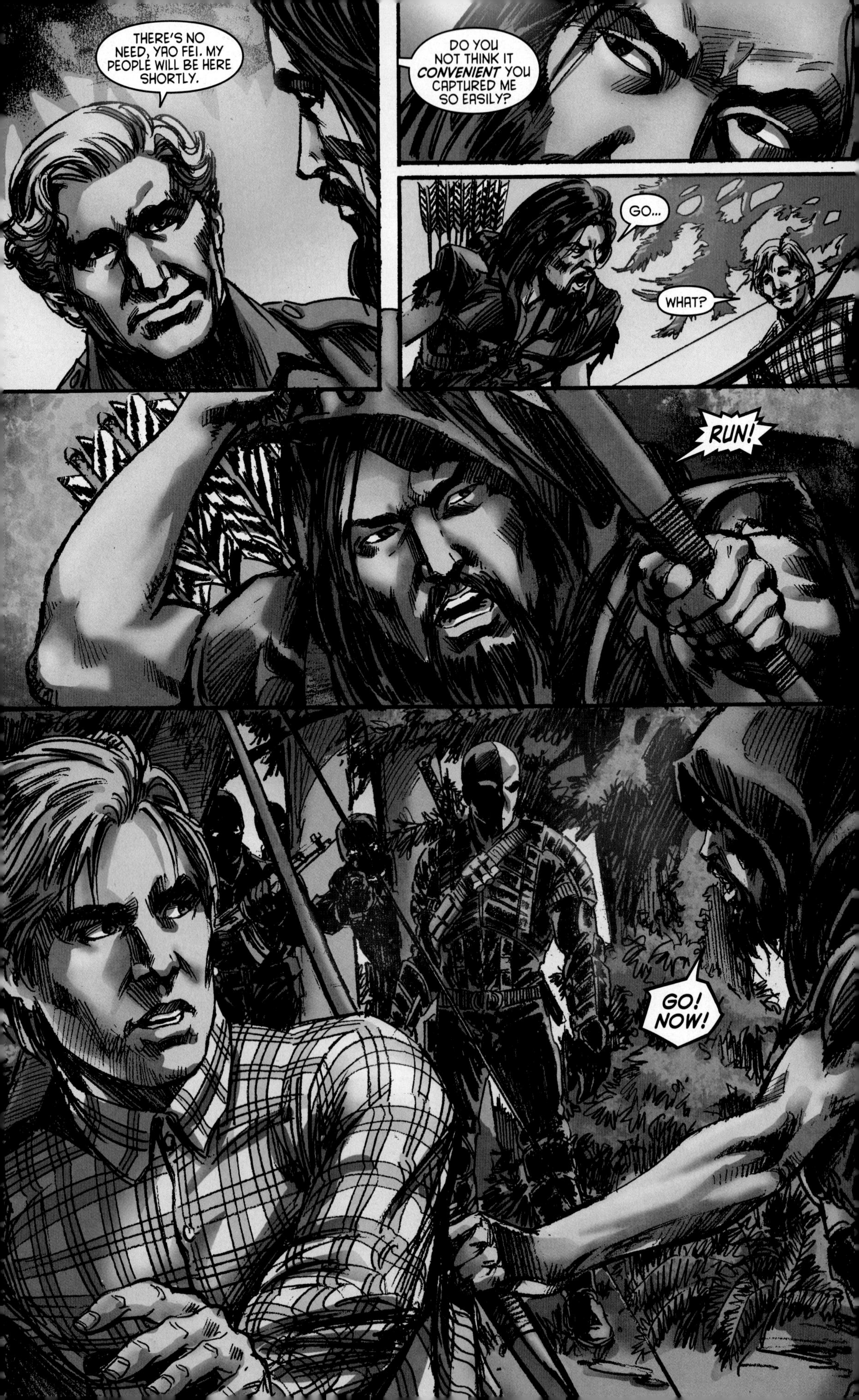
THERE'S NO NEED, YAO FEI. MY PEOPLE WILL BE HERE SHORTLY.
DO YOU NOT THINK IT CONVENIENT YOU CAPTURED ME SO EASILY?
GO...
WHAT?
RUN!
GO! NOW!

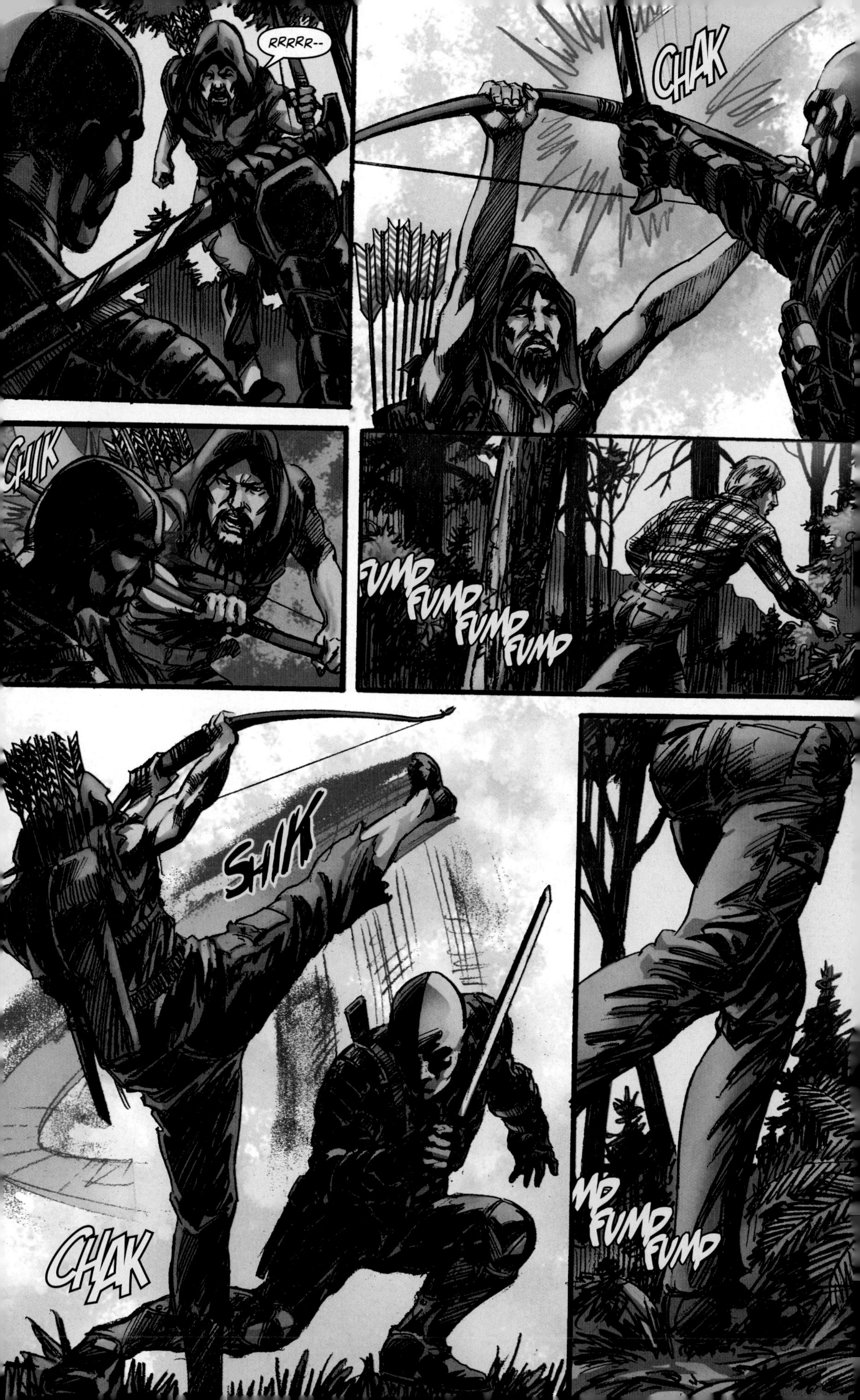
RRRRR--
CHAK
CHIK
FUMP FUMP FUMP FUMP
SHIK
CHAK
FUMP FUMP

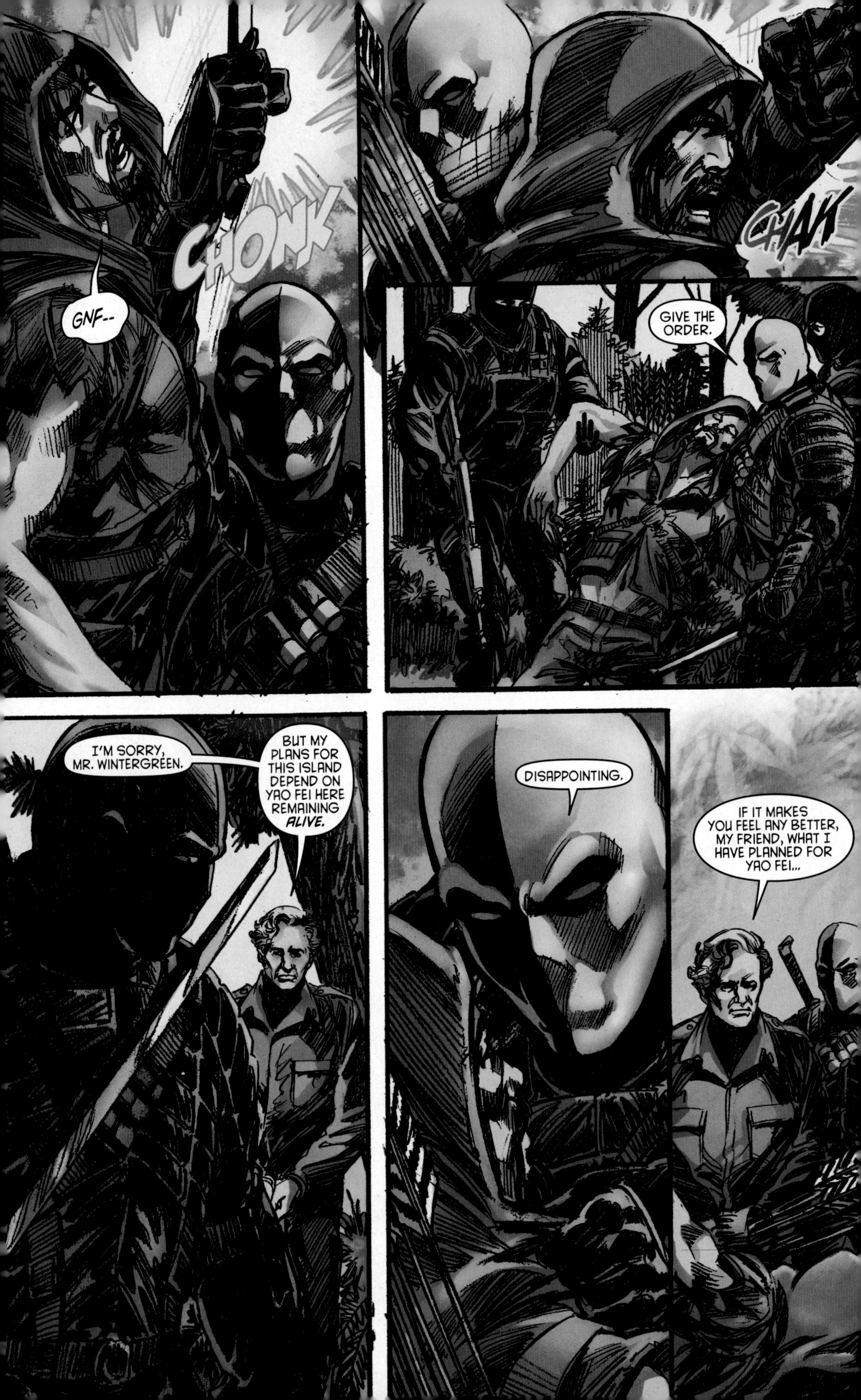
CHONK
GNF--
CHAK
GIVE THE ORDER.
I'M SORRY, MR. WINTERGREEN.
BUT MY PLANS FOR THIS ISLAND DEPEND ON YAO FEI HERE REMAINING *ALIVE*.
DISAPPOINTING.
IF IT MAKES YOU FEEL ANY BETTER, MY FRIEND, WHAT I HAVE PLANNED FOR YAO FEI...

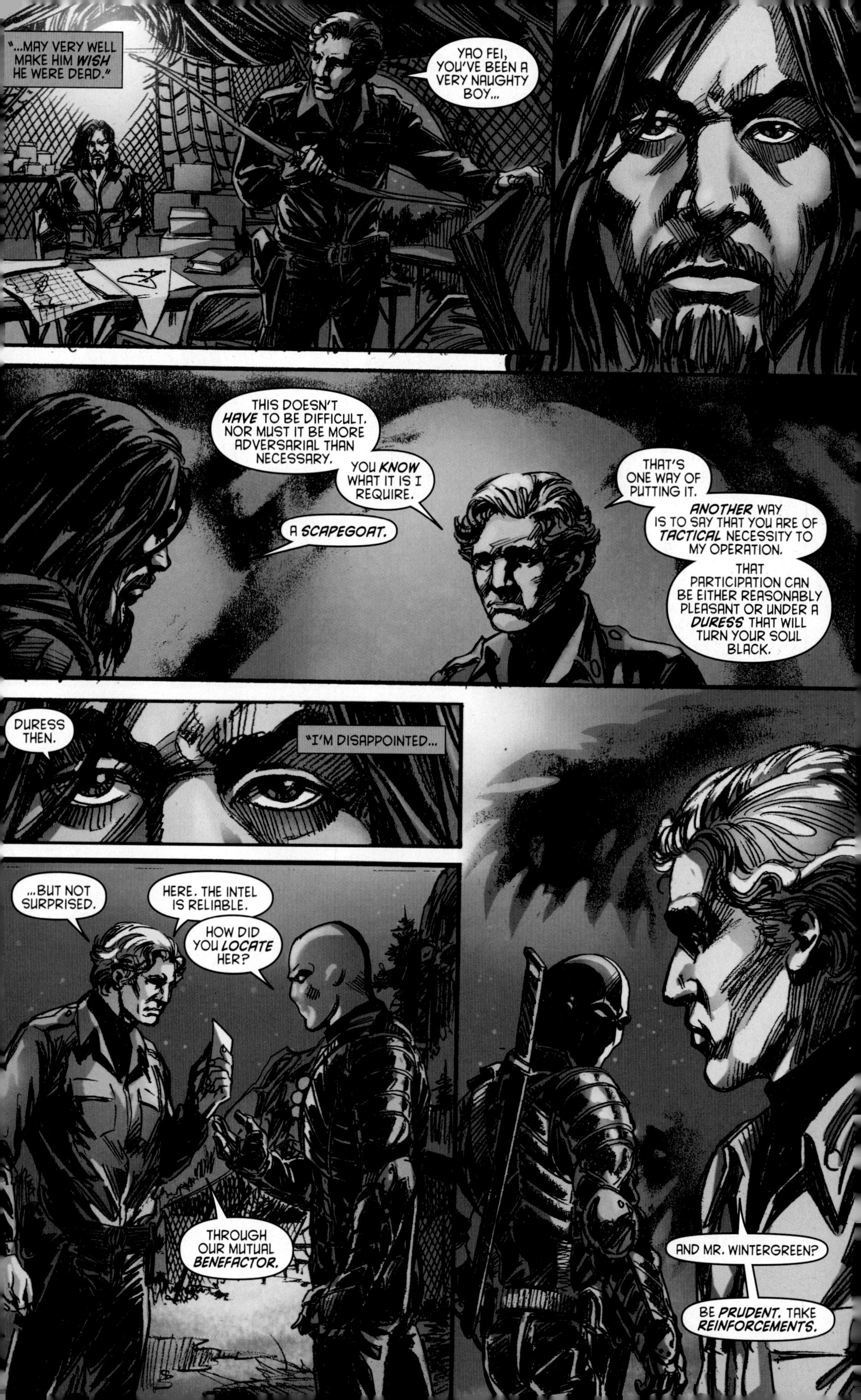
"...MAY VERY WELL MAKE HIM WISH HE WERE DEAD."
YAO FEI, YOU'VE BEEN A VERY NAUGHTY BOY...
THIS DOESN'T HAVE TO BE DIFFICULT. NOR MUST IT BE MORE ADVERSARIAL THAN NECESSARY.
YOU KNOW WHAT IT IS I REQUIRE.
A SCAPEGOAT.
THAT'S ONE WAY OF PUTTING IT.
ANOTHER WAY IS TO SAY THAT YOU ARE OF TACTICAL NECESSITY TO MY OPERATION.
THAT PARTICIPATION CAN BE EITHER REASONABLY PLEASANT OR UNDER A DURESS THAT WILL TURN YOUR SOUL BLACK.
DURESS THEN.
"I'M DISAPPOINTED...
...BUT NOT SURPRISED.
HERE. THE INTEL IS RELIABLE.
HOW DID YOU LOCATE HER?
THROUGH OUR MUTUAL BENEFACTOR.
AND MR. WINTERGREEN?
BE PRUDENT. TAKE REINFORCEMENTS.

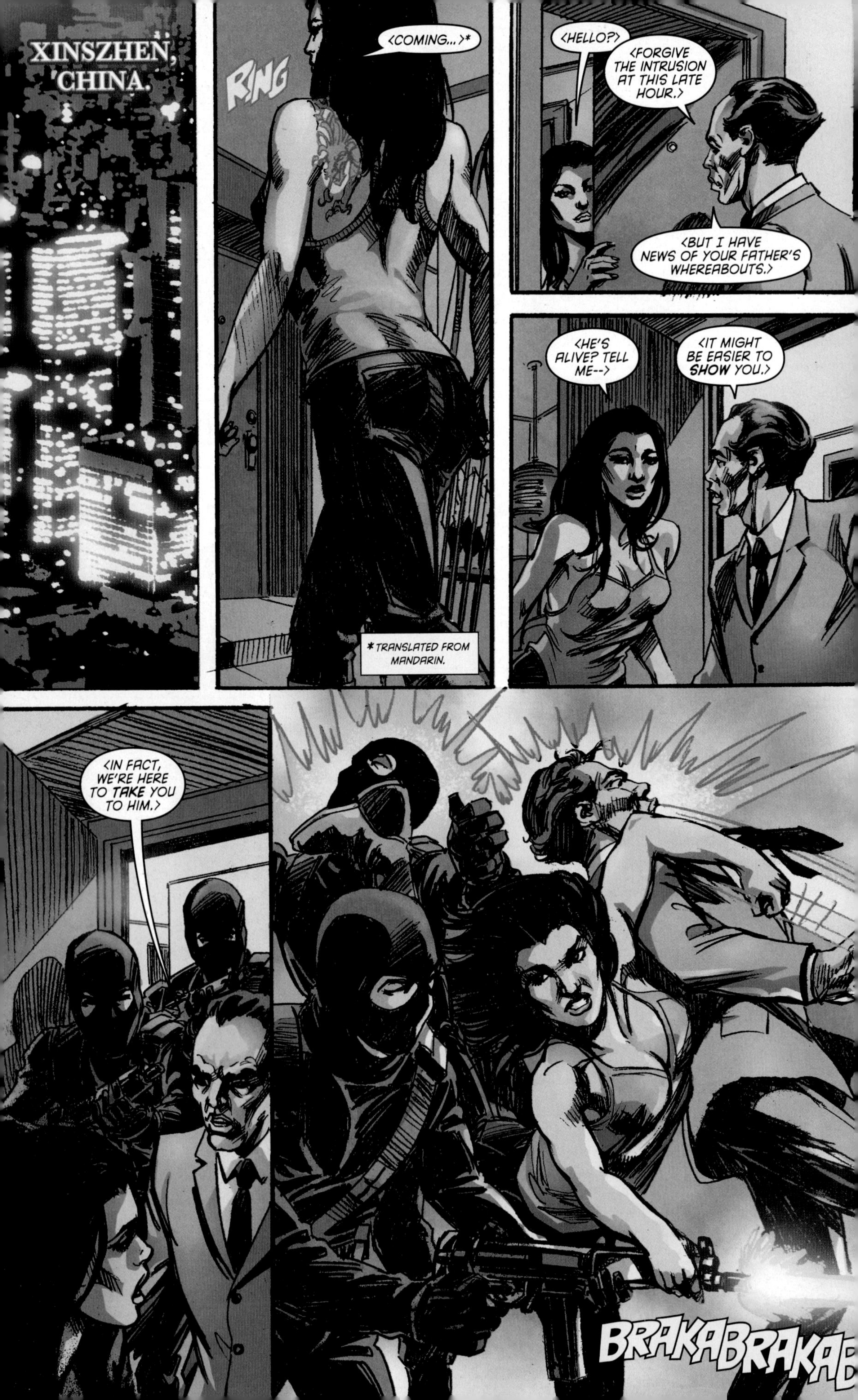
XINSZHEN, CHINA.
RING
<COMING...>*
*TRANSLATED FROM MANDARIN.
<HELLO?>
<FORGIVE THE INTRUSION AT THIS LATE HOUR.>
<BUT I HAVE NEWS OF YOUR FATHER'S WHEREABOUTS.>
<HE'S ALIVE? TELL ME-->
<IT MIGHT BE EASIER TO SHOW YOU.>
<IN FACT, WE'RE HERE TO TAKE YOU TO HIM.>
BRAKABRAKAB

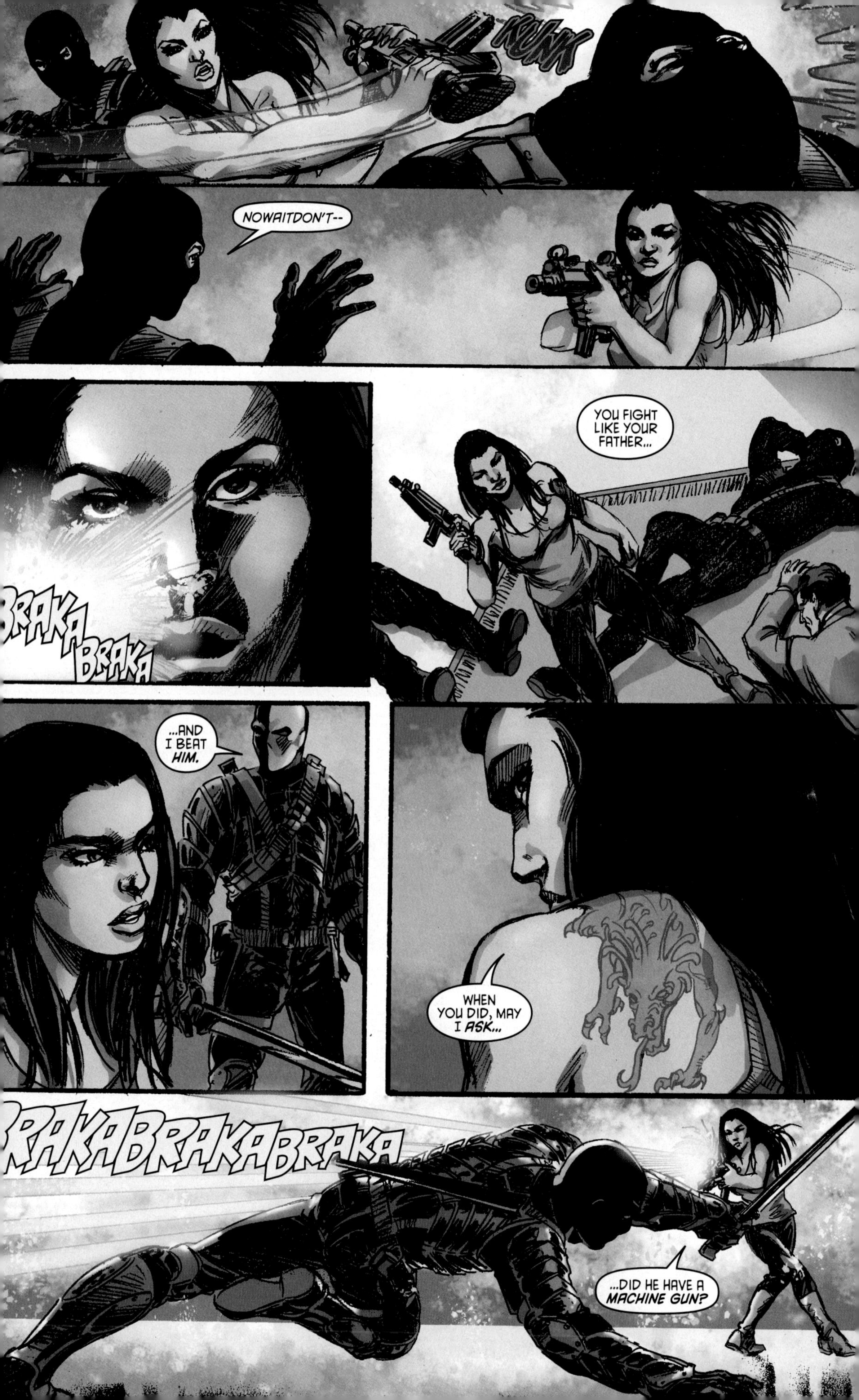
KUNK
NOWAITDON'T--
BRAKA BRAKA
YOU FIGHT LIKE YOUR FATHER...
...AND I BEAT HIM.
WHEN YOU DID, MAY I ASK...
BRAKABRAKABRAKA
...DID HE HAVE A MACHINE GUN?

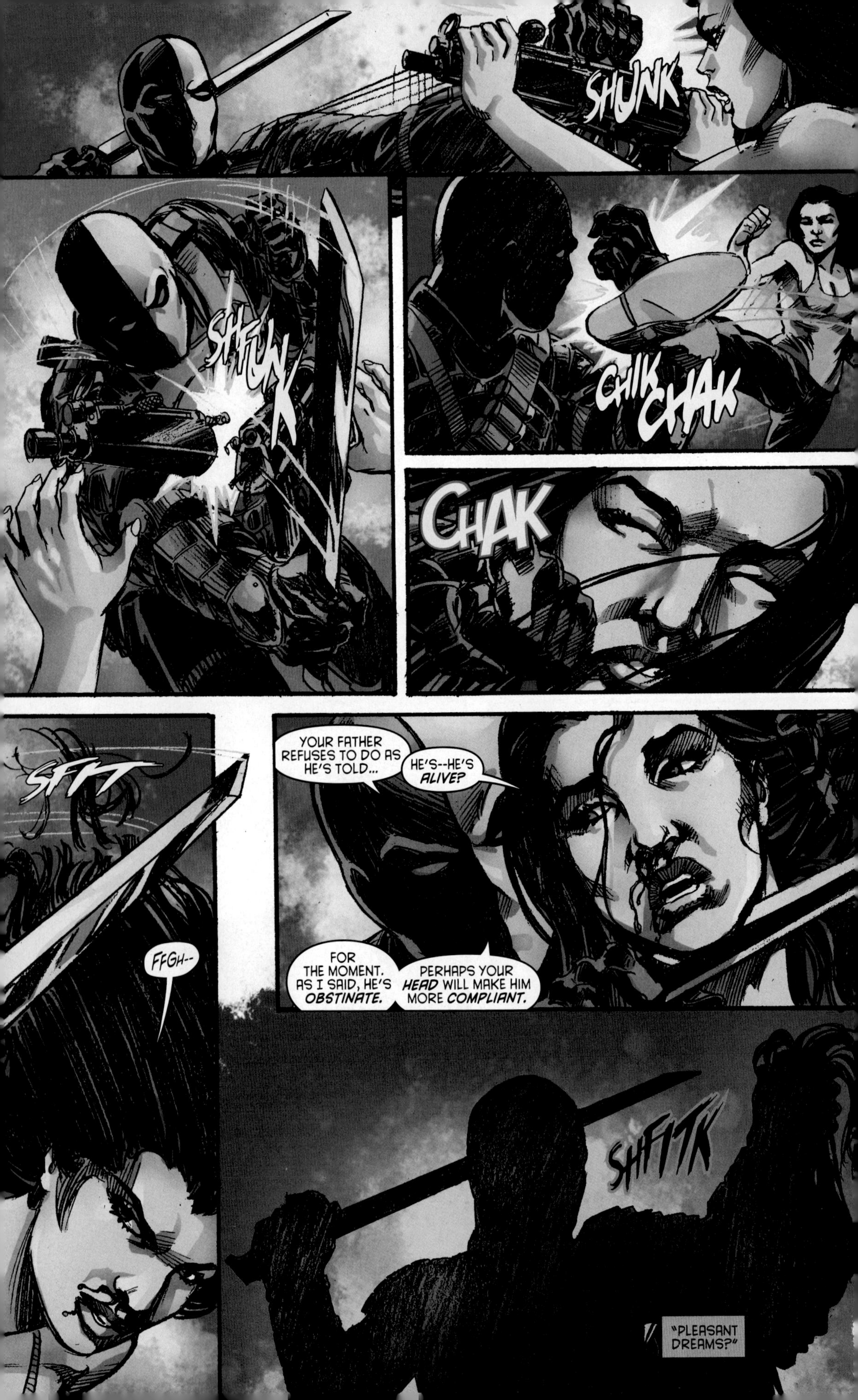
SHUNK
SHFUNK
CHIK CHAK
CHAK
SFFT
YOUR FATHER REFUSES TO DO AS HE'S TOLD...
HE'S--HE'S ALIVE?
FOR THE MOMENT. AS I SAID, HE'S OBSTINATE.
PERHAPS YOUR HEAD WILL MAKE HIM MORE COMPLIANT.
FFGH--
SHFITK
"PLEASANT DREAMS?"

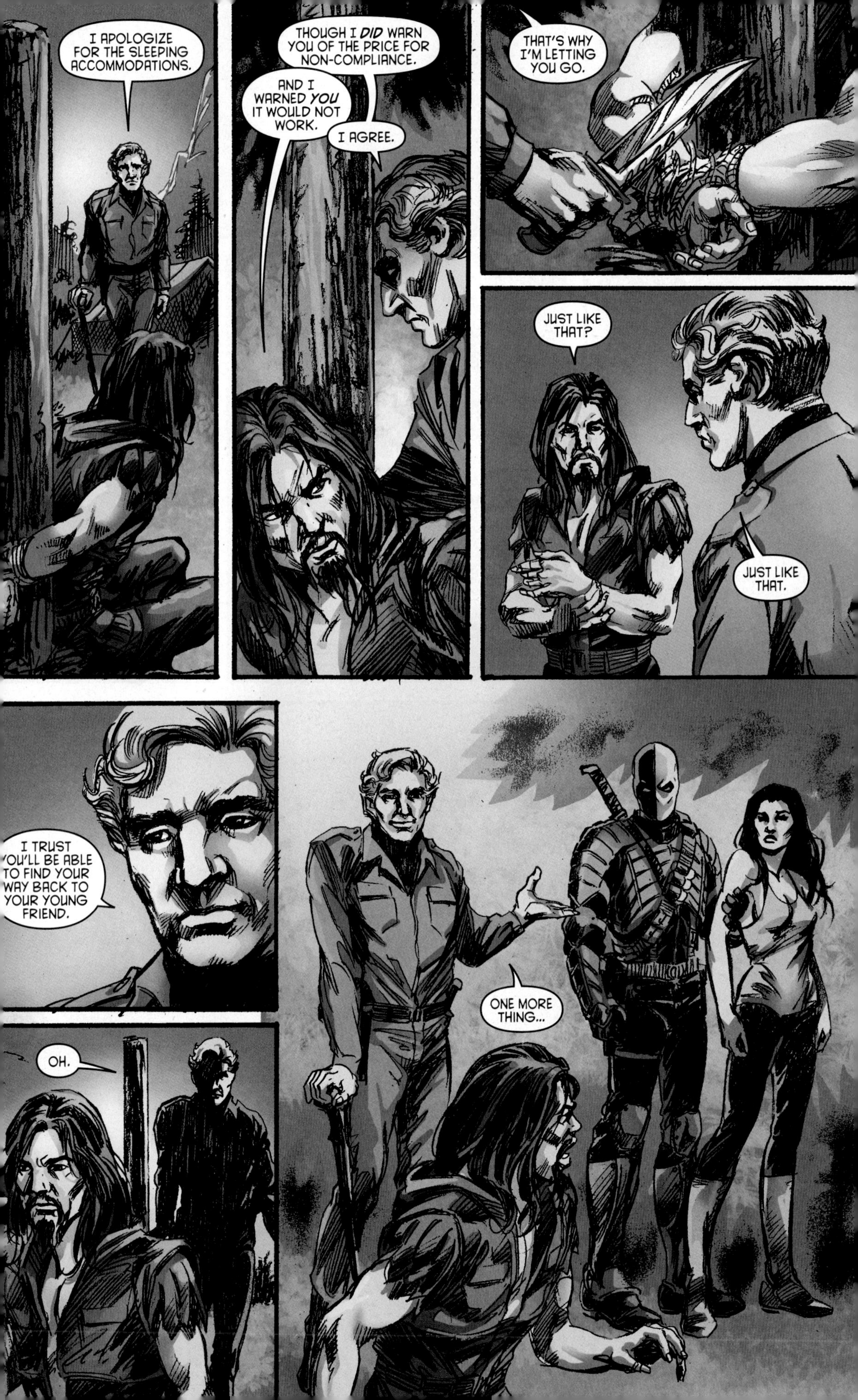
I APOLOGIZE FOR THE SLEEPING ACCOMMODATIONS.
THOUGH I *DID* WARN YOU OF THE PRICE FOR NON-COMPLIANCE.
AND I WARNED *YOU* IT WOULD NOT WORK.
I AGREE.
THAT'S WHY I'M LETTING YOU GO.
JUST LIKE THAT?
JUST LIKE THAT.
I TRUST YOU'LL BE ABLE TO FIND YOUR WAY BACK TO YOUR YOUNG FRIEND.
OH.
ONE MORE THING...

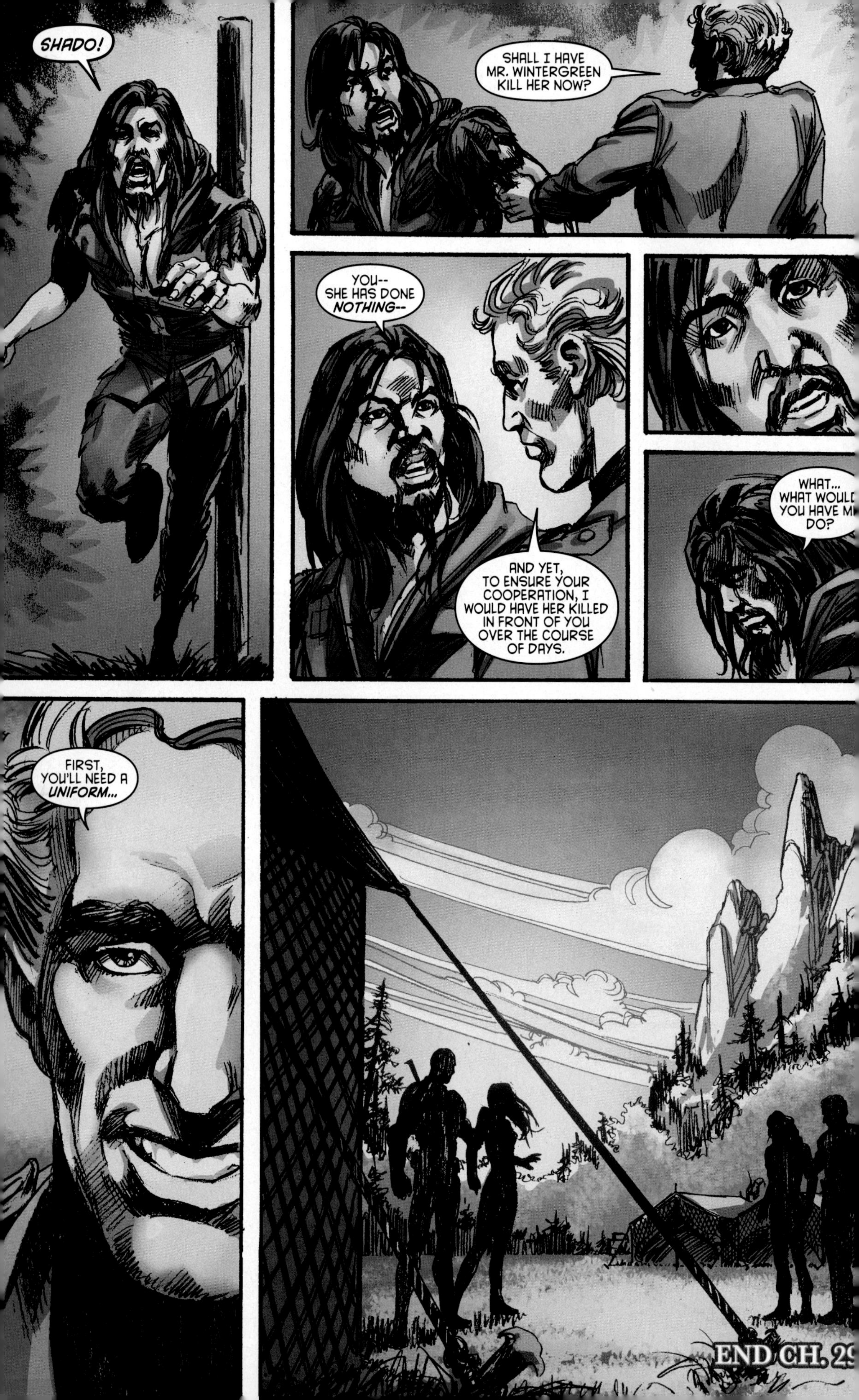
SHADO!
SHALL I HAVE MR. WINTERGREEN KILL HER NOW?
YOU-- SHE HAS DONE NOTHING--
AND YET, TO ENSURE YOUR COOPERATION, I WOULD HAVE HER KILLED IN FRONT OF YOU OVER THE COURSE OF DAYS.
WHAT... WHAT WOULD YOU HAVE ME DO?
FIRST, YOU'LL NEED A UNIFORM...
END CH. 29

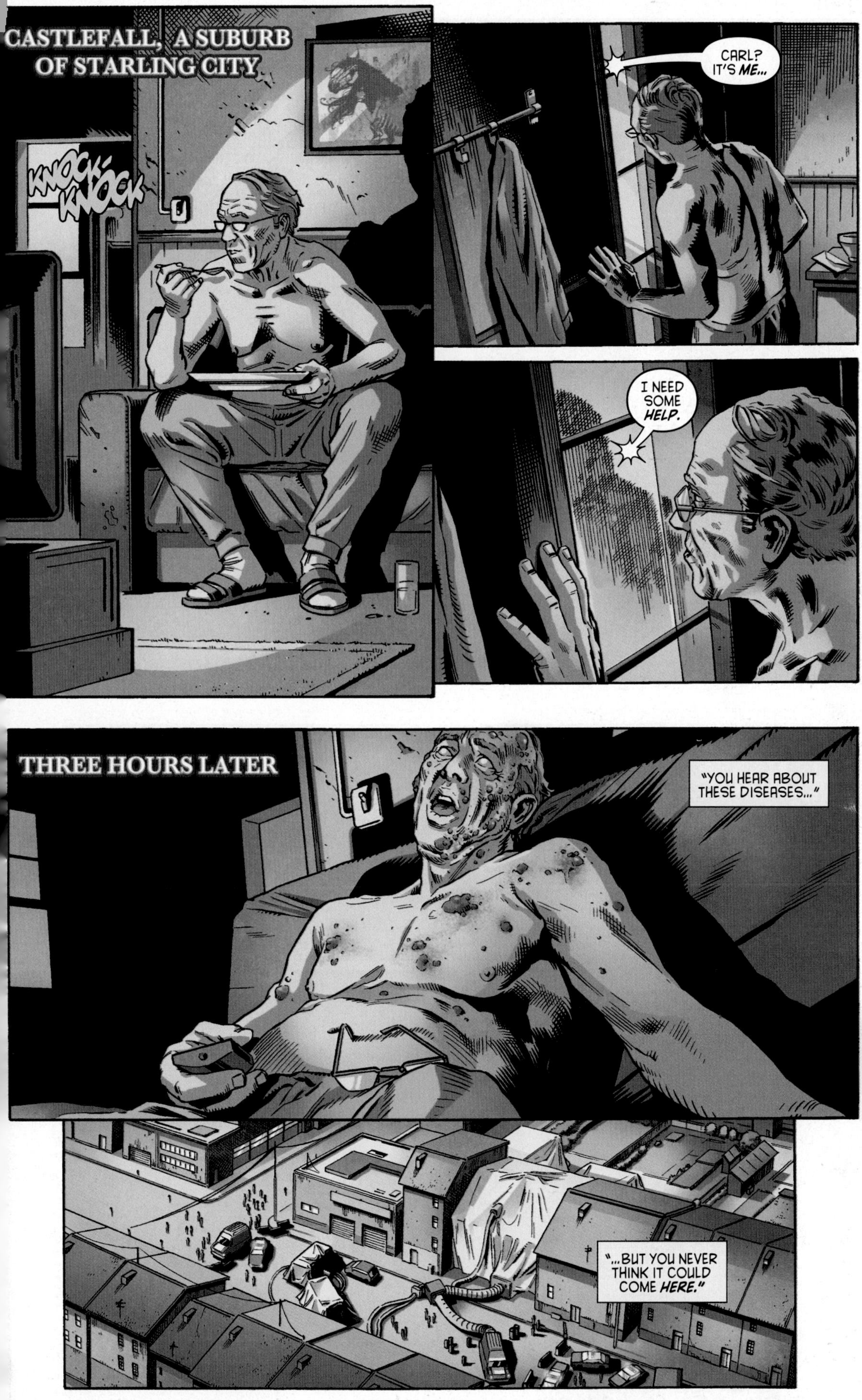
CASTLEFALL, A SUBURB OF STARLING CITY
KNOCK-KNOCK
CARL? IT'S ME...
I NEED SOME HELP.
THREE HOURS LATER
"YOU HEAR ABOUT THESE DISEASES..."
"...BUT YOU NEVER THINK IT COULD COME HERE."

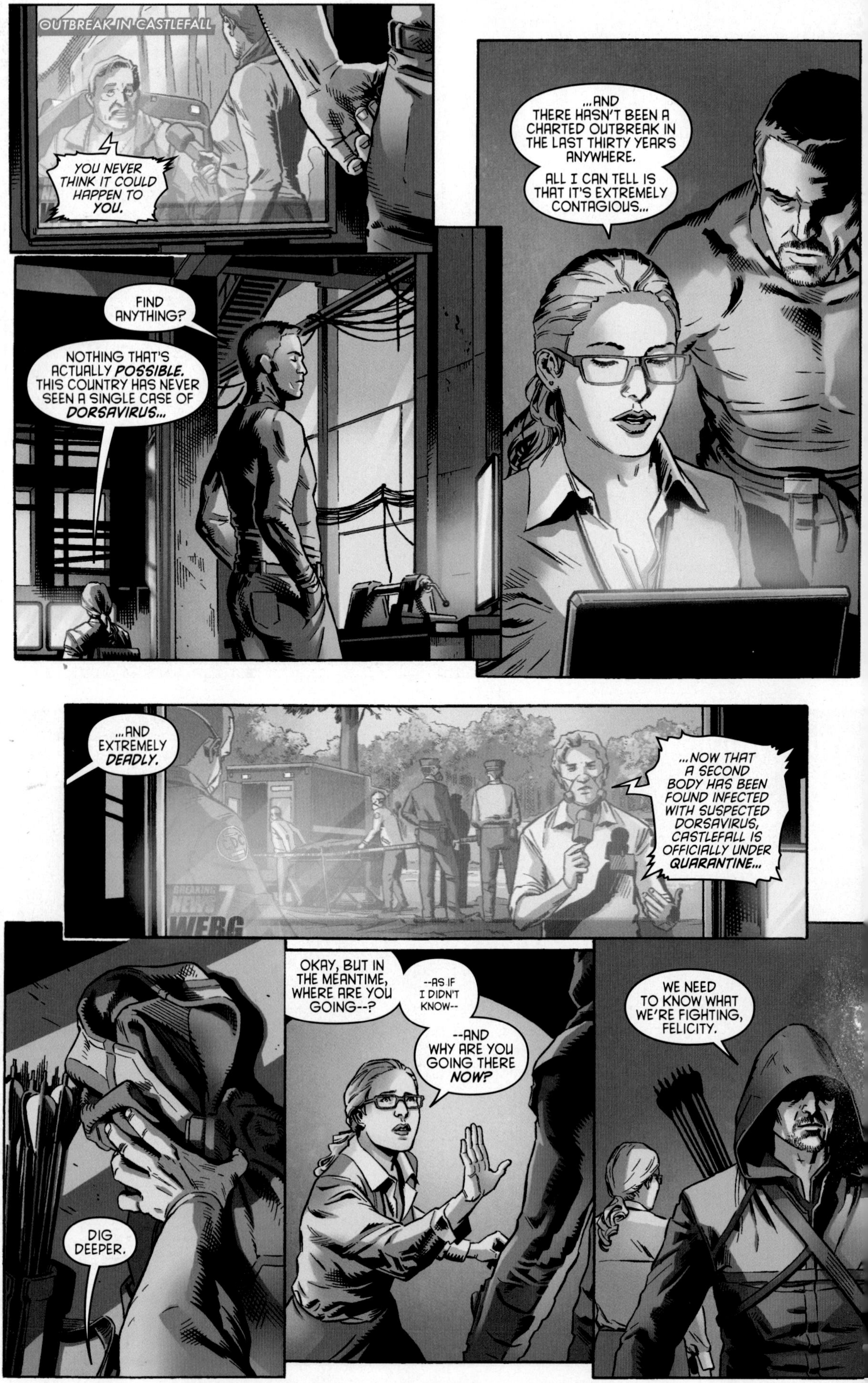
OUTBREAK IN CASTLEFALL
YOU NEVER THINK IT COULD HAPPEN TO YOU.
FIND ANYTHING?
NOTHING THAT'S ACTUALLY POSSIBLE. THIS COUNTRY HAS NEVER SEEN A SINGLE CASE OF DORSAVIRUS...
...AND THERE HASN'T BEEN A CHARTED OUTBREAK IN THE LAST THIRTY YEARS ANYWHERE.
ALL I CAN TELL IS THAT IT'S EXTREMELY CONTAGIOUS...
...AND EXTREMELY DEADLY.
...NOW THAT A SECOND BODY HAS BEEN FOUND INFECTED WITH SUSPECTED DORSAVIRUS, CASTLEFALL IS OFFICIALLY UNDER QUARANTINE...
BREAKING NEWS 7
WERG
DIG DEEPER.
OKAY, BUT IN THE MEANTIME, WHERE ARE YOU GOING--?
--AS IF I DIDN'T KNOW--
--AND WHY ARE YOU GOING THERE NOW?
WE NEED TO KNOW WHAT WE'RE FIGHTING, FELICITY.

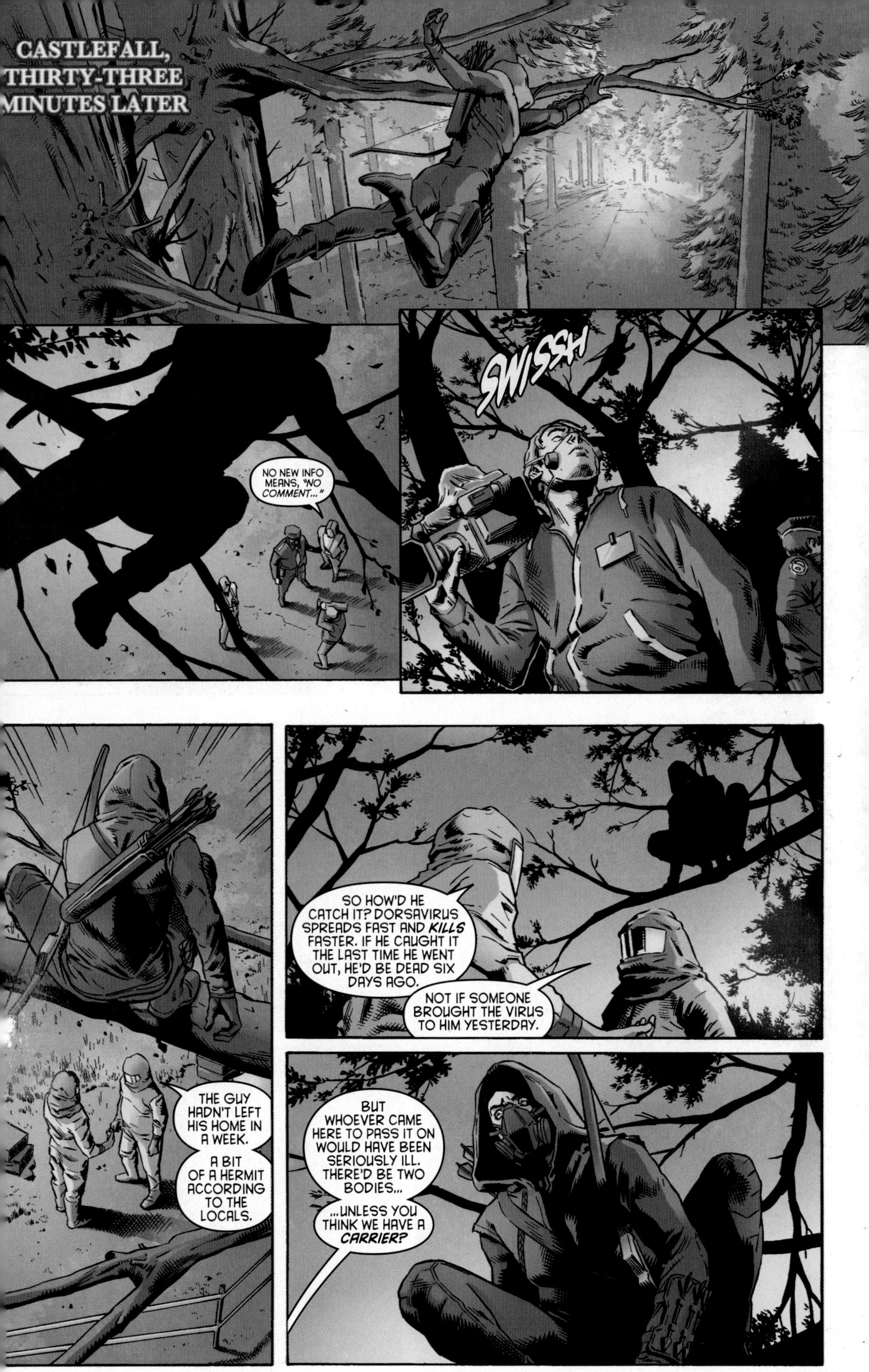
CASTLEFALL, THIRTY-THREE MINUTES LATER
NO NEW INFO MEANS, "NO COMMENT..."
SWISSH
THE GUY HADN'T LEFT HIS HOME IN A WEEK.
A BIT OF A HERMIT ACCORDING TO THE LOCALS.
SO HOW'D HE CATCH IT? DORSAVIRUS SPREADS FAST AND KILLS FASTER. IF HE CAUGHT IT THE LAST TIME HE WENT OUT, HE'D BE DEAD SIX DAYS AGO.
NOT IF SOMEONE BROUGHT THE VIRUS TO HIM YESTERDAY.
BUT WHOEVER CAME HERE TO PASS IT ON WOULD HAVE BEEN SERIOUSLY ILL. THERE'D BE TWO BODIES...
...UNLESS YOU THINK WE HAVE A CARRIER?

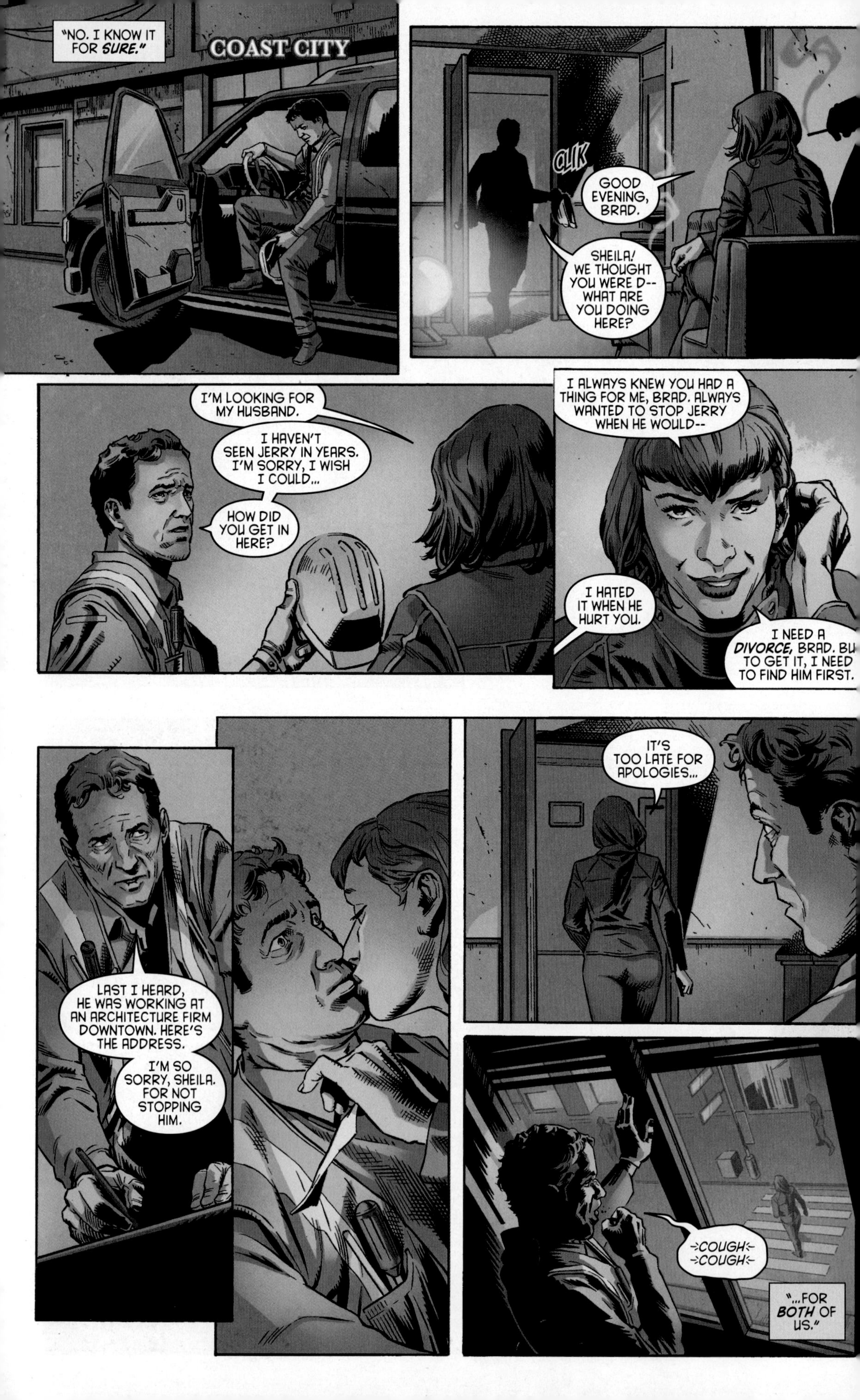
"NO. I KNOW IT FOR *SURE.*"
COAST CITY
CLIK
GOOD EVENING, BRAD.
SHEILA! WE THOUGHT YOU WERE D-- WHAT ARE YOU DOING HERE?
I'M LOOKING FOR MY HUSBAND.
I HAVEN'T SEEN JERRY IN YEARS. I'M SORRY, I WISH I COULD...
HOW DID YOU GET IN HERE?
I ALWAYS KNEW YOU HAD A THING FOR ME, BRAD. ALWAYS WANTED TO STOP JERRY WHEN HE WOULD--
I HATED IT WHEN HE HURT YOU.
I NEED A *DIVORCE,* BRAD. BU
TO GET IT, I NEED TO FIND HIM FIRST.
LAST I HEARD, HE WAS WORKING AT AN ARCHITECTURE FIRM DOWNTOWN. HERE'S THE ADDRESS.
I'M SO SORRY, SHEILA. FOR NOT STOPPING HIM.
IT'S TOO LATE FOR APOLOGIES...
>COUGH< >COUGH<
"...FOR *BOTH* OF US."

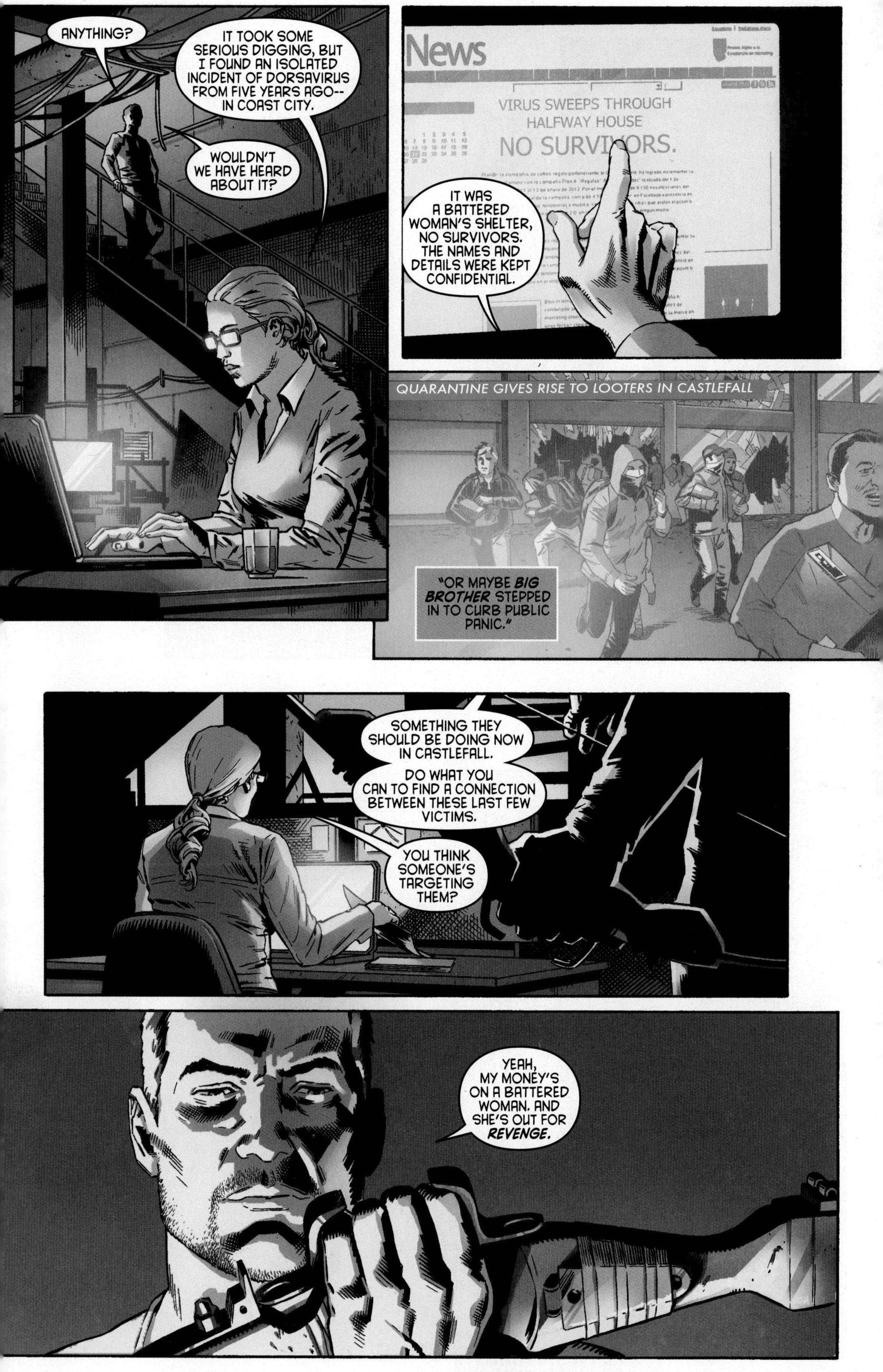
ANYTHING?
IT TOOK SOME SERIOUS DIGGING, BUT I FOUND AN ISOLATED INCIDENT OF DORSAVIRUS FROM FIVE YEARS AGO-- IN COAST CITY.
WOULDN'T WE HAVE HEARD ABOUT IT?
News
VIRUS SWEEPS THROUGH HALFWAY HOUSE
NO SURVIVORS.
IT WAS A BATTERED WOMAN'S SHELTER, NO SURVIVORS. THE NAMES AND DETAILS WERE KEPT CONFIDENTIAL.
QUARANTINE GIVES RISE TO LOOTERS IN CASTLEFALL
"OR MAYBE *BIG BROTHER* STEPPED IN TO CURB PUBLIC PANIC."
SOMETHING THEY SHOULD BE DOING NOW IN CASTLEFALL.
DO WHAT YOU CAN TO FIND A CONNECTION BETWEEN THESE LAST FEW VICTIMS.
YOU THINK SOMEONE'S TARGETING THEM?
YEAH, MY MONEY'S ON A BATTERED WOMAN. AND SHE'S OUT FOR *REVENGE*.

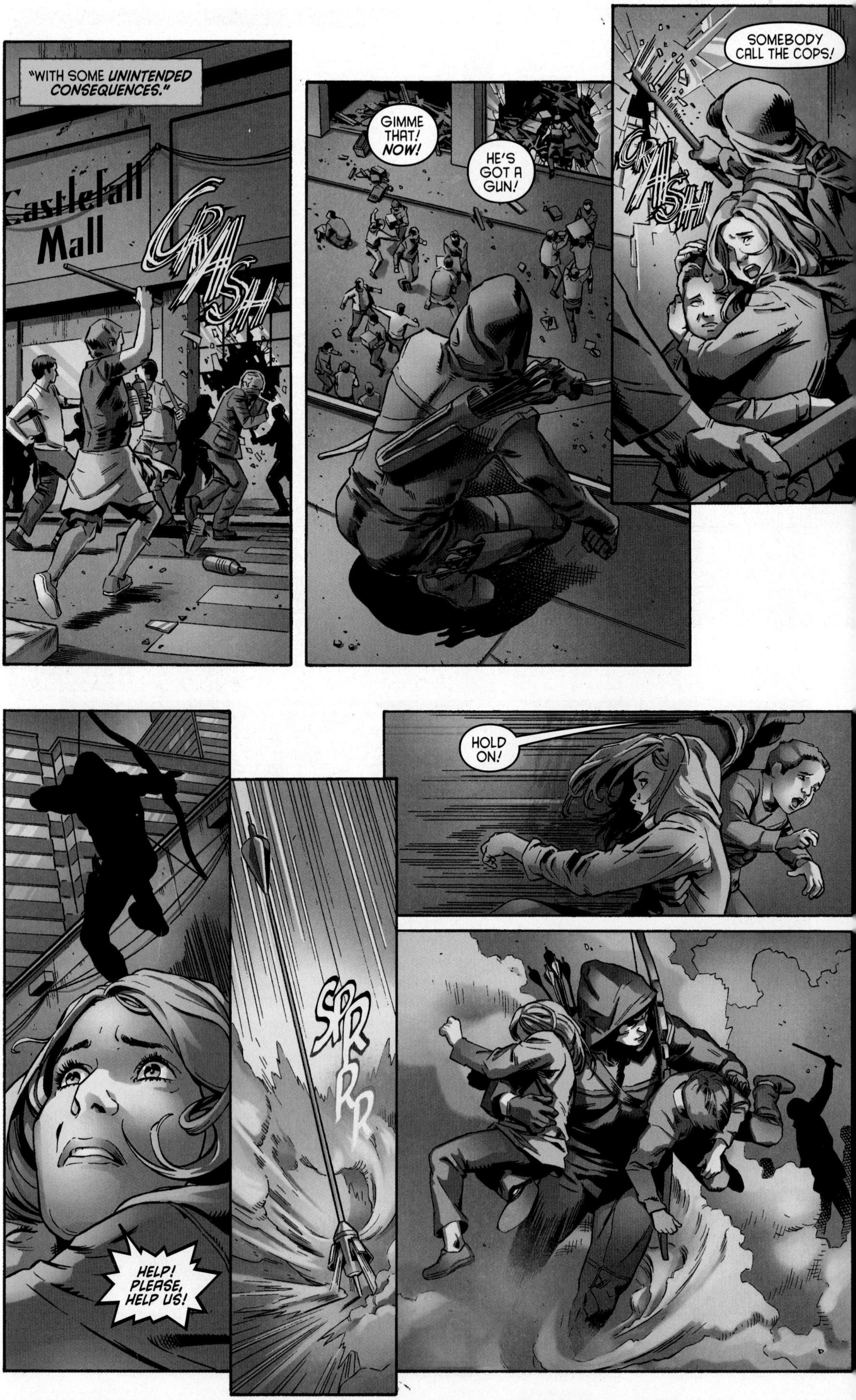
"WITH SOME UNINTENDED CONSEQUENCES."
Castlefall Mall
CRASH
GIMME THAT! NOW!
HE'S GOT A GUN!
SOMEBODY CALL THE COPS!
CRASH
HELP! PLEASE, HELP US!
SPRRR
HOLD ON!

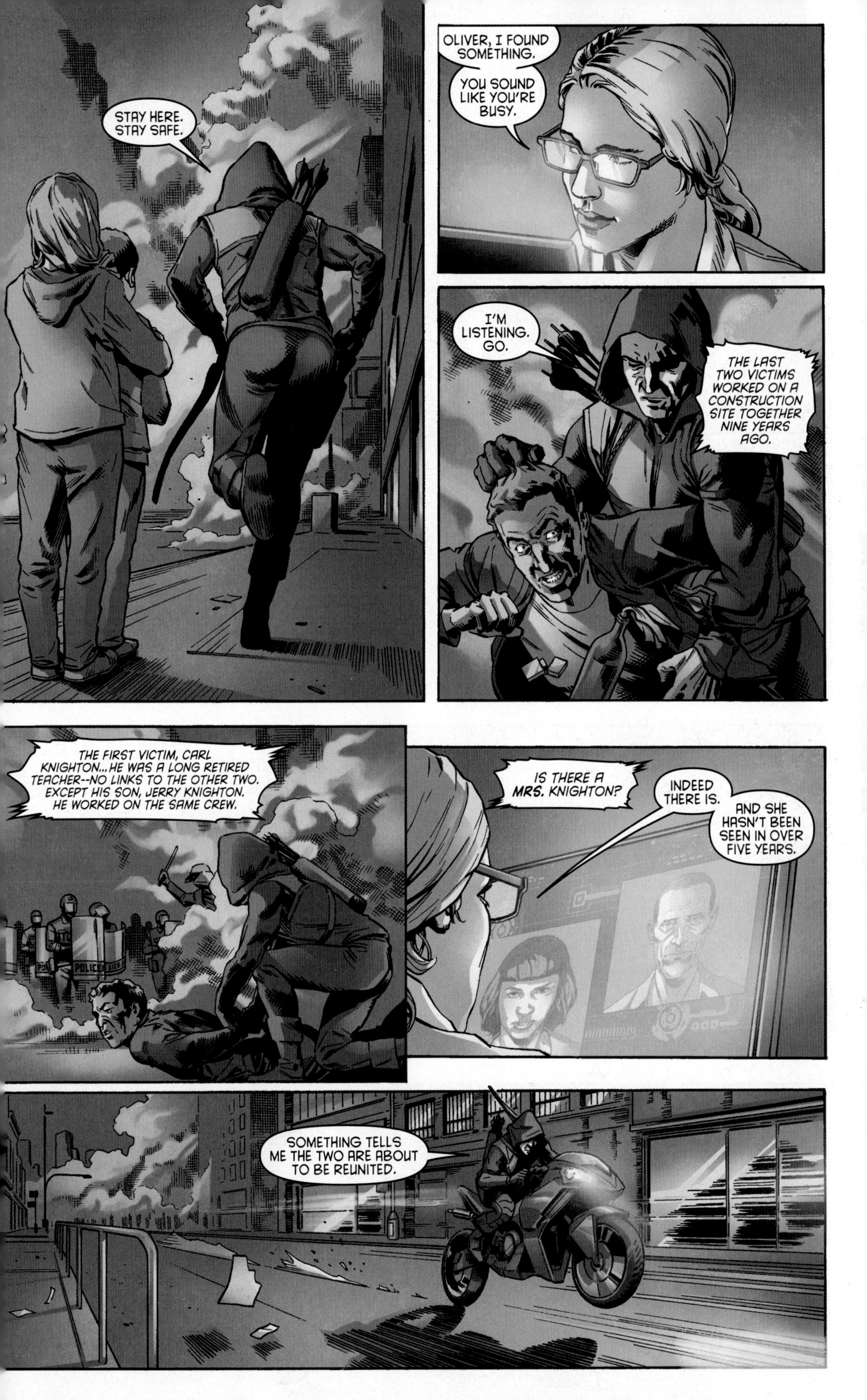
STAY HERE. STAY SAFE.
OLIVER, I FOUND SOMETHING.
YOU SOUND LIKE YOU'RE BUSY.
I'M LISTENING. GO.
THE LAST TWO VICTIMS WORKED ON A CONSTRUCTION SITE TOGETHER NINE YEARS AGO.
THE FIRST VICTIM, CARL KNIGHTON... HE WAS A LONG RETIRED TEACHER--NO LINKS TO THE OTHER TWO. EXCEPT HIS SON, JERRY KNIGHTON. HE WORKED ON THE SAME CREW.
POLICE
IS THERE A MRS. KNIGHTON?
INDEED THERE IS.
AND SHE HASN'T BEEN SEEN IN OVER FIVE YEARS.
SOMETHING TELLS ME THE TWO ARE ABOUT TO BE REUNITED.

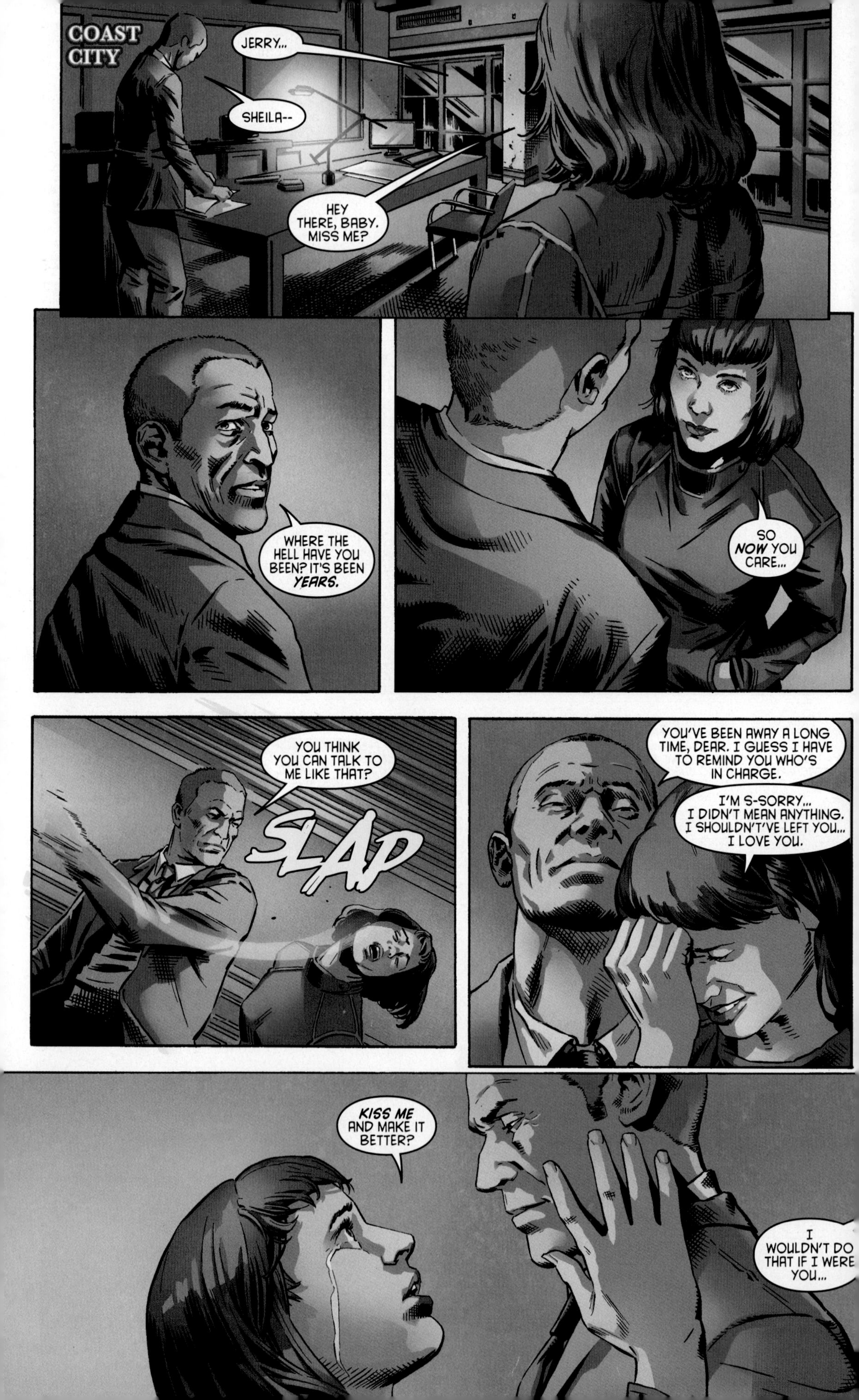
COAST CITY
JERRY...
SHEILA--
HEY THERE, BABY. MISS ME?
WHERE THE HELL HAVE YOU BEEN? IT'S BEEN YEARS.
SO NOW YOU CARE...
YOU THINK YOU CAN TALK TO ME LIKE THAT?
SLAP
YOU'VE BEEN AWAY A LONG TIME, DEAR. I GUESS I HAVE TO REMIND YOU WHO'S IN CHARGE.
I'M S-SORRY... I DIDN'T MEAN ANYTHING. I SHOULDN'T'VE LEFT YOU... I LOVE YOU.
KISS ME AND MAKE IT BETTER?
I WOULDN'T DO THAT IF I WERE YOU...

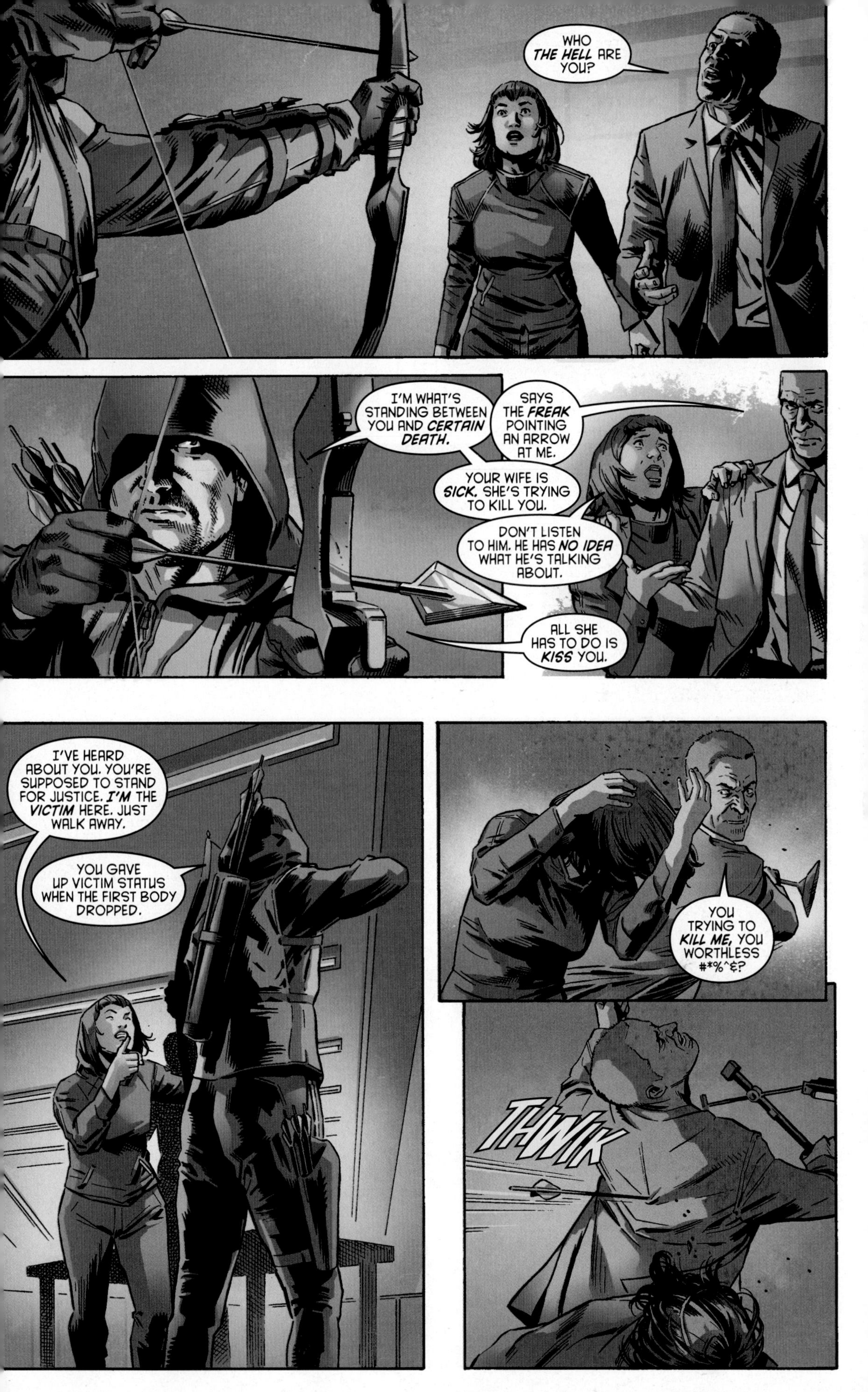
WHO THE HELL ARE YOU?
I'M WHAT'S STANDING BETWEEN YOU AND CERTAIN DEATH.
SAYS THE FREAK POINTING AN ARROW AT ME.
YOUR WIFE IS SICK. SHE'S TRYING TO KILL YOU.
DON'T LISTEN TO HIM. HE HAS NO IDEA WHAT HE'S TALKING ABOUT.
ALL SHE HAS TO DO IS KISS YOU.
I'VE HEARD ABOUT YOU. YOU'RE SUPPOSED TO STAND FOR JUSTICE. I'M THE VICTIM HERE. JUST WALK AWAY.
YOU GAVE UP VICTIM STATUS WHEN THE FIRST BODY DROPPED.
YOU TRYING TO KILL ME, YOU WORTHLESS #*%^&?
THWIK

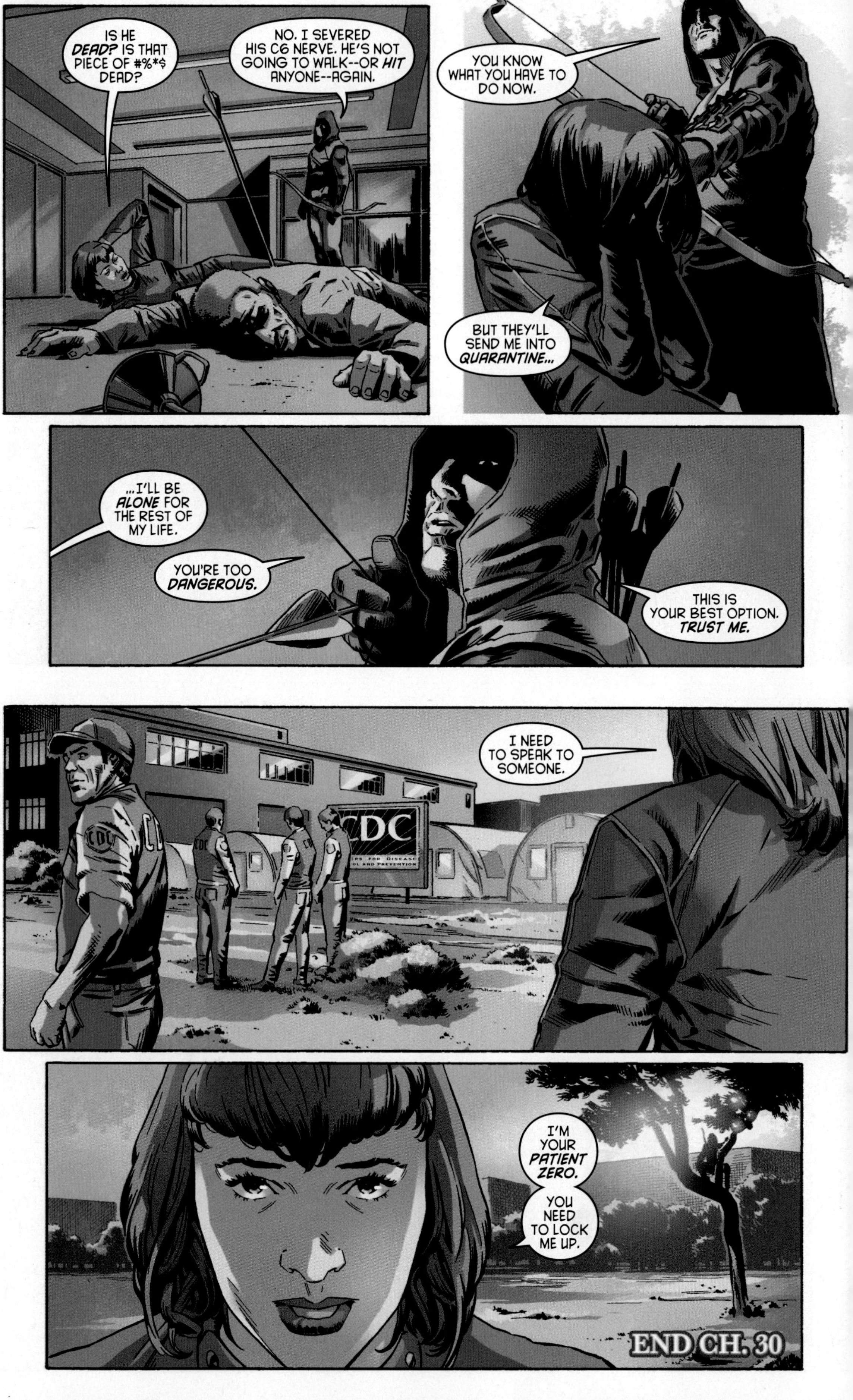
IS HE DEAD? IS THAT PIECE OF #%*$ DEAD?
NO. I SEVERED HIS C6 NERVE. HE'S NOT GOING TO WALK--OR HIT ANYONE--AGAIN.
YOU KNOW WHAT YOU HAVE TO DO NOW.
BUT THEY'LL SEND ME INTO QUARANTINE...
...I'LL BE ALONE FOR THE REST OF MY LIFE.
YOU'RE TOO DANGEROUS.
THIS IS YOUR BEST OPTION. TRUST ME.
CDC
I NEED TO SPEAK TO SOMEONE.
I'M YOUR PATIENT ZERO.
YOU NEED TO LOCK ME UP.
END CH. 30

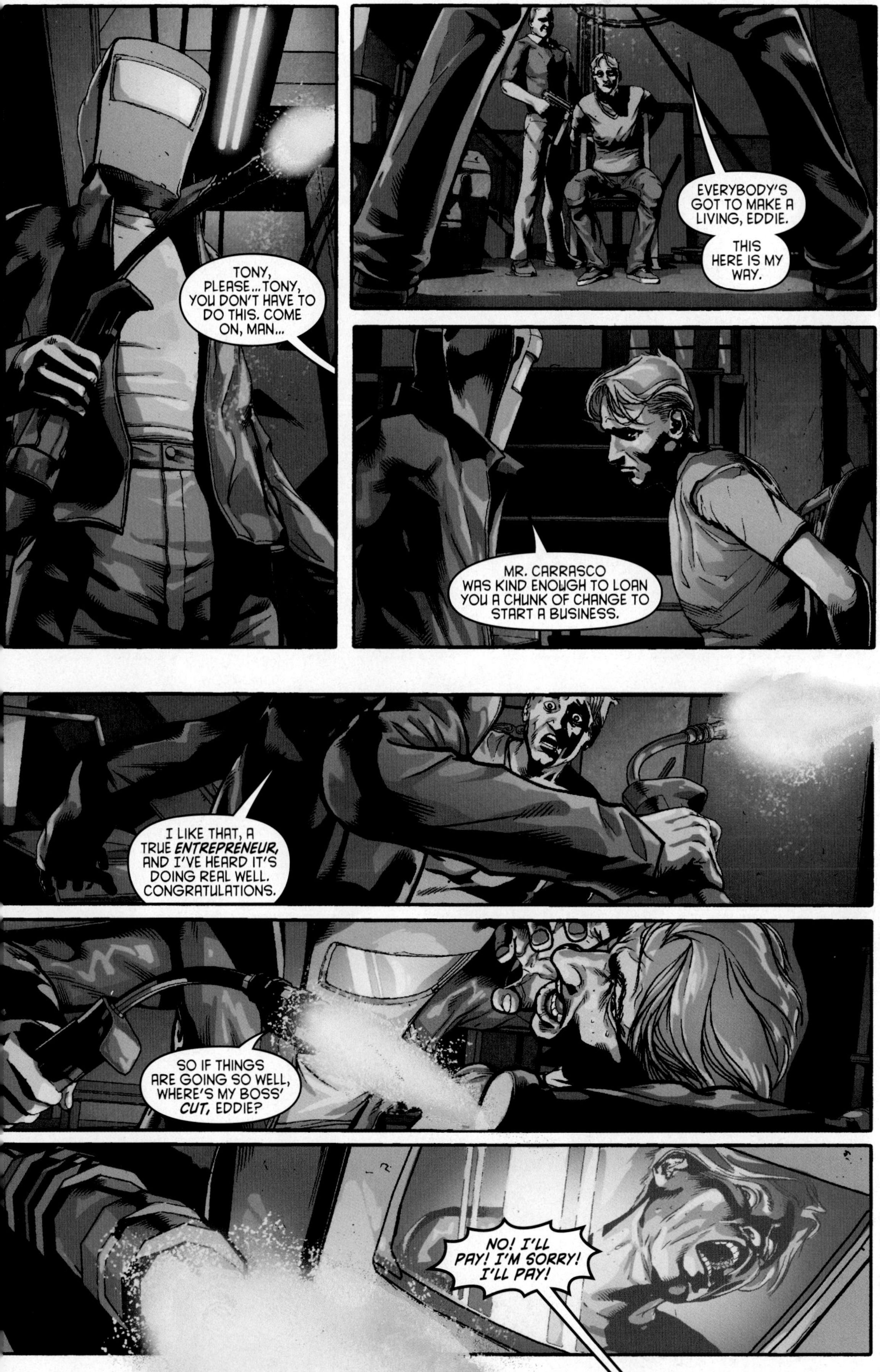
TONY, PLEASE...TONY, YOU DON'T HAVE TO DO THIS. COME ON, MAN...
EVERYBODY'S GOT TO MAKE A LIVING, EDDIE.
THIS HERE IS MY WAY.
MR. CARRASCO WAS KIND ENOUGH TO LOAN YOU A CHUNK OF CHANGE TO START A BUSINESS.
I LIKE THAT, A TRUE *ENTREPRENEUR,* AND I'VE HEARD IT'S DOING REAL WELL. CONGRATULATIONS.
SO IF THINGS ARE GOING SO WELL, WHERE'S MY BOSS' *CUT,* EDDIE?
NO! I'LL PAY! I'M SORRY! I'LL PAY!

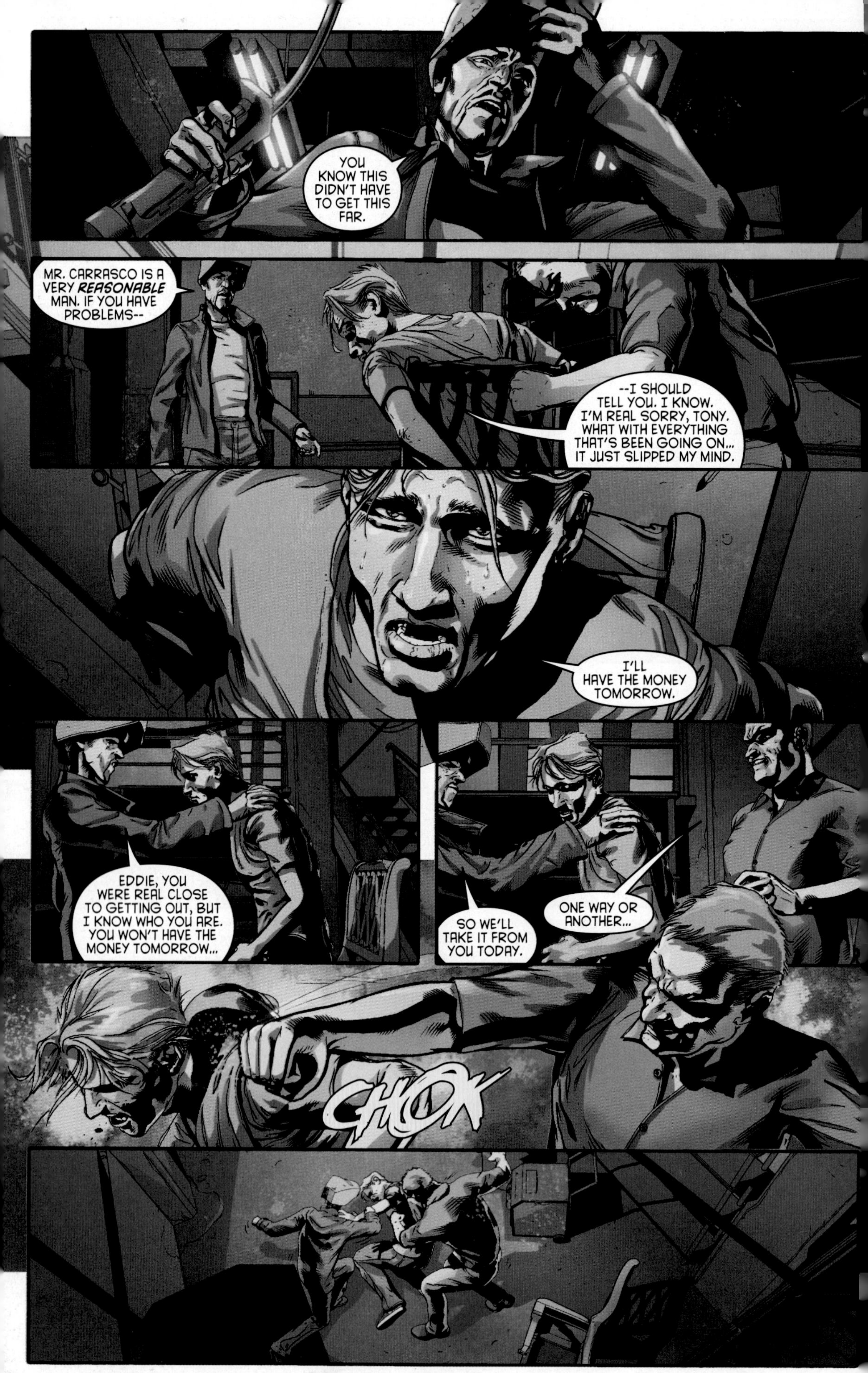
YOU KNOW THIS DIDN'T HAVE TO GET THIS FAR.
MR. CARRASCO IS A VERY *REASONABLE* MAN. IF YOU HAVE PROBLEMS--
--I SHOULD TELL YOU. I KNOW. I'M REAL SORRY, TONY. WHAT WITH EVERYTHING THAT'S BEEN GOING ON... IT JUST SLIPPED MY MIND.
I'LL HAVE THE MONEY TOMORROW.
EDDIE, YOU WERE REAL CLOSE TO GETTING OUT, BUT I KNOW WHO YOU ARE. YOU WON'T HAVE THE MONEY TOMORROW...
SO WE'LL TAKE IT FROM YOU TODAY.
ONE WAY OR ANOTHER...
CHOK

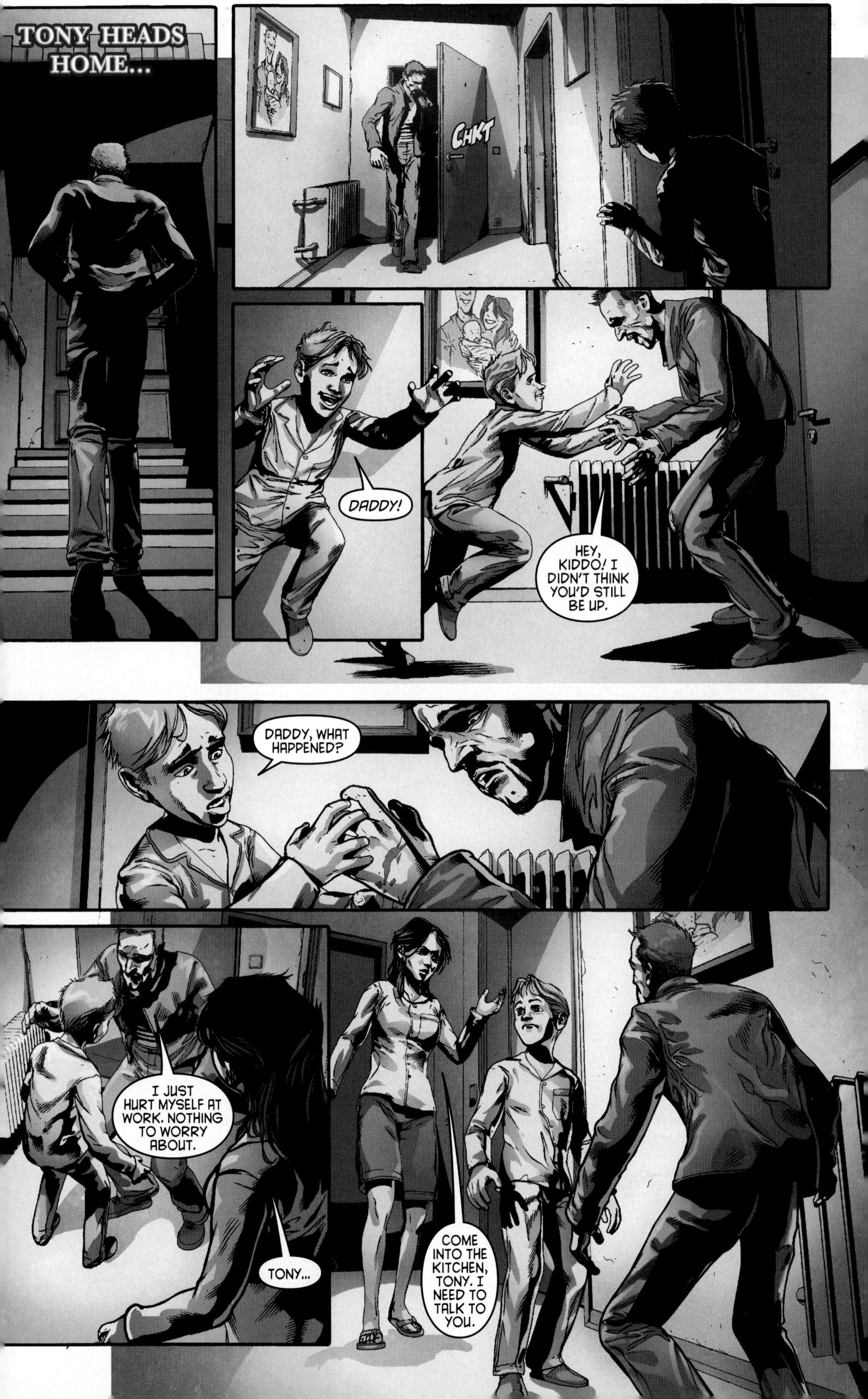
TONY HEADS HOME...
CHKT
DADDY!
HEY, KIDDO! I DIDN'T THINK YOU'D STILL BE UP.
DADDY, WHAT HAPPENED?
I JUST HURT MYSELF AT WORK. NOTHING TO WORRY ABOUT.
TONY...
COME INTO THE KITCHEN, TONY. I NEED TO TALK TO YOU.

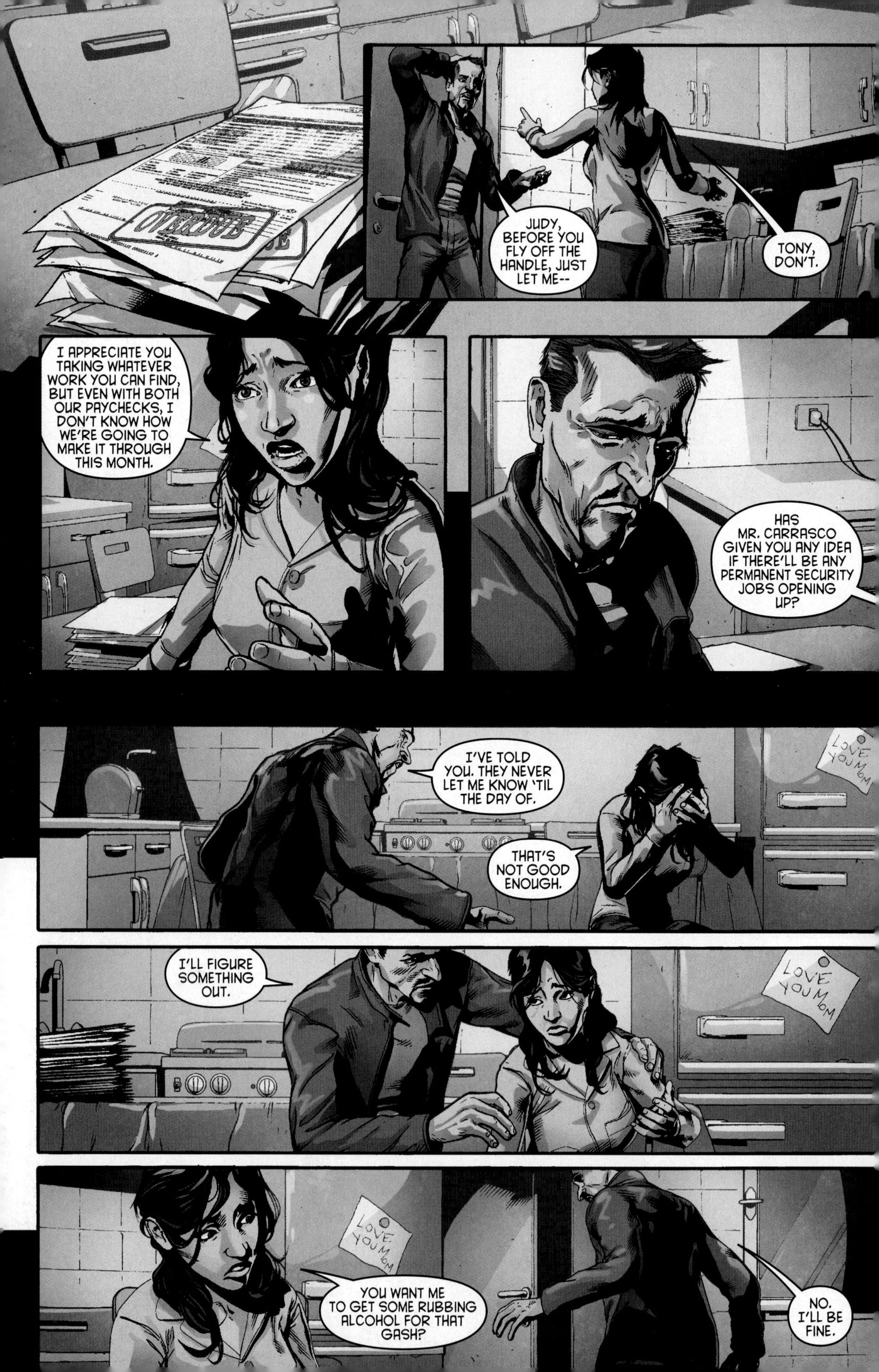
OVERDUE
JUDY, BEFORE YOU FLY OFF THE HANDLE, JUST LET ME--
TONY, DON'T.
I APPRECIATE YOU TAKING WHATEVER WORK YOU CAN FIND, BUT EVEN WITH BOTH OUR PAYCHECKS, I DON'T KNOW HOW WE'RE GOING TO MAKE IT THROUGH THIS MONTH.
HAS MR. CARRASCO GIVEN YOU ANY IDEA IF THERE'LL BE ANY PERMANENT SECURITY JOBS OPENING UP?
I'VE TOLD YOU. THEY NEVER LET ME KNOW 'TIL THE DAY OF.
LOVE YOU MOM
THAT'S NOT GOOD ENOUGH.
I'LL FIGURE SOMETHING OUT.
LOVE YOU MOM
LOVE YOU MOM
YOU WANT ME TO GET SOME RUBBING ALCOHOL FOR THAT GASH?
NO. I'LL BE FINE.

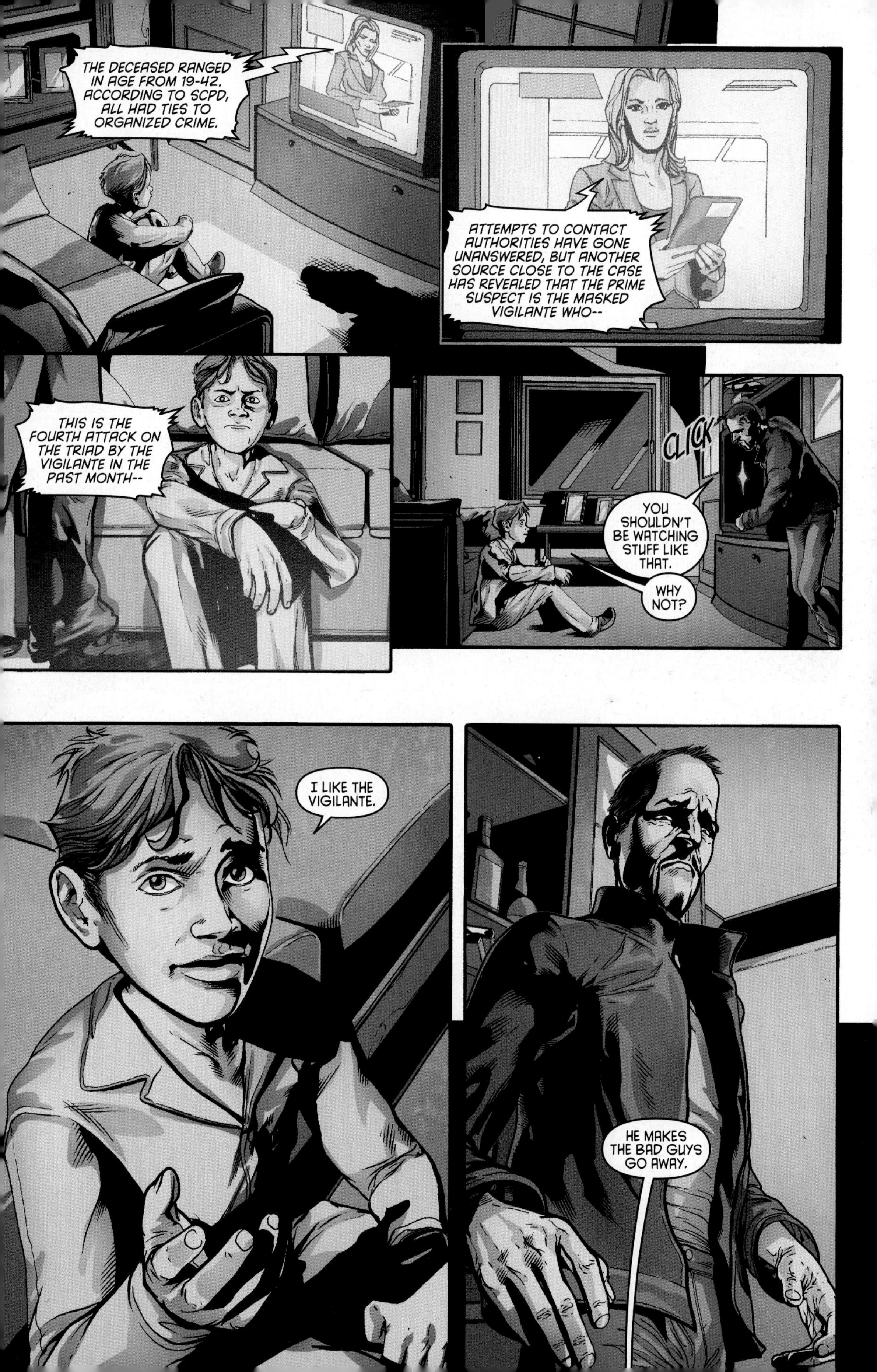
THE DECEASED RANGED IN AGE FROM 19-42. ACCORDING TO SCPD, ALL HAD TIES TO ORGANIZED CRIME.
ATTEMPTS TO CONTACT AUTHORITIES HAVE GONE UNANSWERED, BUT ANOTHER SOURCE CLOSE TO THE CASE HAS REVEALED THAT THE PRIME SUSPECT IS THE MASKED VIGILANTE WHO--
THIS IS THE FOURTH ATTACK ON THE TRIAD BY THE VIGILANTE IN THE PAST MONTH--
CLICK
YOU SHOULDN'T BE WATCHING STUFF LIKE THAT.
WHY NOT?
I LIKE THE VIGILANTE.
HE MAKES THE BAD GUYS GO AWAY.

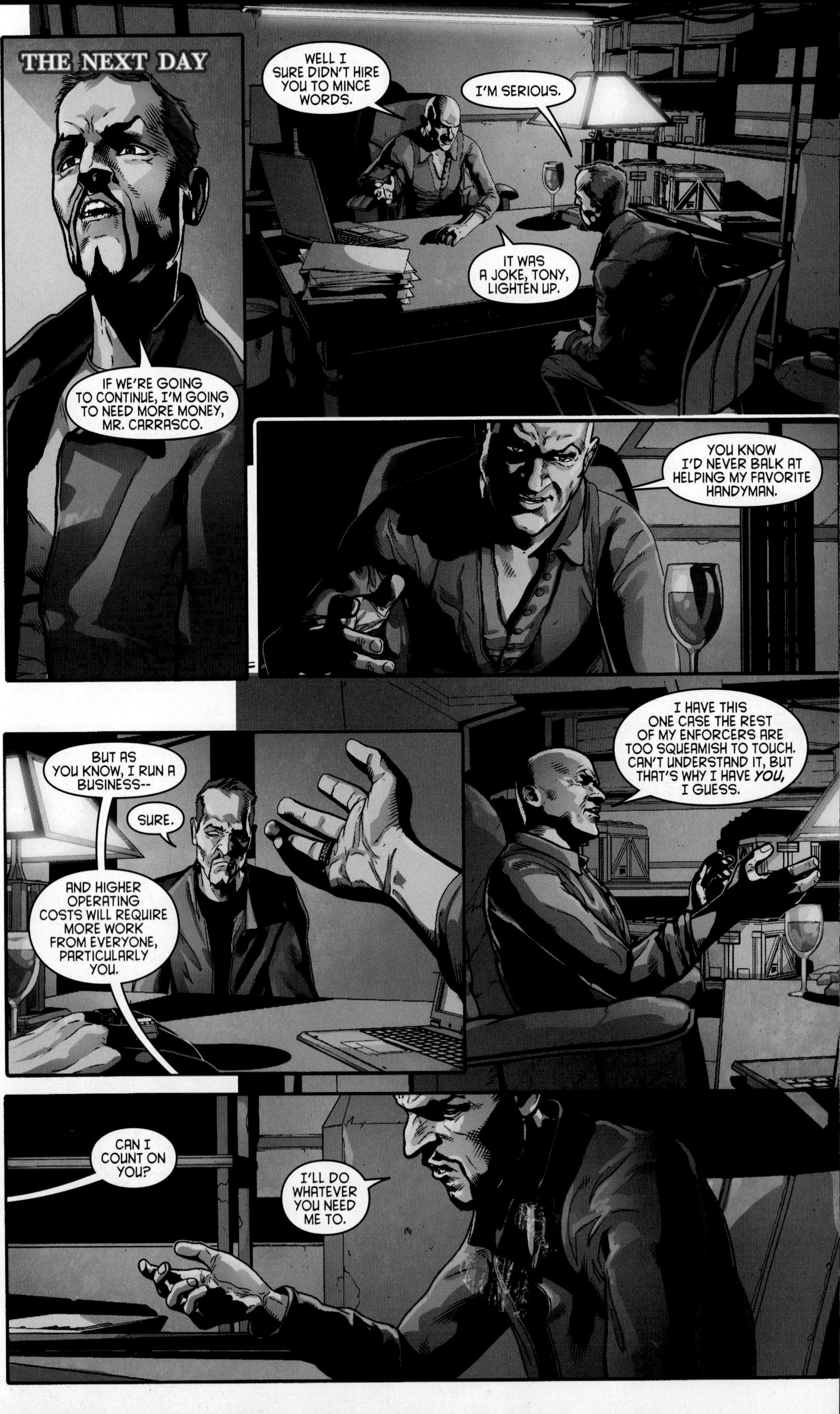
THE NEXT DAY
IF WE'RE GOING TO CONTINUE, I'M GOING TO NEED MORE MONEY, MR. CARRASCO.
WELL I SURE DIDN'T HIRE YOU TO MINCE WORDS.
I'M SERIOUS.
IT WAS A JOKE, TONY, LIGHTEN UP.
YOU KNOW I'D NEVER BALK AT HELPING MY FAVORITE HANDYMAN.
BUT AS YOU KNOW, I RUN A BUSINESS--
SURE.
AND HIGHER OPERATING COSTS WILL REQUIRE MORE WORK FROM EVERYONE, PARTICULARLY YOU.
I HAVE THIS ONE CASE THE REST OF MY ENFORCERS ARE TOO SQUEAMISH TO TOUCH. CAN'T UNDERSTAND IT, BUT THAT'S WHY I HAVE YOU, I GUESS.
CAN I COUNT ON YOU?
I'LL DO WHATEVER YOU NEED ME TO.

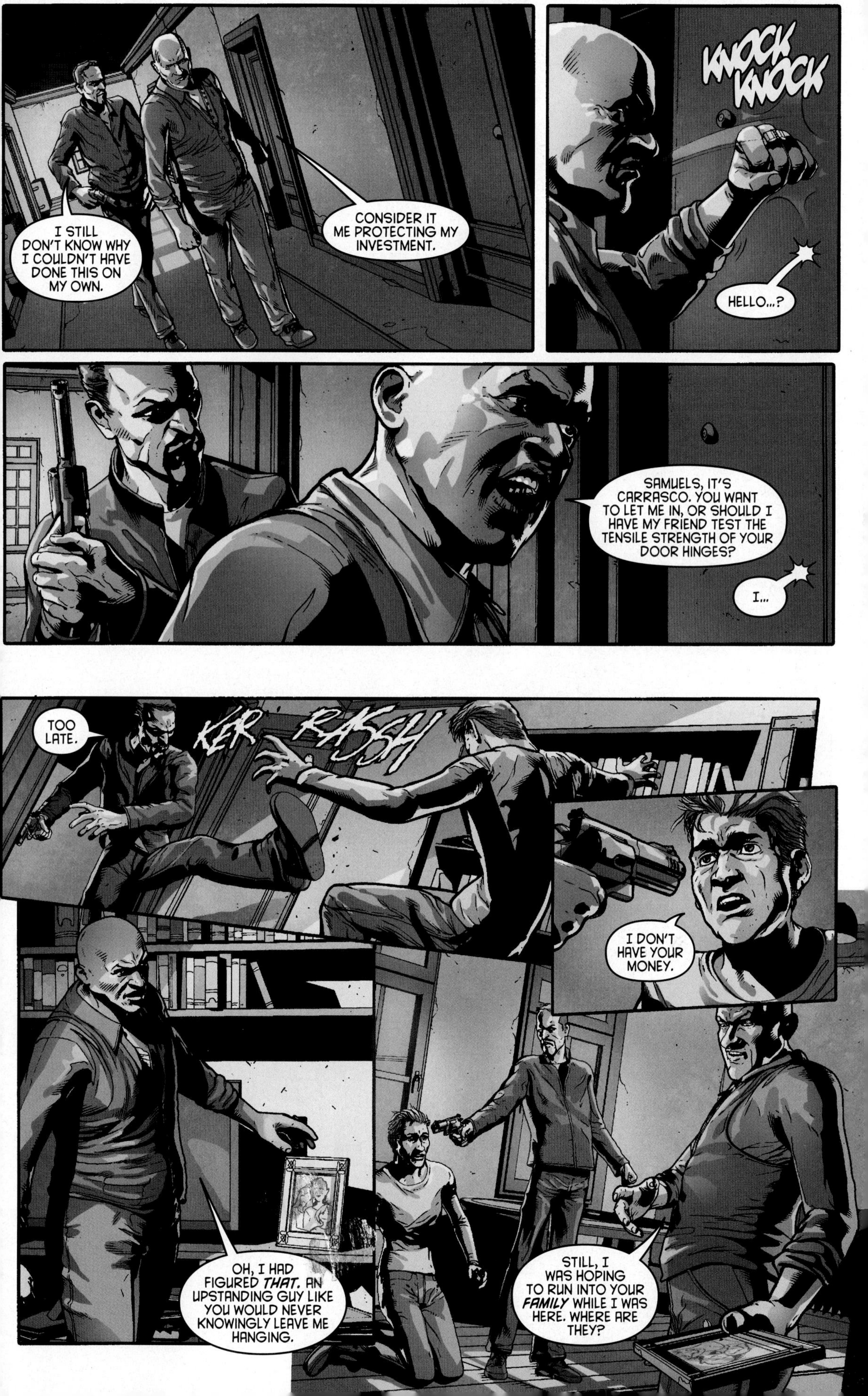
I STILL DON'T KNOW WHY I COULDN'T HAVE DONE THIS ON MY OWN.
CONSIDER IT ME PROTECTING MY INVESTMENT.
KNOCK KNOCK
HELLO...?
SAMUELS, IT'S CARRASCO. YOU WANT TO LET ME IN, OR SHOULD I HAVE MY FRIEND TEST THE TENSILE STRENGTH OF YOUR DOOR HINGES?
I...
TOO LATE.
KER RASSH
I DON'T HAVE YOUR MONEY.
OH, I HAD FIGURED *THAT*. AN UPSTANDING GUY LIKE YOU WOULD NEVER KNOWINGLY LEAVE ME HANGING.
STILL, I WAS HOPING TO RUN INTO YOUR *FAMILY* WHILE I WAS HERE. WHERE ARE THEY?

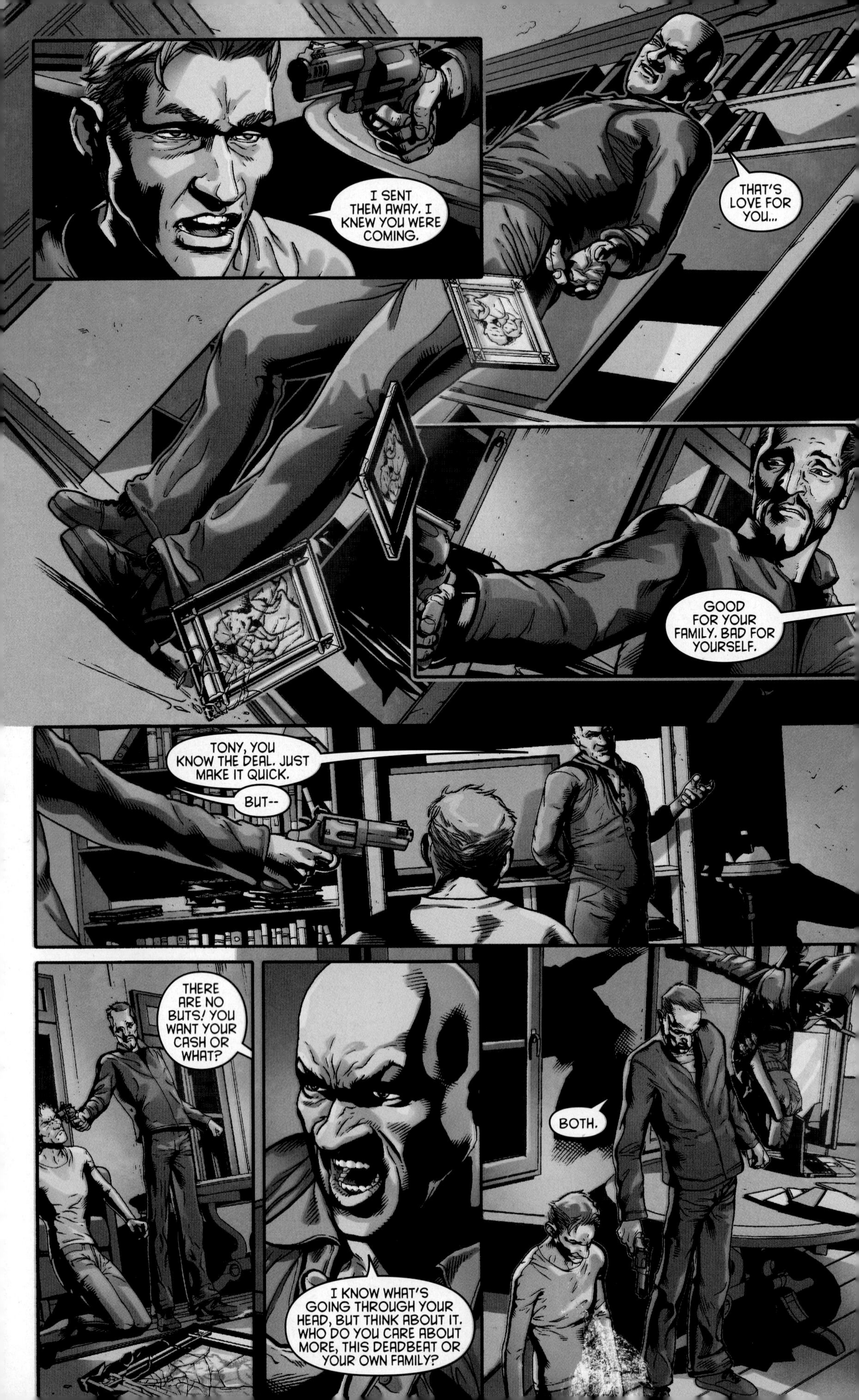
I SENT THEM AWAY. I KNEW YOU WERE COMING.
THAT'S LOVE FOR YOU...
GOOD FOR YOUR FAMILY. BAD FOR YOURSELF.
TONY, YOU KNOW THE DEAL. JUST MAKE IT QUICK.
BUT--
THERE ARE NO BUTS! YOU WANT YOUR CASH OR WHAT?
I KNOW WHAT'S GOING THROUGH YOUR HEAD, BUT THINK ABOUT IT. WHO DO YOU CARE ABOUT MORE, THIS DEADBEAT OR YOUR OWN FAMILY?
BOTH.

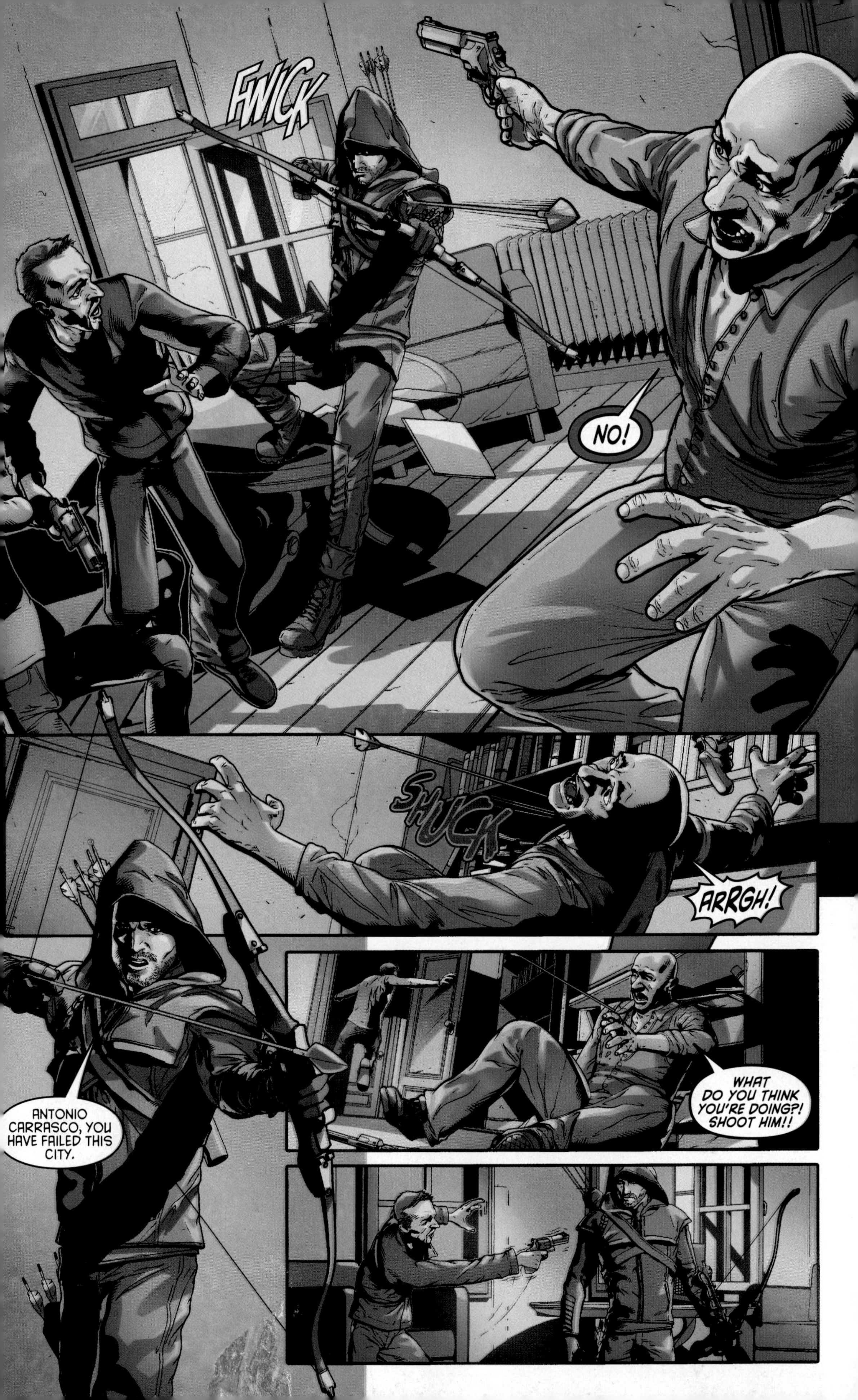
FWICK
NO!
SHUCK
ARRGH!
WHAT DO YOU THINK YOU'RE DOING?! SHOOT HIM!!
ANTONIO CARRASCO, YOU HAVE FAILED THIS CITY.

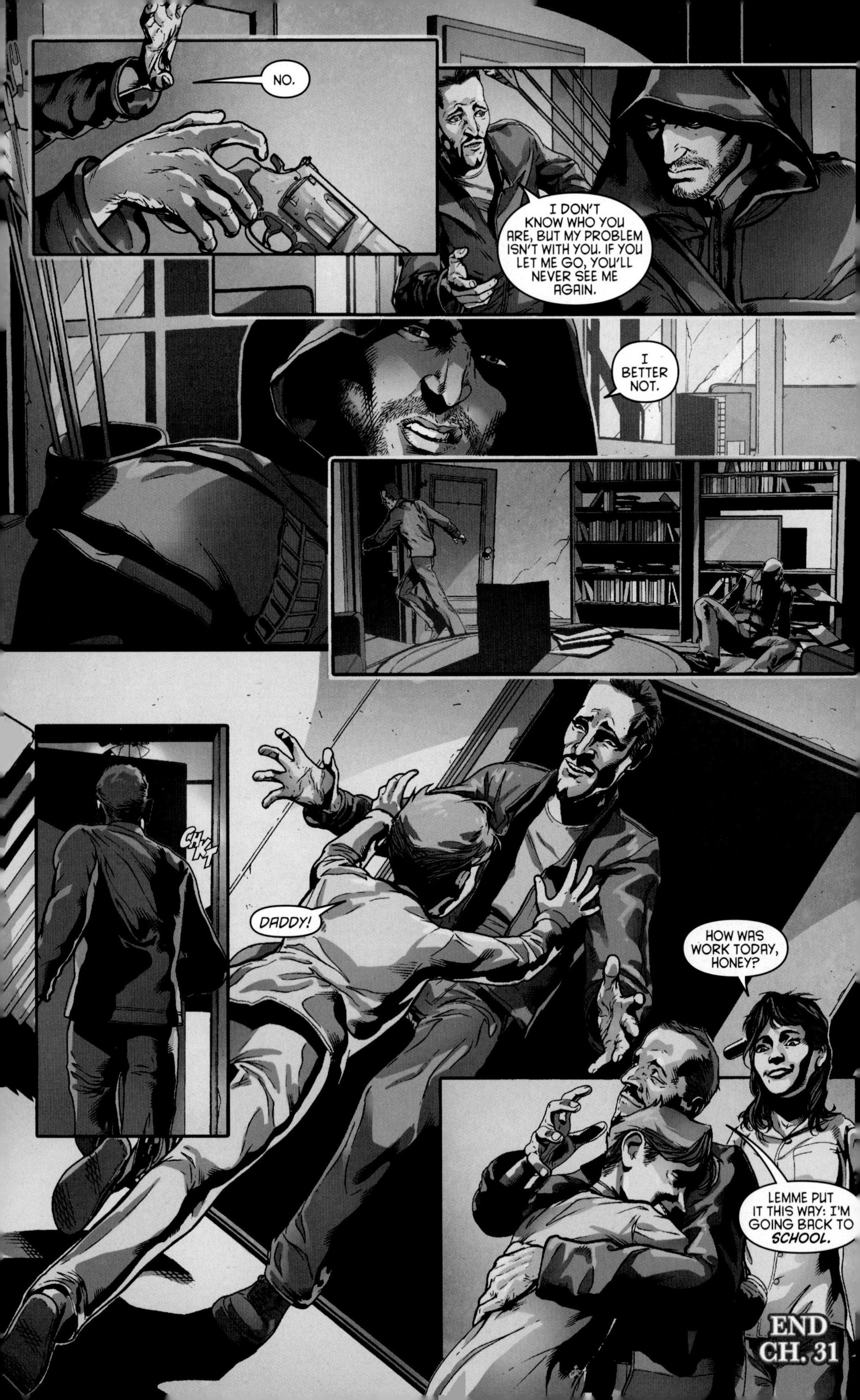
NO.
I DON'T KNOW WHO YOU ARE, BUT MY PROBLEM ISN'T WITH YOU. IF YOU LET ME GO, YOU'LL NEVER SEE ME AGAIN.
I BETTER NOT.
CHKT
DADDY!
HOW WAS WORK TODAY, HONEY?
LEMME PUT IT THIS WAY: I'M GOING BACK TO SCHOOL.
END CH. 31

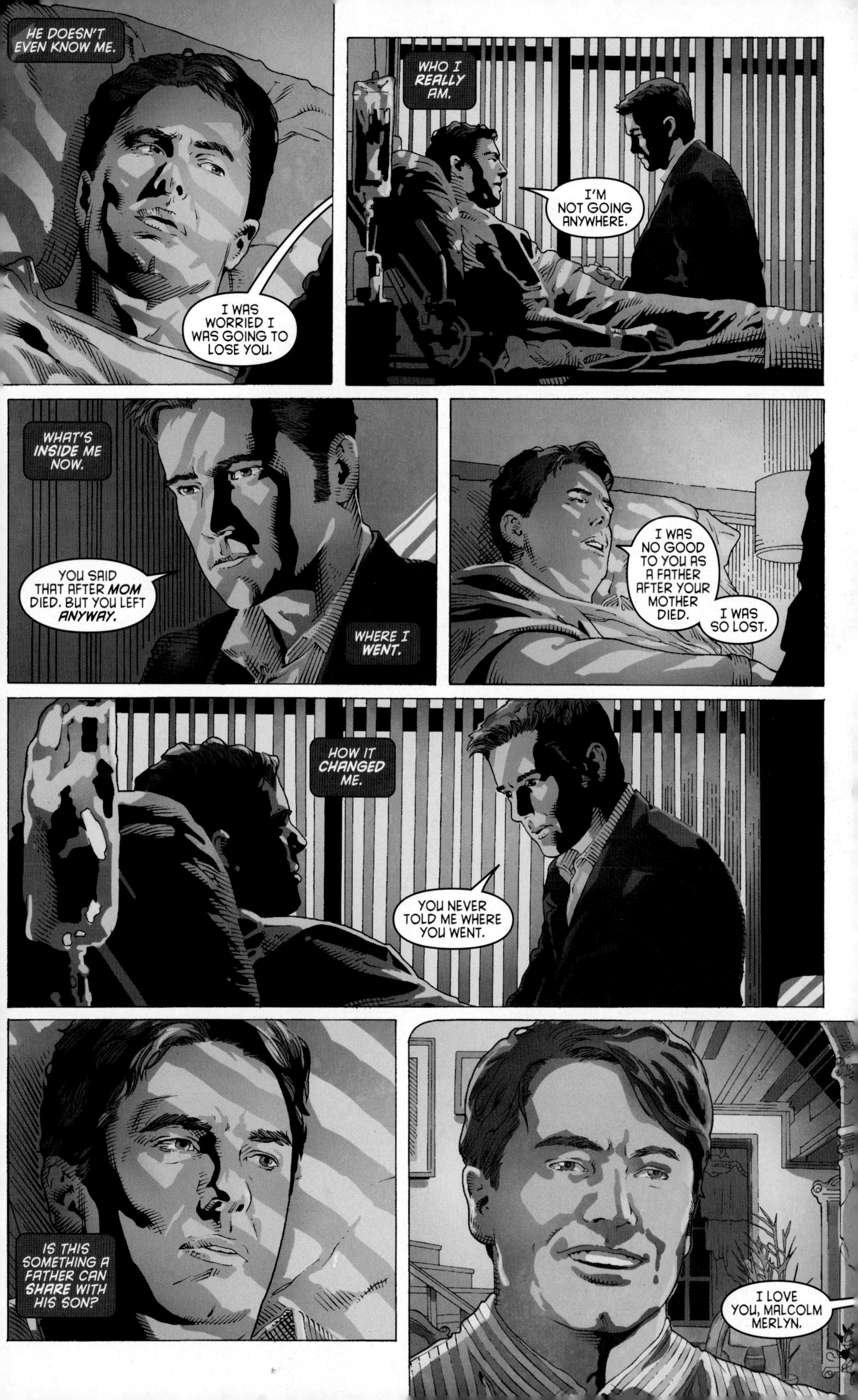
HE DOESN'T EVEN KNOW ME.
I WAS WORRIED I WAS GOING TO LOSE YOU.
WHO I REALLY AM.
I'M NOT GOING ANYWHERE.
WHAT'S INSIDE ME NOW.
YOU SAID THAT AFTER MOM DIED. BUT YOU LEFT ANYWAY.
WHERE I WENT.
I WAS NO GOOD TO YOU AS A FATHER AFTER YOUR MOTHER DIED.
I WAS SO LOST.
HOW IT CHANGED ME.
YOU NEVER TOLD ME WHERE YOU WENT.
IS THIS SOMETHING A FATHER CAN SHARE WITH HIS SON?
I LOVE YOU, MALCOLM MERLYN.

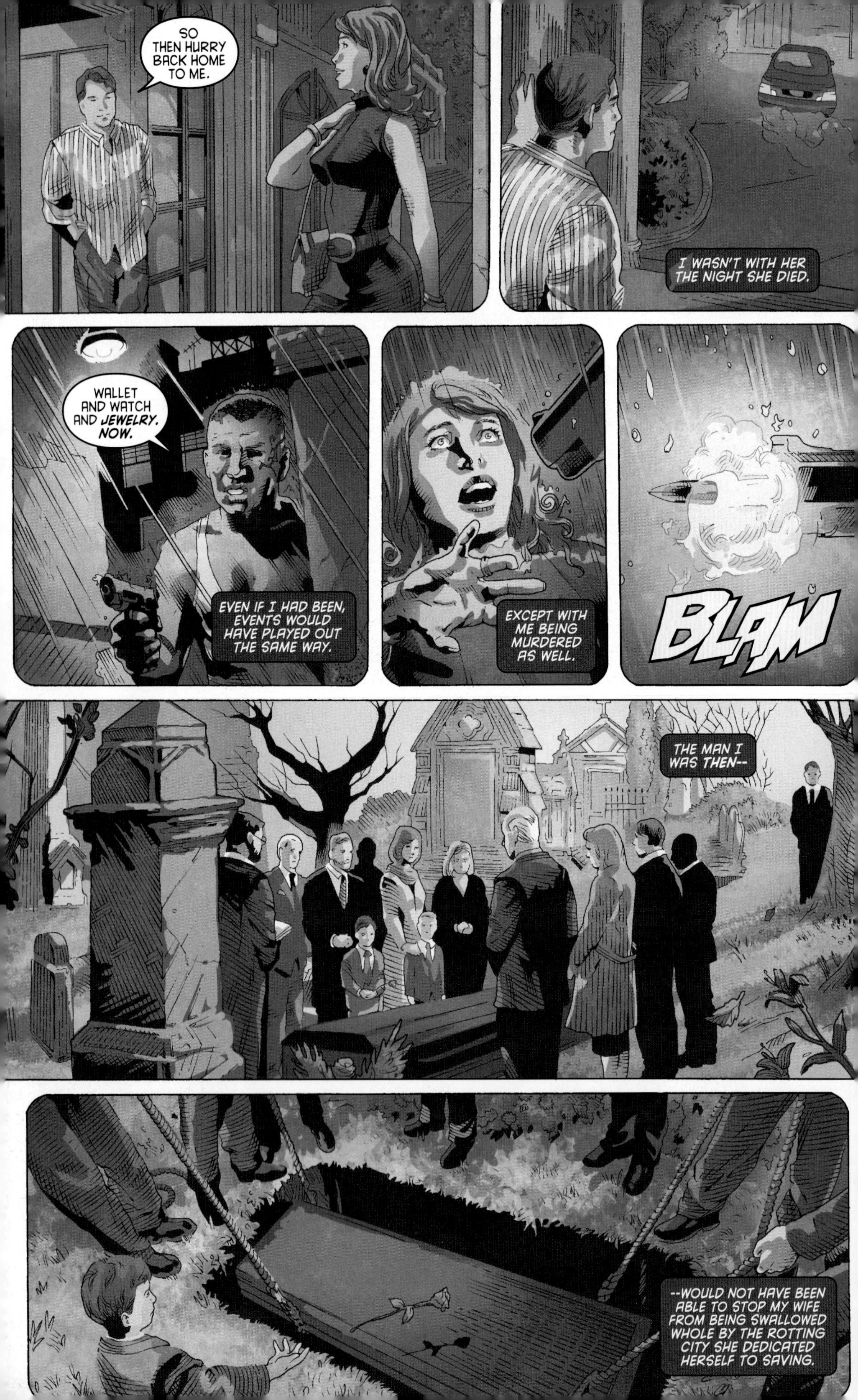
SO THEN HURRY BACK HOME TO ME.
I WASN'T WITH HER THE NIGHT SHE DIED.
WALLET AND WATCH AND JEWELRY. NOW.
EVEN IF I HAD BEEN, EVENTS WOULD HAVE PLAYED OUT THE SAME WAY.
EXCEPT WITH ME BEING MURDERED AS WELL.
BLAM
THE MAN I WAS THEN--
--WOULD NOT HAVE BEEN ABLE TO STOP MY WIFE FROM BEING SWALLOWED WHOLE BY THE ROTTING CITY SHE DEDICATED HERSELF TO SAVING.

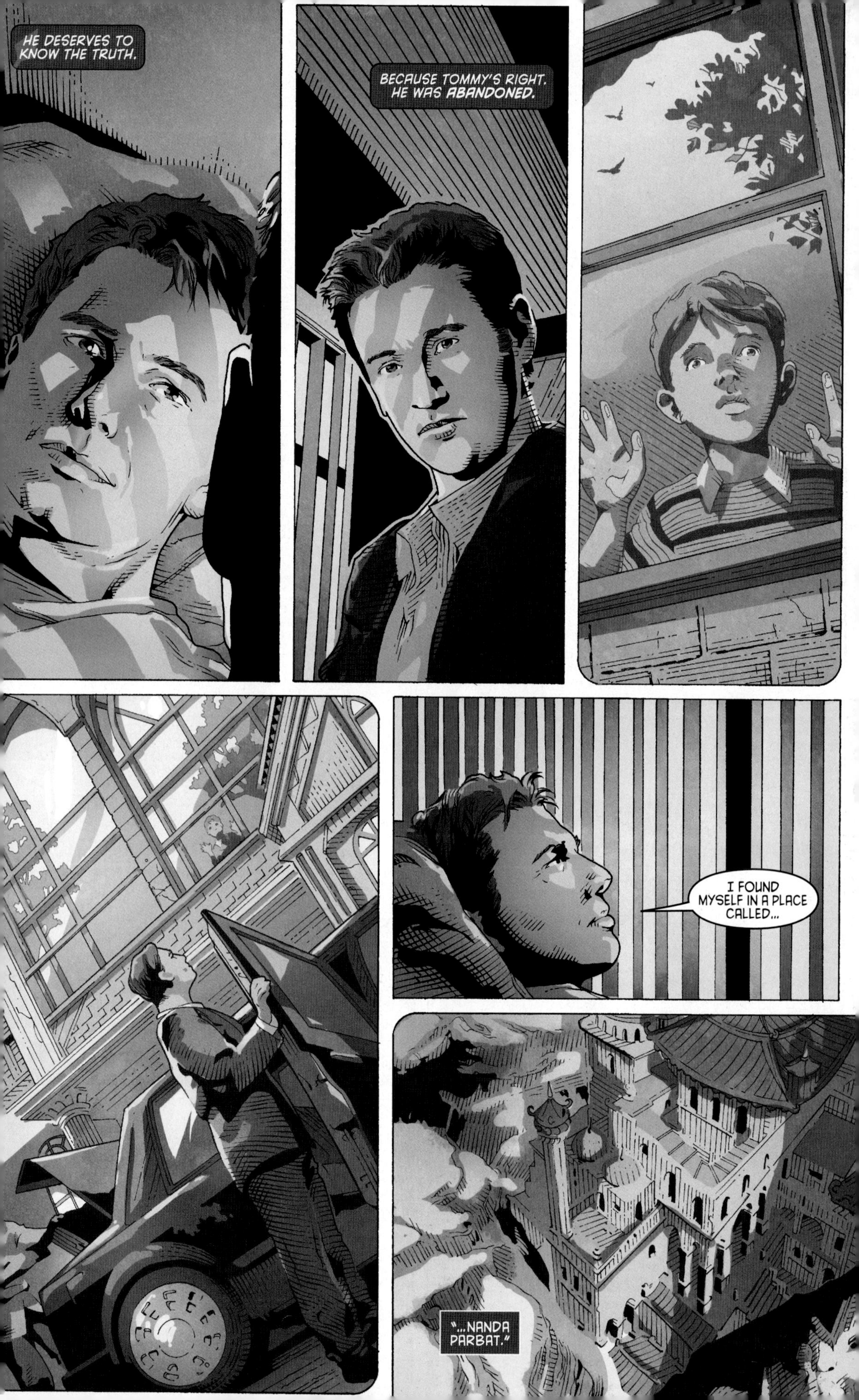
HE DESERVES TO KNOW THE TRUTH.
BECAUSE TOMMY'S RIGHT. HE WAS ABANDONED.
I FOUND MYSELF IN A PLACE CALLED...
"...NANDA PARBAT."

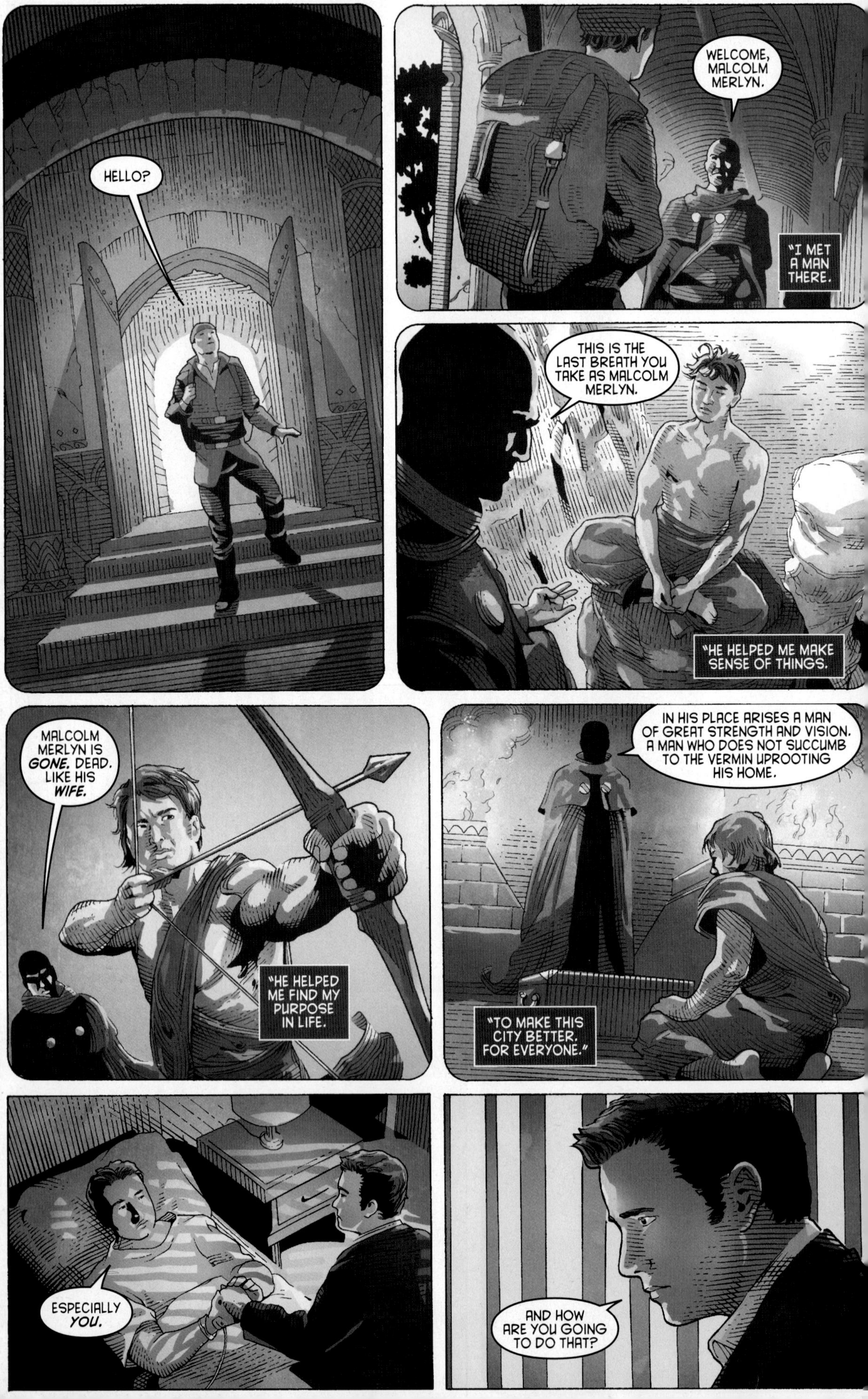
HELLO?
WELCOME, MALCOLM MERLYN.
"I MET A MAN THERE.
THIS IS THE LAST BREATH YOU TAKE AS MALCOLM MERLYN.
"HE HELPED ME MAKE SENSE OF THINGS.
MALCOLM MERLYN IS *GONE.* DEAD. LIKE HIS *WIFE.*
"HE HELPED ME FIND MY PURPOSE IN LIFE.
IN HIS PLACE ARISES A MAN OF GREAT STRENGTH AND VISION. A MAN WHO DOES NOT SUCCUMB TO THE VERMIN UPROOTING HIS HOME.
"TO MAKE THIS CITY BETTER. FOR EVERYONE."
ESPECIALLY *YOU.*
AND HOW ARE YOU GOING TO DO THAT?

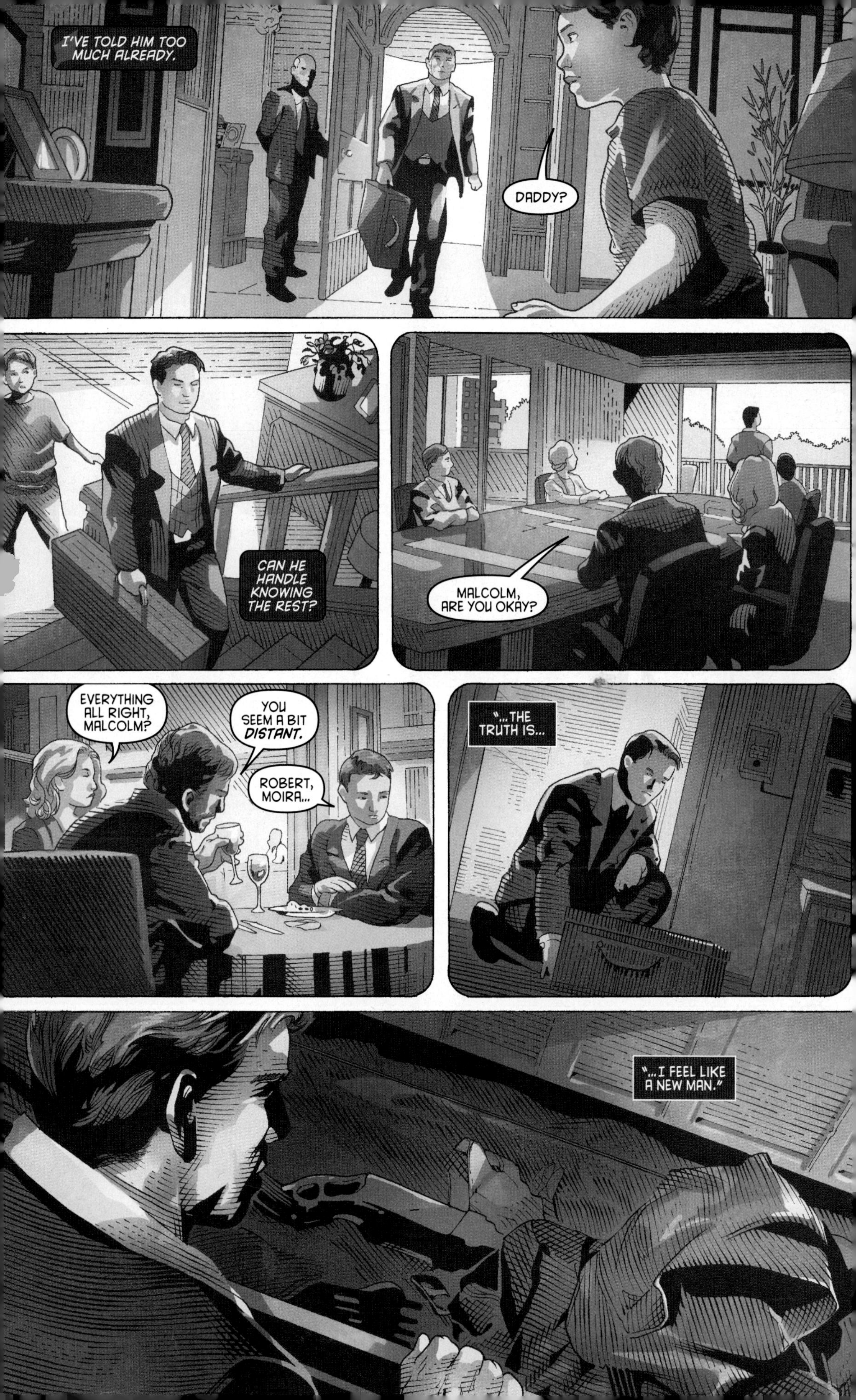
I'VE TOLD HIM TOO MUCH ALREADY.
DADDY?
CAN HE HANDLE KNOWING THE REST?
MALCOLM, ARE YOU OKAY?
EVERYTHING ALL RIGHT, MALCOLM?
YOU SEEM A BIT DISTANT.
ROBERT, MOIRA...
"...THE TRUTH IS...
"...I FEEL LIKE A NEW MAN."

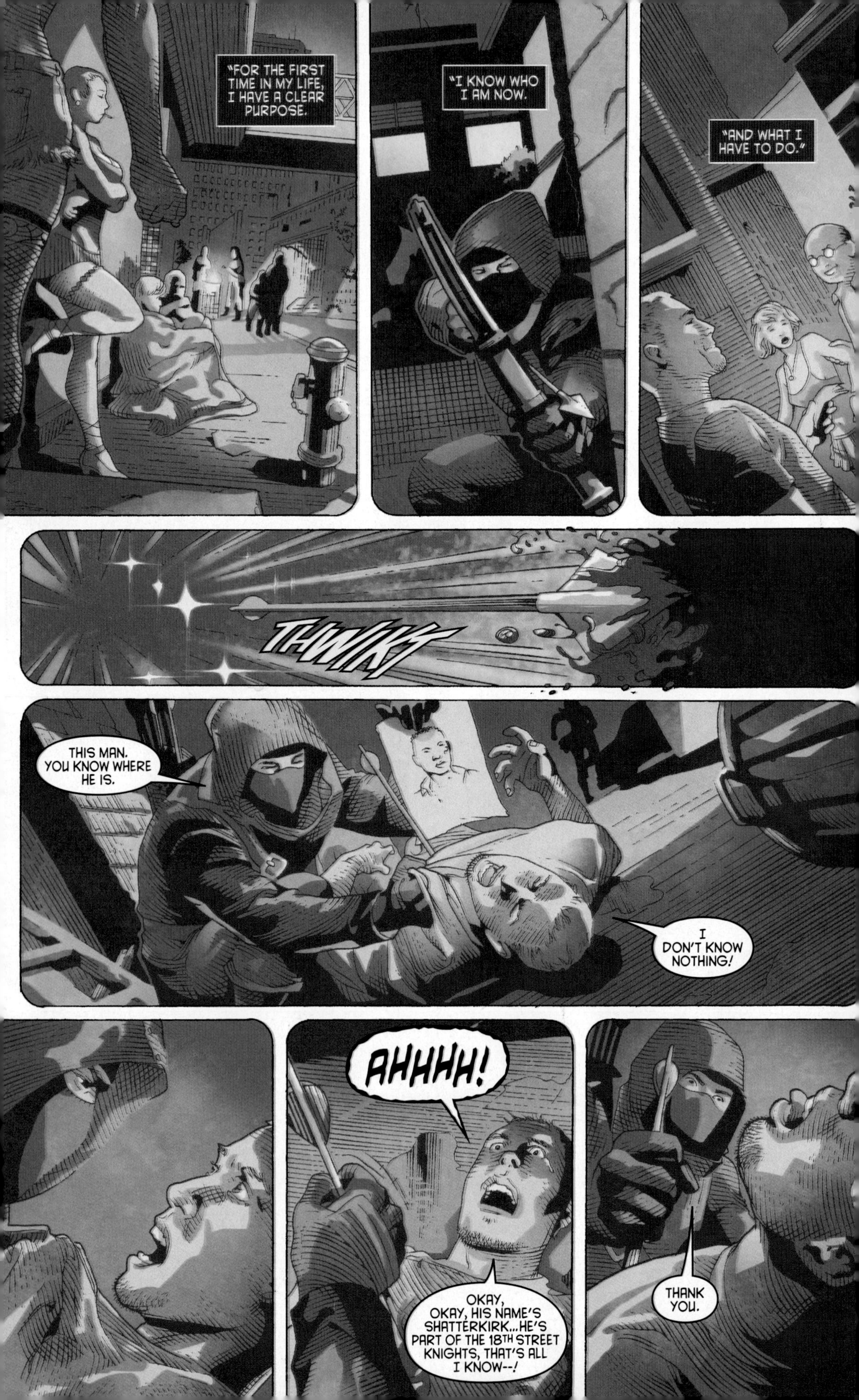
"FOR THE FIRST TIME IN MY LIFE, I HAVE A CLEAR PURPOSE.
"I KNOW WHO I AM NOW.
"AND WHAT I HAVE TO DO."
THWKT
THIS MAN. YOU KNOW WHERE HE IS.
I DON'T KNOW NOTHING!
AHHHH!
OKAY, OKAY, HIS NAME'S SHATTERKIRK...HE'S PART OF THE 18TH STREET KNIGHTS, THAT'S ALL I KNOW--!
THANK YOU.

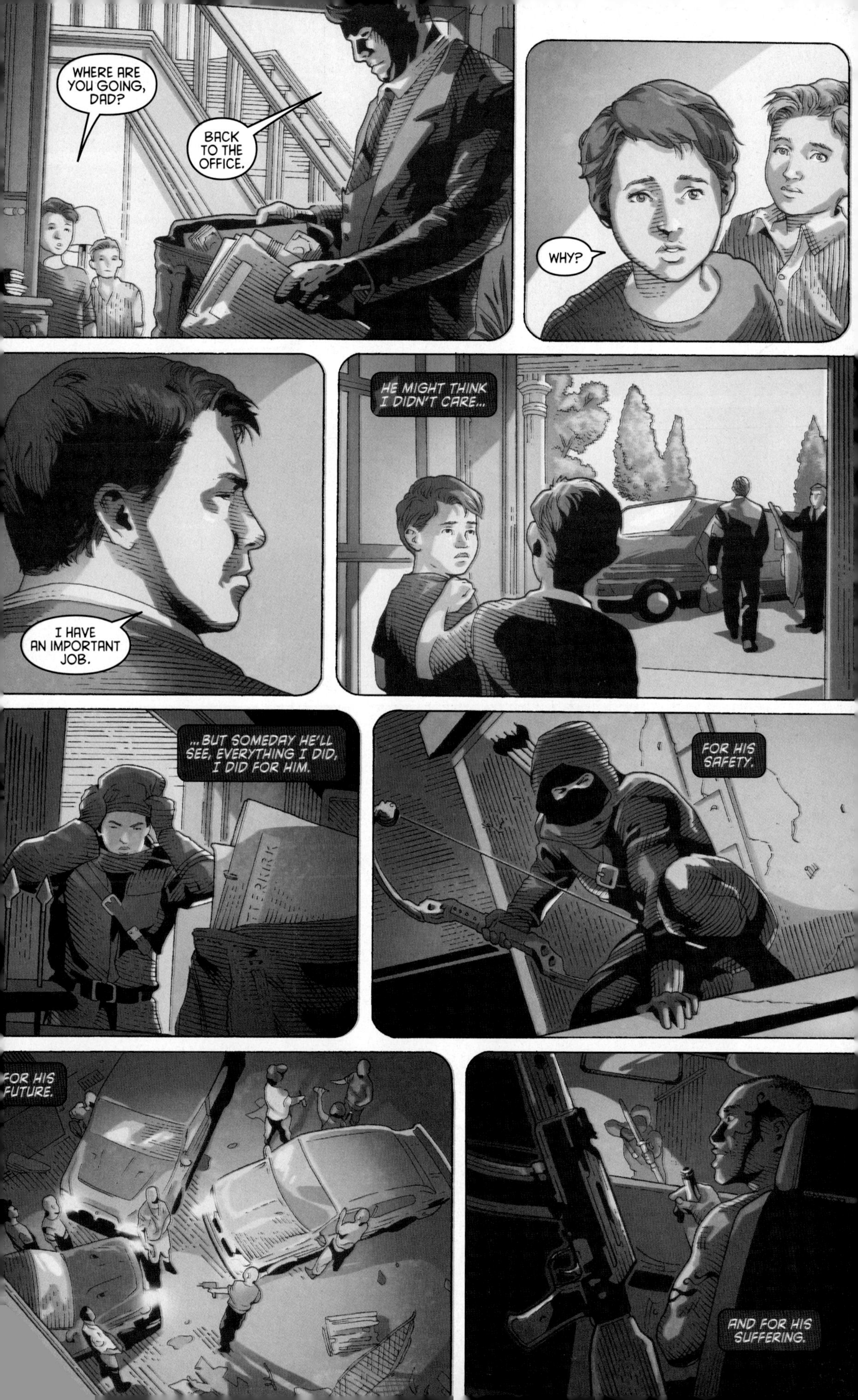
WHERE ARE YOU GOING, DAD?
BACK TO THE OFFICE.
WHY?
I HAVE AN IMPORTANT JOB.
HE MIGHT THINK I DIDN'T CARE...
...BUT SOMEDAY HE'LL SEE, EVERYTHING I DID, I DID FOR HIM.
FOR HIS SAFETY.
FOR HIS FUTURE.
AND FOR HIS SUFFERING.

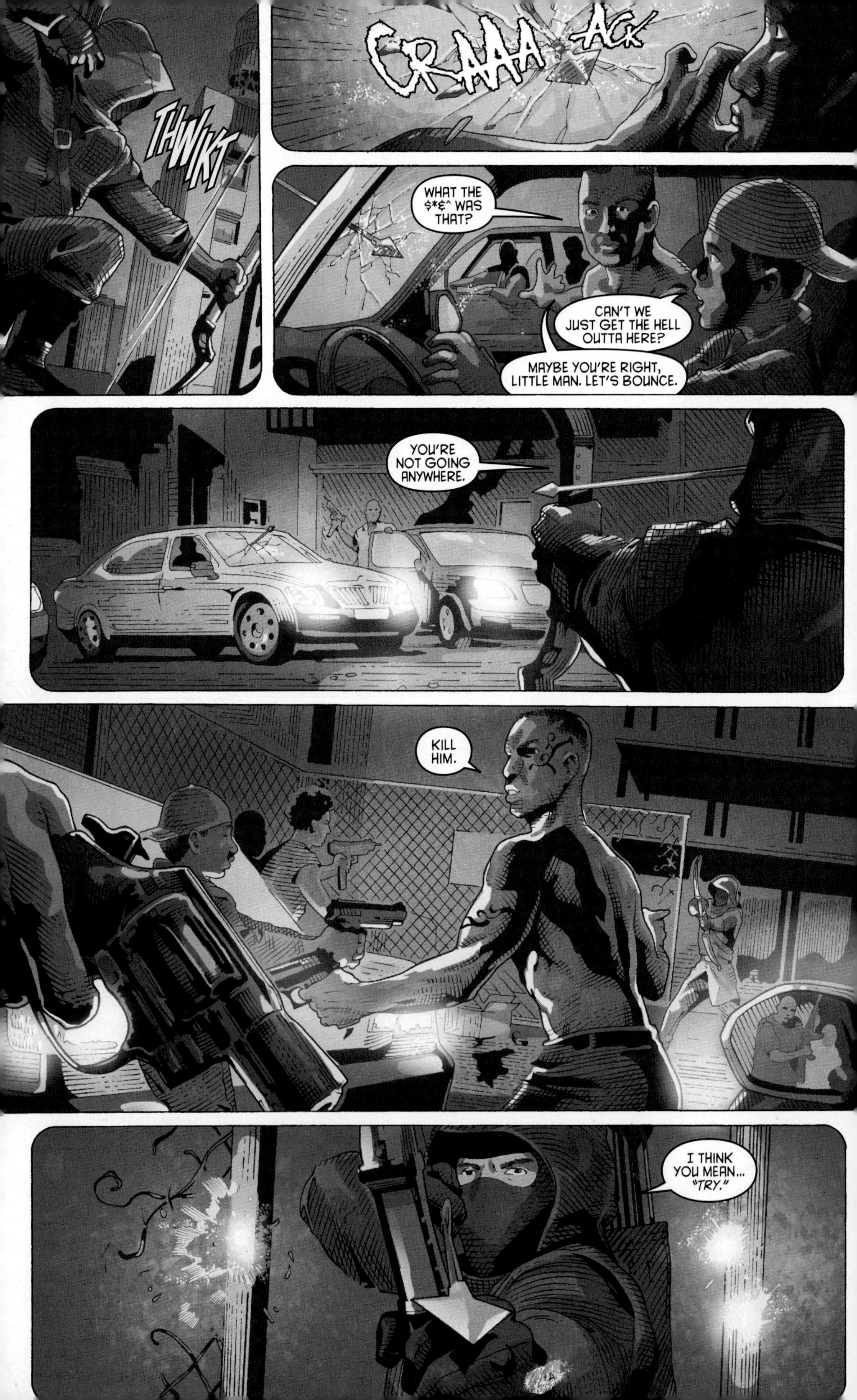
THWIKT
CRAAAA-ACK
WHAT THE $*&^ WAS THAT?
CAN'T WE JUST GET THE HELL OUTTA HERE?
MAYBE YOU'RE RIGHT, LITTLE MAN. LET'S BOUNCE.
YOU'RE NOT GOING ANYWHERE.
KILL HIM.
I THINK YOU MEAN... "TRY."

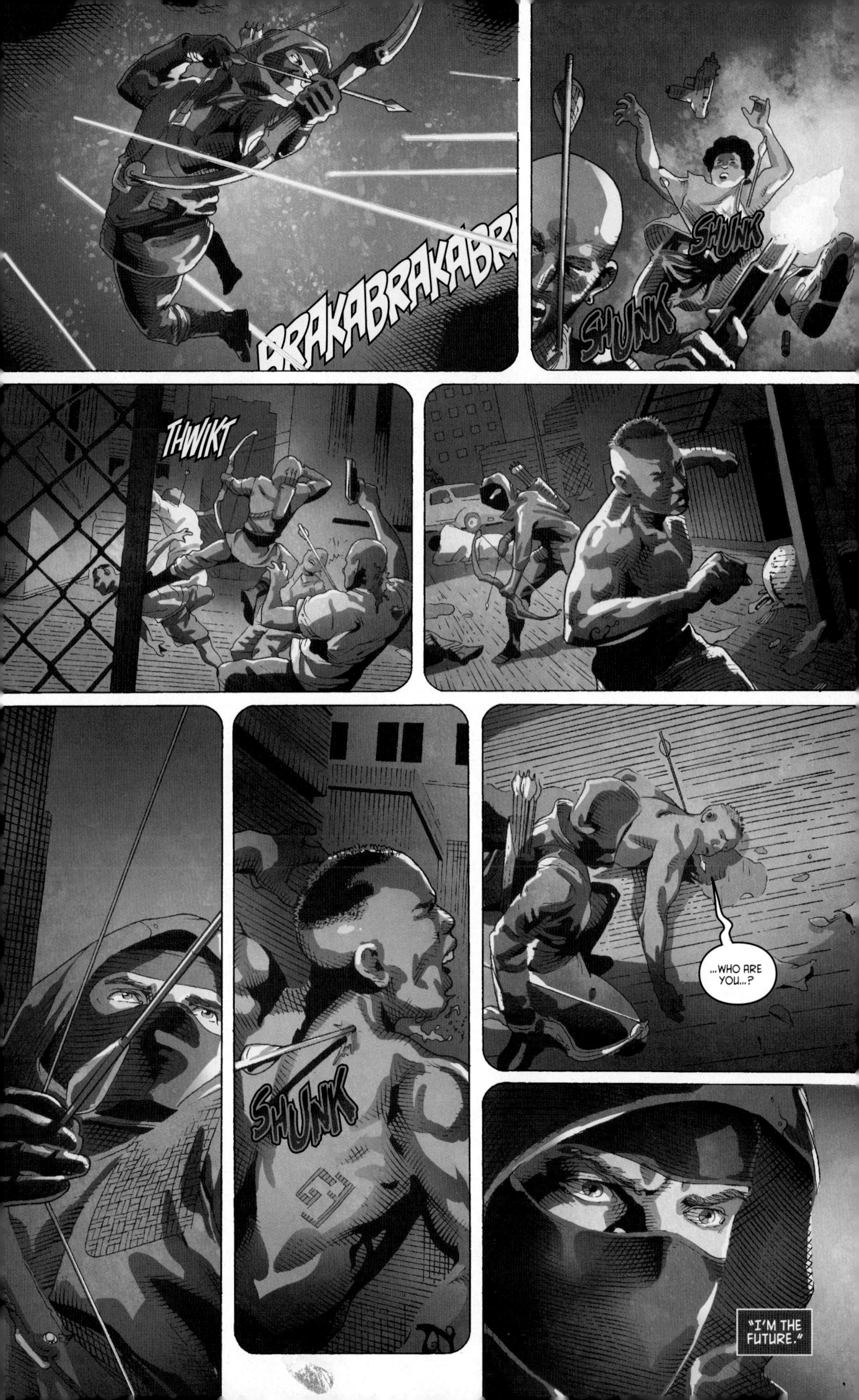
BRAKABRAKABR
SHUNK
SHUNK
THWIKT
SHUNK
...WHO ARE YOU...?
"I'M THE FUTURE."

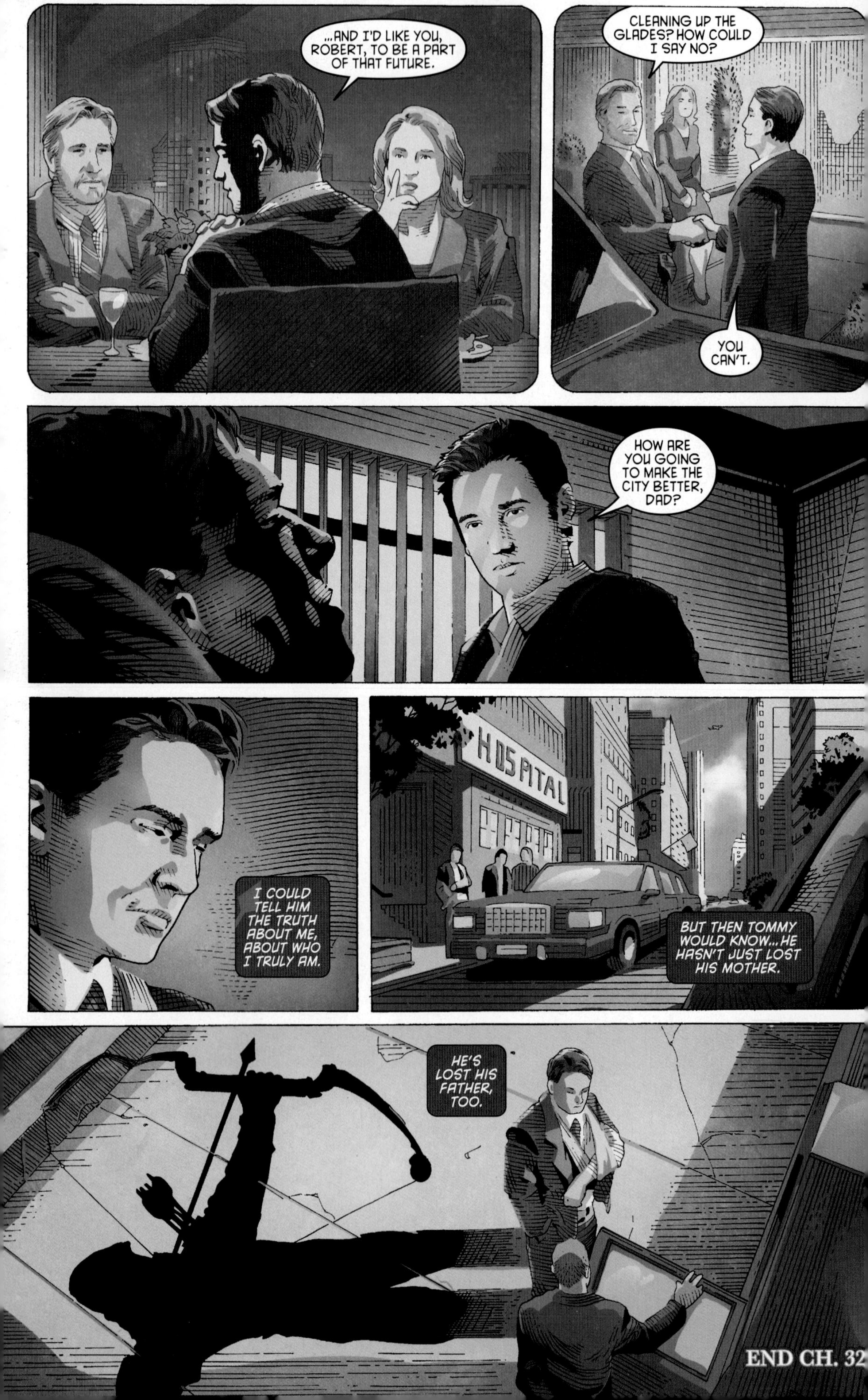
...AND I'D LIKE YOU, ROBERT, TO BE A PART OF THAT FUTURE.
CLEANING UP THE GLADES? HOW COULD I SAY NO?
YOU CAN'T.
HOW ARE YOU GOING TO MAKE THE CITY BETTER, DAD?
I COULD TELL HIM THE TRUTH ABOUT ME, ABOUT WHO I TRULY AM.
HOSPITAL
BUT THEN TOMMY WOULD KNOW... HE HASN'T JUST LOST HIS MOTHER.
HE'S LOST HIS FATHER, TOO.
END CH. 32

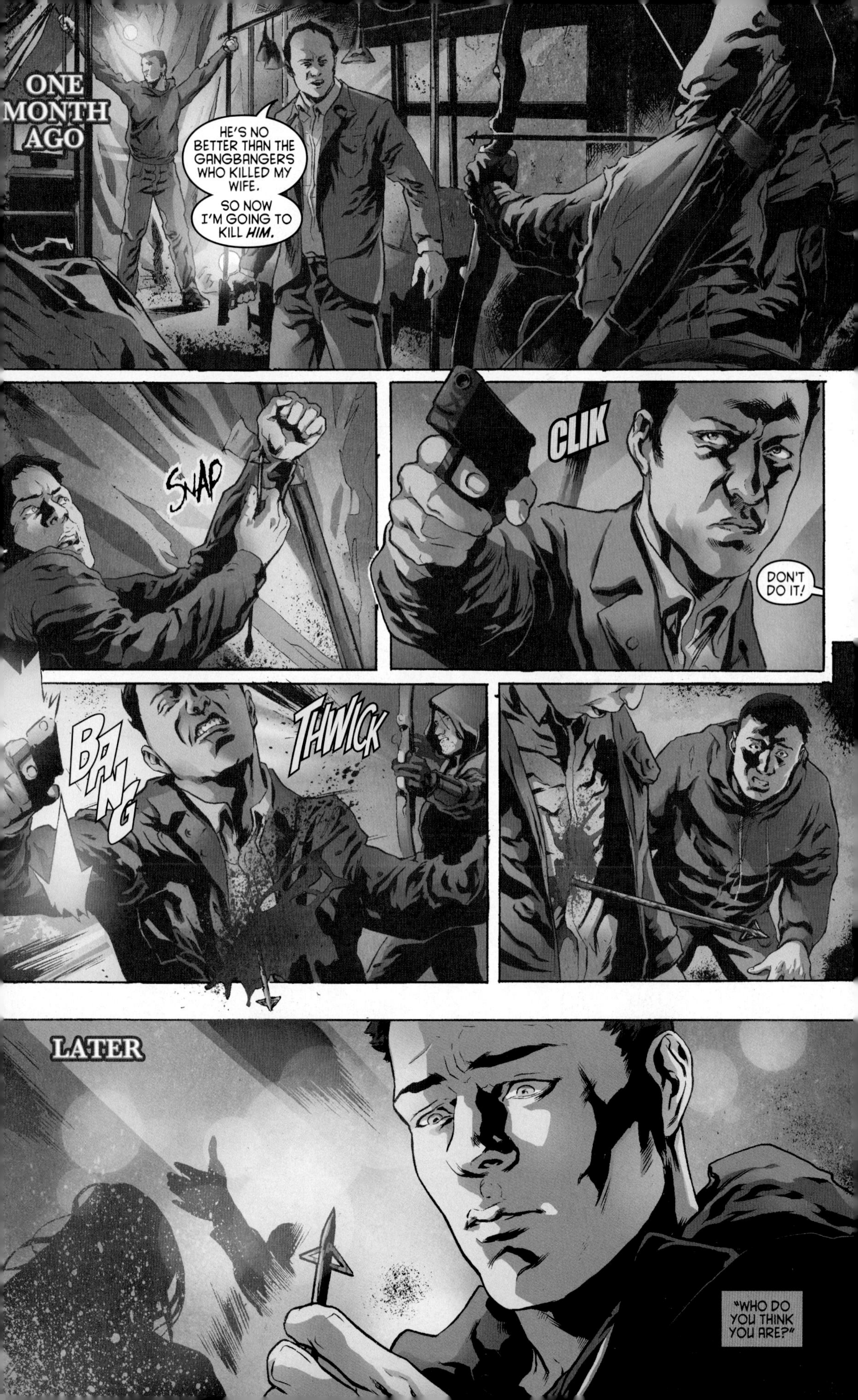
ONE MONTH AGO
HE'S NO BETTER THAN THE GANGBANGERS WHO KILLED MY WIFE.
SO NOW I'M GOING TO KILL *HIM.*
SNAP
CLIK
DON'T DO IT!
BANG
THWICK
LATER
"WHO DO YOU THINK YOU ARE?"

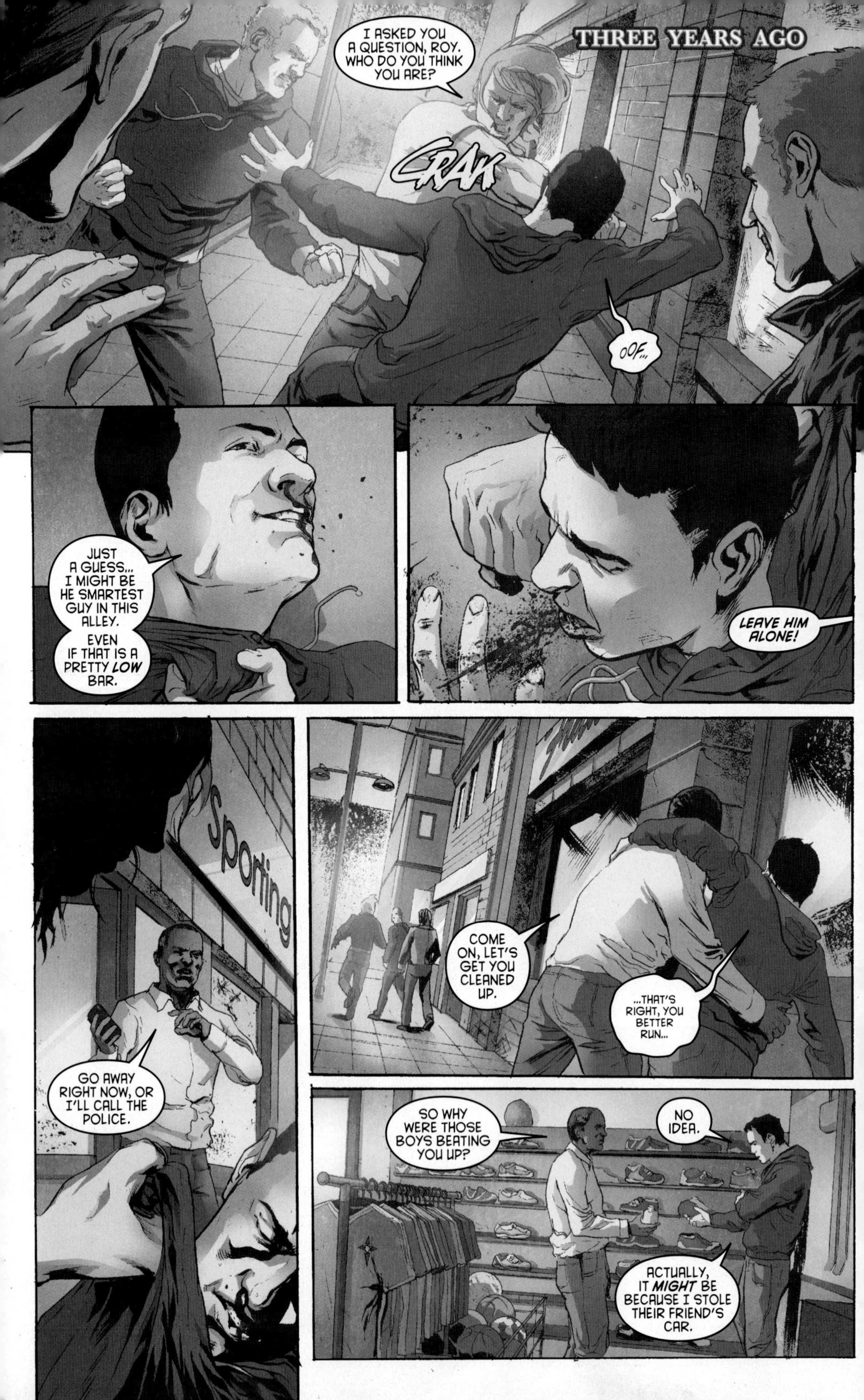
THREE YEARS AGO
I ASKED YOU A QUESTION, ROY. WHO DO YOU THINK YOU ARE?
CRAK
OOF...
JUST A GUESS... I MIGHT BE HE SMARTEST GUY IN THIS ALLEY.
EVEN IF THAT IS A PRETTY LOW BAR.
LEAVE HIM ALONE!
Sporting
GO AWAY RIGHT NOW, OR I'LL CALL THE POLICE.
COME ON, LET'S GET YOU CLEANED UP.
...THAT'S RIGHT, YOU BETTER RUN...
SO WHY WERE THOSE BOYS BEATING YOU UP?
NO IDEA.
ACTUALLY, IT MIGHT BE BECAUSE I STOLE THEIR FRIEND'S CAR.

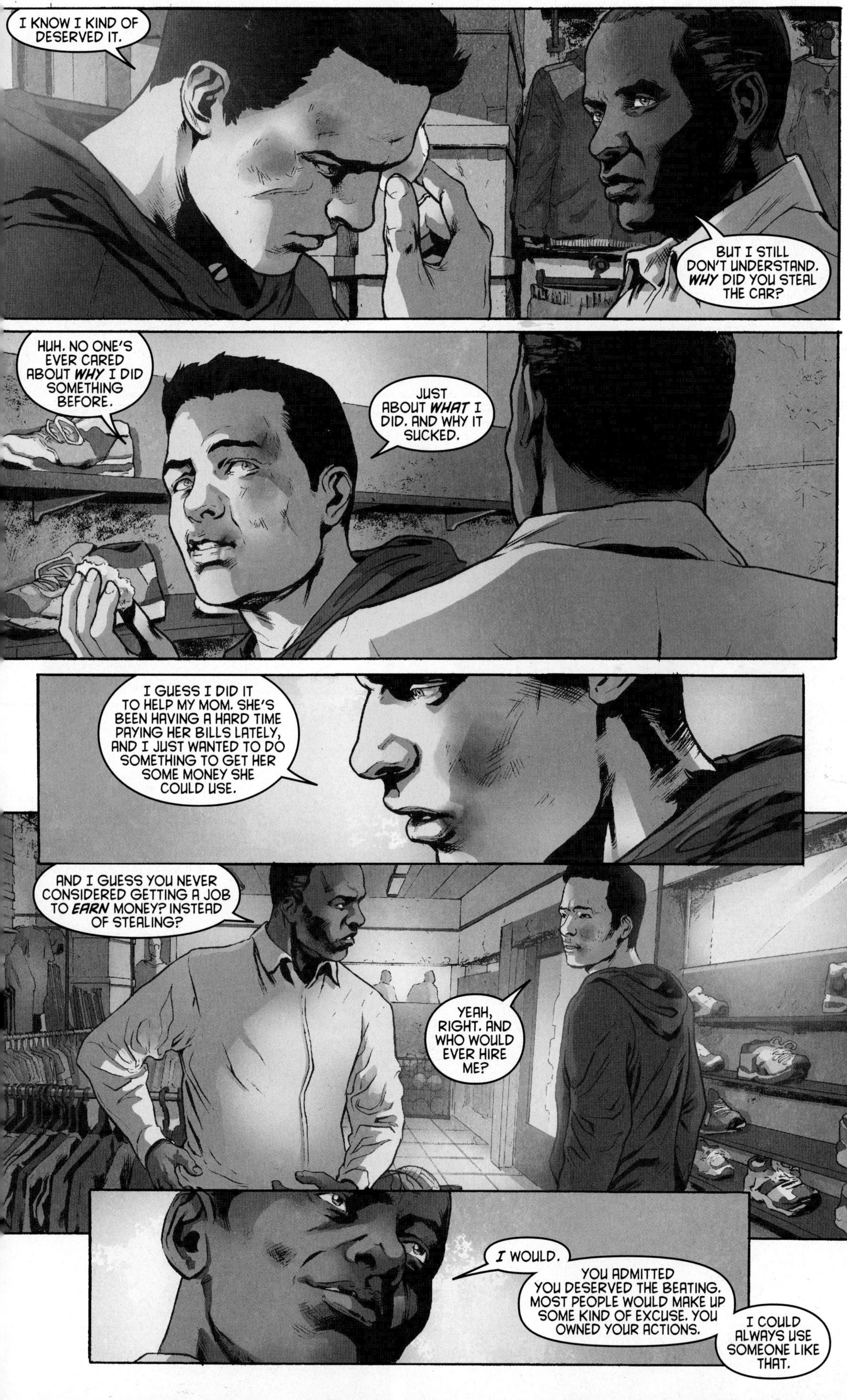
I KNOW I KIND OF DESERVED IT.
BUT I STILL DON'T UNDERSTAND. WHY DID YOU STEAL THE CAR?
HUH. NO ONE'S EVER CARED ABOUT WHY I DID SOMETHING BEFORE.
JUST ABOUT WHAT I DID. AND WHY IT SUCKED.
I GUESS I DID IT TO HELP MY MOM. SHE'S BEEN HAVING A HARD TIME PAYING HER BILLS LATELY, AND I JUST WANTED TO DO SOMETHING TO GET HER SOME MONEY SHE COULD USE.
AND I GUESS YOU NEVER CONSIDERED GETTING A JOB TO EARN MONEY? INSTEAD OF STEALING?
YEAH, RIGHT. AND WHO WOULD EVER HIRE ME?
I WOULD.
YOU ADMITTED YOU DESERVED THE BEATING. MOST PEOPLE WOULD MAKE UP SOME KIND OF EXCUSE. YOU OWNED YOUR ACTIONS.
I COULD ALWAYS USE SOMEONE LIKE THAT.

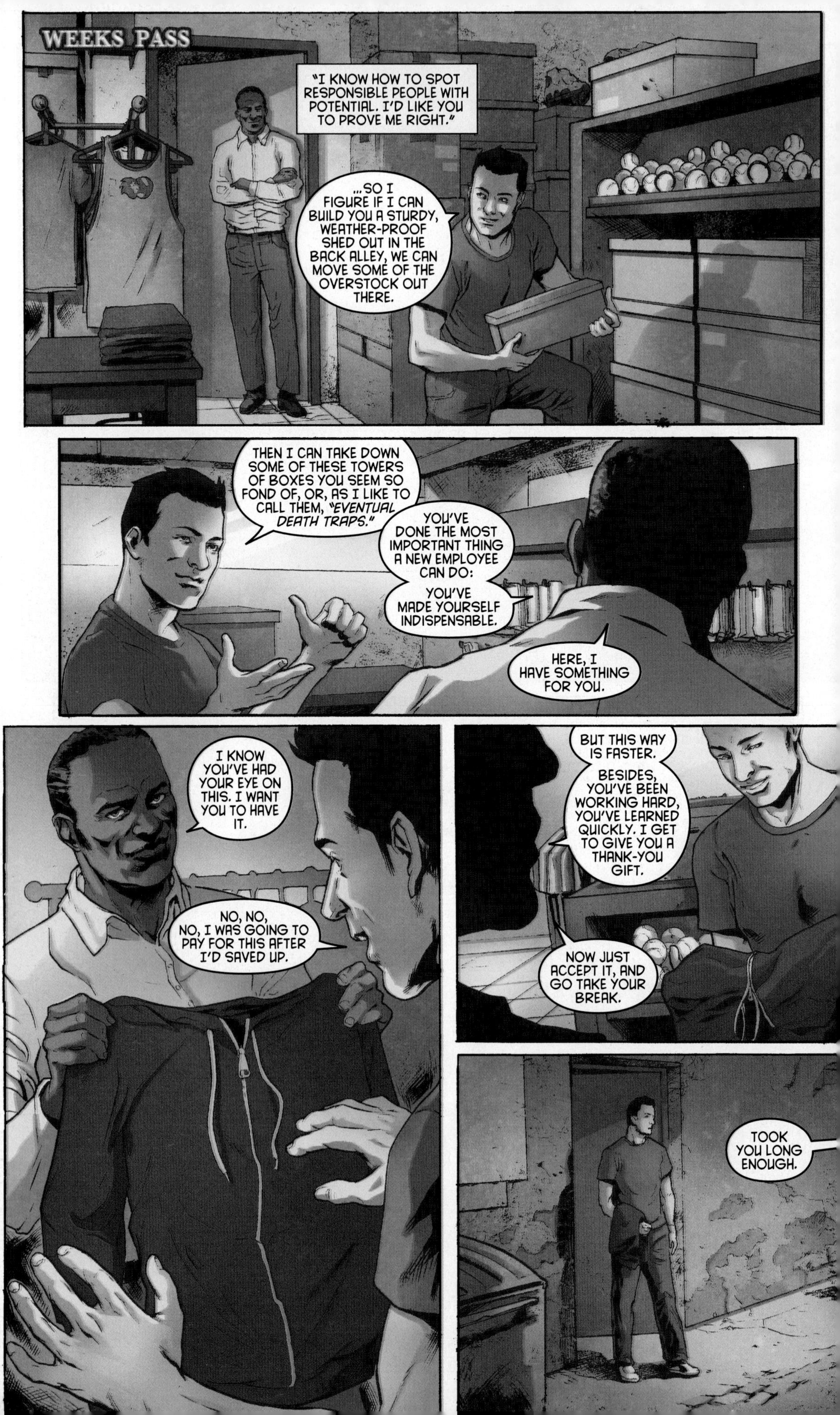
WEEKS PASS
"I KNOW HOW TO SPOT RESPONSIBLE PEOPLE WITH POTENTIAL. I'D LIKE YOU TO PROVE ME RIGHT."
...SO I FIGURE IF I CAN BUILD YOU A STURDY, WEATHER-PROOF SHED OUT IN THE BACK ALLEY, WE CAN MOVE SOME OF THE OVERSTOCK OUT THERE.
THEN I CAN TAKE DOWN SOME OF THESE TOWERS OF BOXES YOU SEEM SO FOND OF, OR, AS I LIKE TO CALL THEM, *"EVENTUAL DEATH TRAPS."*
YOU'VE DONE THE MOST IMPORTANT THING A NEW EMPLOYEE CAN DO:
YOU'VE MADE YOURSELF INDISPENSABLE.
HERE, I HAVE SOMETHING FOR YOU.
I KNOW YOU'VE HAD YOUR EYE ON THIS. I WANT YOU TO HAVE IT.
NO, NO, NO, I WAS GOING TO PAY FOR THIS AFTER I'D SAVED UP.
BUT THIS WAY IS FASTER.
BESIDES, YOU'VE BEEN WORKING HARD, YOU'VE LEARNED QUICKLY. I GET TO GIVE YOU A THANK-YOU GIFT.
NOW JUST ACCEPT IT, AND GO TAKE YOUR BREAK.
TOOK YOU LONG ENOUGH.

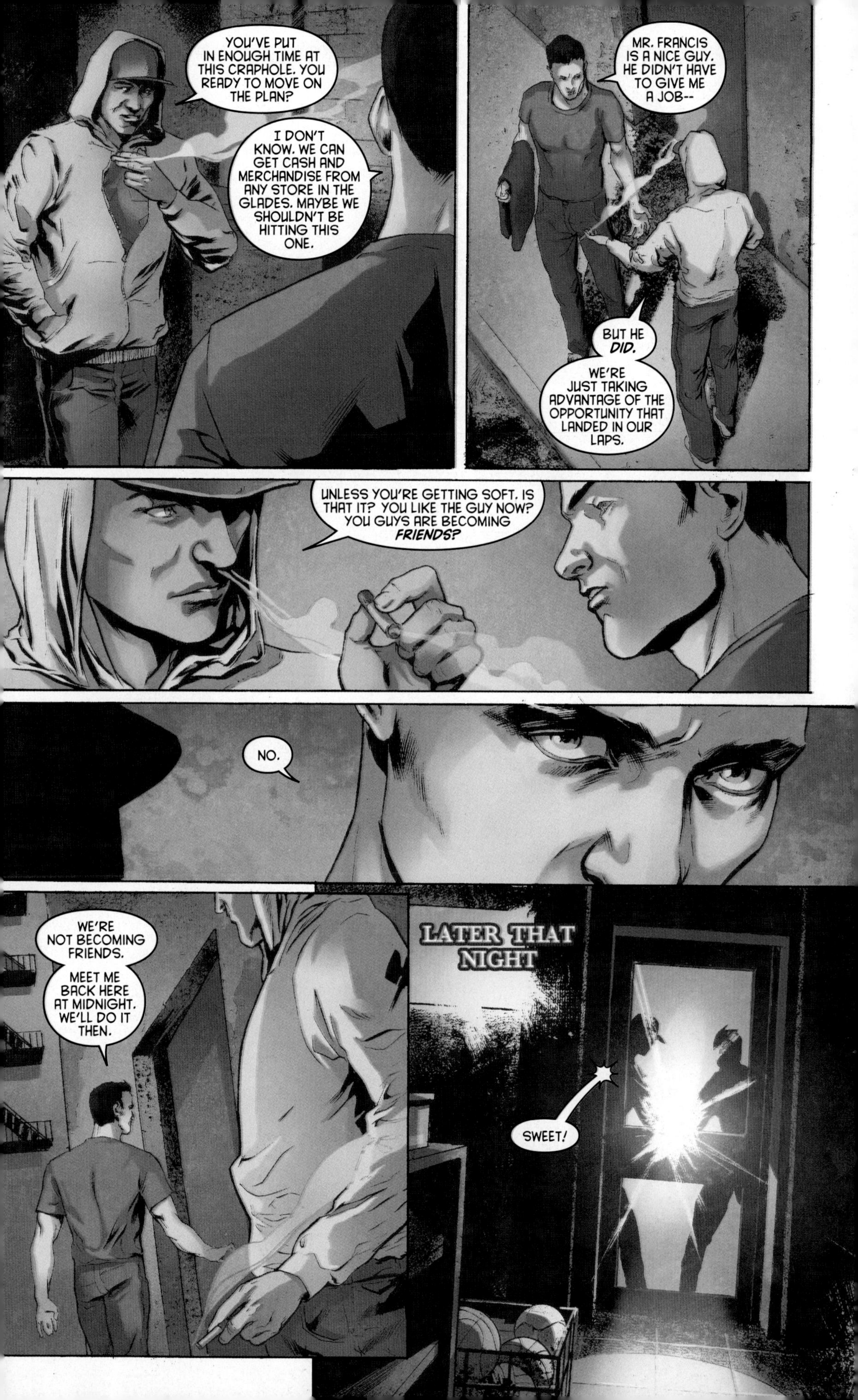
YOU'VE PUT IN ENOUGH TIME AT THIS CRAPHOLE. YOU READY TO MOVE ON THE PLAN?
I DON'T KNOW. WE CAN GET CASH AND MERCHANDISE FROM ANY STORE IN THE GLADES. MAYBE WE SHOULDN'T BE HITTING THIS ONE.
MR. FRANCIS IS A NICE GUY. HE DIDN'T HAVE TO GIVE ME A JOB--
BUT HE *DID.*
WE'RE JUST TAKING ADVANTAGE OF THE OPPORTUNITY THAT LANDED IN OUR LAPS.
UNLESS YOU'RE GETTING SOFT. IS THAT IT? YOU LIKE THE GUY NOW? YOU GUYS ARE BECOMING *FRIENDS?*
NO.
WE'RE NOT BECOMING FRIENDS.
MEET ME BACK HERE AT MIDNIGHT. WE'LL DO IT THEN.
LATER THAT NIGHT
SWEET!

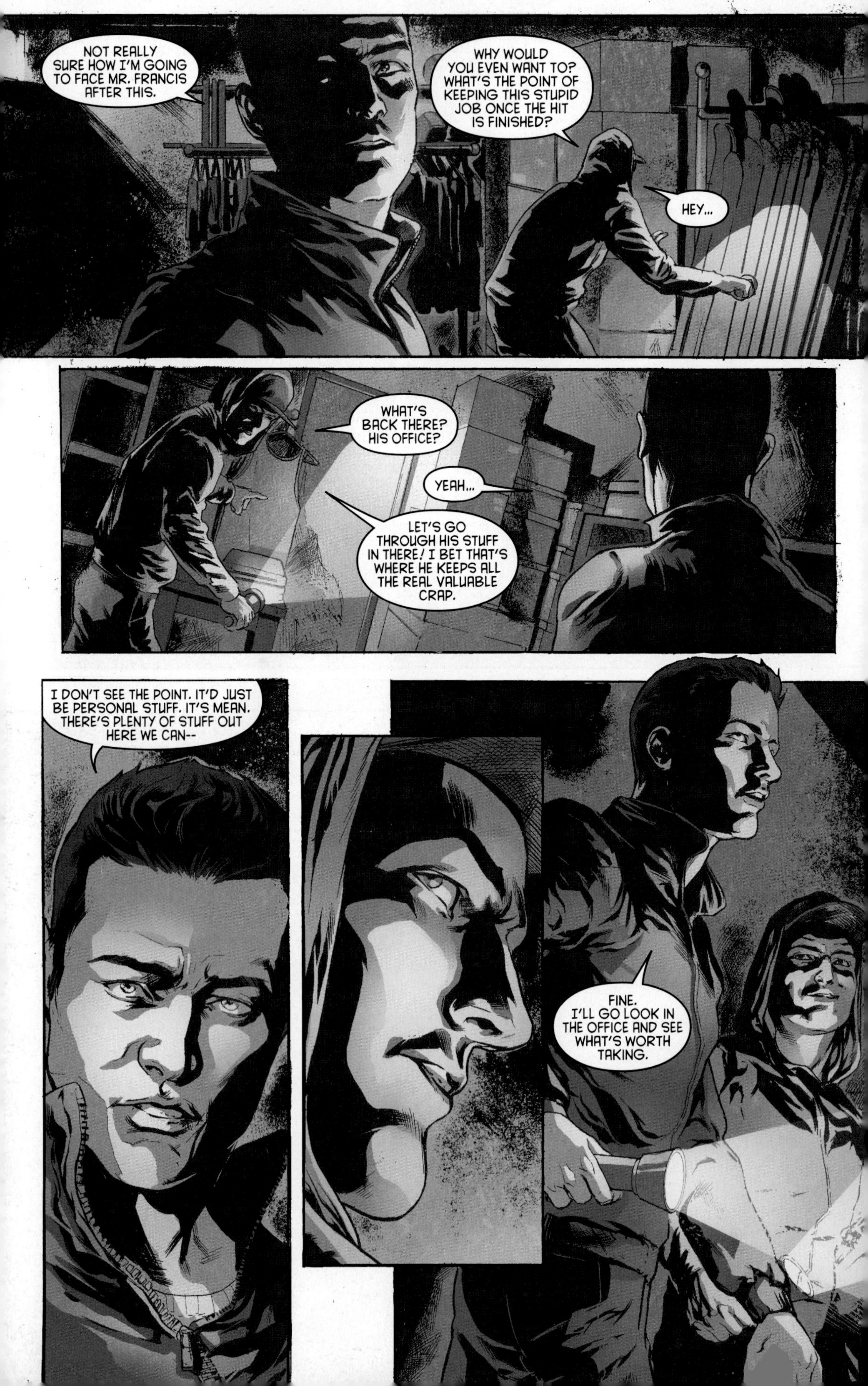
NOT REALLY SURE HOW I'M GOING TO FACE MR. FRANCIS AFTER THIS.
WHY WOULD YOU EVEN WANT TO? WHAT'S THE POINT OF KEEPING THIS STUPID JOB ONCE THE HIT IS FINISHED?
HEY...
WHAT'S BACK THERE? HIS OFFICE?
YEAH...
LET'S GO THROUGH HIS STUFF IN THERE! I BET THAT'S WHERE HE KEEPS ALL THE REAL VALUABLE CRAP.
I DON'T SEE THE POINT. IT'D JUST BE PERSONAL STUFF. IT'S MEAN. THERE'S PLENTY OF STUFF OUT HERE WE CAN--
FINE. I'LL GO LOOK IN THE OFFICE AND SEE WHAT'S WORTH TAKING.

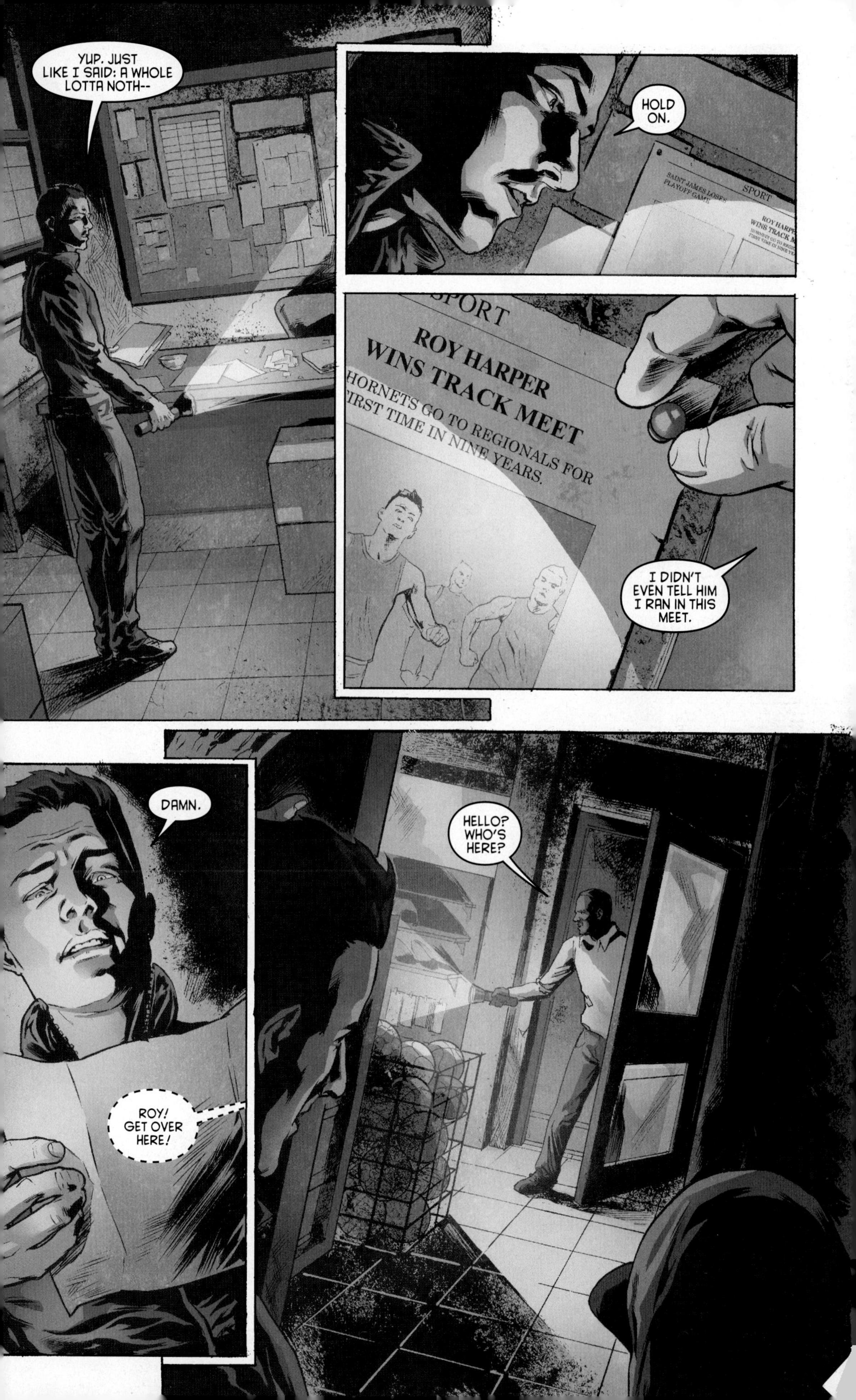
YUP. JUST LIKE I SAID: A WHOLE LOTTA NOTH--
HOLD ON.
SPORT
ROY HARPER WINS TRACK MEET
I DIDN'T EVEN TELL HIM I RAN IN THIS MEET.
DAMN.
ROY! GET OVER HERE!
HELLO? WHO'S HERE?

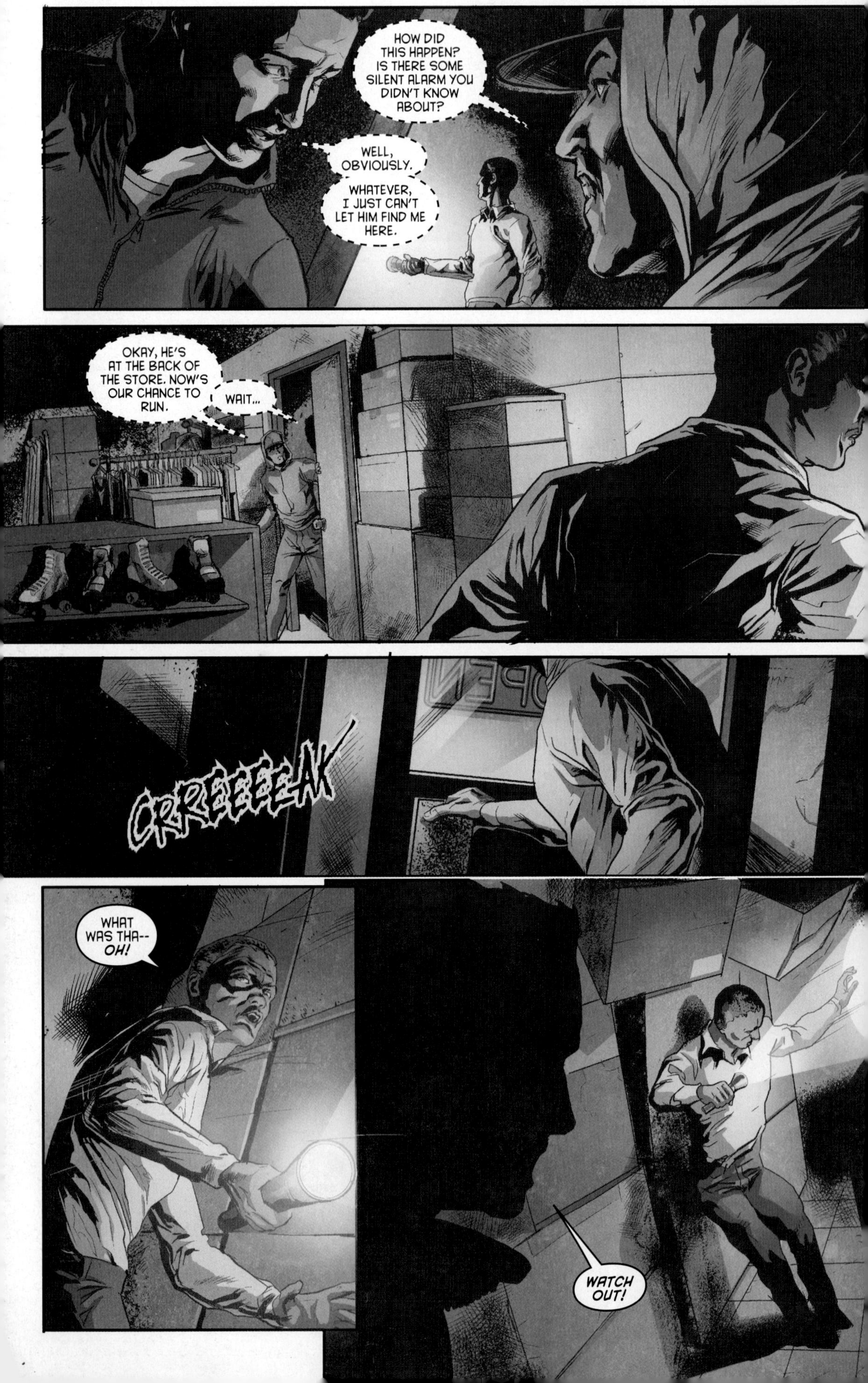
HOW DID THIS HAPPEN? IS THERE SOME SILENT ALARM YOU DIDN'T KNOW ABOUT?
WELL, OBVIOUSLY.
WHATEVER, I JUST CAN'T LET HIM FIND ME HERE.
OKAY, HE'S AT THE BACK OF THE STORE. NOW'S OUR CHANCE TO RUN.
WAIT...
CRREEEEAK
WHAT WAS THA-- OH!
WATCH OUT!

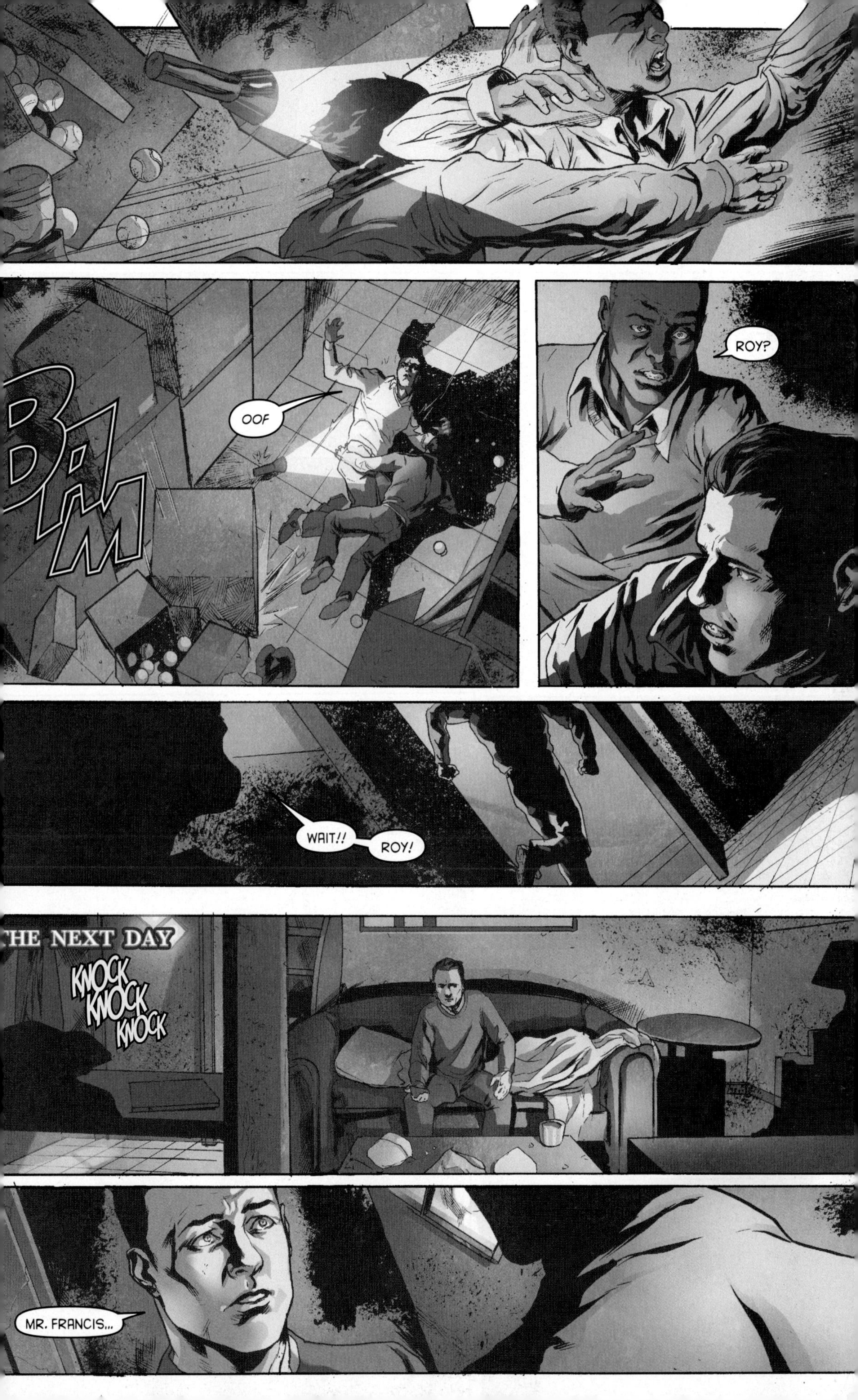
BAM
OOF
ROY?
WAIT!!
ROY!
THE NEXT DAY
KNOCK KNOCK KNOCK
MR. FRANCIS...

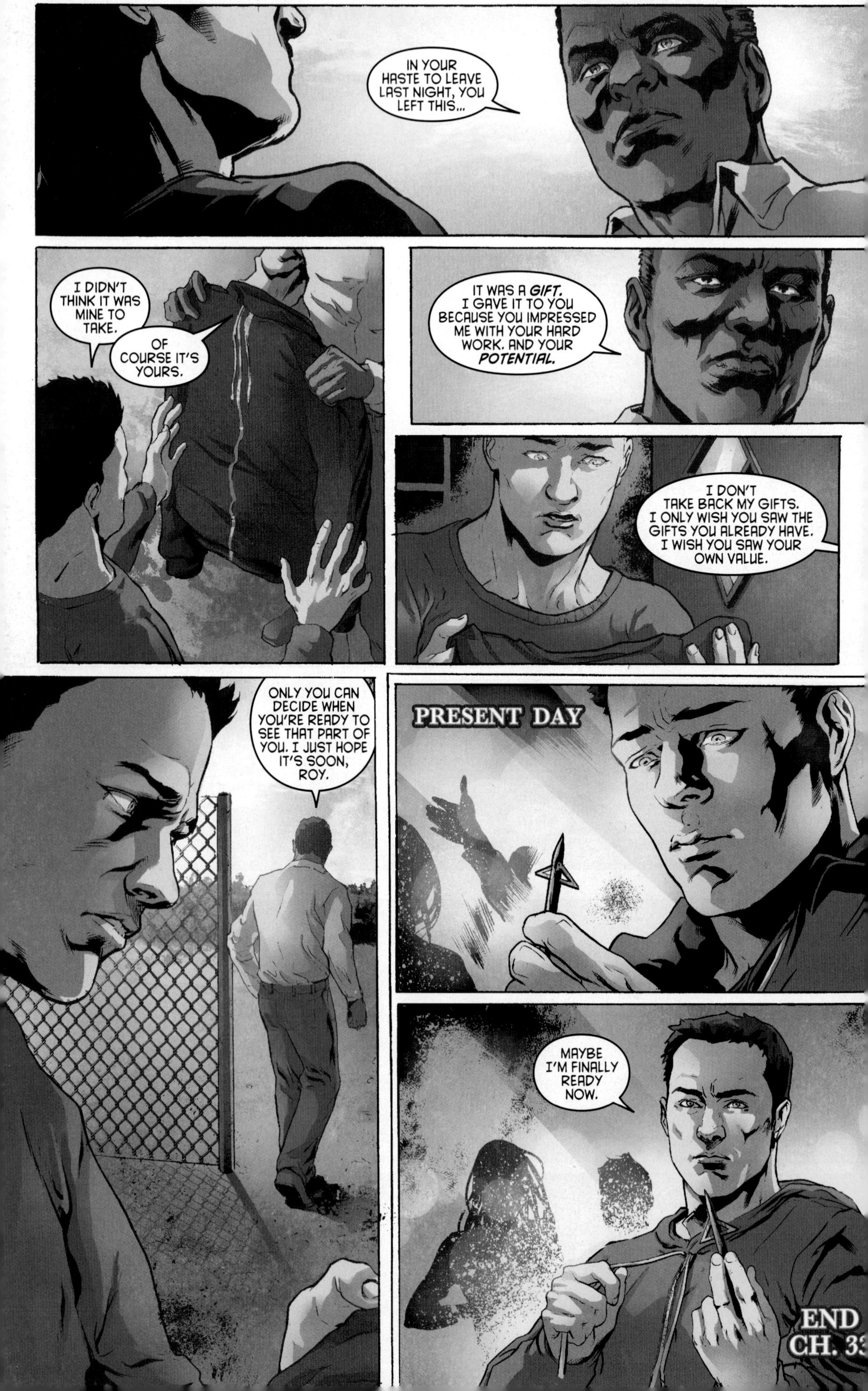
IN YOUR HASTE TO LEAVE LAST NIGHT, YOU LEFT THIS...
I DIDN'T THINK IT WAS MINE TO TAKE.
OF COURSE IT'S YOURS.
IT WAS A *GIFT.* I GAVE IT TO YOU BECAUSE YOU IMPRESSED ME WITH YOUR HARD WORK. AND YOUR *POTENTIAL.*
I DON'T TAKE BACK MY GIFTS. I ONLY WISH YOU SAW THE GIFTS YOU ALREADY HAVE. I WISH YOU SAW YOUR OWN VALUE.
ONLY YOU CAN DECIDE WHEN YOU'RE READY TO SEE THAT PART OF YOU. I JUST HOPE IT'S SOON, ROY.
PRESENT DAY
MAYBE I'M FINALLY READY NOW.
END CH. 33

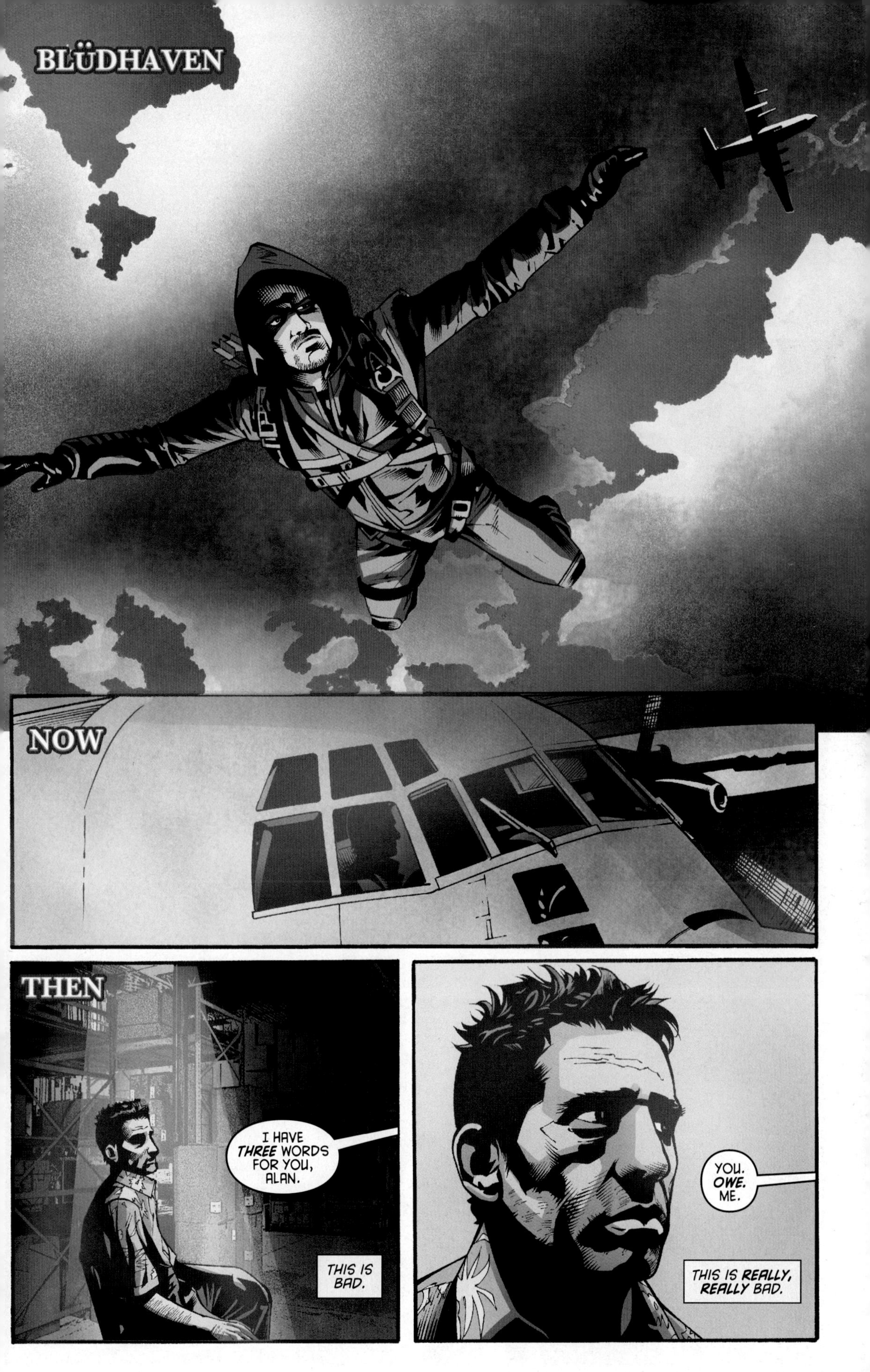
BLÜDHAVEN
NOW
THEN
I HAVE THREE WORDS FOR YOU, ALAN.
THIS IS BAD.
YOU. OWE. ME.
THIS IS REALLY, REALLY BAD.

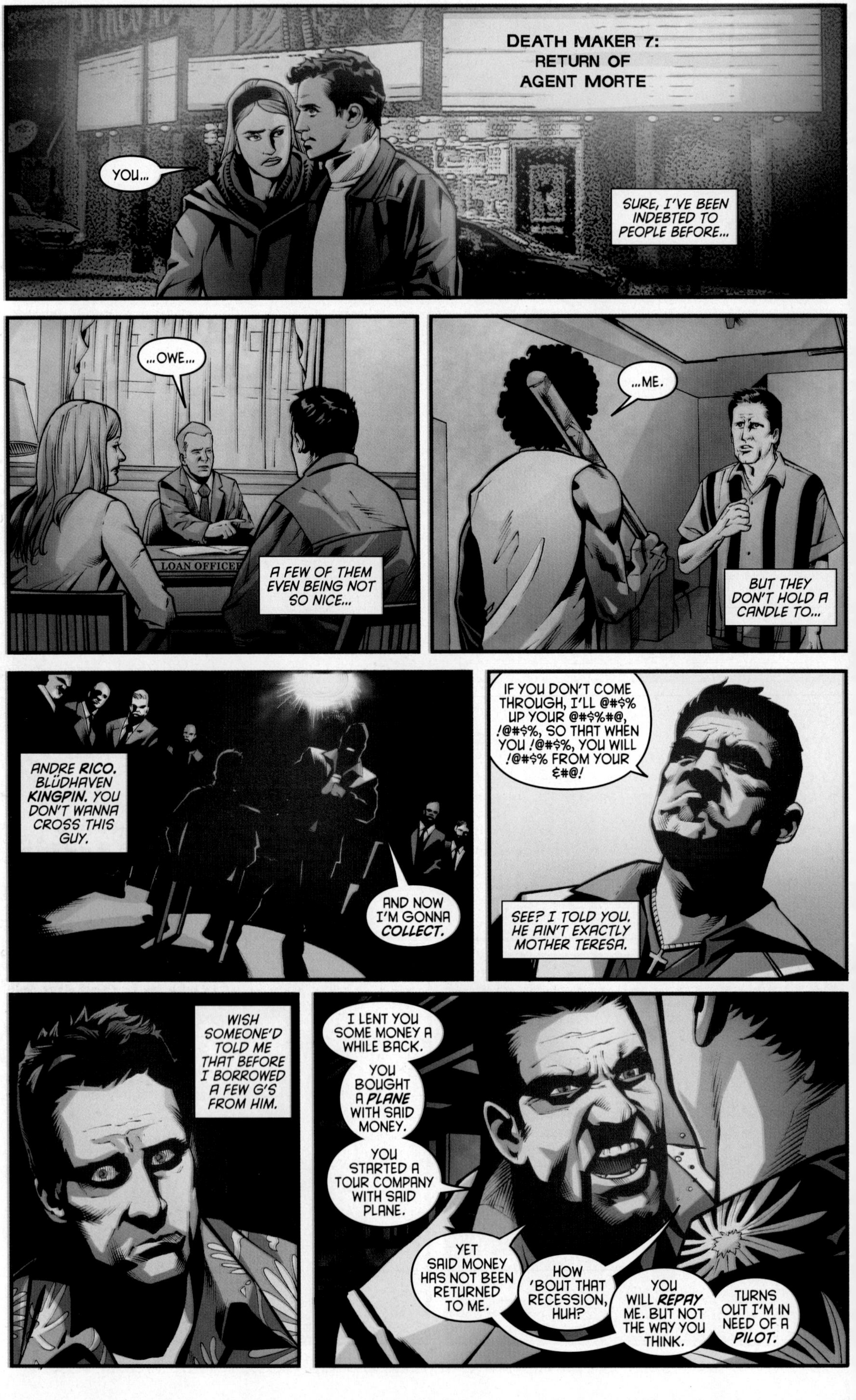

DEATH MAKER 7: RETURN OF AGENT MORTE
YOU...
SURE, I'VE BEEN INDEBTED TO PEOPLE BEFORE...
...OWE...
LOAN OFFICER
A FEW OF THEM EVEN BEING NOT SO NICE...
...ME.
BUT THEY DON'T HOLD A CANDLE TO...
ANDRE RICO. BLÜDHAVEN KINGPIN. YOU DON'T WANNA CROSS THIS GUY.
AND NOW I'M GONNA COLLECT.
IF YOU DON'T COME THROUGH, I'LL @#$% UP YOUR @#$%#@, !@#$%, SO THAT WHEN YOU !@#$%, YOU WILL !@#$% FROM YOUR &#@!
SEE? I TOLD YOU. HE AIN'T EXACTLY MOTHER TERESA.
WISH SOMEONE'D TOLD ME THAT BEFORE I BORROWED A FEW G'S FROM HIM.
I LENT YOU SOME MONEY A WHILE BACK.
YOU BOUGHT A PLANE WITH SAID MONEY.
YOU STARTED A TOUR COMPANY WITH SAID PLANE.
YET SAID MONEY HAS NOT BEEN RETURNED TO ME.
HOW 'BOUT THAT RECESSION, HUH?
YOU WILL REPAY ME. BUT NOT THE WAY YOU THINK.
TURNS OUT I'M IN NEED OF A PILOT.

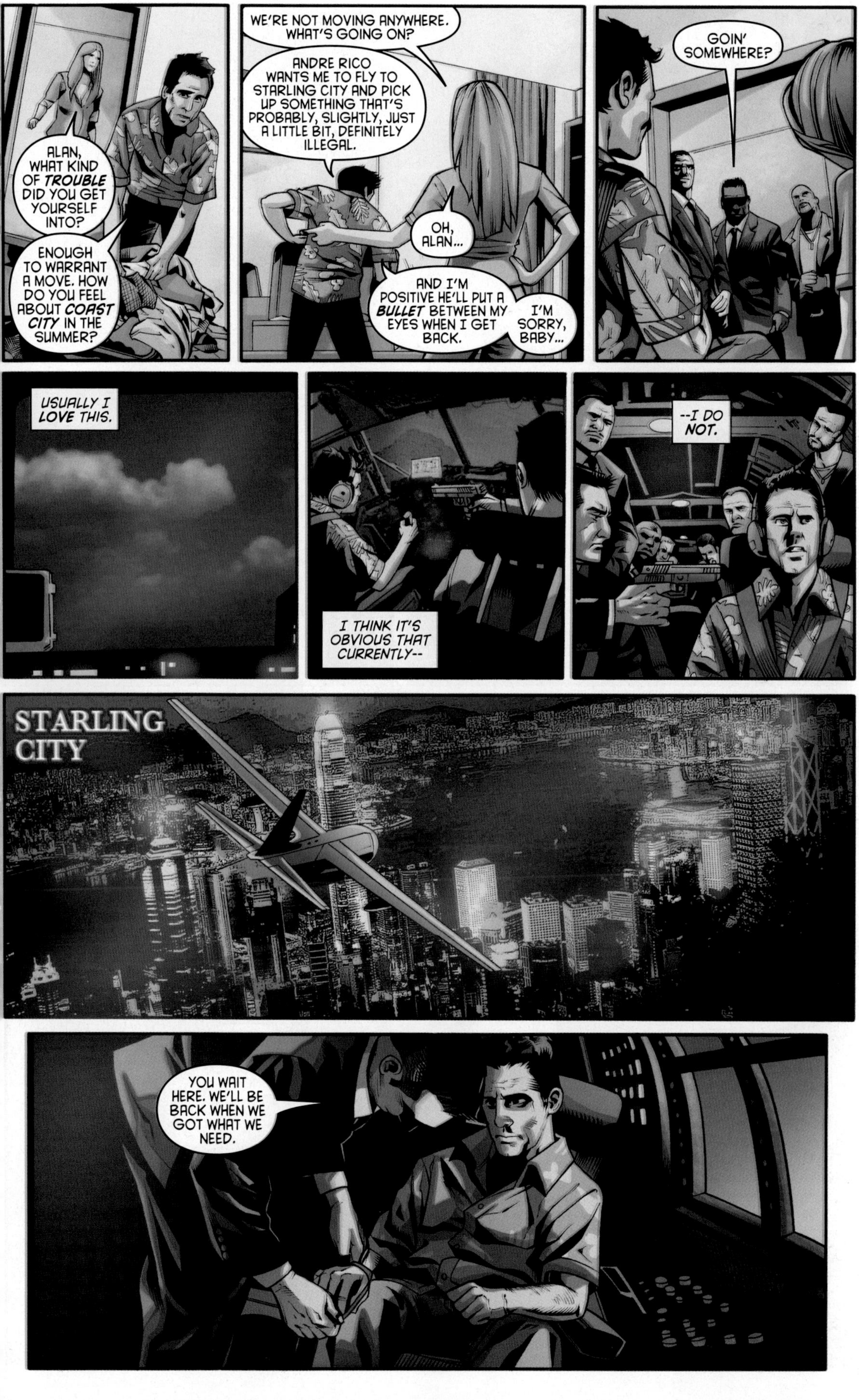
ALAN, WHAT KIND OF *TROUBLE* DID YOU GET YOURSELF INTO?
ENOUGH TO WARRANT A MOVE. HOW DO YOU FEEL ABOUT *COAST CITY* IN THE SUMMER?
WE'RE NOT MOVING ANYWHERE. WHAT'S GOING ON?
ANDRE RICO WANTS ME TO FLY TO STARLING CITY AND PICK UP SOMETHING THAT'S PROBABLY, SLIGHTLY, JUST A LITTLE BIT, DEFINITELY ILLEGAL.
OH, ALAN...
AND I'M POSITIVE HE'LL PUT A *BULLET* BETWEEN MY EYES WHEN I GET BACK.
I'M SORRY, BABY...
GOIN' SOMEWHERE?
USUALLY I ***LOVE*** *THIS.*
I THINK IT'S OBVIOUS THAT CURRENTLY--
--I DO ***NOT.***
STARLING CITY
YOU WAIT HERE. WE'LL BE BACK WHEN WE GOT WHAT WE NEED.

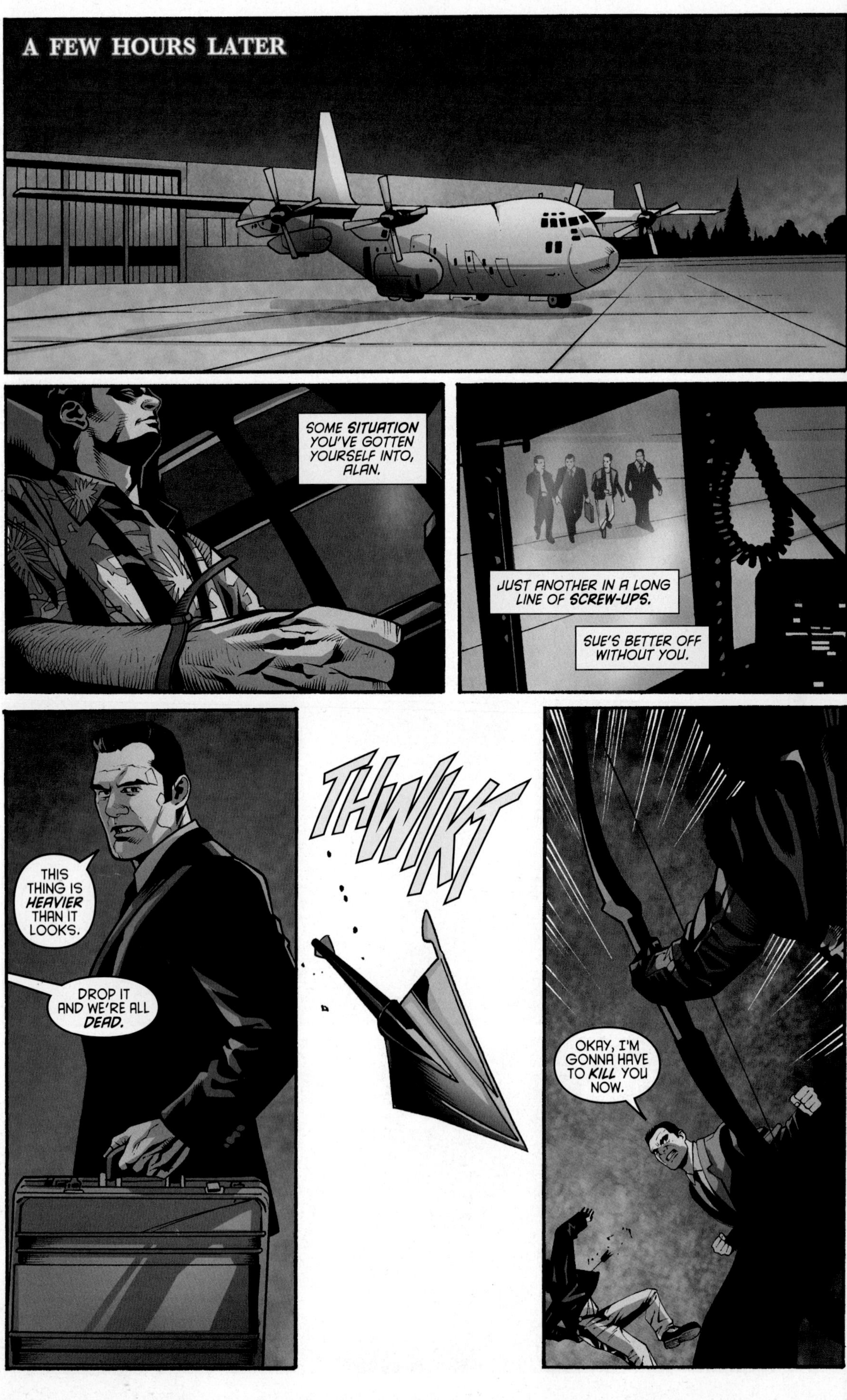
A FEW HOURS LATER
SOME SITUATION YOU'VE GOTTEN YOURSELF INTO, ALAN.
JUST ANOTHER IN A LONG LINE OF SCREW-UPS.
SUE'S BETTER OFF WITHOUT YOU.
THIS THING IS HEAVIER THAN IT LOOKS.
DROP IT AND WE'RE ALL DEAD.
THWIKT
OKAY, I'M GONNA HAVE TO KILL YOU NOW.

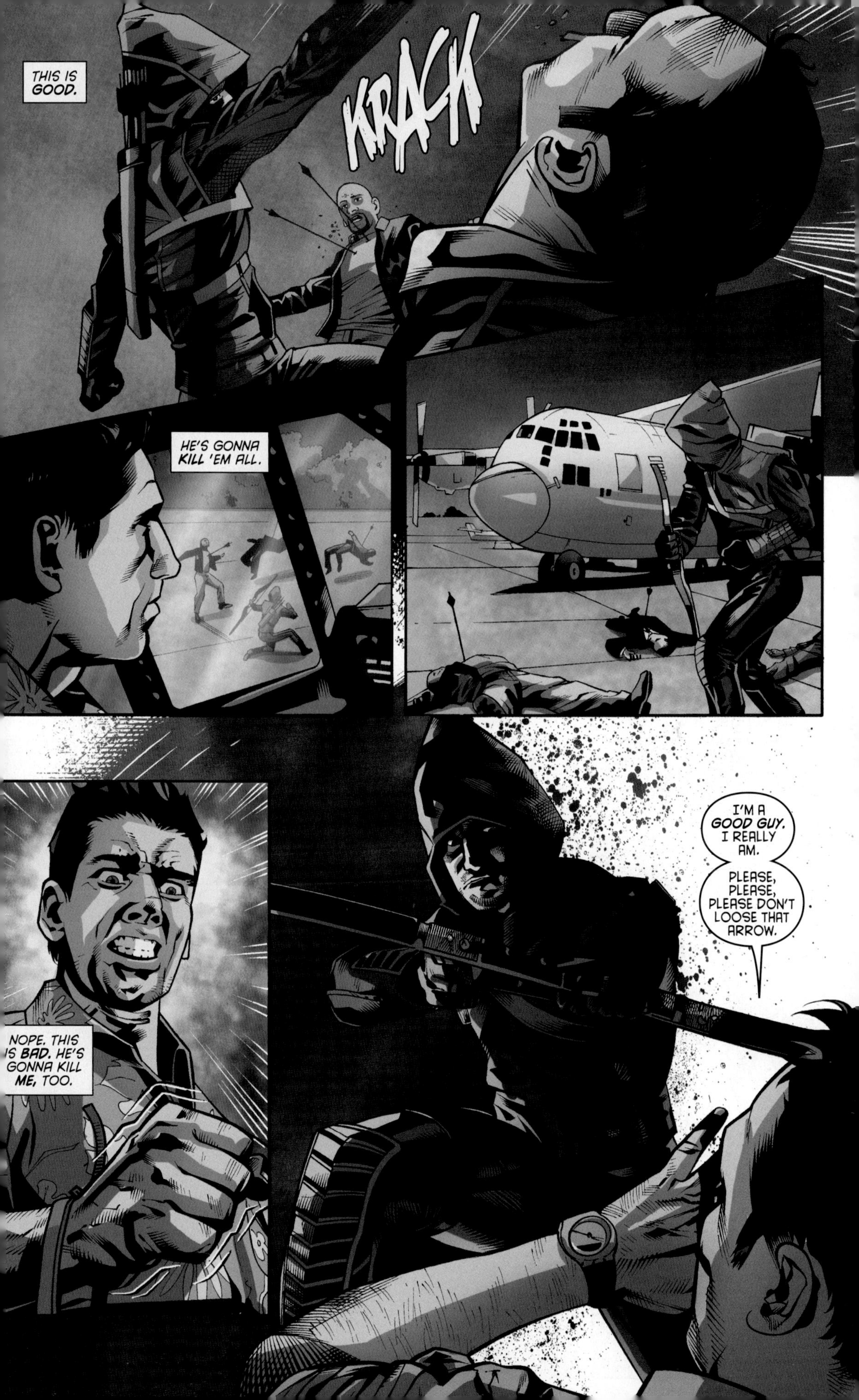
THIS IS GOOD.
KRACK
HE'S GONNA KILL 'EM ALL.
NOPE. THIS IS BAD. HE'S GONNA KILL ME, TOO.
I'M A GOOD GUY. I REALLY AM.
PLEASE, PLEASE, PLEASE DON'T LOOSE THAT ARROW.

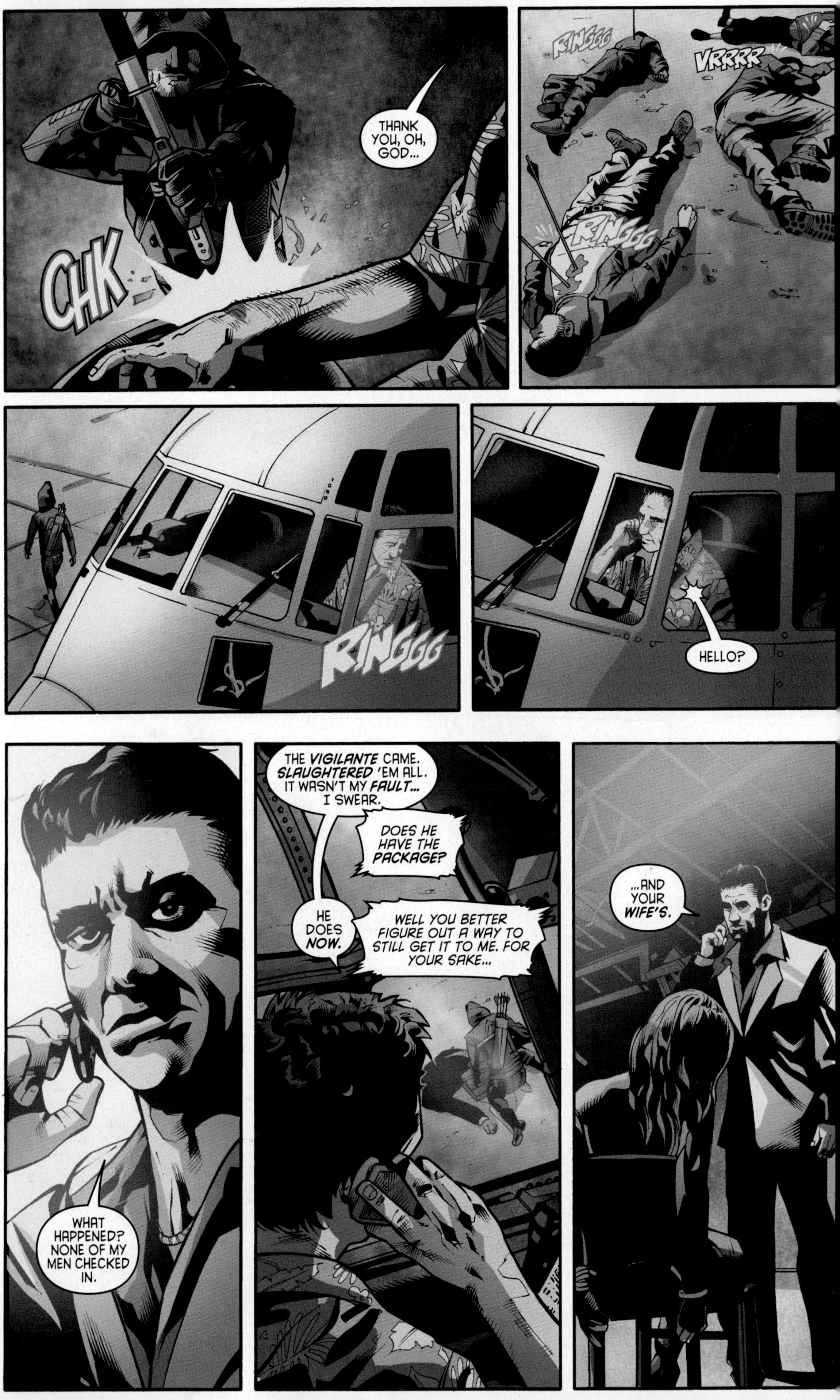
THANK YOU, OH, GOD...
CHK
RINGGG
VRRRR
RINGGG
RINGGG
HELLO?
WHAT HAPPENED? NONE OF MY MEN CHECKED IN.
THE VIGILANTE CAME. SLAUGHTERED 'EM ALL. IT WASN'T MY FAULT... I SWEAR.
DOES HE HAVE THE PACKAGE?
HE DOES NOW.
WELL YOU BETTER FIGURE OUT A WAY TO STILL GET IT TO ME. FOR YOUR SAKE...
...AND YOUR WIFE'S.

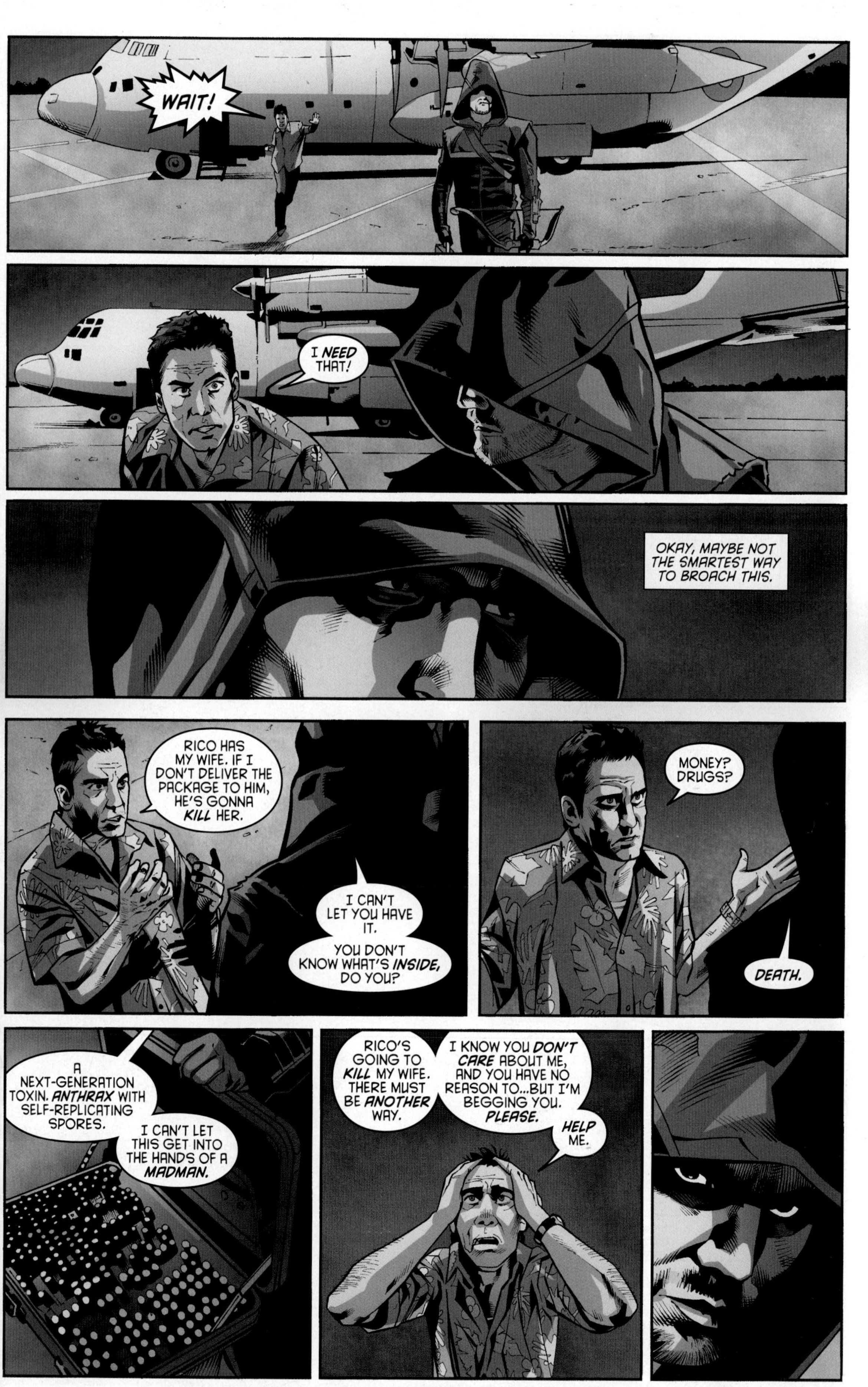
WAIT!
I NEED THAT!
OKAY, MAYBE NOT THE SMARTEST WAY TO BROACH THIS.
RICO HAS MY WIFE. IF I DON'T DELIVER THE PACKAGE TO HIM, HE'S GONNA KILL HER.
I CAN'T LET YOU HAVE IT.
YOU DON'T KNOW WHAT'S INSIDE, DO YOU?
MONEY? DRUGS?
DEATH.
A NEXT-GENERATION TOXIN. ANTHRAX WITH SELF-REPLICATING SPORES.
I CAN'T LET THIS GET INTO THE HANDS OF A MADMAN.
RICO'S GOING TO KILL MY WIFE. THERE MUST BE ANOTHER WAY.
I KNOW YOU DON'T CARE ABOUT ME, AND YOU HAVE NO REASON TO...BUT I'M BEGGING YOU. PLEASE.
HELP ME.

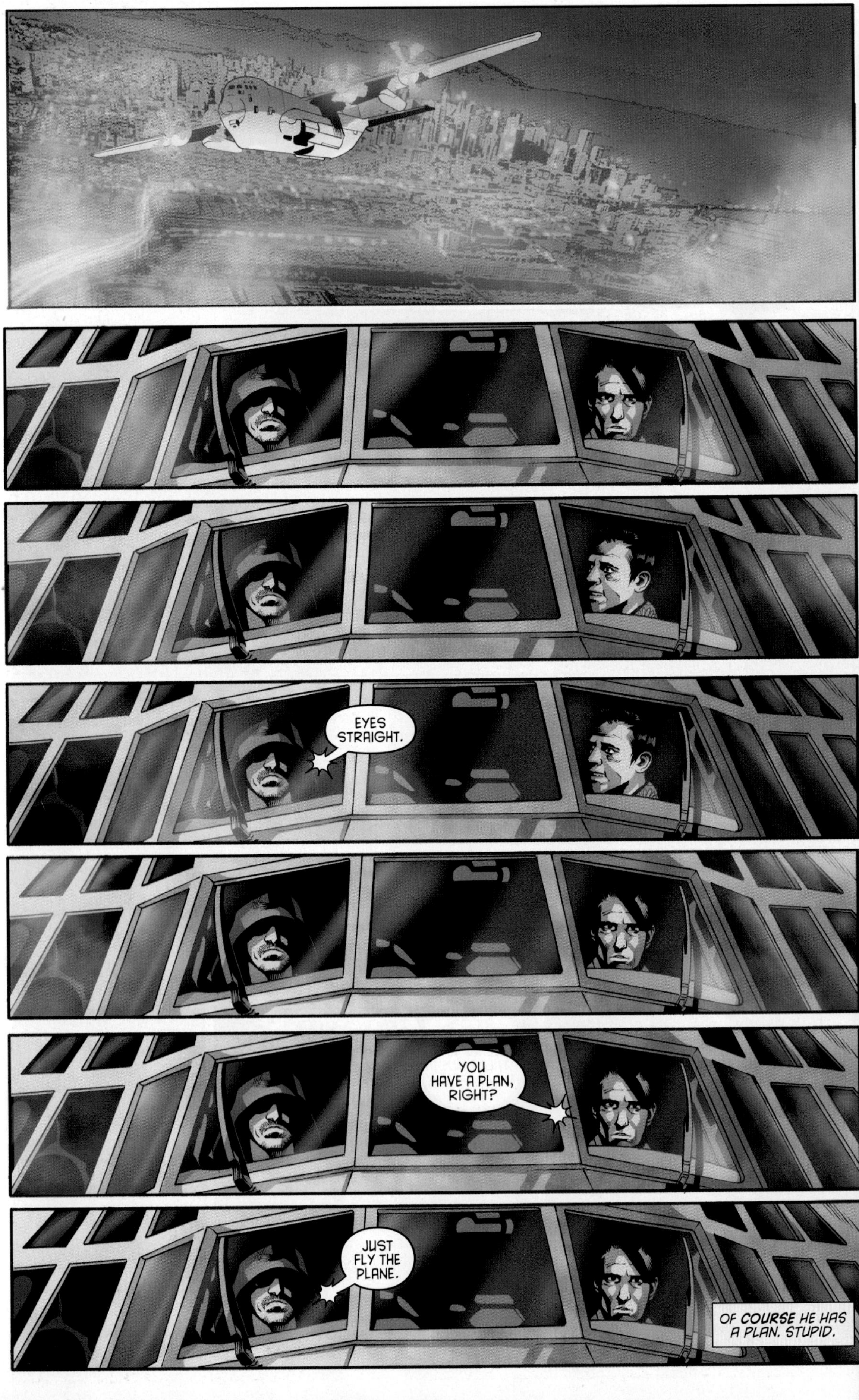
EYES STRAIGHT.
YOU HAVE A PLAN, RIGHT?
JUST FLY THE PLANE.
OF **COURSE** HE HAS A PLAN. STUPID.

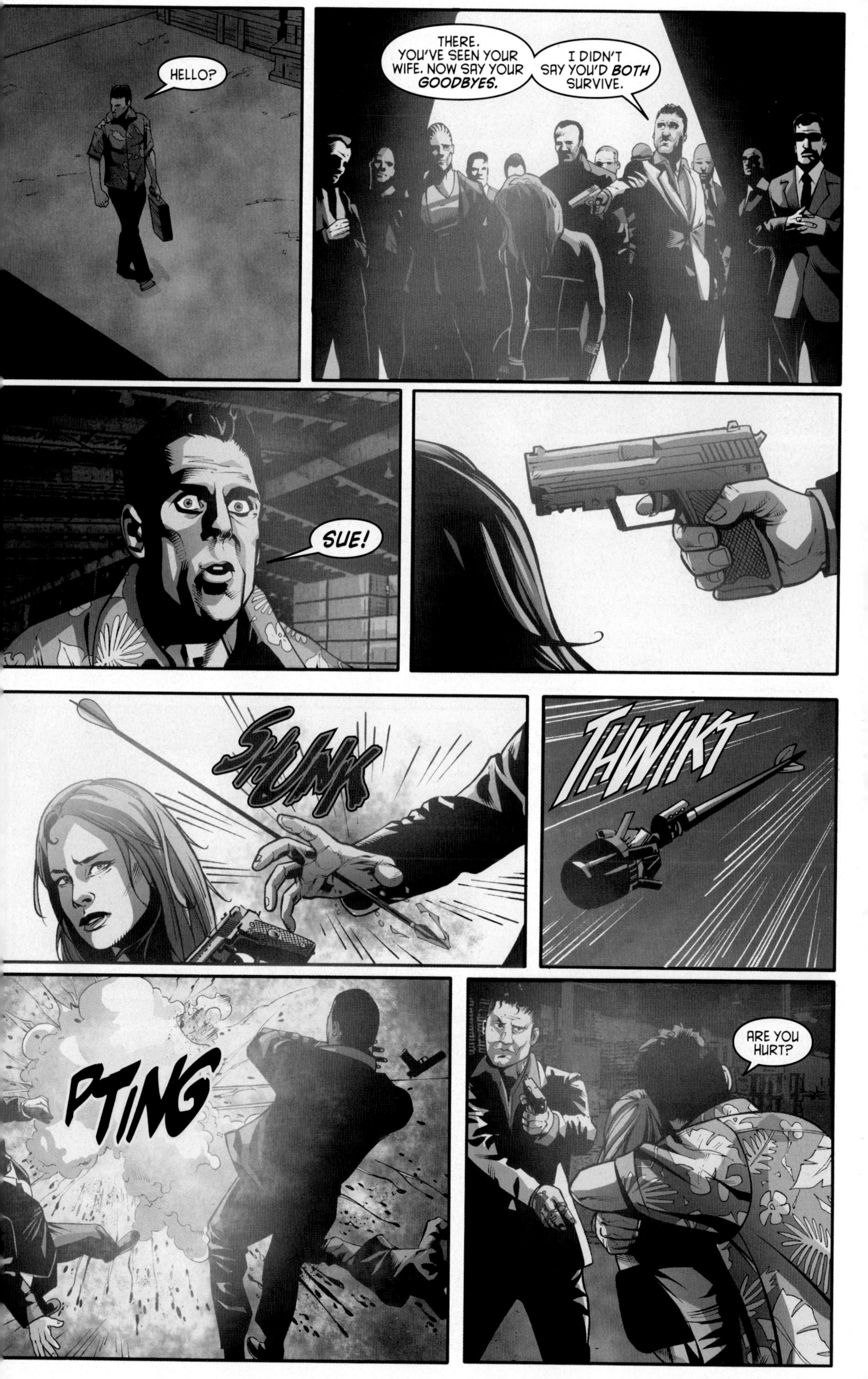
HELLO?
THERE. YOU'VE SEEN YOUR WIFE. NOW SAY YOUR GOODBYES.
I DIDN'T SAY YOU'D BOTH SURVIVE.
SUE!
SHUNK
THWIKT
PTING
ARE YOU HURT?

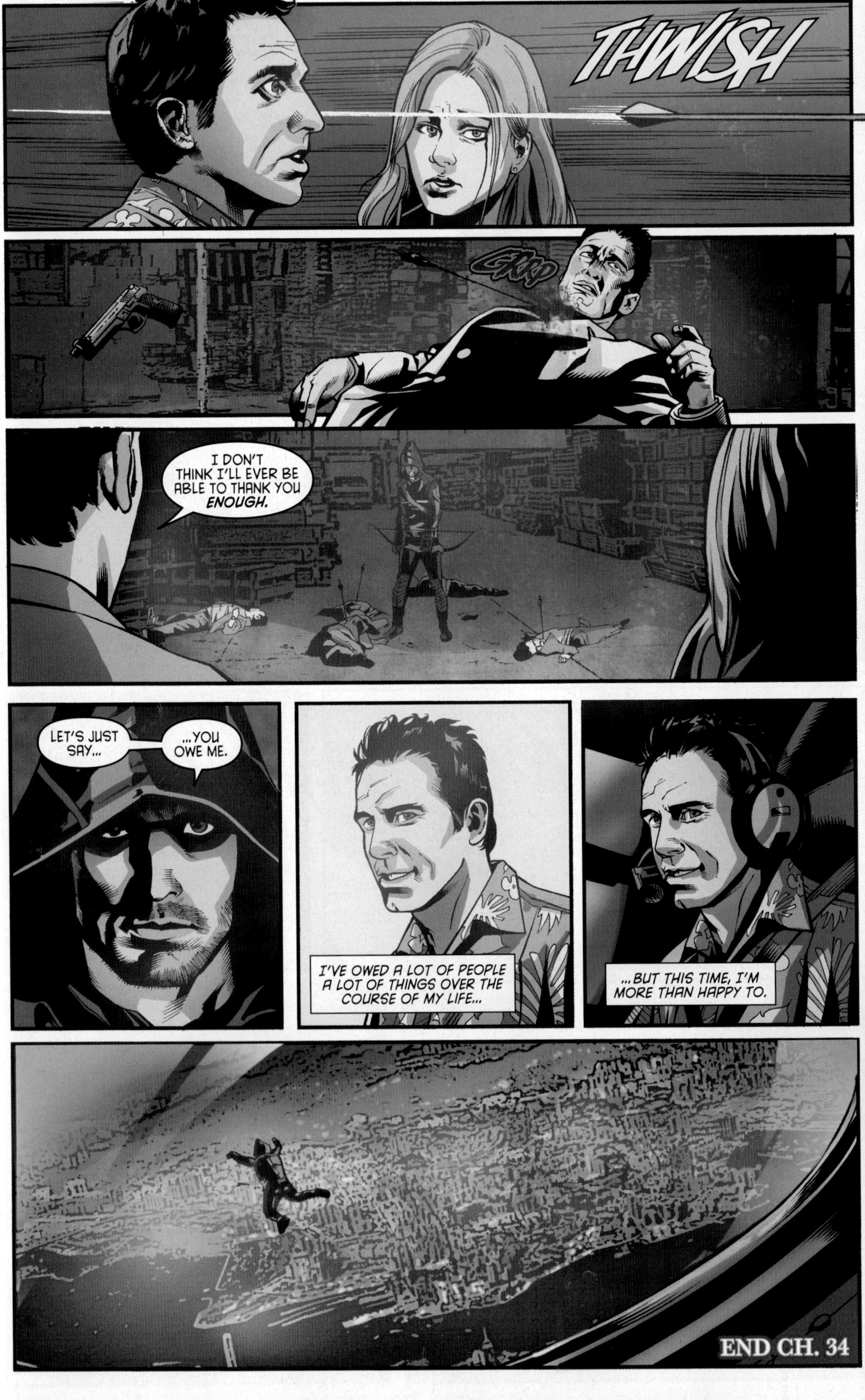
THWISH
GRKP
I DON'T THINK I'LL EVER BE ABLE TO THANK YOU *ENOUGH.*
LET'S JUST SAY...
...YOU OWE ME.
I'VE OWED A LOT OF PEOPLE A LOT OF THINGS OVER THE COURSE OF MY LIFE...
...BUT THIS TIME, I'M MORE THAN HAPPY TO.
END CH. 34

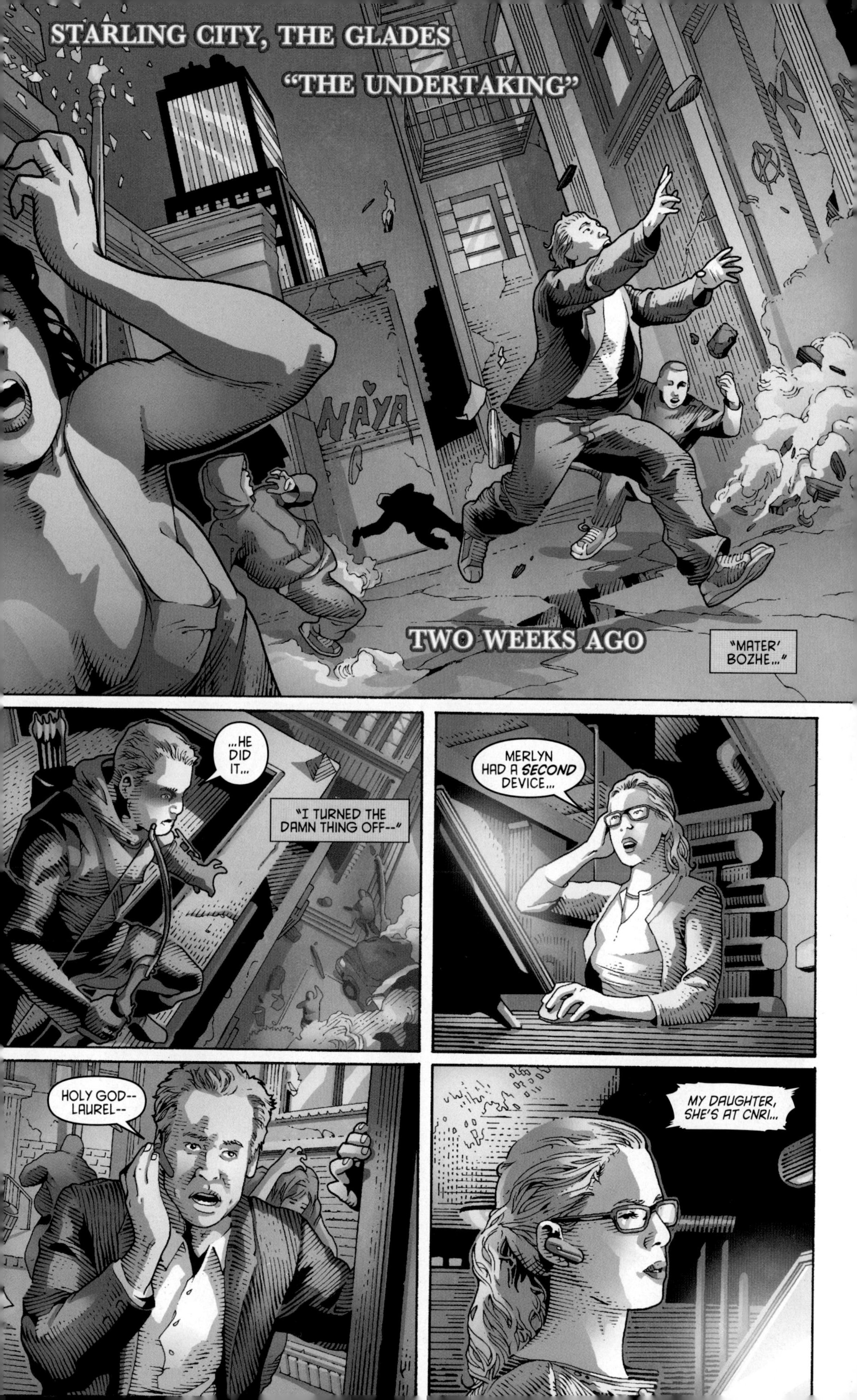
STARLING CITY, THE GLADES
"THE UNDERTAKING"
TWO WEEKS AGO
"MATER' BOZHE..."
...HE DID IT...
"I TURNED THE DAMN THING OFF--"
MERLYN HAD A SECOND DEVICE...
HOLY GOD-- LAUREL--
MY DAUGHTER, SHE'S AT CNRI...

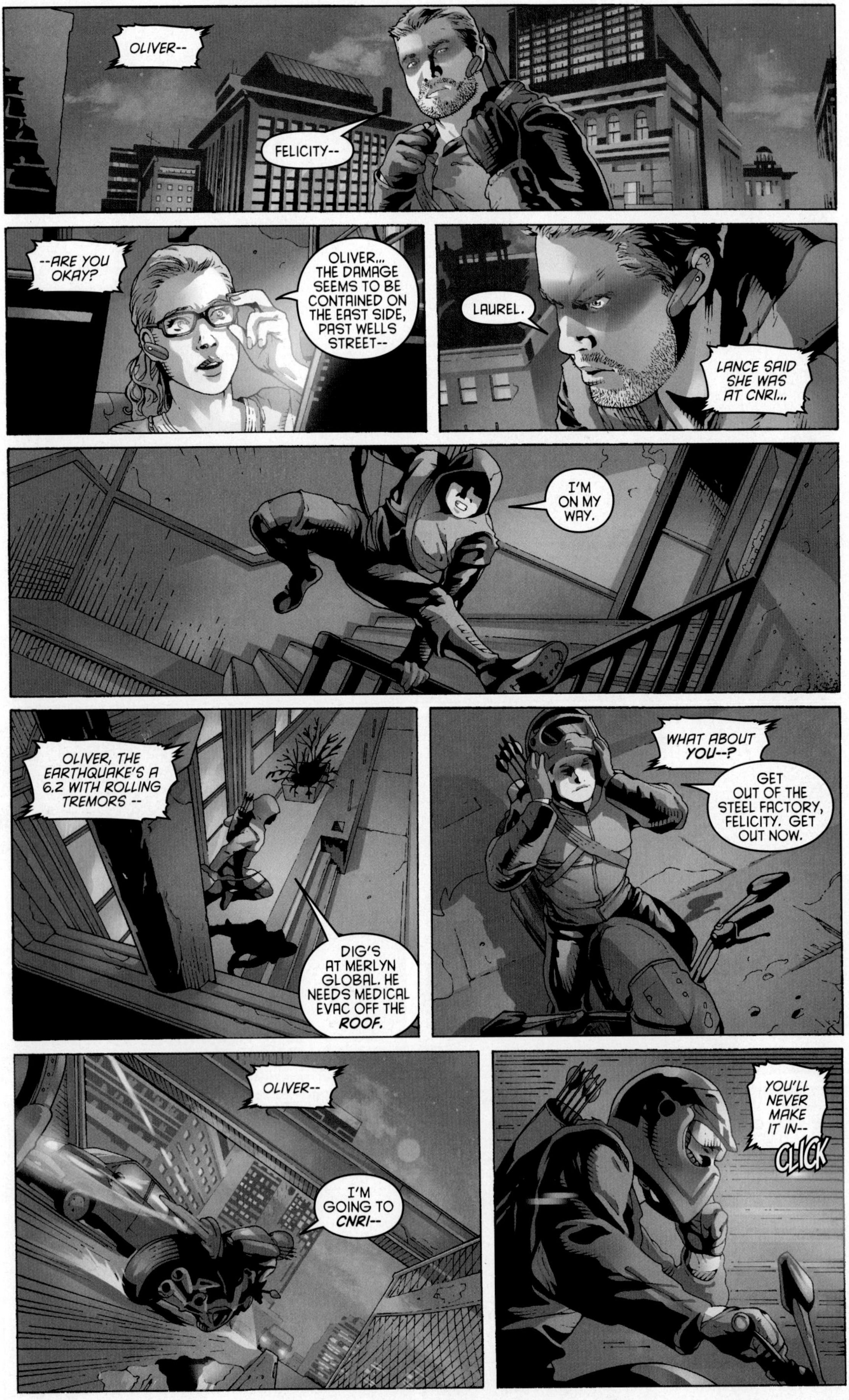
OLIVER--
FELICITY--
--ARE YOU OKAY?
OLIVER... THE DAMAGE SEEMS TO BE CONTAINED ON THE EAST SIDE, PAST WELLS STREET--
LAUREL.
LANCE SAID SHE WAS AT CNRI...
I'M ON MY WAY.
OLIVER, THE EARTHQUAKE'S A 6.2 WITH ROLLING TREMORS --
DIG'S AT MERLYN GLOBAL. HE NEEDS MEDICAL EVAC OFF THE ROOF.
WHAT ABOUT YOU--?
GET OUT OF THE STEEL FACTORY, FELICITY. GET OUT NOW.
OLIVER--
I'M GOING TO CNRI--
YOU'LL NEVER MAKE IT IN--
CLICK

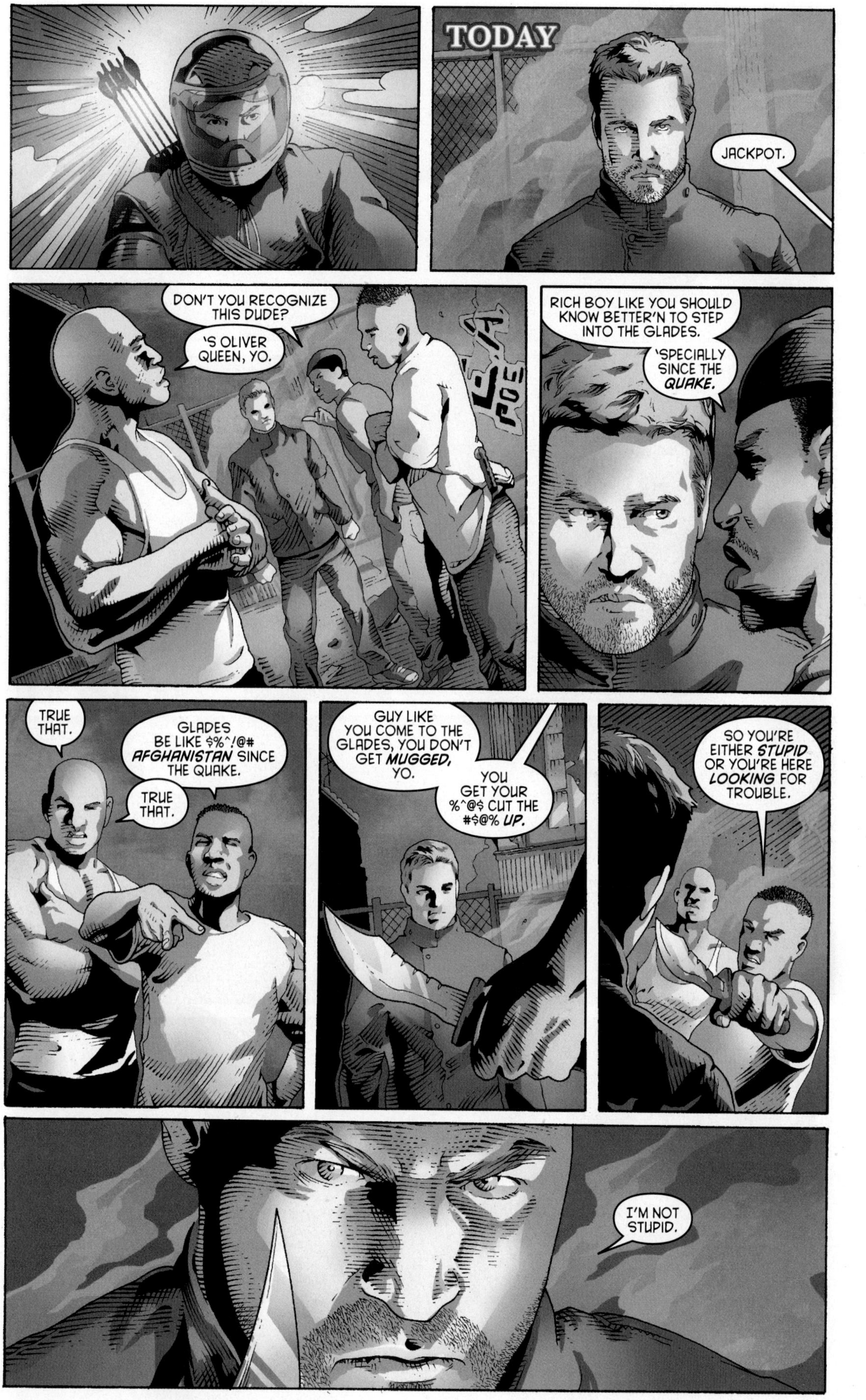
TODAY
JACKPOT.
DON'T YOU RECOGNIZE THIS DUDE?
'S OLIVER QUEEN, YO.
RICH BOY LIKE YOU SHOULD KNOW BETTER'N TO STEP INTO THE GLADES.
'SPECIALLY SINCE THE QUAKE.
TRUE THAT.
GLADES BE LIKE $%^!@# AFGHANISTAN SINCE THE QUAKE.
TRUE THAT.
GUY LIKE YOU COME TO THE GLADES, YOU DON'T GET MUGGED, YO.
YOU GET YOUR %^@$ CUT THE #$@% UP.
SO YOU'RE EITHER STUPID OR YOU'RE HERE LOOKING FOR TROUBLE.
I'M NOT STUPID.

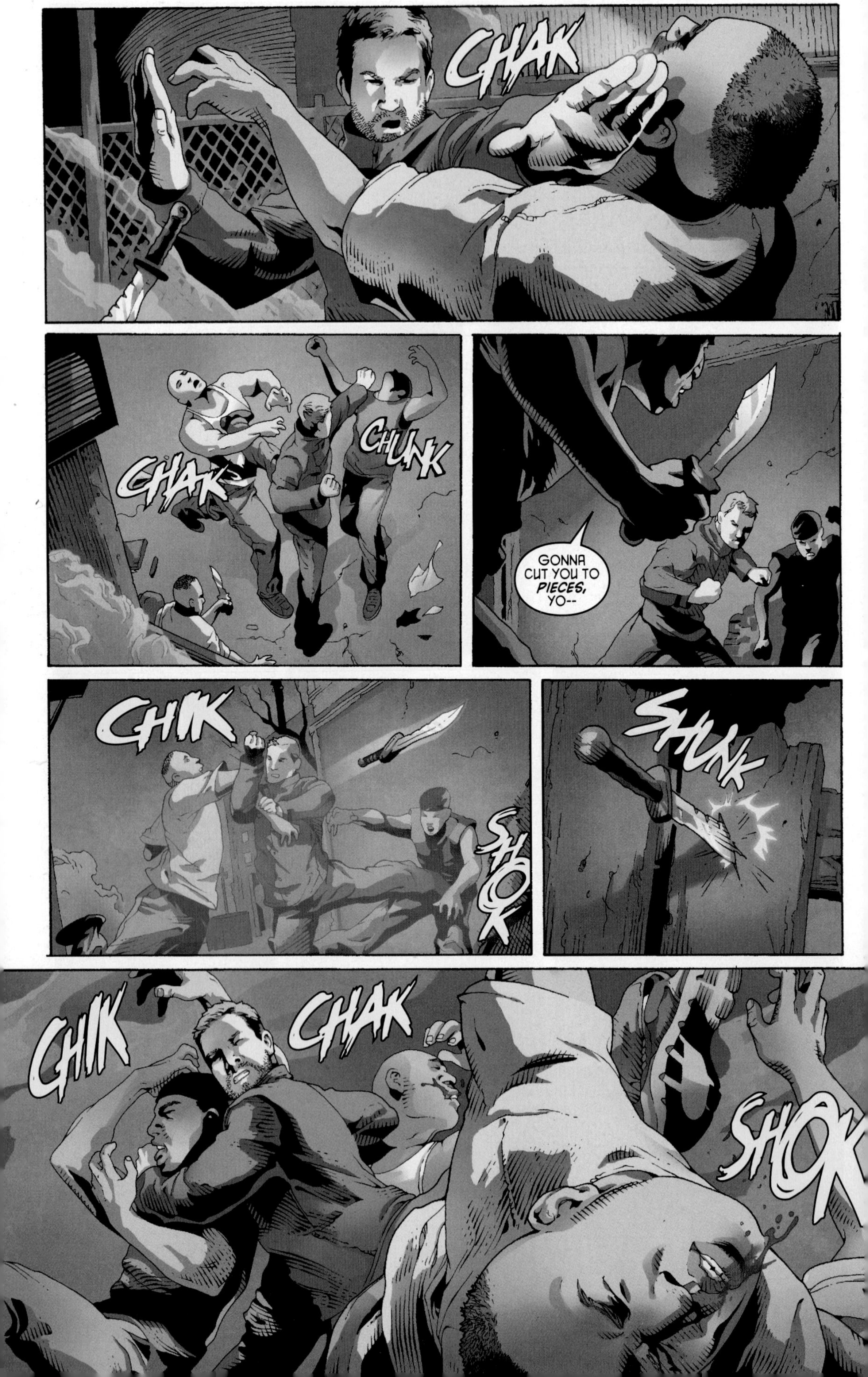
CHAK
CHAK
CHUNK
GONNA CUT YOU TO PIECES, YO--
CHIK
SHOK
SHUNK
CHIK
CHAK
SHOK

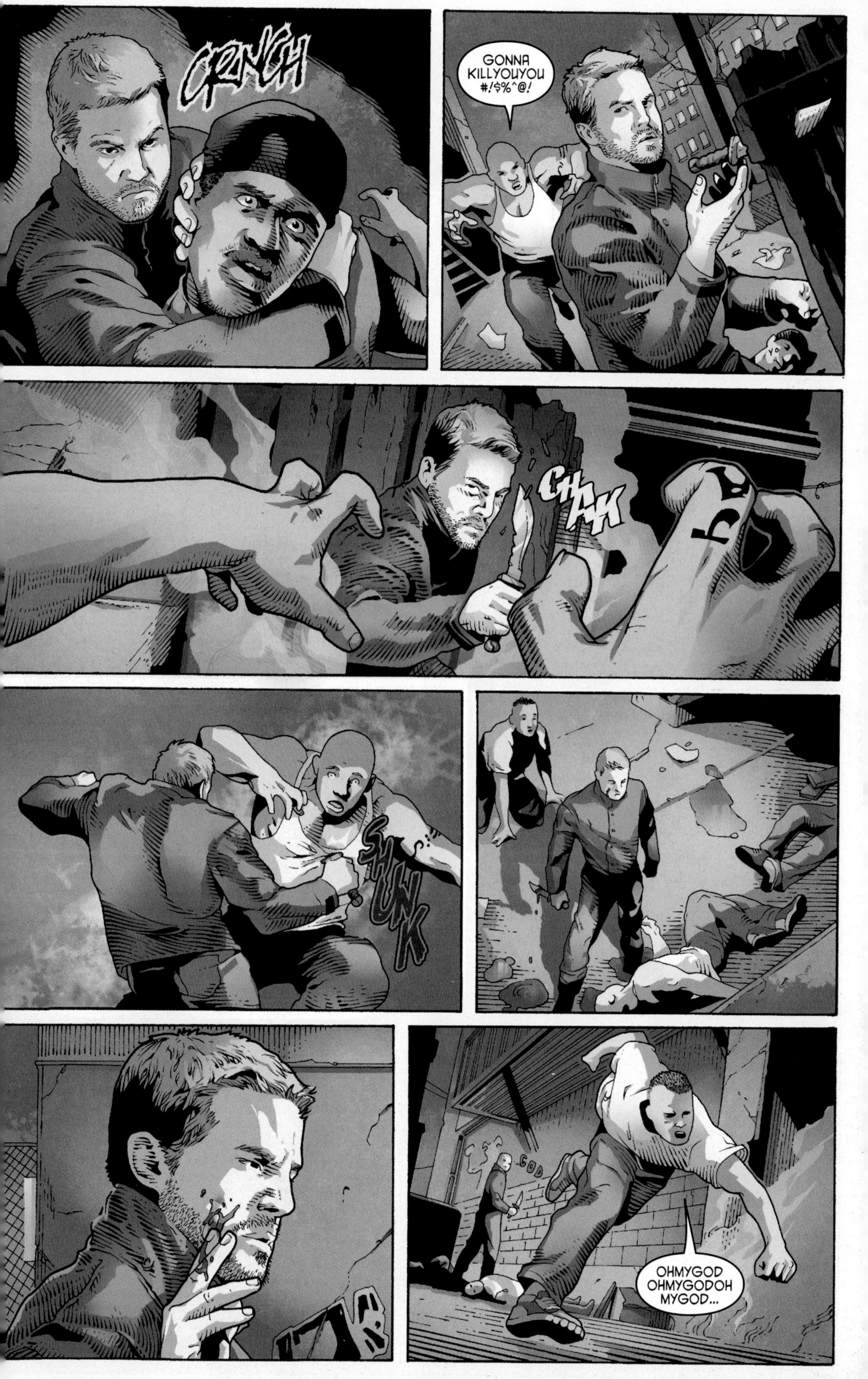
CRUNCH
GONNA KILLYOUYOU #!$%^@!
CHAK
SHUNK
OHMYGOD OHMYGODOH MYGOD...

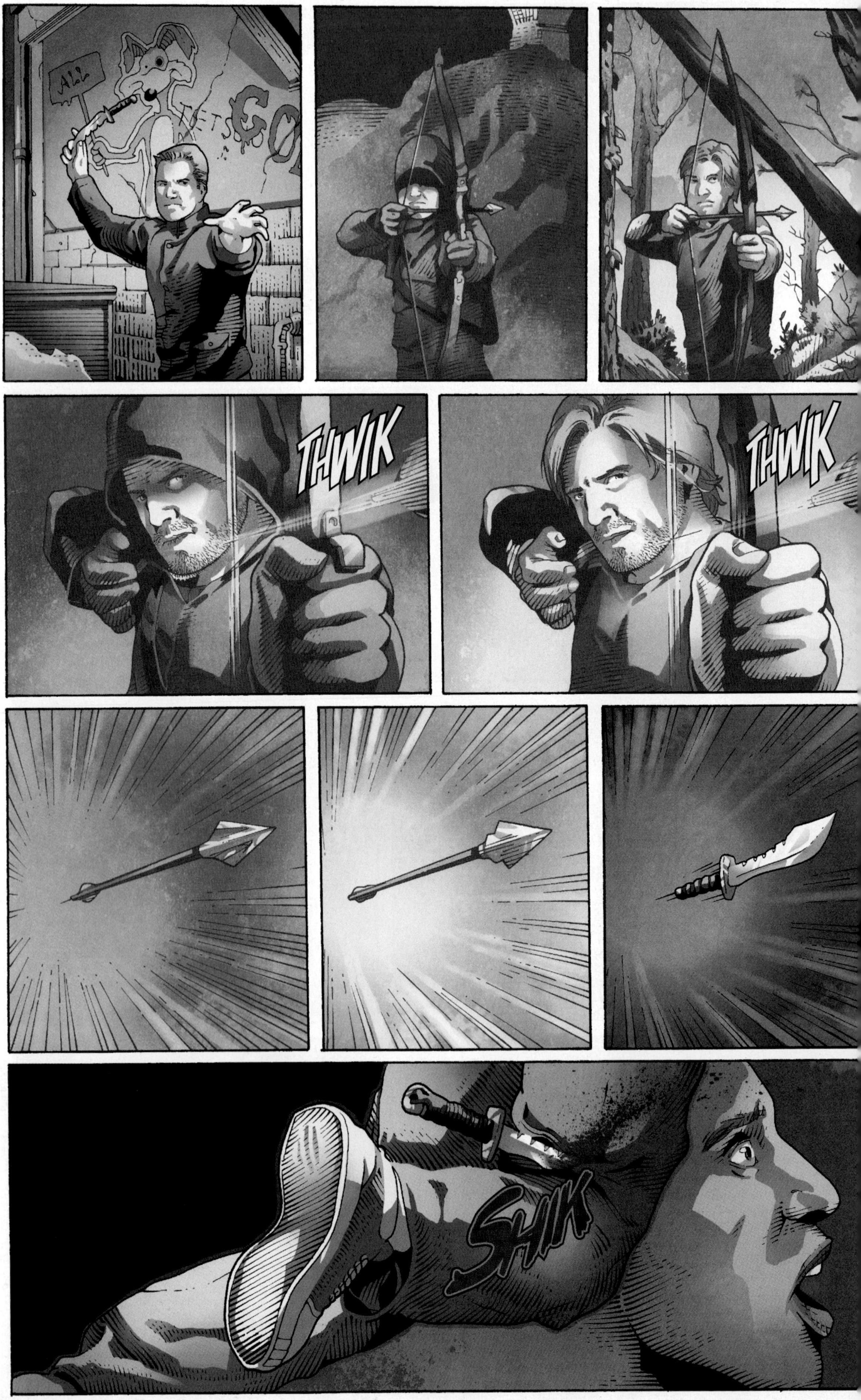
THWIK
THWIK
SHIK

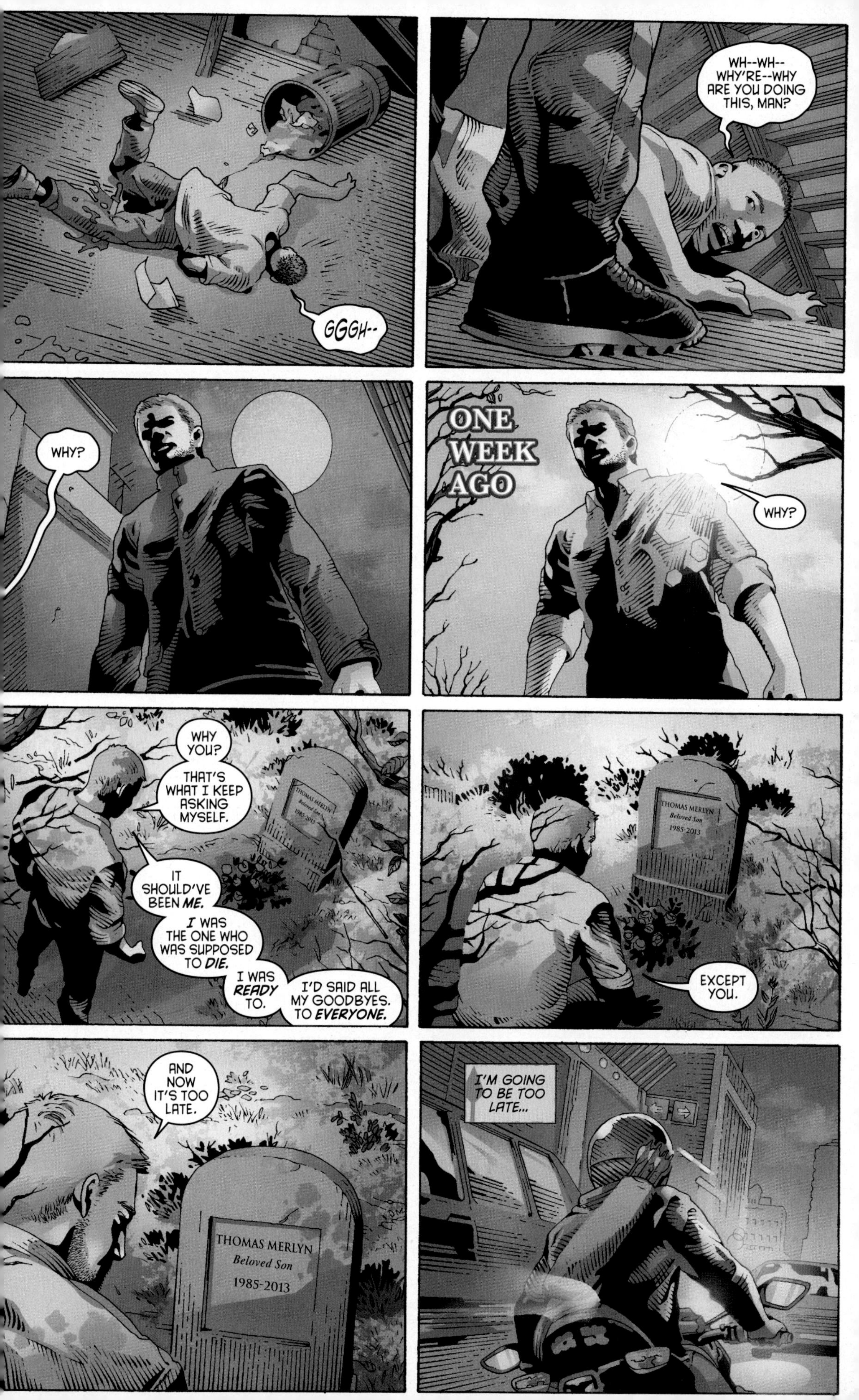
GGGH--
WH--WH--
WHY'RE--WHY
ARE YOU DOING
THIS, MAN?
WHY?
ONE WEEK AGO
WHY?
WHY YOU?
THAT'S WHAT I KEEP ASKING MYSELF.
IT SHOULD'VE BEEN ME.
I WAS THE ONE WHO WAS SUPPOSED TO DIE.
I WAS READY TO.
I'D SAID ALL MY GOODBYES. TO EVERYONE.
THOMAS MERLYN Beloved Son 1985-2013
EXCEPT YOU.
AND NOW IT'S TOO LATE.
THOMAS MERLYN Beloved Son 1985-2013
I'M GOING TO BE TOO LATE...

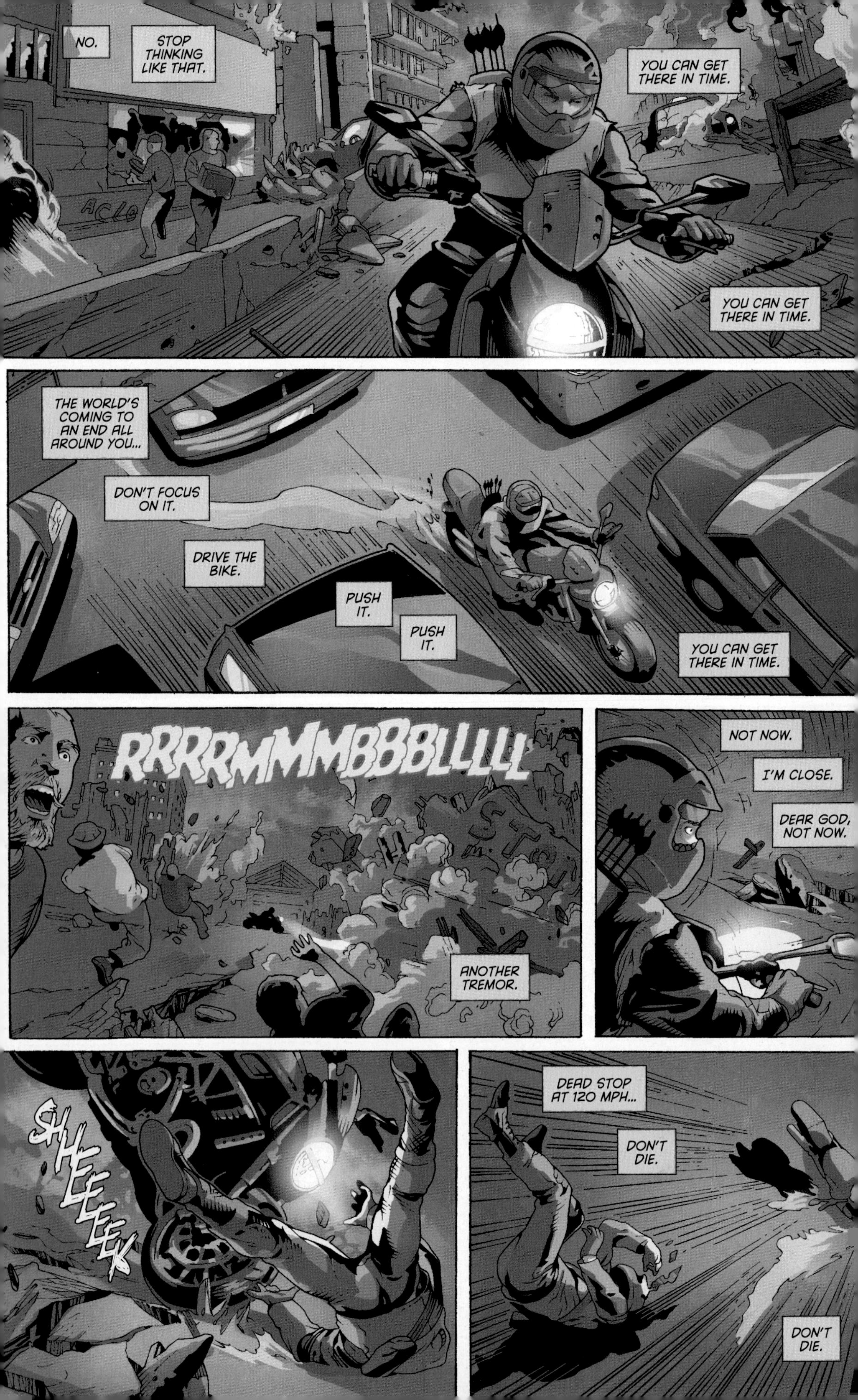

NO.
STOP THINKING LIKE THAT.
YOU CAN GET THERE IN TIME.
YOU CAN GET THERE IN TIME.
THE WORLD'S COMING TO AN END ALL AROUND YOU...
DON'T FOCUS ON IT.
DRIVE THE BIKE.
PUSH IT.
PUSH IT.
YOU CAN GET THERE IN TIME.
RRRRMMMBBBLLLLL
ANOTHER TREMOR.
NOT NOW.
I'M CLOSE.
DEAR GOD, NOT NOW.
SHHEEEEK
DEAD STOP AT 120 MPH...
DON'T DIE.
DON'T DIE.

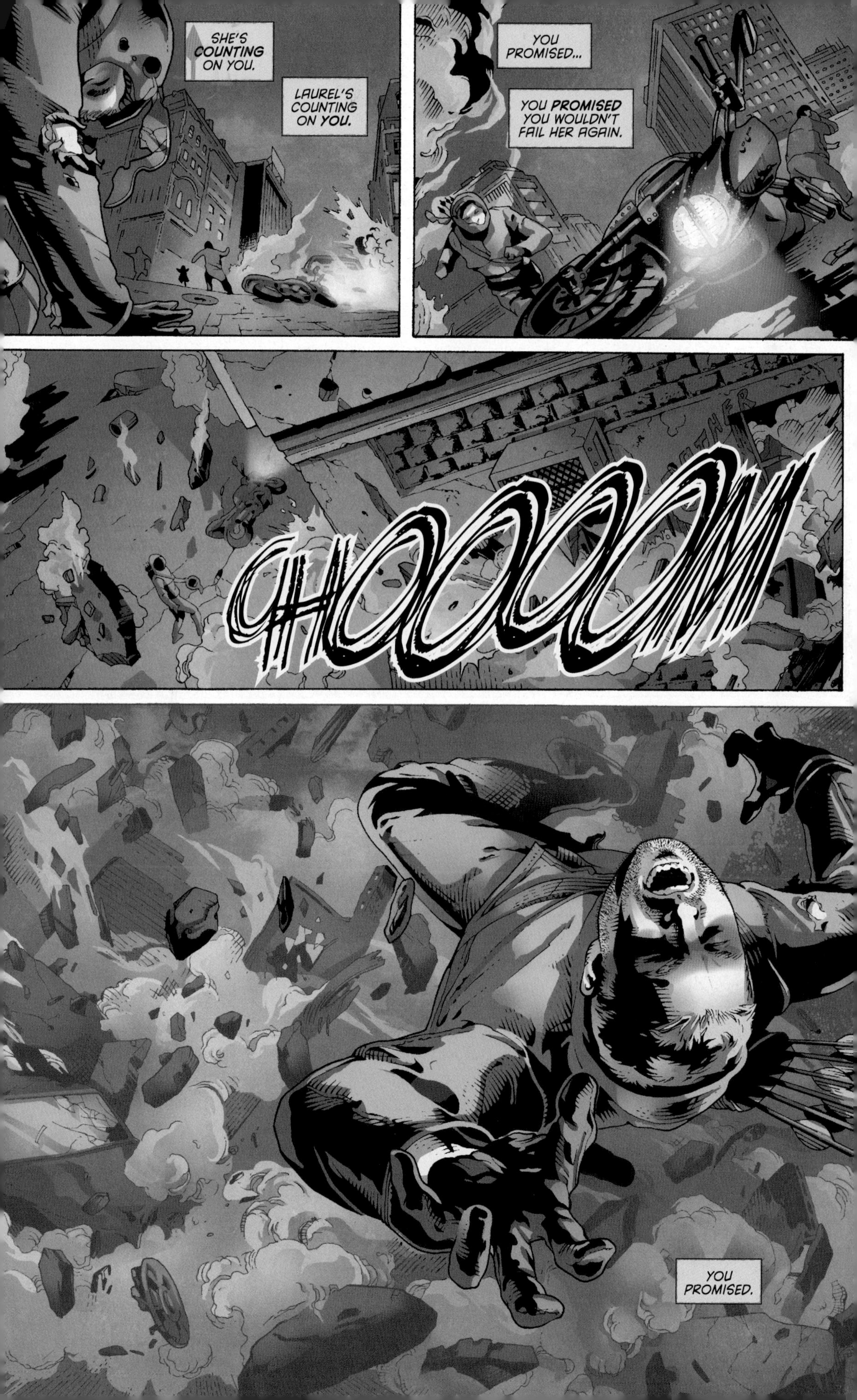
SHE'S COUNTING ON YOU.
LAUREL'S COUNTING ON YOU.
YOU PROMISED...
YOU PROMISED YOU WOULDN'T FAIL HER AGAIN.
CHOOOOM
YOU PROMISED.

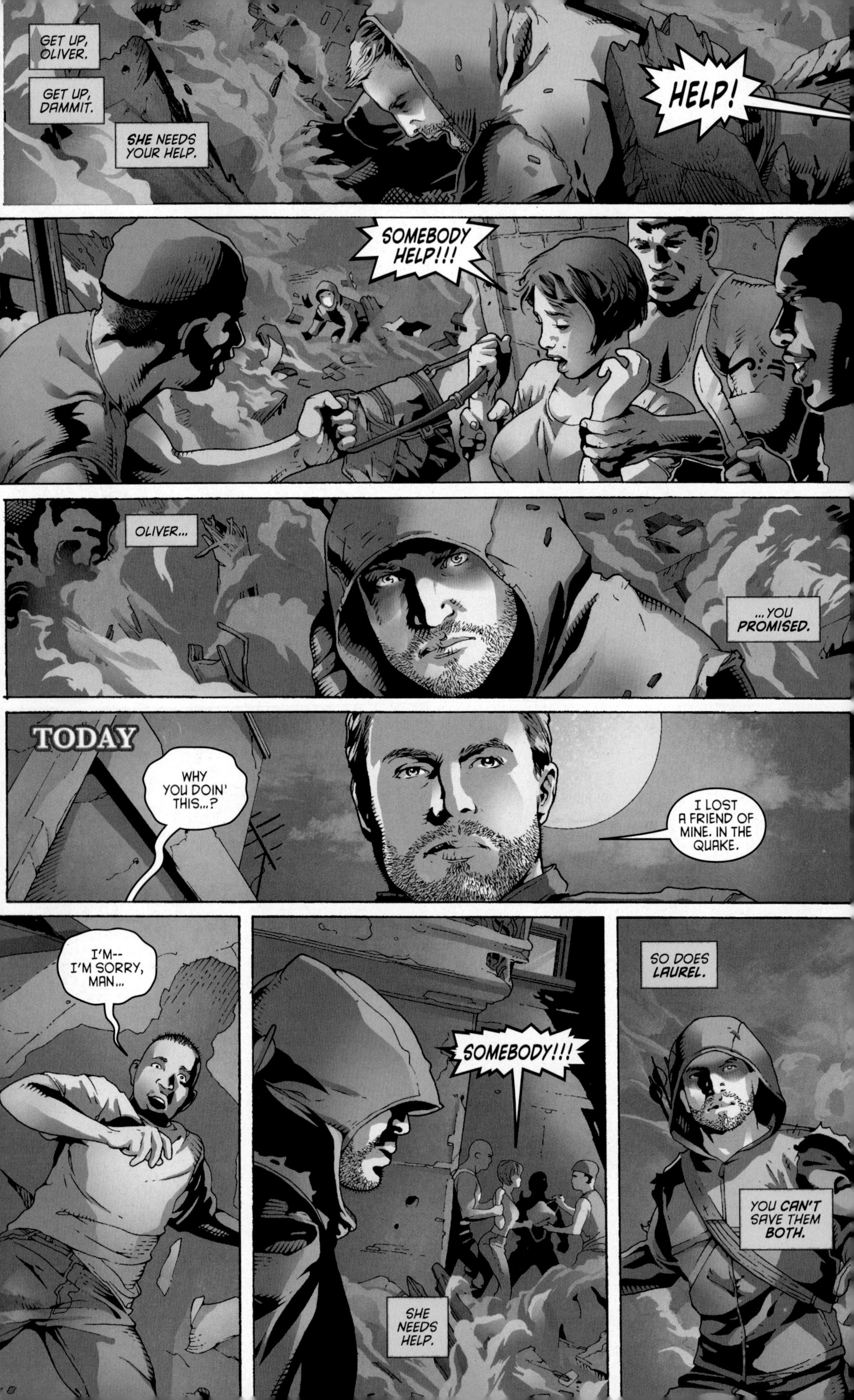
GET UP, OLIVER.
GET UP, DAMMIT.
SHE NEEDS YOUR HELP.
HELP!
SOMEBODY HELP!!!
OLIVER...
...YOU PROMISED.
TODAY
WHY YOU DOIN' THIS...?
I LOST A FRIEND OF MINE. IN THE QUAKE.
I'M-- I'M SORRY, MAN...
SOMEBODY!!!
SHE NEEDS HELP.
SO DOES LAUREL.
YOU CAN'T SAVE THEM BOTH.

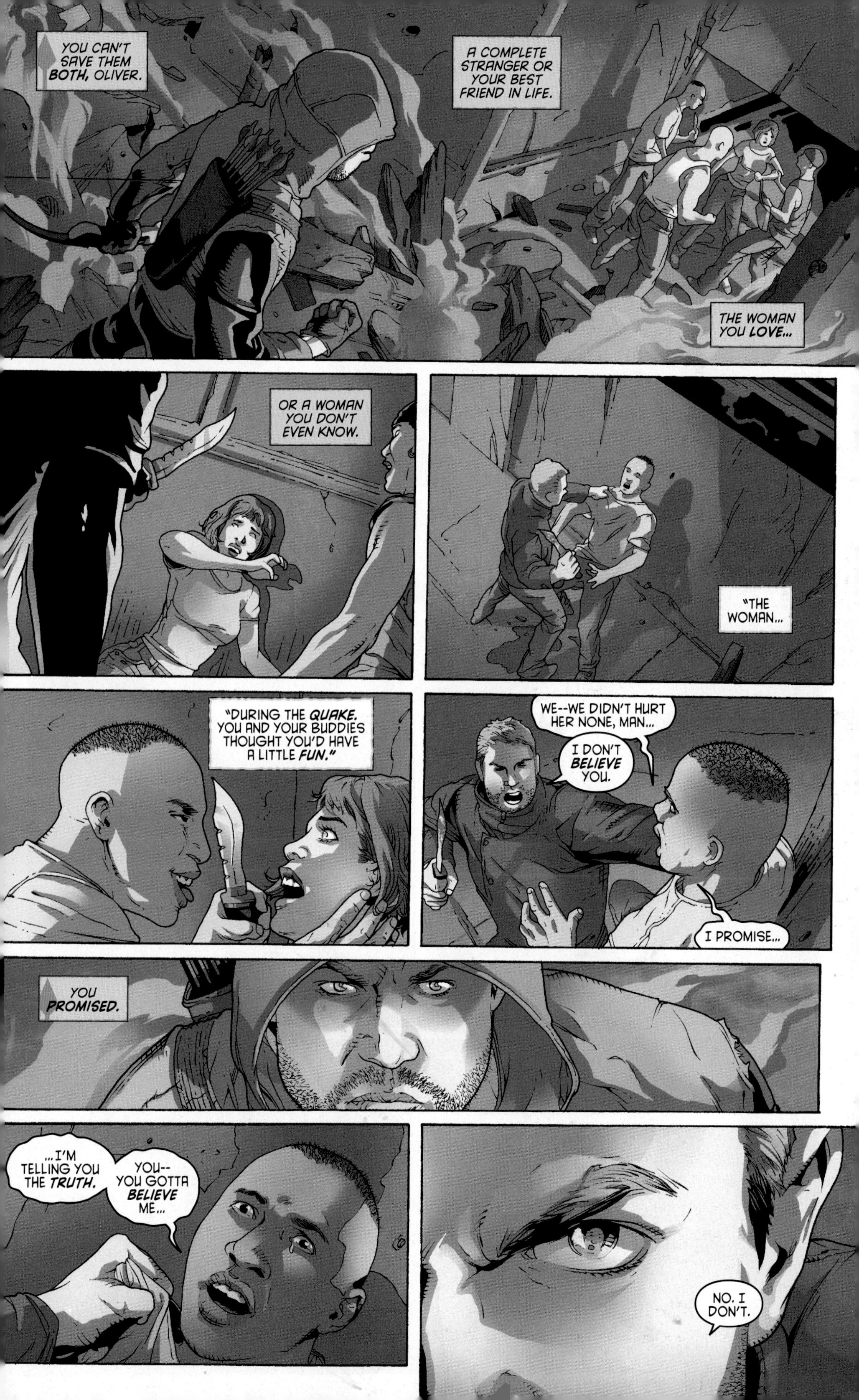

YOU CAN'T SAVE THEM BOTH, OLIVER.
A COMPLETE STRANGER OR YOUR BEST FRIEND IN LIFE.
THE WOMAN YOU LOVE...
OR A WOMAN YOU DON'T EVEN KNOW.
"THE WOMAN...
"DURING THE QUAKE. YOU AND YOUR BUDDIES THOUGHT YOU'D HAVE A LITTLE FUN."
WE--WE DIDN'T HURT HER NONE, MAN...
I DON'T BELIEVE YOU.
I PROMISE...
YOU PROMISED.
...I'M TELLING YOU THE TRUTH.
YOU--YOU GOTTA BELIEVE ME...
NO. I DON'T.

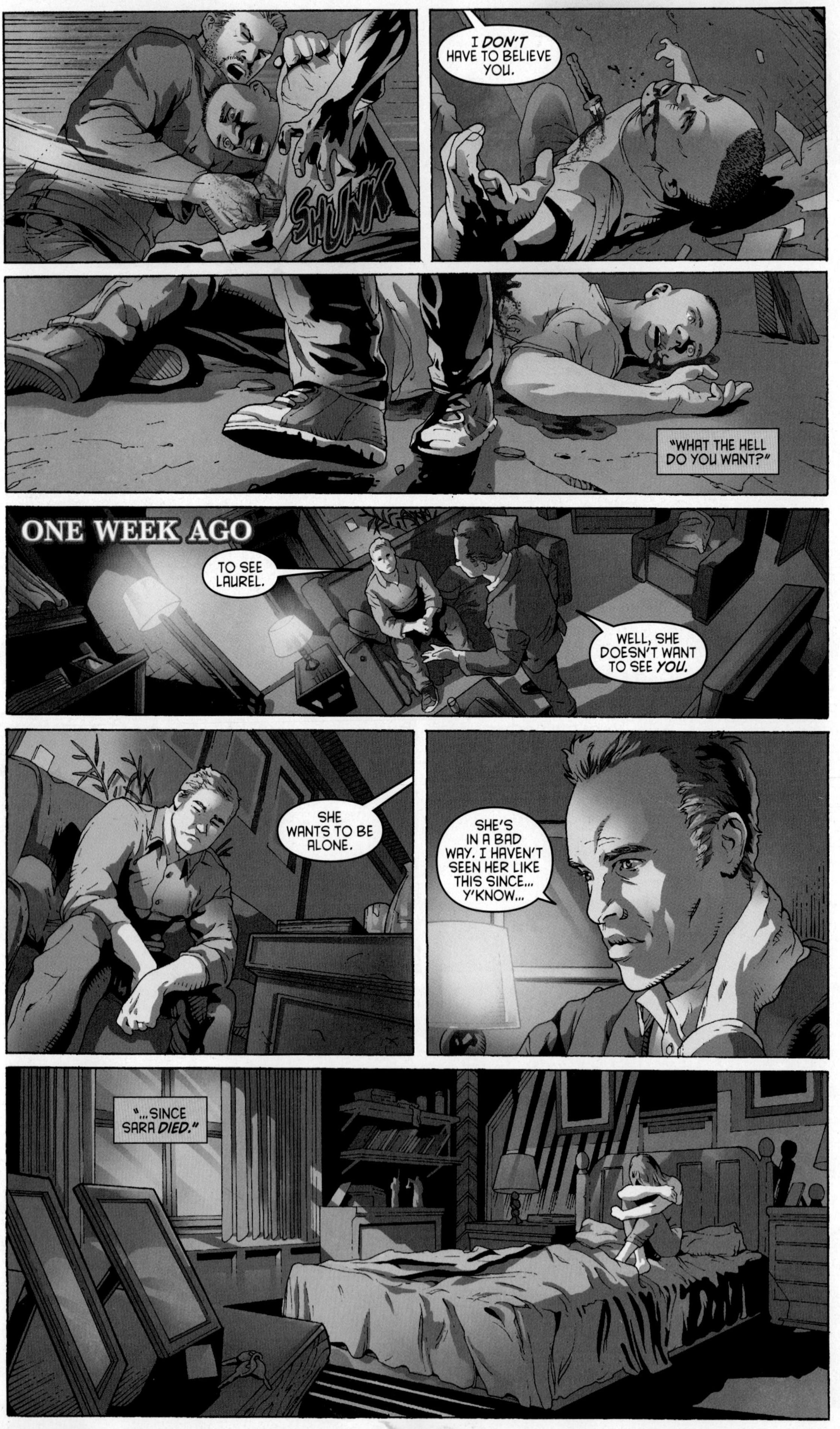
SHUNK
I DON'T HAVE TO BELIEVE YOU.
"WHAT THE HELL DO YOU WANT?"
ONE WEEK AGO
TO SEE LAUREL.
WELL, SHE DOESN'T WANT TO SEE YOU.
SHE WANTS TO BE ALONE.
SHE'S IN A BAD WAY. I HAVEN'T SEEN HER LIKE THIS SINCE... Y'KNOW...
"...SINCE SARA DIED."

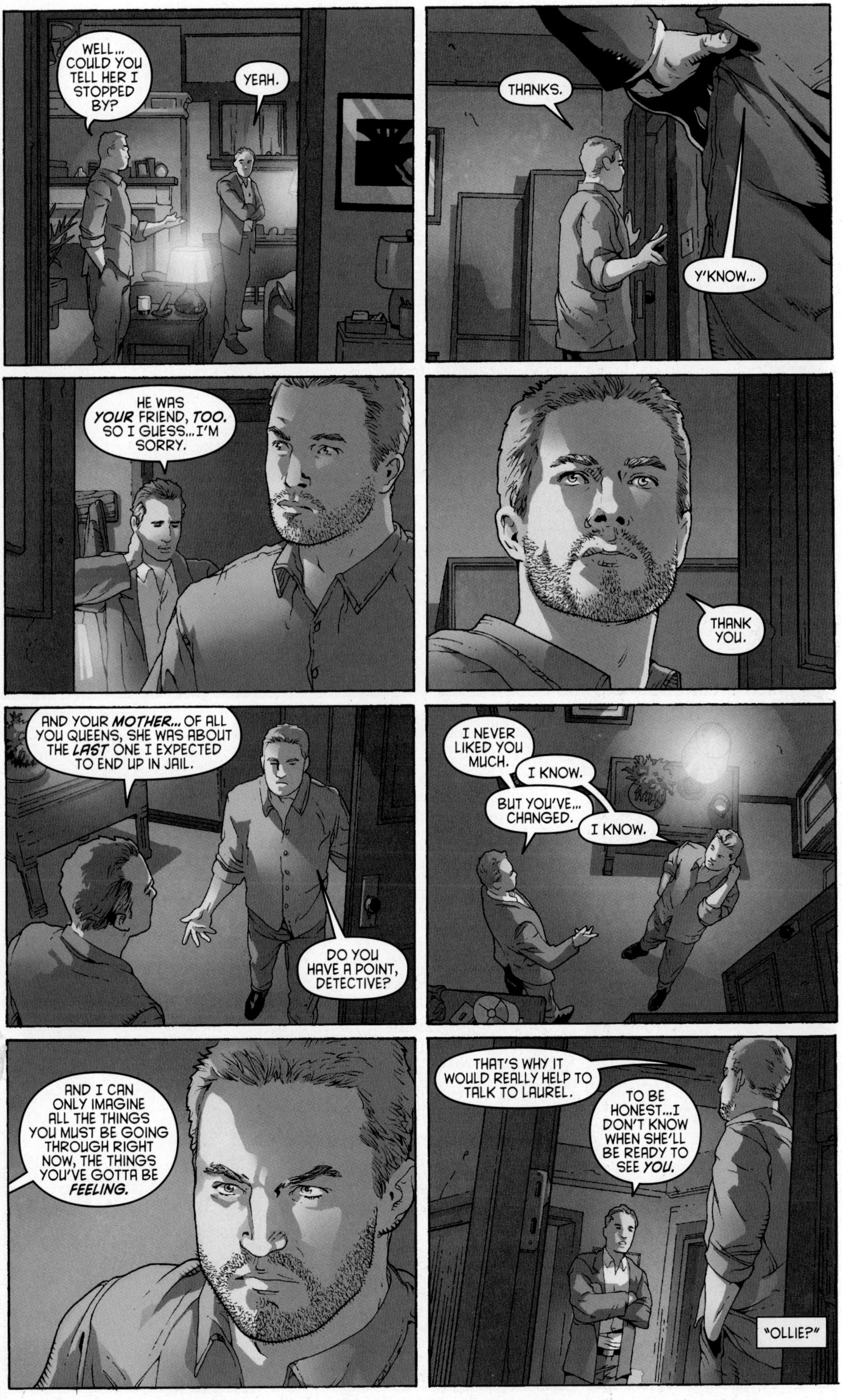

WELL... COULD YOU TELL HER I STOPPED BY?
YEAH.
THANKS.
Y'KNOW...
HE WAS *YOUR* FRIEND, *TOO.* SO I GUESS...I'M SORRY.
THANK YOU.
AND YOUR *MOTHER...* OF ALL YOU QUEENS, SHE WAS ABOUT THE *LAST* ONE I EXPECTED TO END UP IN JAIL.
DO YOU HAVE A POINT, DETECTIVE?
I NEVER LIKED YOU MUCH.
I KNOW.
BUT YOU'VE... CHANGED.
I KNOW.
AND I CAN ONLY IMAGINE ALL THE THINGS YOU MUST BE GOING THROUGH RIGHT NOW, THE THINGS YOU'VE GOTTA BE *FEELING.*
THAT'S WHY IT WOULD REALLY HELP TO TALK TO LAUREL.
TO BE HONEST...I DON'T KNOW WHEN SHE'LL BE READY TO SEE *YOU.*
"OLLIE?"

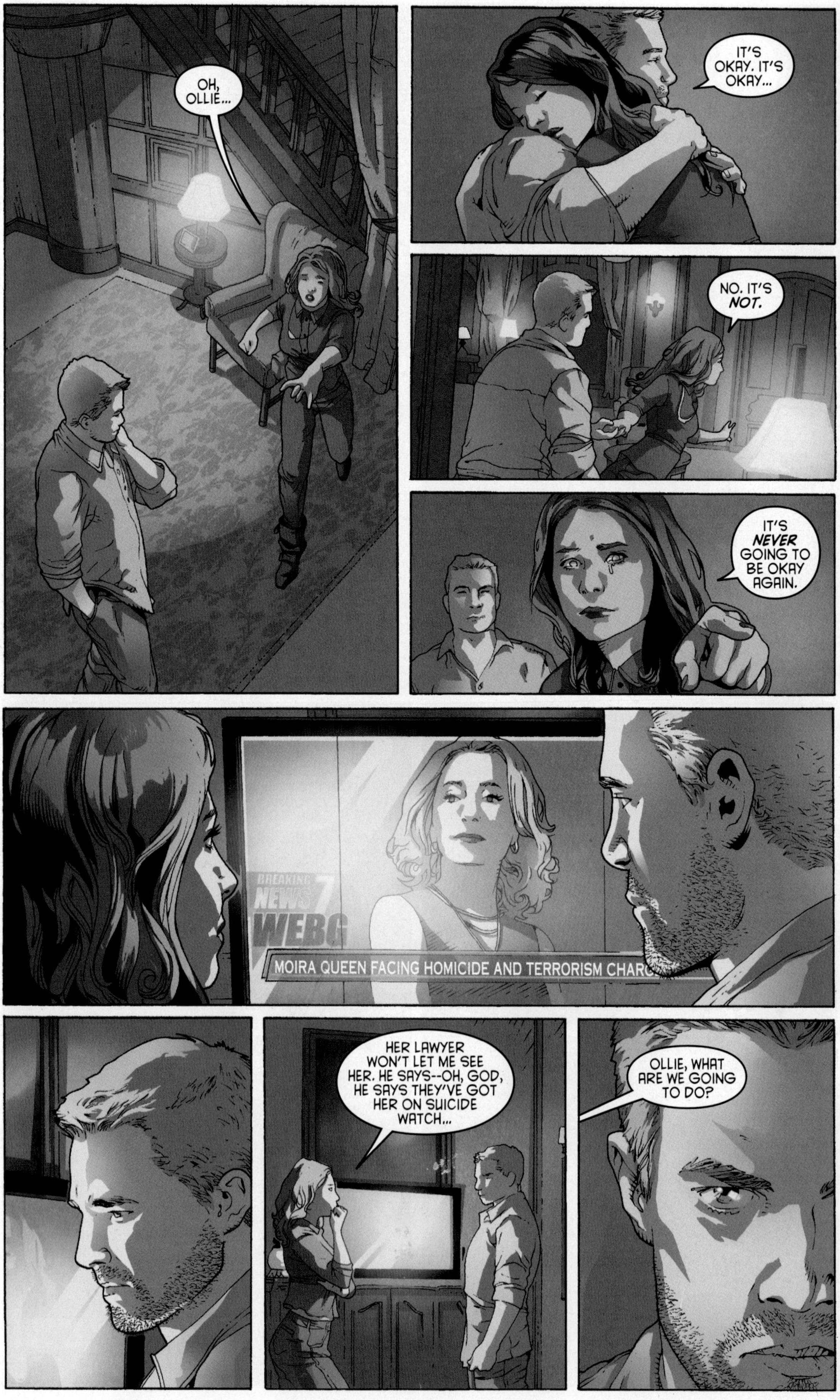

OH, OLLIE...
IT'S OKAY. IT'S OKAY...
NO. IT'S *NOT.*
IT'S *NEVER* GOING TO BE OKAY AGAIN.
BREAKING NEWS 7 WEBG
MOIRA QUEEN FACING HOMICIDE AND TERRORISM CHARG
HER LAWYER WON'T LET ME SEE HER. HE SAYS--OH, GOD, HE SAYS THEY'VE GOT HER ON SUICIDE WATCH...
OLLIE, WHAT ARE WE GOING TO DO?

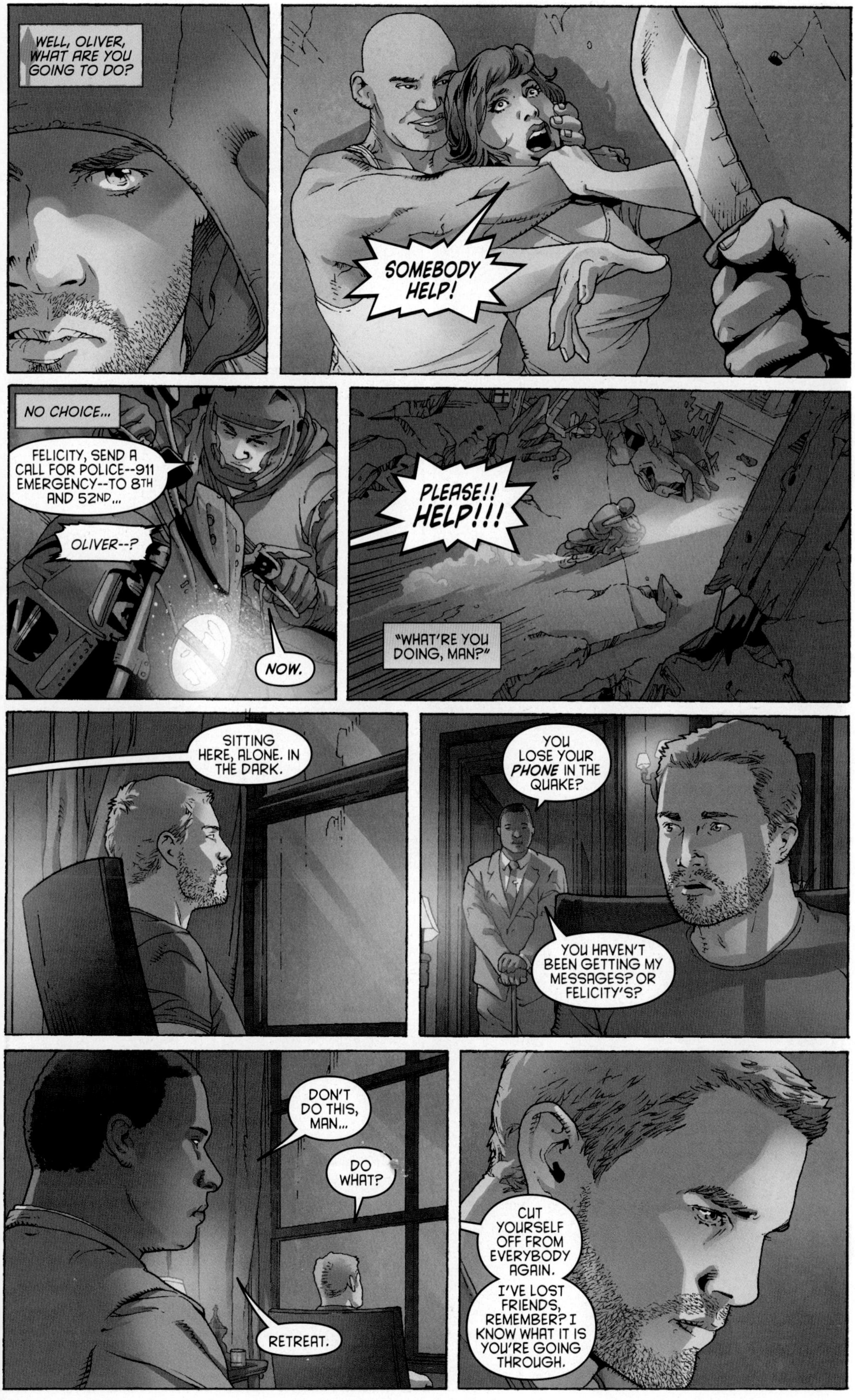
WELL, OLIVER, WHAT ARE YOU GOING TO DO?
SOMEBODY HELP!
NO CHOICE...
FELICITY, SEND A CALL FOR POLICE--911 EMERGENCY--TO 8TH AND 52ND...
OLIVER--?
NOW.
PLEASE!! HELP!!!
"WHAT'RE YOU DOING, MAN?"
SITTING HERE, ALONE. IN THE DARK.
YOU LOSE YOUR PHONE IN THE QUAKE?
YOU HAVEN'T BEEN GETTING MY MESSAGES? OR FELICITY'S?
DON'T DO THIS, MAN...
DO WHAT?
RETREAT.
CUT YOURSELF OFF FROM EVERYBODY AGAIN.
I'VE LOST FRIENDS, REMEMBER? I KNOW WHAT IT IS YOU'RE GOING THROUGH.

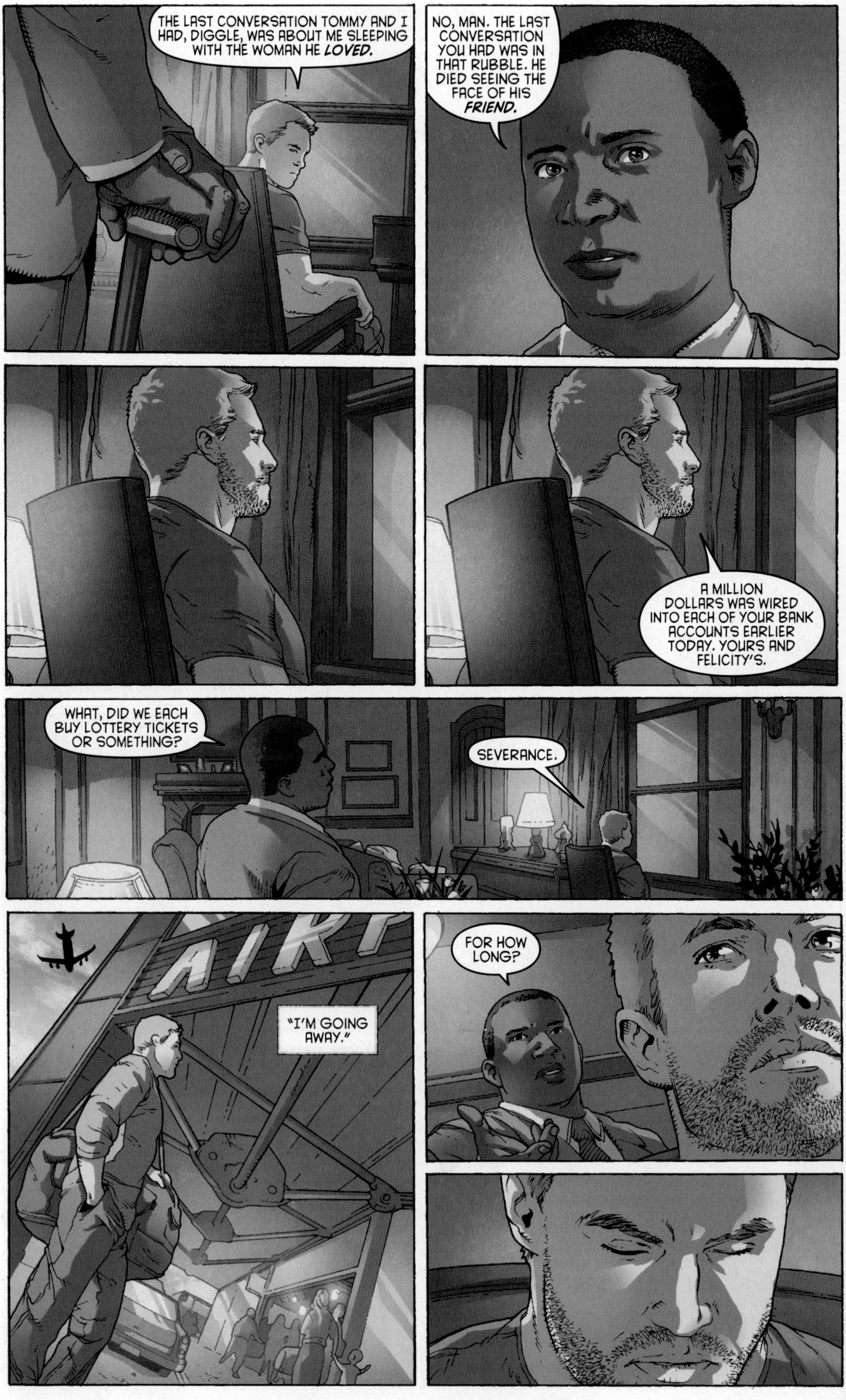
THE LAST CONVERSATION TOMMY AND I HAD, DIGGLE, WAS ABOUT ME SLEEPING WITH THE WOMAN HE *LOVED.*
NO, MAN. THE LAST CONVERSATION YOU HAD WAS IN THAT RUBBLE. HE DIED SEEING THE FACE OF HIS *FRIEND.*
A MILLION DOLLARS WAS WIRED INTO EACH OF YOUR BANK ACCOUNTS EARLIER TODAY. YOURS AND FELICITY'S.
WHAT, DID WE EACH BUY LOTTERY TICKETS OR SOMETHING?
SEVERANCE.
"I'M GOING AWAY."
FOR HOW LONG?

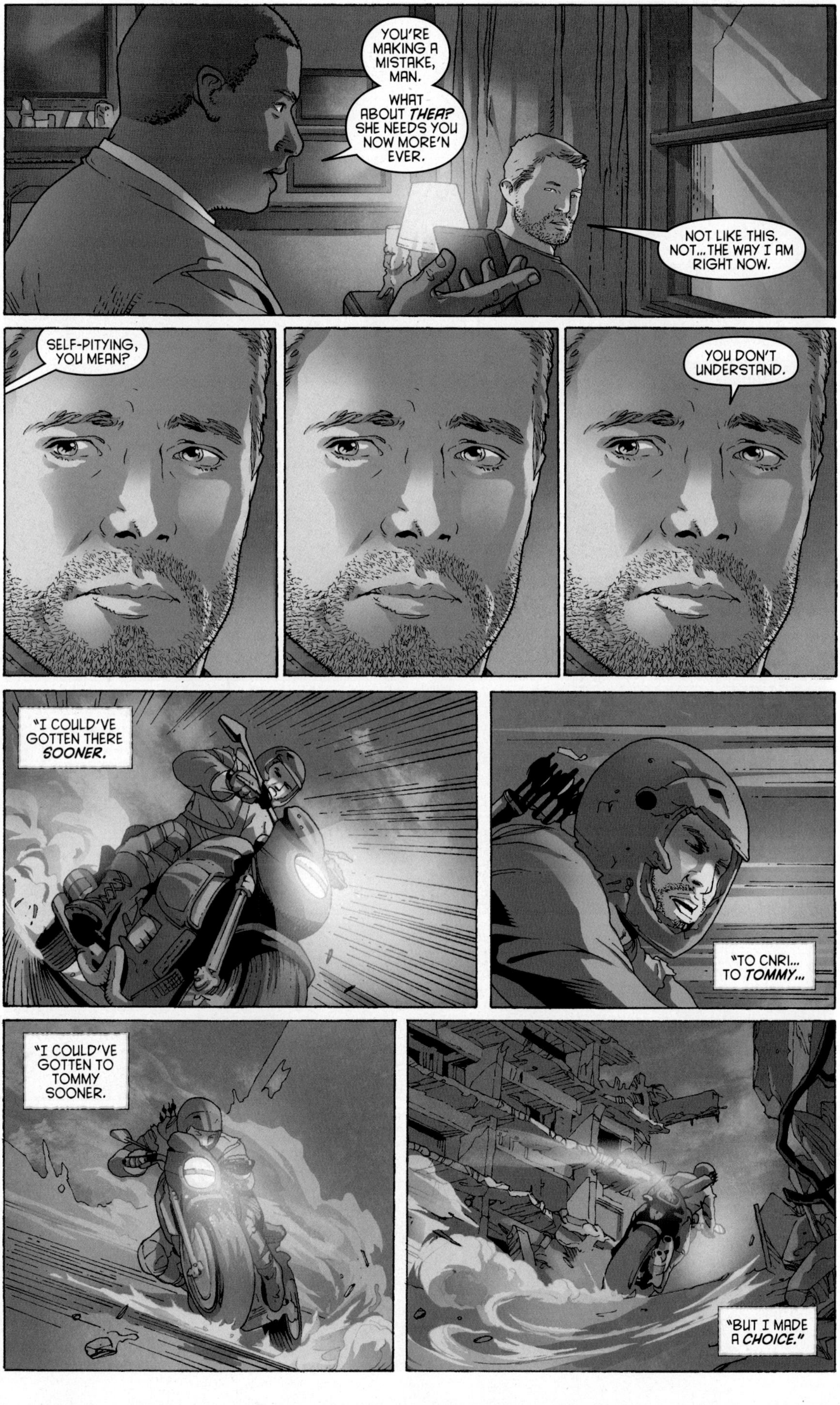
YOU'RE MAKING A MISTAKE, MAN.
WHAT ABOUT THEA? SHE NEEDS YOU NOW MORE'N EVER.
NOT LIKE THIS. NOT...THE WAY I AM RIGHT NOW.
SELF-PITYING, YOU MEAN?
YOU DON'T UNDERSTAND.
"I COULD'VE GOTTEN THERE SOONER.
"TO CNRI... TO TOMMY...
"I COULD'VE GOTTEN TO TOMMY SOONER.
"BUT I MADE A CHOICE."

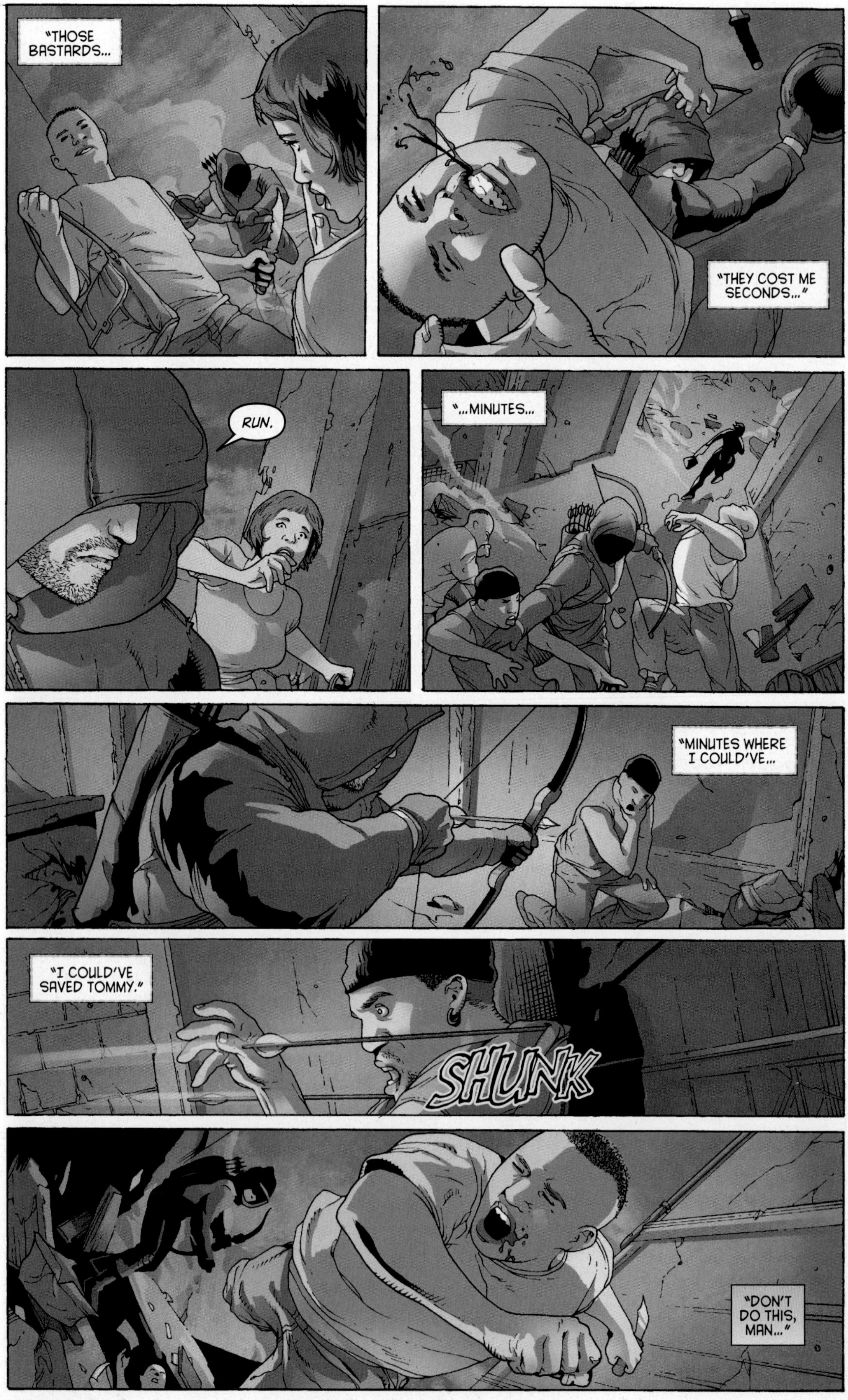
"THOSE BASTARDS...
"THEY COST ME SECONDS..."
RUN.
"...MINUTES...
"MINUTES WHERE I COULD'VE...
"I COULD'VE SAVED TOMMY."
SHUNK
"DON'T DO THIS, MAN..."

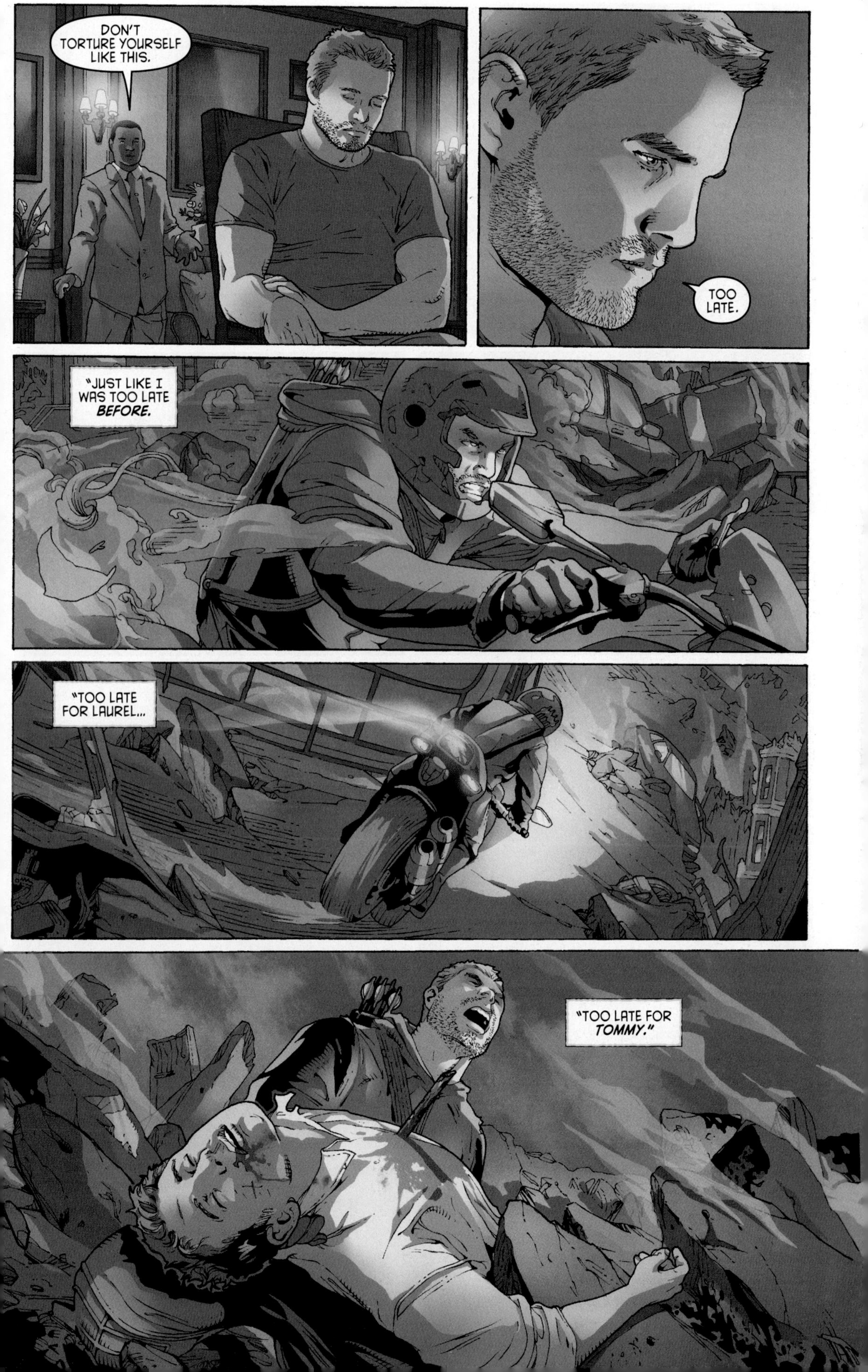
DON'T TORTURE YOURSELF LIKE THIS.
TOO LATE.
"JUST LIKE I WAS TOO LATE *BEFORE.*
"TOO LATE FOR LAUREL...
"TOO LATE FOR *TOMMY."*

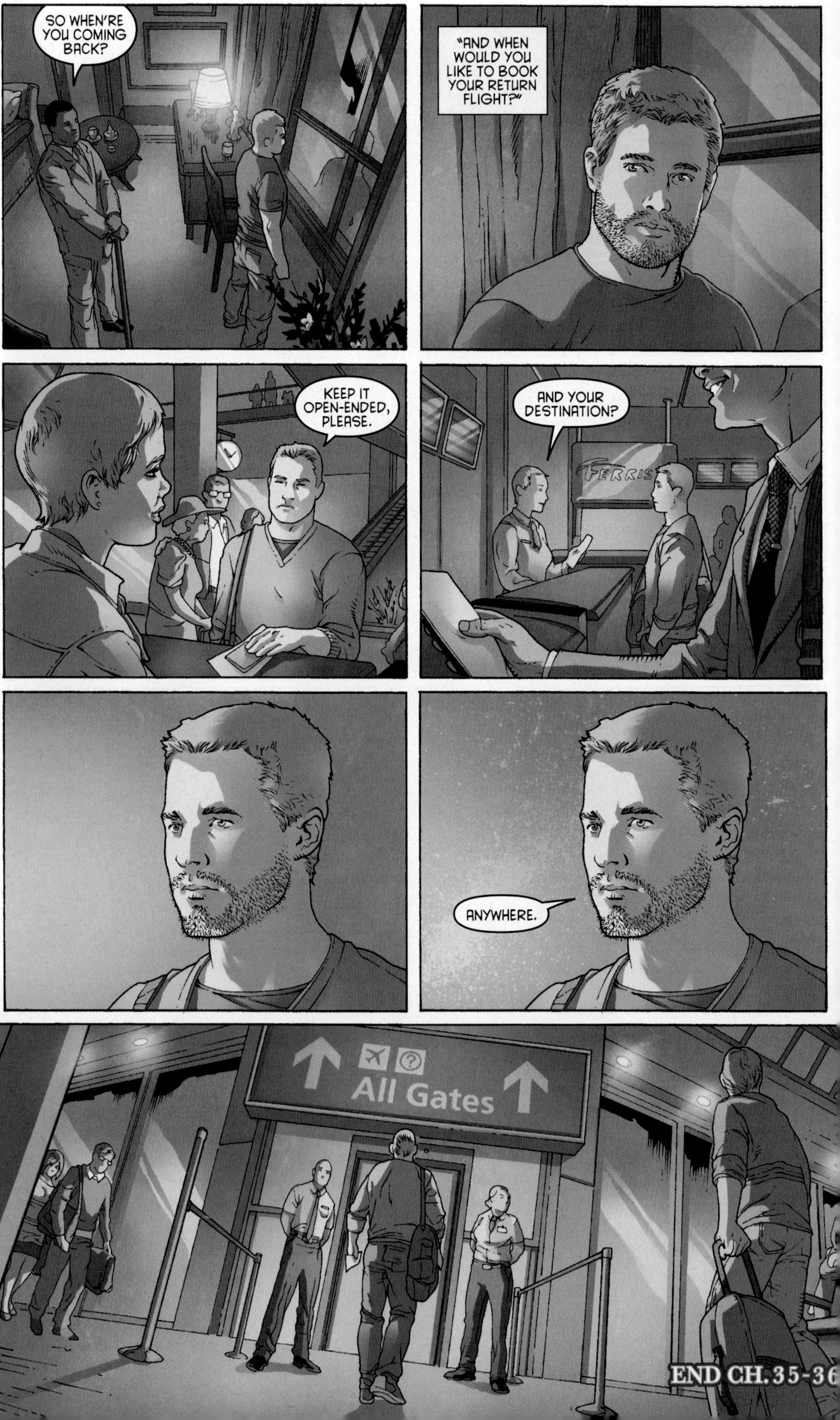
SO WHEN'RE YOU COMING BACK?
"AND WHEN WOULD YOU LIKE TO BOOK YOUR RETURN FLIGHT?"
KEEP IT OPEN-ENDED, PLEASE.
AND YOUR DESTINATION?
FERRIS
ANYWHERE.
All Gates
END CH. 35-36

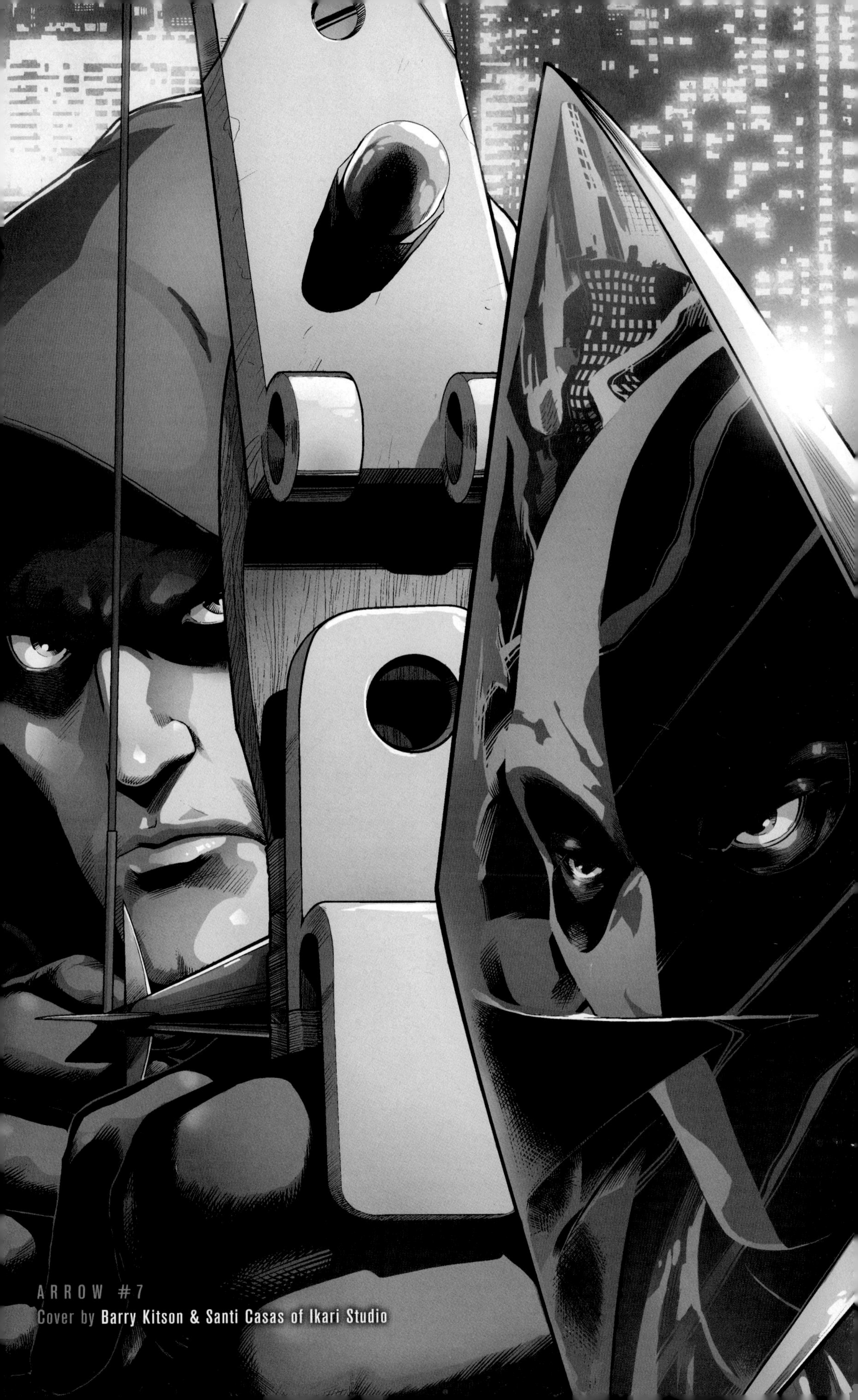

ARROW #7
Cover by **Barry Kitson & Santi Casas of Ikari Studio**

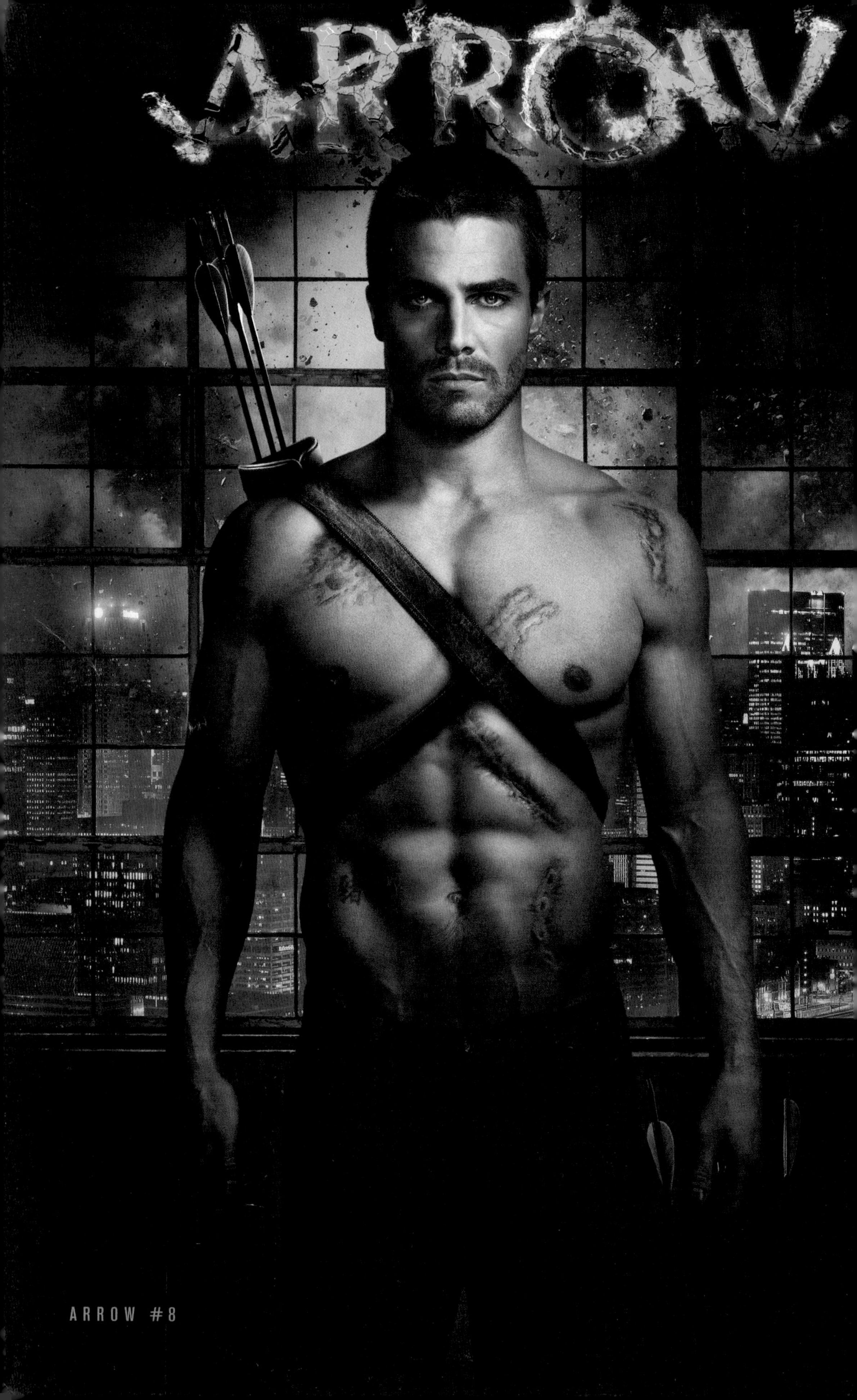
ARROW
ARROW #8

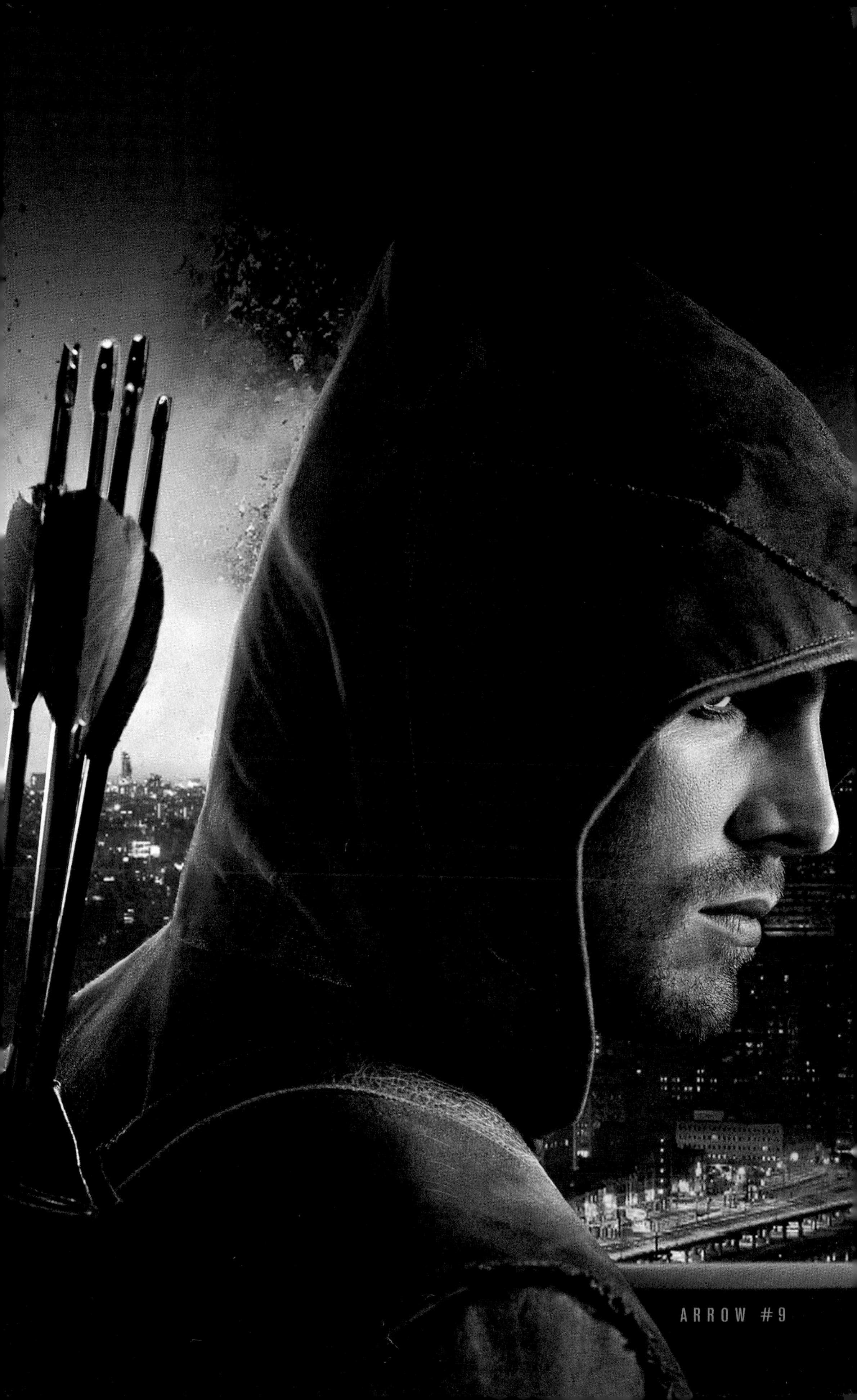
ARROW #9

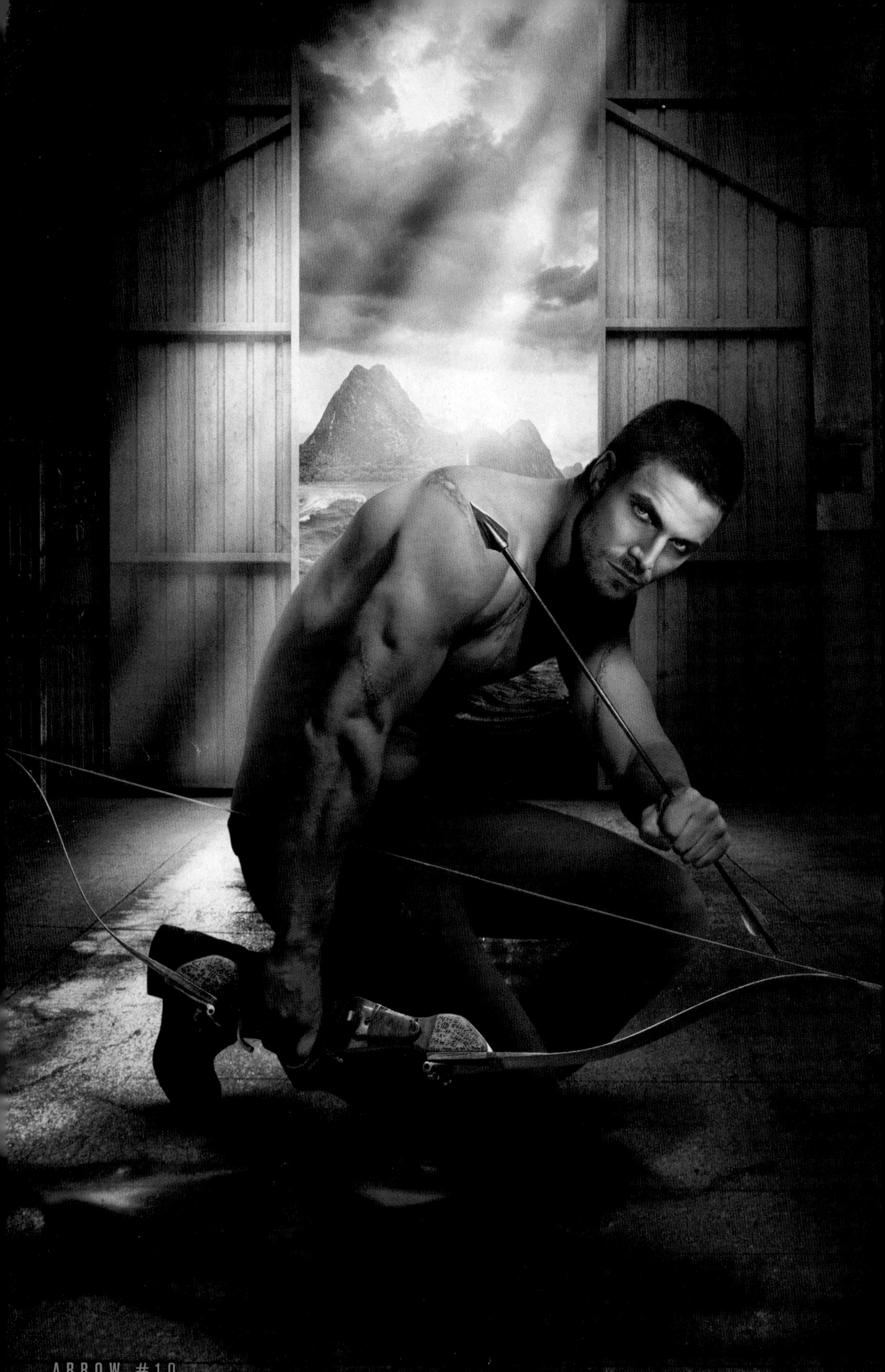

ARROW #10

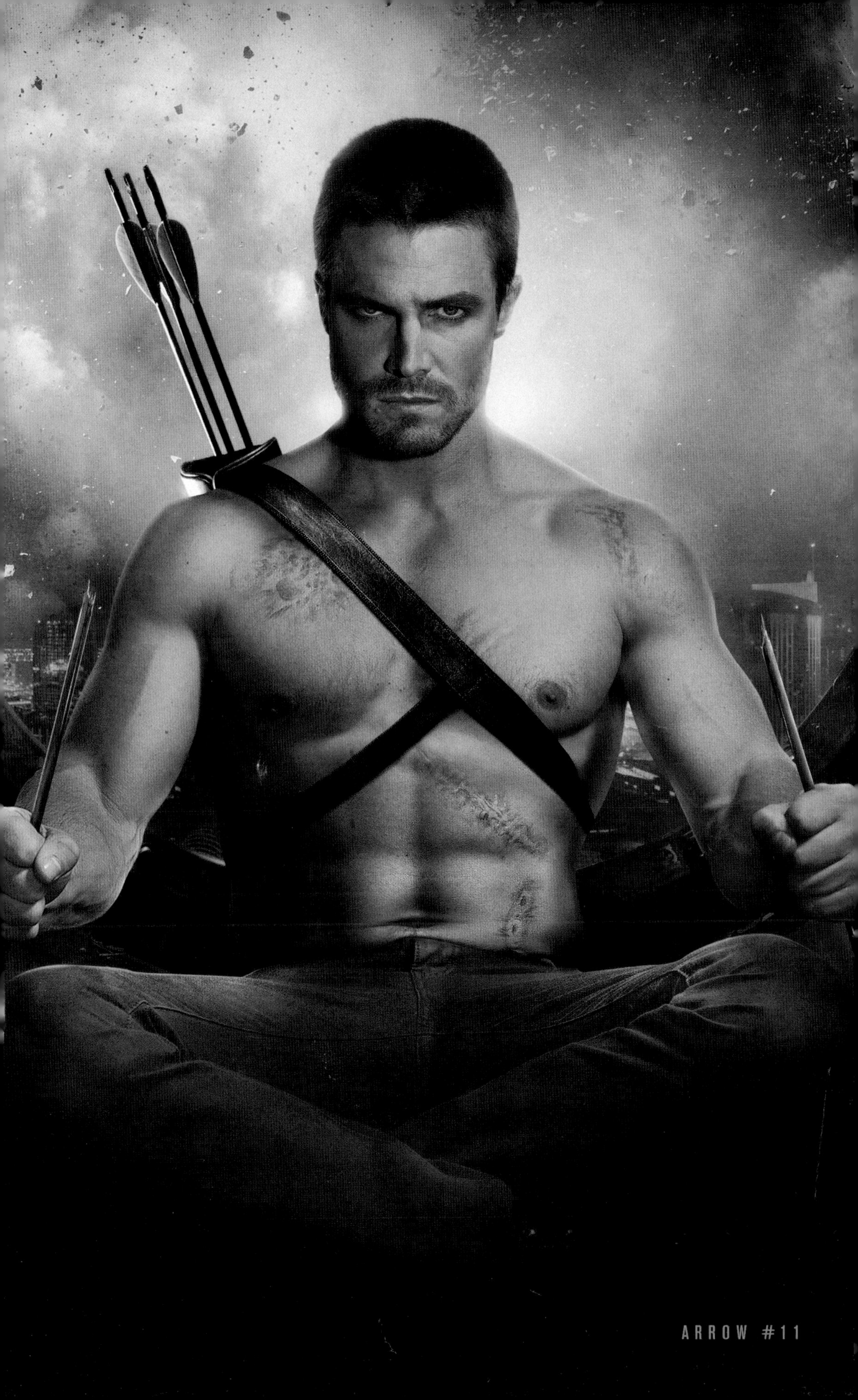

ARROW #11

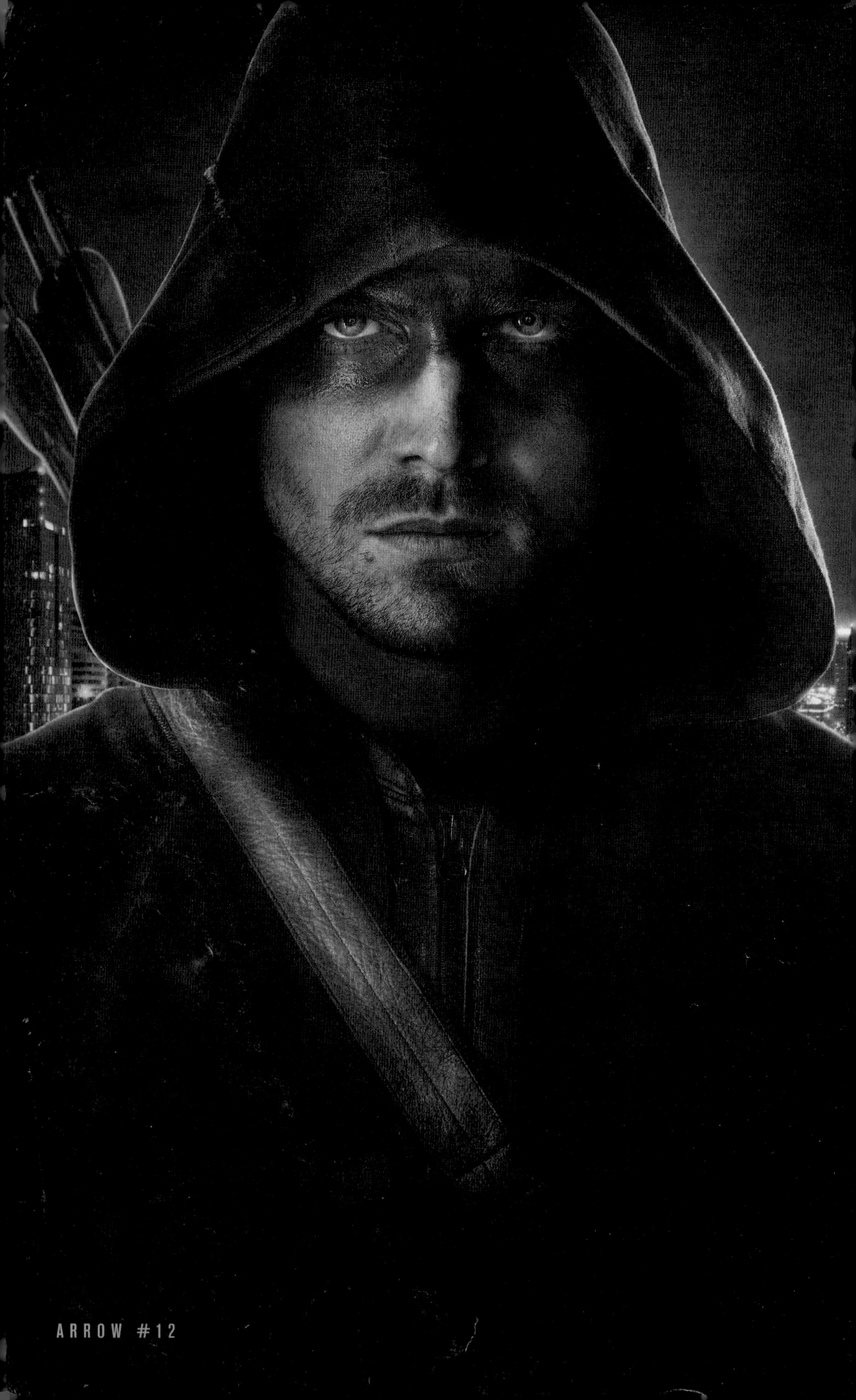

ARROW #12

C
OMICS™

"THE IDENTITY CRISIS mystery involves the biggest DC heroes and will use all of Mr. Meltzer's skills as a thriller novelist." —THE NEW YORK TIMES

"Refreshing. Underscore[s] that these are very human characters in a very risky business." —ENTERTAINMENT WEEKLY

"Mystery novelist Brad Meltzer shows that even superheroes have reasons to be afraid." —SPIN MAGAZINE

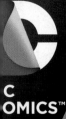

FROM THE *NEW YORK TIMES* #1 BEST-SELLING AUTHOR

BRAD MELTZER
with RAGS MORALES

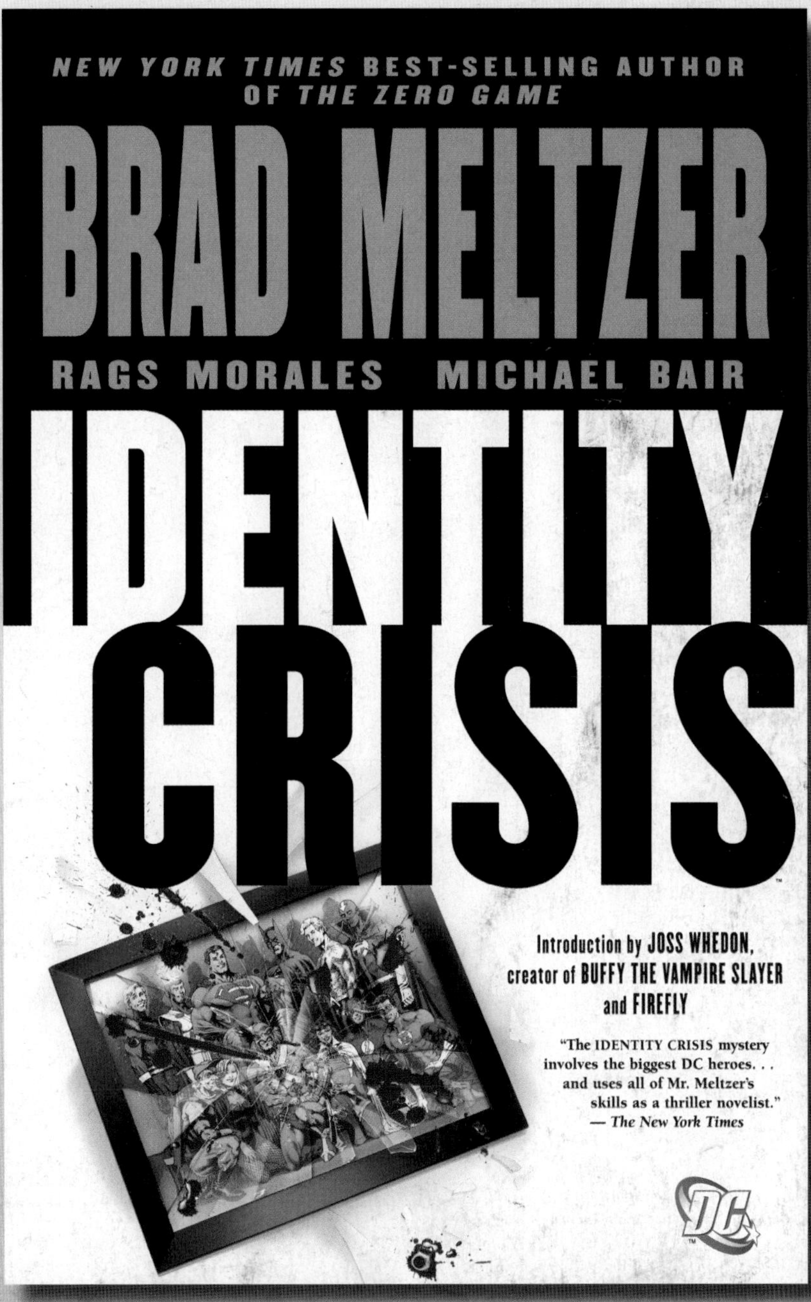
NEW YORK TIMES BEST-SELLING AUTHOR OF THE ZERO GAME
BRAD MELTZER
RAGS MORALES MICHAEL BAIR
IDENTITY CRISIS
Introduction by JOSS WHEDON, creator of BUFFY THE VAMPIRE SLAYER and FIREFLY
"The IDENTITY CRISIS mystery involves the biggest DC heroes. . . and uses all of Mr. Meltzer's skills as a thriller novelist." — The New York Times

JUSTICE LEAGUE OF AMERICA: THE TORNADO'S PATH

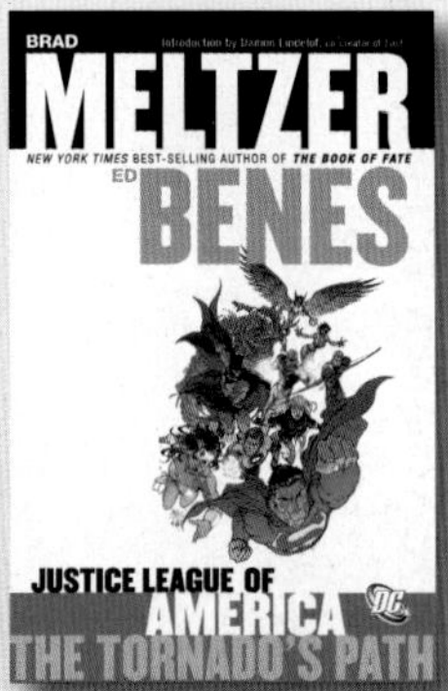
BRAD
MELTZER
ED
BENES
JUSTICE LEAGUE OF AMERICA
THE TORNADO'S PATH

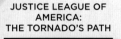

with ED BENES

JUSTICE LEAGUE OF AMERICA: THE LIGHTING SAGA

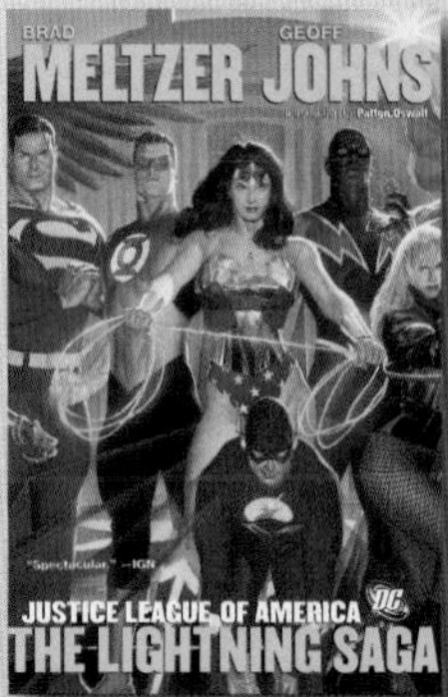
BRAD
MELTZER
GEOFF
JOHNS
JUSTICE LEAGUE OF AMERICA
THE LIGHTNING SAGA

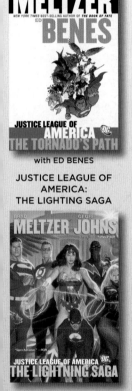

w/ ED BENES & GEOFF JOHNS

GREEN ARROW: THE ARCHER'S QUEST

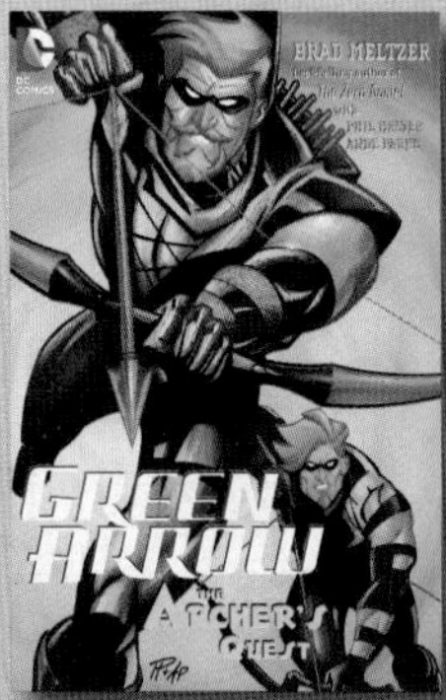
BRAD MELTZER
GREEN ARROW
THE ARCHER'S QUEST

with PHIL HESTER